Third Edition

Psychological Consultation

Introduction to
Theory and Practice

Duane Brown
Walter B. Pryzwansky
Ann C. Schulte
University of North Carolina, Chapel Hill

Allyn and Bacon
Boston • London • Toronto • Sydney • Tokyo • Singapore

Series Editor: Raymond Short
Marketing Manager: Ellen Mann
Production Administrator: Marjorie Payne
Editorial Assistant: Christine Shaw
Cover Administrator: Linda Knowles
Composition/Pre-press Buyer: Linda Cox
Editorial-Production Service: Chestnut Hill Enterprises

Copyright © 1995, 1991, 1987 by Allyn & Bacon
A Simon & Schuster Company
Needham Heights, Massachusetts 02194

Library of Congress Cataloging-in-Publication Data

Brown, Duane.
    Psychological consultation   :   introduction to theory and practice /
Duane Brown, Walter B. Pryzwansky, Ann C. Schulte. — 3rd ed.
        p.   cm.
    Includes bibliographical references and index.
    ISBN 0–205–15921–4
    1. Psychological consultation.   I. Pryzwansky, Walter B.
    II. Schulte, Ann C.   III. Title.
    BF637.C56B76   1995   94-11090
    158'.3—dc20   CIP

Printed in the United States of America

10   9   8   7   6   5   4   3   2   99   98   97   96   95

To
Our Parents,
Lester W. and Mary Ruth Brown
John M. and Joan H. Schulte
and to
David and Scott Pryzwansky

Contents

Preface to the Third Edition

In 1991, we observed that the interest in psychological consultation had intensified since the publication of the first edition in 1987, and we expected that interest to grow unabated. In fact the growth in the interest in consultation has exceeded our expectations. One indication of this interest is the number of books being published in this area. New books dealing with consultation by counselors, school psychologists, special educators, and social workers have been published in the last three years. Special editions of journals and presentations at professional meetings have also attested to the increased interest in consultation. Clearly consultation is increasingly being recognized as a viable intervention for a variety of problems ranging from organizational problems to deficiencies in learning.

In preparing the second edition we added two new applied chapters: consultation with teachers and with parents. While consultation with teachers has long been a concern of consultants, consultation with parents is an emerging area, and that chapter was particularly timely because of the current attention on preschool interventions with parents. Those two chapters have been updated and remain as solid outlines for practitioners working in this area. We have also added a brief section in each chapter titled "Tips for the Practitioner" that is intended to add another applied dimension to this edition. In the "Tips" section we attempt to provide concrete suggestions that will aid the reader to apply the material that has been discussed in that chapter to the real world of consulting.

One chapter from the first and second editions has been deleted, the chapter on training consultants. It has been replaced with a discussion of a topic that has been largely ignored in other books and by us in the first two editions: the consultant. Chapter Seven, "The Characteristics and Skills of the Consultant," raises questions regarding the characteristics of effective consultants and the minimum skills needed to be effective. It attempts to provide tentative answers to the questions raised.

All other chapters have been updated in this revision. However, Chapter Twelve, "Ethical and Legal Considerations," has been extensively revised to reflect changing ethical standards that have been developed to guide practitioners. These revisions bring the content from the second edition to the cutting edge of present practice. We have also tried to look into the future of consultation in Chapter Thirteen, "Issues in Consultation." Because consultation is in a state of flux, readers will want to pay particular attention to this area.

Once again we want to thank our colleagues for their response to both the first and second editions. Many of them have called and written to make suggestions, and many of these suggestions have been incorporated into this edition. We invite people who use this edition to continue to comment on its contents and its usefulness to students.

We also want to thank our support staff for their efforts to bring this edition to fruition. Karen Thigpen, Ericka Simon, and Cadie Blaylock were all instrumental in the preparation of this edtion.

Preface to the Second Edition

In 1987, we introduced the first edition of *Psychological Consultation* by observing that consultation as a helping process is receiving increasing attention from psychologists, counselors, social workers, and other human services workers. It is satisfying to report that this interest has intensified in the last three years and seems likely to continue to do so in the foreseeable future. The major purposes of this second edition, like those of the first, are to provide an overview of the current status of psychological consultation and to focus on unresolved issues in the field. It is also our goal to provide prospective consultants with the knowledge bases and skills they need to practice successfully.

With this latter goal in mind, we have added two applied chapters to this edition: one chapter focusing on consultation with teachers and the other chapter focusing on consultation with parents. These chapters were added, partially because our colleagues who have used the book suggested that more attention needed to be paid to the applied aspects of consultation and partly because our own experiences as consultants, trainers, and supervisors of counselors and psychologists indicate that consultants need skills in working with these groups. We could have chosen to focus on other groups of caregivers such as nursing home personnel or upon administrative groups such as school principals. However, space precludes including chapters on all potential consultees and we believe that the material in this edition will allow consultants to generalize to other groups of consultees.

Just as we did in the first edition, we have tried to provide a balance among theory, practice, and research although this volume is decidedly more applied because of the addition of the chapters previously mentioned. Although we make the point throughout the book, we will begin here by saying that there is limited empirical basis for consultation, but happily there are an increasing number of empirical indicators that suggest strategies that can be employed by consultants. In the research sections of the book, we have tried to summarize these succinctly; thus, the theory and practice sections of the book make up a vast majority of its contents.

We wish to thank our colleagues for their responses to the first edition, particularly those that provided suggestions for improving our work. William Erchul of North Carolina State University deserves special mention because of his help. Our students have also been helpful in providing feedback and we are indebted to them. Finally, we are most appreciative of the efforts of Melody Vaitkus and Susan Eller who conducted library research and Karen Thigpen, Jane Trexler, Cadie Blaylock, and Evelyn Ross who handled correspondence, typed the new chapters as well as the inserts, and conducted the myriad of other activities necessary to bring this project to fruition.

Preface to the First Edition

Consultation as a helping process has become a topic of increasing interest among human services researchers, theoreticians, and practitioners alike. As a result, our knowledge base in this area has expanded tremendously since Gerald Caplan published his landmark work *The Theory and Practice of Mental Health Consultation* in 1970. Two purposes of *Psychological Consultation* are to provide an overview of the growth and current status of consultation in this country and to outline the issues that remain to be addressed in this fledgling field. A third purpose is to provide students in the human services fields of psychology, counseling, and social work with a comprehensive look at the various models of consultation and the processes involved in consultation practice. A final aim of the presentation is to help students acquire the knowledge and skills needed to successfully engage in consultation.

This book, like others, makes several assumptions with regard to its intended audience. One assumption is that consultation will be but one of the intervention strategies used. Another is that the professional identity of the audience will be developed around their individual field of study (psychology or counseling) and thus they will seek to become psychologists, counselors, or social workers, not professional consultants. Finally, it is generally presumed that readers have little experience as consultants and, in fact, are just beginning to develop their knowledge and skills in this area. This is not to say that the experienced consultant cannot learn much from reading this material, but it does suggest that neophyte consultants may profit more from the content of the book.

A considerable amount of *Psychological Consultation* is spent summarizing the contributions to consultation of such individuals as Gerald Caplan, John Bergan, and others. However, much more space is devoted to presenting new materials such as a social learning model of consultation and the legal issues in consultation and to providing thoughtful syntheses of the current literature on issues such as the consultee as a variable in consultation, cross cultural consultation issues, and the efficacy of consultation as an intervention.

The approach used throughout the book provides a balance among theory, research, and practice with the ultimate concern being application. Students are provided with advanced organizers, intext learning exercises, and review questions designed to focus their learning and sharpen their insight into the complex processes surrounding consultation. However, we have not tried to provide simplistic answers to complicated problems, and students should come away with an additional insight: There are many unresolved issues regarding consultation.

No book on consultation can claim that it alone provides the knowledge and skills needed for a reader to become a proficient consultant. *Psychological Consultation* provides the student with a foundation for moving toward that goal along with a clear sense of the status of consultation theory, research, and practice at this historical juncture.

We would like to express our gratitude to four individuals who contributed significantly to the completion of this project. Our magnificent secretaries, Jane Trexler and Lyda Beemer, deciphered handwriting and persevered diligently through the many drafts of the book. Alan Cameron, a graduate student in counseling psychology, also contributed to this work by providing editorial assistance and experiences from his own practice as a consultant that have been incorporated into the volume. Finally, William Erchul shared his resources and his insight regarding consultation throughout the preparation of the manuscript.

$$Chapter \quad 1$$

Introduction to Consultation

Goal of the Chapter

The goal of this chapter is to introduce, define, and differentiate consultation from other intervention strategies employed by human service workers such as counselors, psychologists, and social workers.

Chapter Preview

1. Various definitions of consultation will be reviewed and will be synthesized into a single definition.
2. Some of the related definitional questions in consultation will be discussed.
3. Consultation will be considered as it relates to the other intervention methods employed by human resource workers.
4. A brief history of human resource consultation will be presented.

Purpose

The purposes of this chapter are four-fold. At the outset, a brief history of consultation in this country will be presented. This will be followed by a discussion of the definition of consultation. The inclusion of an entire section devoted to defining consultation may seem a bit odd, but in spite of the widespread use of the term, it is not well understood even among human services workers. In part, the definition of consultation will be pursued by contrasting it with other interventions employed by counselors, psychologists, and social workers. The third objective of this chapter is to present some conjecture about the future of consultation, and the fourth is to set the stage for the remainder of the book by providing an overview of the remaining content.

Consultation: The History and the Promise

Human services consultation has a multifaceted history. Its oldest antecedent lies in clinical consultation, an approach practiced systematically by physicians since the middle of the nineteenth century. Consultation among mental health workers may have begun in this country with the work of Witmer (Levine & Levine, 1970) just after the turn of the century and was widely practiced by the 1920s (Gallessich, 1982). However, it was not until Gerald Caplan's seminal work, *The Theory and Practice of Mental Health Consultation*, was published that mental health consultation gained great impetus. Kurt Lewin's (1951) field theory and his emphasis on action research (Huse, 1980) stimulated a human relations approach to organizational development, although consultation with organizations can be traced to the turn of the twentieth century (Stryker, 1982). More recently, behaviorally-oriented consultants such as Bergan have begun to influence the consultation movement. Of particular note is Bergan's (1977) presentation of a well-developed, behavioral model of consultation. Other important influences can be traced to community psychologists such as Heller (Heller & Monahan, 1977; Heller, Price, Reinberg, Roger, & Wandersman, 1984).

In post–World War II Israel, Gerald Caplan labored with other mental health professionals to provide services to thousands of refugee children. It soon became apparent that the rather small staff of professionals could not possibly provide the direct services needed by the flood of clients coming for help. Caplan and his associates found that counseling the professional staff members about the nature of mental health service could change perspectives and reduce the direct service workload. During this period, mental health consultation as we know it today was born. Three aspects of Caplan's model delineated it clearly from the clinical approach: (1) the egalitarian relationship between the consultee and consultant, (2) theme interference, and (3) his taxonomy of approaches to consultation which included client-centered, consultee-centered, program-centered administrative, and consultee-centered administrative consultation. Each type will be discussed in more detail later. The only controversial aspect of Caplan's model rests in his idea of theme interference, which can be characterized as mild confrontation of stereotypical ideas held by the consultee. The result of Caplan's well conceived approach to consultation is that it is perhaps the most influential model of consultation today in the mental health arena.

As medicine became more specialized, it became common practice for physicians to request assistance in diagnosing medical problems. The clinical model, as it was performed by physicians and in medical schools, is practiced today by mental health consultants involved in the diagnosis of a problem, prescription of a treatment, and withdrawal of the consultant, leaving the consultee to implement the approach (Meyers, Parsons, and Martin, 1979). It is not uncommon for human services agencies to employ consultants to assist in case diagnosis and management, thus perpetuating the clinical model, which was on the decline until recently. The reasons for this decline were three-fold: (1) diagnosis had lost its allure to many, simply because there was little relationship between diagnosis and treatment; (2) the clinical model emphasized abnormality and the diagnostic labels placed on clients were offensive to many; and (3) the relationship was viewed primarily as expert to neophyte rather than the collegial relationship valued by many mental health professionals.

The rise of behaviorism as an influence on consultation has breathed new life into the clinical consultation model. However, behaviorists do not employ traditional labels. They

do see problems as learned and thus capable of being unlearned in reasonably straightforward ways, and they link treatment to diagnosis. Moreover, Bergan's (1977) model of consultation and later iterations of it by Bergan and Kratochwill (1990) and Martens (1993) feature relationships that are more egalitarian than the traditional clinical model. With this said it must be recognized that proponents of this approach still maintain the stance that consultants should dominate the relationship because of their expertise (Erchul & Chewning, 1990). As will be shown in Chapter Three, cognitive behavioral approaches depart from many aspects of the traditional behavioral view, even the idea that the consultant must control the consulting relationship.

Similarly, the community psychology perspective is likely to have an increasing influence on consultation models and the role of the consultant. Heller (1985) has taken issue with some of Caplan's ideas such as consultation only occurs between professionals and that it only pertains to work-related concerns. His view is not unlike the macroperspective taken by social workers in which aspects of the community are seen as producing mental health problems and thus need to be attacked by the collaborative efforts of both community groups and mental health agency professionals to eliminate the source of the problem. If this view becomes more widely accepted, and we suspect that it will, the consultation function will become more widely applied to mental health concerns.

Even a cursory glance at the professional literature will show that interest in consultation is gaining momentum both from the vantage point of the consultant and the consultee. Increased technology and the resulting specialization of professionals increase the need for consultation. So does the recognition of the relationship between meeting human needs and organizational effectiveness. Lippitt and Lippitt (1986) also suggest that there is a growing awareness of the paucity of human energy in our society, and increasingly consultation is being viewed as a tool for freeing that energy. To restate their ideas in somewhat different terms, our society is awakening to the realization that the potential of our young and old alike is constrained by practices that impair mental health in families, schools, work environments, and governmental agencies. Consultation is viewed as a viable method of removing these impediments to mental health and, perhaps more important, preventing them from occurring in the first place.

The demand for consultation services is already causing at least two major trends among helping professionals. Some are becoming professional consultants and either joining the growing number of consulting firms or forming their own businesses. Others are finding that they spend increasing amounts of their time in consultation activities. There is no reason to expect that these trends will abate in the foreseeable future.

Consultation is not a panacea for all the ills of an ailing society, however. It is only one of the tools that can be applied to eliminating these ills in some instances and preventing them in others. And, more specifically, consultation cannot totally replace direct services, although if properly practiced it can probably reduce the need for counseling and psychotherapy. Consultation should be viewed, as it is in this volume, as one of many means to the end of improving mental health and mental health services.

Since 1970 a number of individuals have made contributions to the growth and development of consultation in human resource organizations. Among the leaders in this area are a number of school psychologists, one of whom has already been mentioned, J. R. Bergan. However, Joel Meyers and his associates (Meyers et al., 1979) reconceptualized mental

health consultation for use in school settings, and R. A. Schmuck has pioneered the application of organizational development principles in schools. Others such as J. C. Alpert, J. C. Conoley, T. B. Gutkin, Jack Bardon, R. R. Abidin, Jr., M. L. Tombari, and T. R. Kratochwill have written influential papers and/or conducted pioneering research on consultation. Frequent references to their work will be found throughout this book.

Other groups such as counselor educators, counseling psychologists, and community psychologists have made significant contributions to the current status of consultation. Notable among these is June Gallessich, whose observations on training and theory building in consultation have played an important role in developing consultation practice. DeWayne Kurpius and Donald Dinkmeyer have influenced consultation by advocating systems perspectives and an Adlerian based approach to consultation, respectively. M. K. Hamilton and C. J. Meade (1979) edited an influential publication on systems approaches to consulting on the college campus. Community psychologists, such as Ira Iscoe, Kenneth Heller, F. V. Mannino, and M. F. Shore have also made considerable contributions to the current body of knowledge about consultation through reviews of the empirical literature, training, and critical reviews of theory and practice. Finally, a number of organizational consultants such as Chris Argyris, Gordon and Ronald Lippitt, and Edgar Schein have been influential in shaping consultation as it is conceptualized and practiced today. Their emphasis upon systems thinking and organizational processes perhaps stands as their greatest contribution.

Consultation Defined

Mannino and Shore (1985, 1986) indicate that confusion exists regarding the definition of consultation and that this state of affairs restricts its advancement. A review of the literature provides a great deal of support for this position. In some instances consultation has been likened to training (Gallessich, 1982) and in others advocacy and consultation have been depicted as complementary processes (Conoley, 1981b). However, these isolated cases are probably not the source of the confusion of which Mannino and Shore speak. It is more likely that consultants working in different fields utilizing different theoretical models have slightly different views of consultation and their respective definitions reflect these views. This situation is not unlike the one that exists whenever a counselor or psychotherapist tries to set forth a global definition of counseling or psychotherapy. It would be virtually impossible to synthesize a definition that would satisfy the various practitioners who provide counseling or therapy from a behavioral, Gestalt, client-centered, or rational emotive frame of reference. Thus, while Mannino and Shore may be correct about the confusion regarding the definition of consultation, they may be incorrect about the confusion retarding the advancement of consultation. The purpose of this section is to examine various definitions of consultation with regard to similarities and differences.

Caplan (1970) set forth one of the most integrated definitions of consultation when he formulated his mental health consultation model. He stipulates that consultation involves a voluntary, nonhierarchical relationship between two professionals who are often of different occupational groups (e.g., psychologists and psychiatric nurses) and is initiated by the consultee for the purpose of solving a work-related problem. The goals of consultation, according to Caplan, are two-fold: to improve the consultee's functioning with a client,

which may be an individual, a group, or an organization, and to develop the consultee's skills to the point that she or he will be able to cope with similar problems independently in the future. Caplan also stipulates that (1) typically the consultant comes from outside the consultee's organization, (2) consultation should not focus on the consultee's personal problems, and (3) the consultee has primary responsibility for implementing any solutions that evolve from the consultation process.

Although many consultants find Caplan's definition too restrictive (Heller, 1985; Meyers et al., 1979; Pryzwansky, 1974; Randolph, 1985), some of his ideas have become widely accepted, such as the triadic nature of the consultant-consultee-client interaction and the collegial nature of the consultant-client relationship (Conoley & Conoley, 1982; Dinkmeyer & Carlson, 1973; Gallessich, 1982; Keller, 1981; Kurpius & Fuqua, 1993; Meyers et al., 1979; Reynolds, Gutkin, Elliot, & Witt, 1984).

Two aspects of Caplan's definition have received a great amount of criticism: the external locus of the consultant and the responsibility of the consultee for implementing solutions generated in the process. Most current authorities on consultation agree that the consultant may belong to the same organization as the consultee (be internal versus external) and may act collaboratively in the implementation of a strategy that grows out of consultation (e.g., Bergan, 1977; Dinkmeyer & Carlson, 1973; Gallessich, 1982; Kurpius & Fuqua, 1993; Lippitt & Lippitt, 1986; Meyers et al., 1979; Randolph, 1985). School counselors, school psychologists, clinical and counseling psychologists, social workers, and psychiatric nurses regularly consult within their own agencies, function collaboratively, and, also in opposition to Caplan's view, consult within their own organization *as well* as with members of other organizations.

Another facet of Caplan's definition that has drawn a great deal of opposition is that consultation can only take place between two professionals. It should be recalled that Caplan's approach was developed in response to a certain set of conditions (that is, the flood of refugee children that overwhelmed professionals in post–World War II Israel), that influenced his consultation model. Consultants working under different circumstances have reached different conclusions. Lippitt and Lippitt (1986) depict the consultation process as one that occurs between a consultant and a wide variety of individuals and systems, including families, voters' organizations, communities, political parties, and so forth. Heller (1985) echoes this sentiment in part when he describes consultation as one means of empowering disenfranchised social groups. Brown, Wyne, Blackburn, and Powell (1979) and Snapp and Davidson (1982) also reflect a portion of the Lippitt and Lippitt (1986) perspective when they indicate students may be consultees.

The implicit question embedded in Caplan's (1970) view and those of Lippitt and Lippitt (1986) and others is, What is the essence of consultation? Is it an independent helpgiving process that can be differentiated on its own merit from other helping processes? Or does the nature of the role-players determine when consultation occurs? Certainly many consultants in addition to Caplan (e.g., Conoley & Conoley, 1992; Gallessich, 1982; Meyers et al., 1979; Parsons & Meyers, 1984) appear to opt for the latter definition. The strength of the position that holds that consultation must occur between two professionals is that it adds precision to the definition. The weakness of this position is that it precludes the use of consultation services with teacher's aides, line supervisors, nonprofessional members of community groups, students, or the groups to which they belong. (Jane Close Conoley has

changed her earlier view somewhat, now holding that it is the process that makes consultation unique, not the parties involved.)

A final area of controversy regarding a definition of consultation is related to the one just discussed. If one accepts the idea of consultation with a family (Brown et al., 1979; Lippitt & Lippitt, 1986; Sheridan, 1993), is the focus a work-related problem? Similarly, if one accepts Heller's (1985) ideas about working with community groups to help them assert their political muscle, is the focus a work-related problem? In the strict Caplanian sense, the answer to both of these questions is no. However, most consultants would agree that the focus of consultation is upon all vital processes engaged in by consultees, including communication, their use of technology, their sources of information and resources, the way information and resources are transformed to achieve goals, and the products produced (Katz & Kahn, 1978; Werner & Tyler, 1993). As an example, consultation with a community group would focus upon the work of that group, broadly conceived. Consultation with a parent might focus on the information he or she has about child rearing, how that information is used, and the result (his or her children's behavior).

It is clearly the position here that Caplan's (1970) definition unduly restricts the utilization of consultation for many. It is equally the case that Caplan's definition is a viable one for the consultant who expects to practice the mental health model he set forth. There are no right and wrong definitions of consultation until one begins to consider the assumptions that underpin the process. However, a broader definition of consultation has been adopted by the authors that is more in keeping with that of Lippitt and Lippitt (1986) and that corresponds more closely to the assumptions we make about consultation in the pages that follow.

Human service consultation is defined as a voluntary problem-solving process that can be initiated and terminated by either the consultant or consultee. It is engaged primarily for the purpose of assisting consultees to develop attitudes and skills that will enable them to function more effectively with a client which can be an individual, group, or organization for which they have responsibility. Thus, the goals of the process are two-fold: enhancing services to third parties and improving the ability of consultees to function in areas of concern to them.

The consultation relationship is an egalitarian one and in its most productive form is characterized by openness, warmth, genuineness, and empathy since authentic communication is essential to the success of the enterprise. Even though the parameters of the consulting relationship in many ways parallel those associated with a therapeutic relationship, including the confidentiality of the communication, consultation does not focus on the psychological problems of consultees directly. The consultant may, however, point to psychological deficits of consultees that restrict their ability to deal with certain problems and suggest courses of actions to deal with them.

During consultation, the consultant may assume various roles. In crisis situations, consultants may shift temporarily to an expert mode, diagnose the problem, and prescribe solutions. At other times, the consultant may simply function as a process observer and help consultees to develop awareness of processes that are impairing their functioning in a subsystem or system. Generally speaking, however, collaboration between the consultant and consultee at each phase of the consultation process is encouraged, with the guiding principle being that consultees are to assume as much responsibility for the process as their current status permits. The consultant's functioning in the expert role for long periods of time is

particularly deleterious to the consultee since it all but precludes her or him from developing the skills needed to gain independence from the consultant. Functioning in the process observation mode can be an effective means of facilitating consultee growth, but a more intense and active collaboration is more likely to achieve the long-term goals of consultation.

Finally, consultation may be delivered equally well by internal or external sources, depending to some degree on the nature of the problem, the consultee, and the environmental variables. The essence of this definition is summarized in the following list.

1. Initiated by either consultee or consultant.
2. Relationship characterized by authentic communication.
3. Consultees may be professionals or nonprofessionals.
4. Provides direct services to consultees, assisting them to develop coping skills that ultimately make them independent of consultant.
5. Is triadic in that it provides indirect services to third parties (clients).
6. Types of problems considered are work related when the concept of work is broadly conceived.
7. Consultant's role varies with consultee's needs.
8. Locus of consultant may be internal or external.
9. All communication between consultant and consultee is confidential.

Consultation Contrasted to Other Helping Relationships

In order to clearly differentiate between consultation and other helping services, it may be useful to contrast consultation with advice giving, supervision, therapy/counseling, teaching, and organizational development. Organizational development (OD) involves a series of processes including training, applied research, and consultation that are utilized by a change agent to enhance the functioning of an organization (Lippitt & Lippitt, 1986; Smith & Corse, 1986). The organizational development specialist may choose from any of these strategies depending upon the needs of the organization. However, an OD specialist who enters an organization as a consultant may employ action research such as surveys of employee perceptions of problems and proposed solutions to those problems. Similarly, training may be used as one of a vast assortment of interventions in the consulting process (Lippitt & Lippitt, 1986). Consulting then, is one of the roles that an OD specialist may assume, although it is interrelated to a large degree with training and action research.

"Teaching is a process of imparting, in a planned systematic way, a specified body of information" (Conoley & Conoley, 1992, p. 4). As noted in the foregoing paragraph, teaching (training) is a tool that consultants employ in the consultation process, usually as a part of an intervention strategy, although it could very well be used in other stages of consultation. Teaching in the traditional sense is often a formal, didactic situation and is rarely collaborative. Much of the so-called teaching that occurs in consultation, however, is more informal and involves various forms of modeling rather than lecturettes and homework (Conoley & Conoley, 1992).

Therapy/counseling is a direct relationship in which the aim is to alter the behavior of the person (client) receiving the service. Like consulting it is usually predicated upon the

assumption that a human relationship characterized by genuineness and trust is necessary for success. Also, like consultation, the goal of therapy/counseling is to produce an independent client. However, the direct nature of the service clearly differentiates it from consultation as does the depth and intensity of the client-therapist relationship and the fact that there is usually a direct focus on the client's defenses. Mental health consultation, which will be discussed in Chapter Two, most closely parallels therapy and counseling because of Caplan's focus on weakening consultee defenses (Conoley & Conoley, 1992).

Supervision also has some similarities with consultation as well as some important differences. Perhaps the most important differences lie in the nature of the relationship. Supervisors are clearly the experts in most supervisory relationships and are often authority figures as well because their evaluations lead to grades, raises, promotions, and so forth. This contrasts with the democratic relationship presupposed here and advocated by most consultants with the exception of Caplan's (1970) client-centered model of mental health consultation. Although supervisors aim to increase the functioning of supervisees, the evaluative nature of the relationship makes it difficult, if not impossible, to establish a totally non-threatening relationship (Caplan, 1970; Conoley & Conoley, 1992; Gallessich, 1982).

Advice giving is probably the process most often confused with consultation. As Gallessich (1982) points out, when we use the term consultation colloquially, we are for the most part referring to seeking or giving advice. However, a number of implicit and explicit aspects of the advice process distinguishes it from consultation. First, one person assumes an expert role. Second, there is no explicit intention to develop expertise in the person receiving the advice. Thus, when a similar situation arises in the future the recipient in all likelihood will have to return to the source of the advice. Third, no particular type of relationship is assumed to exist between the advice giver and receiver, although it is certainly one of expert to novice.

Recently it has become fashionable to use the terms *collaboration* and *consultation* together as in *collaborative consultation* (Reyes & Jason, 1993; West & Idol, 1993). Schulte (1993) reminds us that collaboration and consultation are two distinct processes. Collaboration is an interactive, planning, decision-making or problem-solving process involving two or more team members, according to West and Idol (1993, p. 679). Consultation, as we have already seen, is also a problem-solving process involving two or more people. However, what is inherent in most definitions of consultation is that it is an *indirect* helping process that empowers the consultee. The collaborative process involves two or more individuals in a *direct* helping process. Given this incongruity, should the two terms be linked? That is, can we actually have collaborative consultation?

Consultation can involve collaboration in several of its stages. For example, consultant and consultee can collaborate in the assessment of the client and in the goal-setting process. Most would agree that unless this occurs the consulting process is doomed to failure. However, if the consultant and the consultee work together to deliver the intervention as Reyes and Jason (1993) suggest, can the relationship still be characterized as consultation? Schulte (1993) thinks not, and historically she is correct. Does calling the relationship between two people collaborative consultation create a new model of consultation as West and Idol (1993) suggest? Probably not. What goes on between two persons focused on helping a third is consultation when the service is delivered by the consultee, and it is collaboration when both collaborators deliver the service.

Student Learning Activity 1.1

Please place an A by each statement that applies to advice, a C by each statement that depicts consultation, a T/C by each that describes therapy or counseling, an S by each that portrays supervision, and a T by each activity that describes teaching or training. In some instances, more than one classification may be appropriate.

Activities	Classification
1. Involves an indirect approach to clients	_____
2. Direct approach that involves primarily one-way communication	_____
3. Evaluation of the person assumed to be a part of the relationship	_____
4. One person assumes an expert role	_____
5. Direct approach that requires two-way communication	_____
6. Aimed at producing an independent recipient of services	_____
7. Does not expect that recipient of the process will become self-sufficient	_____
8. Triadic relationship	_____
9. Relationship is assumed to be between equals	_____
10. Process not based upon facilitative relationship	_____

Some Definitional Issues

As we have already seen, many differences arise when consultation is defined. A number of conflicting issues exist in other aspects of consultation as well. A few of the more important ones will be discussed briefly at this point.

Terminology

Three chief actors have been identified in relationship to the human services consultation process: consultant, consultee, and client. The consultant, working directly with the consultee, provides indirect services to a third party, a client. This terminology is for the most part in keeping with that employed traditionally by consultants working in human service agencies. However, a vast body of literature exists that focuses upon consulting in business and industry. In this literature (e.g., Lippitt, 1982; Lippitt & Lippitt, 1986; Steele, 1975) the client is the person with whom the consultant actually works. No rationale for this discrep-

ancy appears in the professional literature. It could be conjectured that because much of the organizational consultation literature was developed by external consultants who consulted for pay, businesses were viewed as clients, or those who pay for services. In a practical sense, this distinction is unimportant and does not serve as a barrier to the literature, as long as the reader is aware that it exists.

Lack of True Theories

Gallessich (1982) critiqued the major approaches to consultation, which she termed clinical, mental health, behavioral, and organizational. The clinical model, sometimes termed the medical or expert service model, grew out of the medical tradition where physicians who possessed more expertise were asked to assist in diagnosing the problems being experienced by other physicians' patients. Gallessich suggests that this model has no cohesive theoretical base. Similarly, she holds that the mental health consultation model (Caplan, 1970), the behavioral model (Bergan, 1977; Russell, 1978), and the organizational consultation model (Lippitt & Lippitt, 1986; Meyers, 1978; Schein, 1969; Steele, 1975) suffer from the same malady: no integrated theoretical base.

Gallessich (1985) contends that the lack of good models has created a crisis in consultation because techniques are not linked to conceptual or empirical foundations. The result, she believes, is that consultants do not use a coherent approach to focus their practice. She fears, and draws support from numerous others (e.g., Bardon, 1985; Bowen, 1977; Glaser, 1981), that the lack of conceptual models will result in harmful consultation processes because atheoretical approaches may not allow for clear role descriptions that are needed by the consultant and consultee. Gallessich also believes that consultation without a clear conceptual base may be technique ridden and may not provide the consultant with adequate boundary parameters. As a result the consultant may inadvertently stray into areas that are "off limits."

While Gallessich's (1985) concerns about the status of conceptual models of consultation appear to have some legitimacy, there is certainly some room for disagreement with such a bleak picture. Dinkmeyer and Carlson (1973) set forth a consultation model based upon the individual psychology of Alfred Adler; Bergan (1977) articulated a carefully conceived approach to consultation anchored primarily in operant learning theory. A third model, Brown & Schulte (1987), which grew out of the tenets of social learning theory (Bandura, 1977b), will be presented in Chapter Three. Recently, Fuqua and Kurpius (1993), Brack, Jones, Smith, White, and Brack (1993), Rockwood (1993) and Rose (1993) have discussed more than a half-dozen models of organizational consultation, and Martens (1993) has clarified the original behavioral model set forth by Bergan. It is undoubtedly the case that each of the current models of consultation is open to criticism, but the field has no shortage of models and theories.

Internal versus External Consultants

Should consultants be a part of the organization to which they provide services (internal) or be brought in from the outside (external)? This question has provided the basis for a spirited debate over the past years, and while the controversy is abating and a number of

individuals (Conoley & Conoley, 1982; Kurpius & Fuqua, 1993; Lippitt & Lippitt, 1986) endorse the concept of both, some concerns remain, particularly about the role of the internal consultant.

Internal consultants are sometimes viewed as being at a disadvantage in the consulting process because they may appear to have less status than external consultants, may be restricted by role definitions (for example, a school counselor may be viewed as one providing direct services) (Conoley & Conoley, 1992), and may seem not to possess the degree of objectivity needed to function effectively in the consultation role because they have adopted the normative structure of the organization of which they are a part (Beer, 1980). On the other hand, internal consultants have distinct advantages because of their familiarity with the organizational processes, an increased knowledge of the sources of different types of records, and an awareness of both the formal and informal power structure of an organization. Data have demonstrated that a variety of different types of internal consultants including school psychologists, (Mannino & Shore, 1986; Medway & Updike, 1985; Sibley, 1986; West & Idol, 1987) school counselors, and business consultants can function effectively. This issue of internal versus external consultants will be addressed in detail throughout this book since it has potential implications for most human resource consultants.

Interventions Utilized by Human Resource Workers

Figure 1.1 is a conceptual model of the functioning of human service professionals. It draws on the earlier work of Morrill, Oetting, and Hurst (1974) and Brown et al. (1979), but extends and redefines to some degree the thinking of both groups. The model retains the four targets of intervention posed by Brown and associates—individuals, groups, organizations, and communities. It also retains the three purposes of intervention posed by Morrill et al., which were remediation, prevention, and development. To be more congruent with current mental health terminology, these have been renamed in the current model to primary, secondary, and tertiary mental health prevention.

Primary prevention is proactive in that it aims at enhancing the mental health of an unidentified group that is assumed to have positive mental health. Primary prevention programs may be aimed at individuals (for example, enhancing coping skills), groups (enhancing communication patterns), organizations (improving decision making), and communities (developing mechanisms to increase community input into governance).

Secondary prevention involves the identification and treatment of problems before they have serious consequences in the life of an individual, group, organization, or community. Early identification and remediation of learning difficulties of children is a secondary prevention activity. So are preventive programs aimed at juveniles who have committed minor crimes, job enrichment programs designed to increase worker morale, and community based programs aimed at improving housing conditions.

Tertiary prevention programs attempt to reduce the impact of debilitating mental health problems. Consultation with the mother of a self-destructive child falls into this category as does consulting with the staff of a mental health agency confronted with numerous adults who have eating disorders. Consultation with organizations where high stress and the often related symptoms of high blood pressure, heart disease, and psychosomatic

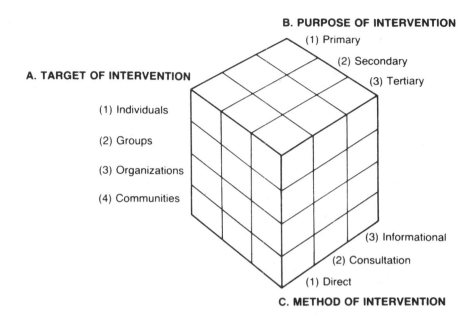

FIGURE 1.1   Reconceptualization of Purposes and Targets of Interventions Used by Counselors, Psychologists, Social Workers, and Other Human Resource Workers

ailments are common would be a tertiary prevention activity if the focus was on those already disabled. So would consultation in the community that focused on drug addicts or alcoholics.

Intervention methods in the current model have been refined somewhat from those offered previously. Direct interventions involve face-to-face contact with target groups. Training interventions, including teaching and supervision, are direct activities that may be used with varying sizes of groups for any of the three purposes. Counseling and therapy are direct interventions employed with individuals or small groups as secondary or tertiary prevention methods.

Consultation is an indirect service engaged in with a consultee or consultees to pursue the primary, secondary, or tertiary prevention of mental health problems with any of the four target groups. In this model consultation is not restricted to a collaborative approach but may include a variety of approaches.

Informational approaches are also indirect, but differ from consultation in that no consultee is involved. Interventions of this type attempt to influence a target group through a number of informational activities including the use of media (Morrill et al., 1974). However, informational approaches are not restricted to the use of computers, newspapers, television, or radio, but also include brochures, books, and other printed materials that focus upon the various target groups for the purposes of preventing and/or treating mental health problems.

Which intervention method should one choose? The obvious bias of the authors is that consultation is the preferred intervention in many instances. However, a variety of

factors enter into this choice including but not limited to the setting in which one works, the skills of the professional, the expectations of colleagues, the nature of the presenting problem, time available, and availability of the client. A rule of thumb for selecting an intervention method *should be* the one that has the greatest likelihood of achieving the intended goal at the least cost. As we shall see, consultation provides a viable alternative to direct service and informational approaches in many instances.

The Perspective of This Book

A review of the professional literature from a variety of applied fields within the social sciences reveals a remarkable theoretical convergence in thinking. This convergence is upon systems theory and its applications to understanding organizations, family therapy, education, transpersonal counseling, community functioning, and so forth. Whether one considers the simple formulation of Lewin (1951), $B = f(P \times E)$ (that is, behavior is a function of a person/environment interaction), Bandura's (1977a) reciprocal determinism, or the interpretation of organizational functioning using systems theory by Katz and Kahn (1978), it is almost impossible to escape the conclusion that an interrelatedness exists among individuals and the small groups to which they belong, and both in turn to larger, more complex social structures such as organizations and communities. The conclusion that interrelatedness exists, and the obvious corollary that understanding individuals or groups requires an understanding of the individual, the groups to which they belong, and the processes by which they interact, is a basic premise of this book. Other points of view will be presented as well because not all consultants have incorporated systems theory into their thinking.

A corollary to the premise of interrelatedness is that consultants cannot afford to think in old-fashioned, linear terms when they consider problems. Causation cannot be attributed to a single source. And just as problems have multiple causes, there are numerous pathways to solutions. Maybe more importantly, solutions designed to alleviate an identified problem in a given area may in turn produce negative consequences in another area. For example, school personnel, recognizing that student achievement was lagging, instituted tough academic programs only to find that dropping out of school increased. Similarly, businesses that have attempted to achieve production goals by utilizing improved technology have found that the potential gains are more than offset by increases in human problems. Thus, we have come full circle to our original premise. Linear thinking must give way to a type of multivariate logic that presupposes multiple causation and solutions and concerns itself with the interrelatedness among individuals, groups, and organizations.

Interrelatedness, multiple causality, and multiple pathways to solutions are three principles of systems thinking. But what is a system? It is an entity that takes various types of resources ranging from information to raw material (input) and through technology transforms the resource to some produce (output) (Katz & Kahn, 1978). A community agency takes in resources from the community, offers programs, and increases mental health among those served. Individuals, families, organizations, and communities can be conceptualized in the same way, as we shall see.

The Remainder of the Book

The three chapters that immediately follow will be devoted to outlining the major models of consultation. Chapter Two will deal with Caplanian ideas about consultation; his four approaches (Caplan, 1970) to consultation will be presented. Chapter Three will cover behavioral models of consultation. In that chapter, two models will be presented, one based primarily on operant learning principles (Bergan, 1977) and the other grounded in social learning theory (Bandura, 1977a; Brown & Schulte, 1987). Chapter Four will provide an overview of systems theory and present three models of organizational consultation: organizational development (Beer, 1980; Huse, 1980; Lippitt, 1982), Schein's (1969) process approach, and Blake and Mouton's (1976) eclectic model.

Process variables in consultation will be examined in Chapters Five and Six. Chapter Five will provide an overview of the consultation process including a description of the stages through which consultation passes and an examination of the techniques employed at each stage. Chapter Six will deal with some of the major concerns that arise in the consultation process. Chapter Seven discusses the skills and characteristics needed to be an effective consultant. Chapter Eight addresses a heretofore largely unexplored but critical factor in the consultation process, the consultee. Chapters Nine and Ten will focus on consultation with parents and teachers, respectively. In this chapter, approaches to the evaluation of consultation will be discussed with some practical suggestions given for evaluating the effectiveness of consultation. Chapter Eleven discusses the processes involved in evaluation and gives guidelines for planning and using these processes.

The last section of the book will deal with some of the issues in consultation. Chapter Twelve will present a number of ethical principles that can guide the consultation effort and address certain legal pitfalls that may confront the consultant. Chapter Thirteen will be devoted to a variety of issues including consultant-consultee similarity in consultation, research needs, and consultation versus other interventions such as psychotherapy.

Summary

Consultation is slowly coming into its own as an intervention strategy among helping professionals. Since it is just receiving widespread attention, many issues remain to be resolved including the very essence of the content and process of consultation. However, numerous models of consultation have evolved and each has a perspective that can be useful to the neophyte consultant. The primary focus of this chapter was to point out definitional issues and lines of demarcation between consultation, counseling, training, advocacy, and supervision.

Tips for the Practitioner

1. Make sure you have a comprehensive definition of consultation before you begin to consult including the

- role of the consultant
- role of the consultee
- nature of the consulting relationship
- expected outcomes of consultation.

2. Practice communicating your definition by first writing it out and then explaining it to a person who knows little about consulting.

Review Questions

1. Contrast the various definitions of consultation using Caplan's definition as the basis for discussion.

2. Identify the salient issues in consultation that exist at this time.

3. Discuss the current status of consultation as an intervention in schools, mental health centers, college counseling centers, and other places where mental health professionals are employed.

References

Bandura, A. (1977a). Self system: Toward a unifying theory of behavioral change. *Psychological Review, 84*, 191–215.

Bandura, A. (1977b). *Social learning theory*. Englewood Cliffs, NJ: Prentice-Hall.

Bardon, J. I. (1982). School psychology's dilemma: A proposal for its resolution. *Professional Psychology, 13*, 955–968.

Bardon J. I. (1985). Toward a consultation meta-theory: On the verge of a breakthrough. *The Counseling Psychologist, 13*(3), 69–72.

Beer, M. (1980). *Organizational change and development: A systems view*. Santa Monica, CA: Goodyear.

Bergan, J. R. (1977). *Behavioral consultation*. Columbus, OH: Charles E. Merrill.

Bowen, D. D. (1977). Values dilemmas in organizational development. *Journal of Applied Behavioral Science, 13*, 545–558.

Brack, G., Jones, E. S., Smith, R. M., White, J., & Brack, C. J. (1993). A primer on consultation theory. *Journal of Counseling and Development, 71*, 619–628.

Brown, D., Wyne, M. D., Blackburn, J., & Powell, C. (1979). *Consultation: Strategy for improving education*. Boston: Allyn & Bacon.

Brown. D., & Schulte, A. (1987). A social learning model of consultation. *Professional psychology: Research and practice, 18*, 283–287.

Caplan, G. (1970). *The theory and practice of mental health consultation*. New York: Basic Books.

Conoley. J. C. (Ed.) (1981a). *Consultation in schools: Theory, research, procedures*. New York: Academic Press.

Conoley, J. C. (1981b). Advocacy consultation: Processes and problems. In W. C. Conoley (Ed.). *Consultation in schools: Theory, research, procedures* (pp. 157–178). New York: Academic Press.

Conoley. J. C., & Conoley, C. W. (1982). *School consultation: A guide to practice and training*. New York: Macmillan.

Dinkmeyer, D., & Carlson, J. (1973). *Consulting: Facilitating human potential and change processes*. Columbus, OH: Charles E. Merrill.

Erchul, W. P., & Chewning, T. G. (1990). Behavioral consultation from a request-centered relational communication perspective. *School Psychology Quarterly, 5*, 1–20.

Fuqua, D. R., & Kurpius, D. J. (1993). Conceptual models of organizational consultation. *Journal of counseling and development, 71*, 607–618.

Gallessich, J. (1982). *The profession and practice of consultation: A handbook for consultants, trainers of consultants and consumers of consultation services*. San Francisco: Jossey-Bass.

Glaser, E. M. (1981). Ethical issues in consultation practice with organizations. *Consultation, 1*(1), 12–16.

Hamilton, M. K., & Meade, C. J. (Eds.). (1979). *Consulting on campus: New directions for student services*. San Francisco: Jossey-Bass.

Heller. K. (1985). Issues in consultation to community groups: Some useful distinctions between social regulations and indigenous citizens groups. *The Counseling Psychologist, 15*, 403–409.

Heller, K., Price, R. H., Reinberg, S., Riger. S., & Wandersman, A. (1984). *Psychology and community change: Challenge of the future* (2nd ed.), Homewood, IL: The Dorsey Press.

Heller, K., & Monahan, J. (1977). *Psychology and community change*. Homewood, IL: The Dorsey Press.

Huse, E. F. (1980). *Organizational development and change*. (2nd ed.) St. Paul, MN: West Publishing Co.

Katz, D., & Kahn, R. L., (1978). *The social psychology of organizations*. New York: Wiley.

Keller, H. R. (1981). Behavioral consultation. In J. C. Conoley (Ed.), *Consultation in schools: Theory, research, procedures* (pp. 59–90). New York: Academic Press.

Kurpius, D. J. (1993). Fundamental issues in defining consultation. *Journal of Counseling and Development, 71*, 598–600.

Levine, M., & Levine, A. (1970). *A social history of helping services*. New York: Appleton-Century-Crofts.

Lewin, K. (1951). *Field theory in social sciences*. New York: Harper & Row.

Lippitt, G. L. (1982). *Organizational renewal*. (2nd ed.) Englewood Cliffs, NJ: Prentice-Hall.

Lippitt, G., & Lippitt, R. (1986). *The consulting process in action* (2nd ed.). San Diego, CA: University Associates.

Mannino, F. V., & Shore, M. F. (1975). Effecting change through consultation. In F. V. Mannino, B. W. MacLennon, & M. F. Shore (Eds.), *The practice of mental health consultation* (pp. 478–499). New York: Garder Press.

Mannino, F. V., & Shore, M. F. (1985). Understanding consultation: Some orienting dimensions. *The Counseling Psychologist, 13*(3), 363–367.

Mannino, F. V., & Shore, M. F. (1986). Introduction. In F. V. Mannino, E. J. Trickett, M. F. Shore, M. G. Kidder, & G. Levine (Eds.), *Handbook of mental health consultation* (pp. xi–xvii). Washington, DC: U.S. Government Printing Office.

Martens, B. K. (1993). A behavioral approach to consultation. In J. E. Zins, T. R. Kratochwill, & S. E. Elliot (Eds.) *Handbook of Consultation Services for Children*. San Francisco: Jossey-Bass.

Medway, F. J., & Updyke, J. F. (1985). Meta-analysis of consultation outcome studies. *American Journal of Community Psychology, 13*, 489–505.

Meyers, J. (1978). Training school psychologists for a consultation role. *School Psychology Digest, 7*(3), 26–31.

Meyers, J., Parsons, R. D., & Martin, R. (1979). *Mental health consultation in the schools*. San Francisco: Jossey-Bass.

Morrill, W. H., Oetting, E. R., & Hurst, J. C. (1974). Dimensions of counselor functioning. *Personnel and Guidance Journal, 52*(6), 354–359.

Parsons, R. D., & Meyers, J. (1984). *Developing consultation skills: A guide to training, development, and assessment for human services professionals*. San Francisco: Jossey-Bass.

Pryzwanksy, W. B. (1974). A reconsideration of the consultation model for delivery of school based psychological services. *American Journal of Orthopsychiatry, 44*, 579–583.

Randolph, D. L. (1985). *Micro consulting: Basic psychological consultation skills for helping professionals*. Johnson City, TN: Institute of Social Sciences and Arts.

Reyes, O., & Jason, L. A. (1993). Collaborating with the community. In J. E. Zins, T. R. Kratochwill, & S. E. Elliot (eds.) *Handbook of Consultation Services for Children*. San Francisco: Jossey-Bass.

Reynolds. C. R., Gutkin, T. B., Elliot, S. N., & Witt, J. C. (1984). *School psychology: Essentials of theory and practice*. New York: John Wiley & Sons.

Rockwood, G. F. (1993). Edgar Schein's process versus content consultation model. *Journal of Counseling and Development, 71*, 636–638.

Ross, G. J. (1993). Peter Block's flawless consulting and the homunculus theory: Within each person is a perfect consultant. *Journal of Counseling and Development, 71*, 639–641.

Russell, M. L. (1978). Behavioral consultation: Theory

and process. *Personnel and Guidance Journal, 56,* 346–350.

Schein, E. H. (1969). *Process consultation: Its role in organizational development.* Reading. MA: Addison-Wesley.

Schulte, A. C. (1993). In the eye of the beholder: Collaborations consultation definition and research. In D. Fuch's (chair) *Questioning Popular Beliefs About Collaborations Consultation.* Paper presented at annual meeting of Council for Exceptional Children. San Antonio, TX.

Sheridan, S. M. (1993). Models for working with parents. In J. E. Zins, T. R. Kratochwill, & S. E. Elliot (eds.) *Handbook of Consultation Services for Children.* San Francisco: Jossey-Bass.

Sibley, S. (1986). *A meta-analysis of school consultation research.* Unpublished doctoral dissertation, Texas Women's University: Denton, TX.

Smith, K. K., & Corse, S. J. (1986). The process of consultation: Critical issues in F. V. Mannino, E. J. Trickett, M. F. Shore, M. G. Kidder, & G. Levin (Eds.). *Handbook of mental health consultation* (pp. 247–278). Washington, DC: U.S. Government Printing Office.

Snapp. M., & Davidson, S. L. (1982). Systems interventions for school psychologists: A case study approach. In C. R. Reynolds & T. B. Gutkin (Eds.), *The handbook of school psychology* (pp. 858–861). New York: John Wiley & Sons.

Steele, F. (1975). *Consulting for organizational change.* Amherst, MA: University of Massachusetts Press.

Stryker, S. C. (1982). *Principles and practices of professional consulting.* Gleneg, MD: Bermont Books.

Werner, J. L., & Tyler, J. M. (1993). *Journal of Counseling and Development, 71,* 689–692.

West, J. F., & Idol, L. (1987). School consultation (Part I): An interdisciplinary perspective on theory, models and research. *Journal of Learning Disabilities, 7,* 388–408.

West, J. F., & Idol, L. (1993). The counselor as a consultant in a collaborative school, *Journal of Counseling and Development, 71,* 673–683.

Chapter *2*

Mental Health Consultation

Goal of the Chapter

The goal of this chapter is to present Caplan's mental health model of consultation and related work by other theorists and researchers.

Chapter Preview

1. The historical events that precipitated the development of mental health consultation are delineated.
2. Mental health consultation is defined and the fundamental assumptions which underlie it are examined.
3. Caplan's description of the process of consultation is summarized.
4. The four types of consultation discussed by Caplan—client-centered case consultation, consultee-centered case consultation, program-centered administrative consultation, and consultee-centered administrative consultation—are described.
5. Consultee-centered consultation and the related concepts of theme interference and theme interference reduction are discussed in detail.
6. Variants of mental health consultation are described, and recent research related to mental health consultation is summarized.

One of the most influential figures in the field of psychological consultation has been Gerald Caplan. A psychiatrist and a leader in the development of community psychiatry, Caplan was one of the first mental health professionals to write about consultation. His ideas still are pervasive in psychological consultation and reflect both an environmental and psychodynamic perspective. In this chapter, Caplan's (1964, 1970, 1974, 1977, 1986; Caplan & Caplan, 1993) approach to psychological consultation, often referred to as mental health

consultation or Caplanian consultation, will be described. In addition, models of consultation that have been based in part on Caplan's ideas, such as Meyers (Meyers, 1981, 1989; Meyers, Brent, Faherty, Modafferi, 1993; Meyers & Kundert, 1988; Meyers, Parsons, & Martin, 1979) and Altrocchi (1972), also will be described. Finally, further developments in Caplan's approach to prevention of mental health problems will be discussed.

Roots of Mental Health Consultation

In the years since World War II a new perspective on mental health and disorders has emerged. Termed the *community* or *preventive* approach, this perspective emphasizes the importance of social support systems within a community in the prevention of psychological disorders (Sarason & Sarason, 1984).

Caplan (1970, 1974) sees consultation as a central component in this preventive approach. In his view, maladaptive behavior and psychological disturbance arise in part because caregivers, family, friends, and community groups within a social system do not provide sufficient direction, support, and stability when an individual is faced with a stressful life event. If the community mechanisms for supporting persons under stress are improved, the incidence of psychological disturbance that requires direct intervention by mental health professionals can be reduced and the overall mental health of a community enhanced.

Caplan views caregiving agents, such as nurses, doctors, teachers, the clergy, and police, as key persons whose actions can affect the mental health of others. By consulting with these agents, community mental health can be enhanced by: (1) helping caregiving agents work out ways to accomplish their professional objectives (for example, teaching, law enforcement) that also promote mental health in their clients, and (2) dealing with personality factors in consultees that interfere with their professional functioning and reduce their effectiveness with clients (Caplan, 1974).

Caplan's emphasis upon the extent to which the personal needs and unresolved conflicts of caregivers interfere with their professional functioning reflects one of two major influences on his approach to consultation, the psychodynamic perspective. But recognition of the importance of social institutions in determining behavior is reflected in Caplan's focus on making social institutions such as schools function more effectively by improving their capacity to deal with the mental health problems of their clients.

Caplan (1970; Caplan & Caplan, 1993) traces his interest in consultation to his work in a child guidance center in Israel after World War II. He was part of a team of psychiatrists, psychologists, and social workers who supervised the mental health of approximately 16,000 new immigrant children who were cared for in over 100 residential institutions throughout Israel. Because of the large geographic area served and the high rate of referrals, traditional mental health services involving referral, diagnosis, and treatment of individual children were not feasible. To provide services, a child guidance staff member would travel to a particular residential institution to deal with a group of referrals. Rather than provide psychotherapy, the staff member would discuss with the child-care staff alternative ways of managing the child that would resolve the child's problems while he or she remained in the residential institution.

Child guidance staff members functioning in this way made several discoveries that pointed to consultation as an important and efficient means of dealing with mental health problems (Rosenfeld & Caplan, 1954). First, specific institutions and childcare workers seemed to have difficulties with particular groups of children. One institution might have a high rate of referrals of children with learning problems while another institution might refer a high rate of aggressive children. This finding suggested that by improving the ability of the staff of an institution to cope with a particular problem, a large number of children's problems could be resolved without direct service to the individual children. Second, consultants noted that many times childcare workers seemed to have developed a rather narrow perspective on children and the problems they presented. A sympathetic and objective discussion with the consultant often allowed staff members to see children as persons with difficulties rather than as problem children, to develop a wider range of action alternatives for dealing with problems, and subsequently to deal with the problems more effectively (Caplan, 1970). Third, consultants found that working in the childcare institution rather than dealing with referred children at the guidance center allowed them to quickly understand the variety of factors within the institution that might be affecting a particular child and caregiving agent. These factors might have been unknown to them had the child been treated at the center. The teachers and other caregivers also seemed more comfortable in their own setting and were more likely to share their perceptions of cases freely with consultants.

Following his experiences in Israel, Caplan journeyed to Harvard to work with Erich Lindemann, another pioneer in preventive psychiatry. There, Caplan continued to develop and refine the techniques of mental health consultation through his work in the Field Training Unit of the Harvard School of Public Health and the Laboratory of Community Psychiatry at Harvard Medical School. Caplan did not see consultation as a new profession, but as an important form of mental health service delivery that had not been formally recognized and distinguished from other forms of mental health services (Caplan, 1970). In his book *The Theory and Practice of Mental Health Consultation* (Caplan, 1970), as well as several related works (Caplan, 1964, 1974, 1977), Caplan sought to formalize and further develop consultation as part of the role of a mental health professional.

Basic Concepts in Mental Health Consultation

Definition of Consultation

Caplan (1970), as well as others (Gallessich, 1982; Reschly, 1976) note that the term consultation is used in many ways. However, in his writing Caplan used consultation in a restricted sense referring to "a process of interaction between two professional persons—the consultant, who is a specialist, and the consultee, who invokes the consultant's help in regard to a current work problem with which he [*sic*] is having some difficulty and which he has decided is within the other's area of specialized competence. The work problem involves the management or treatment of one or more clients of the consultee, or the planning or implementation of a program to cater to such clients" (Caplan, 1970, p. 19).

Consultation is a service provided to caregiving professionals such as doctors, nurses, teachers, lawyers, welfare workers, probation officers, police, and clergy to assist them in

dealing with the psychological aspects of a current work problem and, most importantly, to deal more effectively with similar problems in the future (Caplan, 1970). Caplan includes both individual and group consultation in his definition, although his emphasis in earlier writings (Caplan, 1970) was on individual consultation.

A fundamental aspect of Caplan's definition of consultation, and one that has had a strong influence on consultation (Gutkin & Curtis, 1990; Meyers, 1981; Meyers et al., 1993), is his conceptualization of the consulting relationship as non-hierarchical and coordinate. Both the consultant and consultee are viewed as experts in their own areas. The consultant has no authority over the consultee—he or she is free to accept or reject any of the consultant's suggestions and maintains sole responsibility for carrying out any interventions. Caplan views a coordinate relationship as important for insuring that the consultee incorporates the knowledge gained in consultation into his or her own system of thinking. Hierarchical relationships in which one party has authority over the other are seen as an impediment to learning because the subordinate may feel coerced to accept the other's suggestions and resist acting on them to preserve his or her autonomy (Caplan, 1970). The following list is Caplan's summary of the basic characteristics of consultation.

1. Mental health consultation is a method for use between two professionals in respect to a lay client or a program for such clients.

2. The consultee's work problem must be defined by him [*sic*] as being in the mental health area—relating to (a) mental disorder or personality idiosyncrasies of the client, (b) promotion of mental health in the client, (c) interpersonal aspects of the work situation. The consultant must have expert knowledge in these areas.

3. The consultant has no administrative responsibility for the consultee's work, or professional responsibility for the outcome of the client's case. He is under no compulsion to modify the consultee's conduct of the case.

4. The consultee is under no compulsion to accept the consultant's ideas or suggestions.

5. The basic relationship between the two is coordinate. There is no built-in hierarchical authority tension. This is a situation that in our culture potentiates the influence of ideas. The freedom of the consultee to accept or reject what the consultant says enables him to take quickly as his own any ideas that appeal to him in his current situation.

6. The coordinate relationship is fostered by the consultant's usually being a member of another profession and coming briefly into the consultee's institution from the outside.

7. It is further supported by the fact that consultation is usually given as a short series of interviews—two or three, on the average—which take place intermittently in response to the consultee's awareness of current need for help with a work problem. The relationship in individual consultation is not maintained and dependency fostered by continuing contact. In group consultation there may be regular meetings, but dependency is reduced by peer support.

8. Consultation is expected to continue indefinitely. Consultees can be expected to encounter unusual work problems throughout their careers. Increasing competence and sophistication of consultees in their own profession increase the likelihood of their recognizing mental health complications and asking for consultation.

9. A consultant has no predetermined body of information that he intends to impart to a particular consultee. He responds only to the segment of the consultee's problems which the

latter exposes in the current work difficulty. The consultant does not seek to remedy other areas of inadequacy in the consultee. He expects other issues to be raised in future consultations.

10. The twin goals of consultation are to help the consultee improve his handling or understanding of the current work difficulty and through this to increase his capacity to master future problems of a similar type.

11. The aim is to improve the consultee's job performance and not his sense of well-being. It is envisaged, however, that since the two are linked, a consultee's feelings of personal worth will probably be increased by a successful consultation, as will also his capacity to deal in a reality-based socially acceptable way with certain of his life difficulties. In other words, a successful consultation may have the secondary effect of being therapeutic to the consultee.

12. Consultation does not focus overtly on personal problems and feelings of the consultee. It respects his privacy. The consultant does not allow the discussion of personal and private material in the consultation interview.

13. This does not mean that the consultant does not pay attention to the feelings of the consultee. He is particularly sensitive to these and to the disturbance of task functioning produced by personal problems. He deals with personal problems, however, in a special way, such as by discussing them in the form in which the consultee has displaced them onto the client's case and the work setting.

14. Consultation is usually only one of the professional functions of a specialist, even if he is formally entitled "consultant." He should utilize the consultation method only when it is appropriate in the situation. At other times he will make use of different methods. It may sometimes occur that the demands of a situation will cause him to put aside his consultation in the middle. For instance, if he gets information during a consultation interview that leads him to judge that the consultee's actions are seriously endangering the client, such as by not preventing suicide or not leading toward investigation and treatment for a dangerous psychosis, he should set aside his consultant role and revert to his basic role as a psychiatrist, psychologist, or social worker. He will then give advice or take action that he does not allow the consultee the freedom to reject. This destroys the coordinate relationship and interrupts the consultation contact in favor of a higher goal. Such dramatic occasions have been rare in my experience, but consultants must constantly keep the possibility in mind as a realization of the realistic limits of this method.

15. Finally, it is worth emphasizing that mental health consultation is a method of communication between a mental health specialist and other professionals. It does not denote a new profession—merely a special way in which existing professionals may operate. The process of this operation has been refined and analyzed and can be systematically taught and learned. The content of the consultation communication will naturally vary in accordance with the specialized knowledge and experience of the consultant. Thus, although psychiatrists, psychologists, psychiatric social workers, and psychiatric nurses should use the same techniques of consultation with a particular consultee, the content of their specialized remarks about the case of the client will differ. The consultant must have specialized knowledge about the topic on which the consultee needs help: and the professional training and experience of the consultant will determine the detailed nature and form of this knowledge. (Source: *The Theory and Practice of Mental Health Consultation* by Gerald

Caplan. Copyright © 1970 by Basic Books, Inc., Publishers. Reprinted with permission Basic Books, Inc., Publishers, New York.)

Caplan distinguishes between four types of consultation based on two major divisions, (1) whether the content focus of consultation is difficulty with a particular client or an administrative difficulty, and (2) whether the primary goal of consultation is providing information in the consultant's area of specialty or improvement of the consultee's problem-solving capacity. Though each type of consultation is discussed in detail in subsequent sections, they are described briefly here.

In *client-centered case consultation* the focus is upon the consultee's management of a particular client or group of clients for whom he or she is responsible. The primary goal in this type of consultation is prescriptive—the consultant assesses the client and provides information to the consultee so that he or she may deal more effectively with the client. *Consultee-centered case consultation* also is concerned with the consultee's management of a particular client or group of clients, but improvement in the client is a secondary goal of this type of consultation. The primary goal is increased skills for the consultee and the focus of consultation is on the consultee's difficulties in dealing with the client (or clients) in question. *Program-centered administrative consultation* is the administrative counterpart of client-centered case consultation. The consultant functions as an expert in mental health and social systems and provides recommendations relevant to program development and administrative concerns for a particular agency. The last type of consultation, *consultee-centered administrative consultation*, also is concerned with program development and administrative concerns, but like consultee-centered case consultation, the focus is on increasing consultee effectiveness rather than consultant-generated solutions to specific organizational concerns.

Fundamental Assumptions in Mental Health Consultation

Before describing the process of mental health consultation, some of the fundamental assumptions that underlie mental health consultation and distinguish it from other types of consultation need to be delineated.

Both intrapsychic and environmental factors are important in explaining and changing behavior. More than any other model of consultation, mental health consultation focuses on intrapsychic variables, such as consultee feelings, attitudes, and beliefs, that are important in behavior change (Meyers, 1981). However, as already noted, Caplan's work also reflects a strong environmental focus, and his conception of the environment is not incompatible with more current, multi-level systems frameworks. Problems are not viewed as residing solely within the client, but as potentially residing at several different levels within and external to an organization. Assessment in mental health consultation focuses on a wide range of factors that may be relevant to a problem, including characteristics of the client, communication between the consultee and client, consultee skill level, consultee perceptions and attitudes, organizational factors that contribute to similarities in problems across consultees and clients, and community concerns and undercurrents that may make selected issues more salient and increase the likelihood that consultees will seek consultation for certain types of problems. Even Caplan's focus on intrapsychic factors within the consultee

reflects an environmental focus because the consultee is seen as an important part of the client's social environment (Meyers, 1981).

More than technical expertise is important in designing effective interventions. The adoption of an intervention technique is not solely a function of its effectiveness, but is influenced by many other factors. As Alpert and Silverstein (1985) state: "Basic to Caplan's method is the concept that each consultee is embedded in a profession with norms, roles, language, and a body of knowledge. Each consultee is also a member of a specific organizational culture. . . . Because of the unique aspects of these contexts, the consultant could not presume to fully understand the consultee's framework, and must assume that any recommendations for change will be adapted by the consultee" (p. 285). In other words, it is unlikely that consultants will be able to design interventions that are appropriate for consultees from other institutions and professions. Despite the consultant's expertise, intervention is left in the hands of the consultee.

Kelly (1993) recognized the importance of this assumption in a recent chapter discussing Caplan's contributions to consultation. He maintained that one of the four most important contributions of Caplan's work to an understanding of the consultation process was his assertion that the success of consultation was measured by the consultant's ability to translate mental health concepts to fit the role requirements of the consultees' profession.

Learning and generalization occur when consultees retain responsibility for action. Within Caplan's model, responsibility for action belongs to consultees. The consultant does not become involved in case management in client-centered case consultation or the implementation of organizational changes in administrative consultation. In Caplan's (1970) view, the direct involvement of consultants in problem resolution diminishes the consultees' feelings of ownership over problems and solutions generated to resolve them. Therefore, they are less likely to incorporate the concepts introduced in consultation into their working style.

Consultation concerning a single case issue also is restricted to two or three short interviews to prevent consultees from relying on the consultant for more than discussion of issues relevant to a problem. Consultants' brief involvement and lack of participation in selecting and implementing interventions or change strategies also communicates the expectation that consultees can manage work problems independently.

Consultee attitudes and affect also are assumed to be important in generalization. Even if consultees possess the skills to deal with a particular problem, they may not apply these skills if they do not perceive the situation objectively, have conflicting needs, or a particular strategy does not fit their own belief system. For example, a physician who has been trained to interact with patients in a paternalistic manner may be reluctant to allow patients to take an active role in treatment decision making even though he or she is aware that allowing the patient more control may lead to greater compliance and feelings of well-being in the patient.

Mental health consultation is a supplement to other problem-solving mechanisms within an organization. Caplan (1970) assumes that there are several ways of addressing difficulties with clients within an organization and that, for many types of problems, procedures other than consultation are more appropriate. For example, skill deficiencies in the consultee should be handled through supervision because the consultant is unlikely to understand the skills involved in another profession.

Student Learning Activity 2.1

List the conditions you believe are most conducive   your assumptions with Caplan's.
to generalization of skills to other settings. Compare

This assumption is important because Caplan's approach to consultation can easily be misinterpreted if it is ignored. Although Caplan (1970) indicates that the most frequent problems brought to consultation involve consultees' lack of objectivity (such as identification with a client), these are also the problems that Caplan considered most appropriate for consultation. Consultants actively work to refer other types of problems to more appropriate persons within an organization. When an organization does not have other problem-solving mechanisms, or when consultation is viewed as serving purposes other than those assumed by Caplan, the consultant can expect different types of problems to be brought to consultation. Caplan cites an extreme example of inadequate problem-solving mechanisms and their effect on the content of consultation in his interactions with antipoverty organizations that emerged as part of the Great Society legislation of the 1960s.

> *Moreover, organizations such as many of those that have recently emerged in the antipoverty and model cities fields are often staffed by people who have not had the opportunity for the systematic acquisition of traditional skills, which, in any case, might not be effective in these settings. Although these workers may ask a consultant to help them to struggle with the overwhelming difficulties they encounter, what they really need is not someone who will increase their capacity to do what they already know, but someone who will assist them to acquire new skills and who will meanwhile plug gaps by temporarily taking over essential tasks in supervision, planning, administration, and even line operations, until the staff can learn to accomplish these functions by themselves. They ask for a consultant, but they need someone who will combine consultation with straightforward teaching, supervision, and collaboration (Caplan, 1970, pp. xi–xii).*

Note that Caplan describes consultation as a process to increase consultee's capacity to *do what they already know*. That is, Caplan assumes consultees possess the skills necessary to perform their professional duties but are blocked by other factors.

Consultee attitudes and affect are important in consultation, but cannot be dealt with directly. As noted earlier, Caplan's approach places considerable emphasis on the thoughts and feelings of the consultee. For example, stereotypes of particular persons or situations may interfere with consultees' understanding of their clients, or unresolved conflicts in the consultees' past or present personal lives are brought out by similarities with current work problems.

Although consultee feelings are important, they cannot be dealt with directly. Instead, the consultant forms hypotheses about the types of personal issues that are interfering with the consultee's functioning and intervenes indirectly, by using the work problem as a metaphor for the consultee's problem. Caplan and Caplan (1993) refer to this as "using the

displacement object." In Caplan's (1970; Caplan & Caplan, 1993) view, direct confrontation would impede consultation for several reasons. First, if the consultant were to point out that consultee attitudes and feelings appear to be blocking effective problem-solving, the coordinate relationship between the consultant and consultee would be upset. Concerns about personal autonomy would interfere with the consultee's ability to benefit from consultation and resolve the work problem. Second, making the consultee aware of his or her apparent feelings would result in loss of face and arouse anxiety and defensiveness, further reducing the consultee's capacity to deal with the problem. Third, the focus of consultation would be off the work problem. By dealing simultaneously with manifest content (the work problem) and latent content (the personal conflict), the consultant is able to assist the consultee in resolving the work problem. As a side effect, the consultee may also find some resolution of conflicts outside of work.

The Consultation Process

Although the process of consultation unfolds somewhat differently within each of Caplan's types of consultation, many concerns and tasks are common to all types. Caplan's original book on consultation (1970) and its updated version (Caplan and Caplan, 1993) provide detailed descriptions of many of the issues faced by the consultant during the course of consultation and how they might be handled. This detailed and pragmatic advice about entering an organization and working with consultees is useful reading for consultants working within any model. Caplan's description of the consultation process from the first contact with an organization to follow-up and evaluation is summarized here to provide the reader with an overview of his approach, before the four types of consultation are described in detail.

Building a Relationship with a Consultee Institution

Caplan notes that establishing ties with an organization that eventually result in consultation can be a lengthy process. The consultant may gradually work into the role of consultant from a more limited, direct-service role. For example, a human services professional from a community mental health center may visit a school first to gather data regarding a child he or she is treating at the center. After several of these contacts, the professional may be asked to provide a workshop. As the organization becomes more familiar with the professional and finds that he or she interacts well with the staff and provides useful information, these contacts may develop into a more formal consultative relationship.

In these initial contacts the consultant works to develop cordial relations with upper-level administrators as well as staff members. A second goal is to establish a reputation as competent, trustworthy, and willing to help, but respectful of the organization's and staff members' own prerogatives (Caplan, 1970). The consultant also tries to understand the organization so that eventual consultation contacts are successful. Caplan notes that each institution has its own unique set of social norms regarding such issues as formality, ways of making appointments, and punctuality that must be understood by the consultant.

Consultation generally is initiated by negotiation of an agreement between the consultant and the consultee organization. The consultant seeks sanction from the highest level

administrator, but also informs and seeks sanction for consultation at all levels of the organization, since lack of support from any source can impede consultation. As the consultant's role changes, the initial contract or agreement is renegotiated to better describe the new role. Thus, consultation agreements are generally explicit, formalized, successive, and negotiated at the highest level of the organization (Caplan & Caplan, 1993; Kelly, 1993).

Establishing Relationships with Consultees

The nature of the consultant's relationships with consultees is a central component of all types of mental health consultation. The consultees must view themselves as active participants in consultation who educate the consultant regarding their professional role and its constraints so that the consultant can make relevant contributions. As discussed earlier, the consultant works to establish a coordinate, non-hierarchical relationship with consultees where professional issues and concerns can be discussed openly. A key issue here is confidentiality. Caplan emphasizes the importance of dealing with confidentiality issues explicitly and repeatedly assuring consultees that their handling of cases will not be discussed with others, particularly their superiors (Caplan & Caplan, 1993).

The consultative relationship is important not only because consultees' feelings of ownership will affect their disposition to act, but a major avenue of skill learning in consultation is the consultees' identification with consultants. That is, a strong, positive relationship makes it more likely that the consultant will serve as a role model to consultees. Caplan lists three general aspects of professional functioning that are modeled by the consultant: (1) empathy toward clients, (2) tolerance of feelings in others and oneself, and (3) a belief that by gathering enough information in a systematic and objective manner, human behavior can be understood.

Status issues are often a concern within consultative relationships and are discussed in detail by Caplan. Although the consultant has no administrative authority over consultees, the latter may feel threatened by the consultant or relate to the consultant as a superior rather than a colleague. Caplan advises the consultant to avoid judgmental statements regarding consultees' actions since these may reinforce the superior/subordinate relationship. Caplan also suggests that the consultant counter consultees' attempts to place him or her in a superior position by responding in kind of self-deprecating actions by the consultee. For example, the consultant who senses that the consultee is overly solicitous might devote more attention to the statements of the consultee and insist on meeting solely at the convenience of the consultee.

Assessment

The responsibility for assessment as well as the type of assessment information collected varies with the type of consultation. However, in all types of consultation the consultant privately assesses, to some extent, both the consultee and organizational factors that may have bearing on the problem and its resolution. This point will be discussed later in more detail with reference to each type of consultation.

One important aspect of assessment is the consultant's examination of the problem with consultees. This form of problem assessment is also an intervention aimed at changing con-

sultees. Through questioning, consultees' views of their problems may be broadened and they also may learn to approach new problems in a similar manner in the future. This technique is summarized by Caplan:

> *His [sic] principal mode of communication is not by stating his assessment of the situations or by giving advice, although when appropriate he may do both, but by the questions he poses about the material. These do not take the form of an interrogation of the consultee. Instead, the consultant sits beside the consultee, as it were, and engages in a joint pondering about the complexities of the problem. His contribution mainly takes the form of widening and deepening the focus of discussion by suggesting new avenues for collecting information, new possibilities for understanding the motivations and reactions of the characters in the case history, and new ways in which the situation might be handled (1970, p. 59).*

Interventions

In all types of mental health consultation, responsibility for action concerning the presenting problem remains with consultees. However, in both types of consultee-centered consultation, the consultant formulates and carries out interventions to remedy shortcomings within the consultee without the consultee's awareness. These interventions may be relatively simple, such as altering a consultee's perception of a case by asking questions dealing with a broad range of topics related to the problem or modeling a rational, problem-solving approach by remaining calm despite a consultee's sense of urgency and anxiety about an issue. Interventions may also be complex. For example, in theme interference reduction, the consultant may decide over the course of a consultation session, (or series of sessions) that a consultee anticipates a disastrous outcome for certain types of cases because of their similarity to unresolved issues in his or her personal life. The consultant then assists the consultee to successfully resolve such a case, demonstrating that the outcome is not inevitable and thereby increasing the consultee's effectiveness with similar cases in the future. Theme interference reduction and other intervention techniques targeted at consultees are described in detail in the section discussing consultee lack of objectivity.

Follow-up and Evaluation

Although responsibility for action rests with consultees, the consultant indicates an interest in knowing the outcome of individual cases or organizational problems that have been

---

Student Learning Activity 2.2

Caplan maintains that consultees problem-solving capabilities can be influenced by the types of questions asked by the consultant. Try his questioning approach in a roleplay of a consultation problem. Do you feel comfortable avoiding direct suggestions about how the problem might be handled? Ask the person who played the consultee to discuss his or her perceptions of the consultation session.

discussed in consultation. Caplan also advises the consultant to attempt to evaluate consultation services as a means of increasing professional effectiveness, and he discusses several evaluation methods. However, he notes the difficulties involved in evaluating consultation, a complex indirect service, where effectiveness depends on successful linkages between the consultant's intervention, change in consultee perceptions and attitudes, change in consultee behavior, change in the client, and change in the organization or consultees' interactions with future clients.

Types of Mental Health Consultation

In this section the four types of consultation delineated by Caplan (1970; Caplan & Caplan, 1993) are described in detail. Table 2.1 contrasts the four types of consultation on a number of dimensions.

Client-centered Case Consultation

Caplan (1970) characterizes client-centered case consultation as the most familiar type of consultation performed by mental health professionals. A consultee encounters difficulty with a client for whom he or she has responsibility and seeks in the consultant a specialist who will assess the client, arrive at a diagnosis, and make recommendations concerning how the consultee might modify his dealings with the client. Frequently, this type of consultation is seen as a means of screening clients for more in-depth diagnosis and treatment. The consultant is to make a recommendation regarding whether referral is warranted and, regardless of that decision, provide suggestions to the consultee regarding his or her day-to-day interactions with the client.

Often, the assessment, diagnosis, and recommendations are summarized in a written report to the consultee. The consultee uses the information provided in the report to develop and implement his or her own plan for dealing with the client with minimal involvement of the consultant. Examples of client-centered case consultation include a psychologist at a hospital who is asked to examine a medical patient and provide insights regarding the mental health aspects of the case or a teacher's request that a school psychologist assess a child who is having difficulty learning to read, provide insight regarding the child's difficulty, and suggest appropriate instructional approaches.

The primary goal of client-centered case consultation is to develop a plan for dealing with the client's difficulties. Education or skill development for the consultee is a secondary focus. Assessment focuses upon the nature of the client's difficulties and much of the consultant's time is spent in direct contact with the client. The consultant also assesses the resources and constraints in the consultee's setting that will affect the type of plan that can be implemented successfully.

Direct assessment of the client often includes formal assessment techniques such as psychological or educational tests or clinical interviews, but the focus of assessment is on providing usable information to the consultee. In the example where the school psychologist is asked to consult with a teacher regarding a child's reading difficulty, the consultant would be more likely to use a criterion-referenced test, which provides information about

TABLE 2.1   Comparisons among Caplan's Four Types of Consultation on Several Dimensions

| | Mental Health Consultation | | | |
	Client-centered Case Consultation	Consultee-centered Case Consultation	Program-centered Administrative Consultation	Consultee-centered Administrative Consultation
Focus	Focuses on developing a plan that will help a specific client.	Focuses on improvement of the consultee's professional functioning in relation to specific cases.	Focuses on improvement of programs or policies.	Focuses on improvement of consultee's professional functioning in relation to specific programs or policies.
Goal	To advise the consultee regarding client treatment.	To educate consultee using his or her problems with the client as a lever.	To help develop a new program or policy or improve an existing one.	To help consultee improve problem-solving skills in dealing with current organizational problems.
Example	School psychologist called in to diagnose a student's reading problem.	School counselor asks for help in dealing with students' drug-related problems.	Nursing home director requests help in developing staff orientation program.	Police chief asks for help in developing ongoing program to deal with interpersonal problems between veteran and new officers.
Consultant's Role and Responsibilities	Usually meets with consultee's client to help diagnose problem.	Never, or rarely, meets with consultee's client.	Meets with groups and individuals in an attempt to accurately assess problems.	Meets with groups and individuals in an attempt to help them develop their problem-solving skills.
	Is responsible for assessing problem and prescribing course of action.	Must be able to recognize source of consultee's difficulties and deal with indirectly.	Is responsible for correctly assessing problem and providing a plan for administrative action.	Must be able to recognize source of organizational difficulty and serve as catalyst for action by administrators.

a child's specific skill deficits, rather than a norm-referenced test, which provides information concerning the child's standing in relation to his or her classmates, but whose results do not translate easily into remedial strategies.

The emphasis on providing usable information for the consultee implies that consultants also must have an understanding of the environment in which a difficulty occurs so that their recommendations are feasible within that setting. Therefore, the resources and constraints operative in the consultee's work setting are examined, such as role expectations, norms, financial and time constraints, and individual consultee strengths and weaknesses that will affect the type of plan that can be implemented. Of particular interest during this

phase of assessment is the consultee/client relationship and how this relationship might be strengthened or altered to improve the problem situation. The consultant looks for misunderstanding and miscommunication that may be blocking problem resolution and then tries to improve communication and understanding by acting as a "communication bridge" (Caplan, 1970, p. 115) between consultee and client. An understanding of the consultee and his or her work setting also aids the consultant in deciding the manner in which information can be communicated most effectively to the consultee. As Caplan points out, this is not just a matter of avoiding technical jargon, but carefully choosing the concepts to be conveyed and the manner in which they are conveyed to suit the consultee's professional role and personal style. For instance, a psychologist making recommendations to a manager about an employee who is under severe home-related stress might discuss a recommendation about dealing with the employee in terms of maintaining his or her productivity rather than relieving the employee's discomfort and improving his or her coping skills, even though both are expected outcomes of the recommendations.

Implementation of the consultant's recommendations is the responsibility of the consultee. However, the consultant may meet with the consultee to discuss the recommendations and insure that the consultee understands them. The consultant may also contact the consultee later to check on the progress of the client, which provides the consultant with a general idea of the accuracy of diagnosis and the usefulness of his or her recommendations.

Consultee-centered Case Consultation

The terms *mental health consultation* and *Caplanian consultation* are sometimes used synonymously in the consultation literature for consultee-centered consultation. This type of consultation is most closely identified with Caplan and, of the four types of consultation Caplan delineates, he devotes the most attention to it. Like its counterpart, client-centered case consultation, consultee-centered case consultation is concerned with difficulties a consultee encounters with a particular client for whom he or she has responsibility in the work setting. However, the primary goal of consultation is remediation of the shortcomings in the consultee's professional functioning that are responsible for difficulties with the present case. Client improvement is viewed as a secondary goal.

Because the focus of this type of consultation is on those characteristics of the consultee that are contributing to his or her difficulty with the client, there is little or no direct assessment of the client. The consultant's primary mode of assessment is careful listening and probing while the consultee describes the case. Through inconsistencies and inaccuracies in the consultee's description of the problem, the consultant is able to identify the cognitive and affective factors that are interfering with consultee functioning.

Caplan divides the sources of consultee difficulty into four major categories that necessitate different actions on the part of the consultant. There are (1) lack of knowledge, (2) lack of skill, (3) lack of self confidence, and (4) lack of objectivity. Each of these sources of consultee difficulty and consultant actions to deal with them are described below.

Lack of Knowledge
When lack of knowledge is contributing to the consultee's present difficulties with a case, he or she may be ignorant of, or fail to see the relevance of, psychological or social factors

pertinent to the case. A nurse may be aware that providing a rationale or explanation for requests increases compliance, but may fail to follow this principle when giving instructions to outpatients regarding medication. Likewise, a teacher may be aware that rehearsal increases the probability that information will be remembered, but may give instructions only once to the class.

Although consultee lack of knowledge can be dealt with by supplying the information to the consultee, Caplan maintains that when the consultant encounters repeated instances of consultation falling in this category, it signals a system-level need or inadequacy for which individual consultation with a specialist represents an expensive, inefficient alternative. In such cases the consultant should provide feedback to the organization regarding the unmet need he or she perceives and suggest alternate ways of dealing with the need such as continuing education, supervision, or group consultation. For example, a school psychologist who repeatedly encounters requests for consultation regarding discipline concerns may suggest to administrators that this is an appropriate topic for an inservice presentation to all interested teachers.

Lack of Skill

The second category, lack of skill, refers to instances in consultation where the consultee appears to understand the relevant factors in dealing with a case, but is unable to find a satisfactory solution to the problem the case presents. Within Caplan's model of consultation, lack of skill on the part of the consultee is not a problem that is ideally suited to consultation because the consultant typically is from another profession and institution and, therefore, is not likely to have complete knowledge of the methods and techniques that are part of the consultee's profession and accepted within his or her organization. Such difficulties are more appropriately handled though supervision because the supervisor is a member of both the consultee's profession and institution. Thus, the plans generated in supervision are more likely to be consonant with the consultee's professional identity and the norms within the work setting.

Caplan suggests that the consultant's role in problems involving consultee lack of skill should be to support the consultee in understanding the issues involved in the case and exploring appropriate avenues for skill development available within the work setting. In instances where means other than consultation are unavailable for dealing with a consultee's lack of skill, Caplan advises that the consultant avoid providing a single solution that may not fit the norms for the consultee's profession and institution. A more desirable procedure is to suggest a variety of alternative actions to the consultee. The difficulties inherent in designing a plan that is compatible with professional and institutional norms that are unknown to a consultant are illustrated in the following example.

> *A consultant whose previous experience had included working with adults trying to break habits or reduce undesirable behaviors (e.g., chronic worrying) by applying mild self-punishment techniques began working in a school and received a request for consultation from a teacher who wanted some of her fourth graders to stay on task. The consultant suggested a behavior control technique in which children applied mild self-punishment when they found themselves off task (snapping a rubber band on one's wrist). Despite the fact that corporal punishment*

was used routinely at this particular elementary school and that the recommended technique was mild in comparison, this particular technique was so foreign to the norms of the school that the implementation of the technique caused considerable uproar among teachers, administrators, and parents. Both the consultant and consultee met with much criticism and the consultant's role and credibility were considerably diminished. While the consultant's judgment in this case is questionable, this example illustrates Caplan's cautionary note about failure to fully appreciate norms operative in a setting.

Lack of Confidence

The third source of consultee difficulty discussed by Caplan is lack of confidence. As with the previous sources of difficulty within the consultee, Caplan does not view lack of confidence as a problem well suited to consultation. When consultants believe that problems stem from lack of confidence, they provide support and assurance to consultees temporarily, while assisting consultees to find other sources of support within their organizations. A psychiatric social worker dealing with his or her first adolescent suicide attempt may be aware of the legal and ethical obligations with regard to parental notification and also be aware of the usual procedures for dealing with suicide attempts, but may still find the case frightening and seek reassurance that the case is handled appropriately. The consultant would provide this support, but would also help the consultee find more senior members of his or her own profession to provide this support in the future.

Lack of Objectivity

The final source of consultee difficulty is lack of objectivity. In Caplan's estimation, when supervisory and administrative mechanisms are functioning well in a human service organization, the majority of consultee-centered consultation cases will fall in this category. This type of consultee difficulty occurs when consultees lose their usual professional distance or objectivity when working with a client and cannot apply their skills to resolve a current problem with a client. In addition, the consultee's failure to resolve the problem independently may exacerbate the consultee's original difficulty. For example, a nurse who has difficulty dealing with uncooperative patients will be even less objective when several attempts to gain compliance from an uncooperative patient have failed. Assessment of consultee lack of objectivity is based primarily on the consultee's description of the case, the factors he or she chooses to emphasize, the reasoning and premises that underlie conclusions the consultee has drawn, and inconsistencies in the facts the consultee relates. Typically, the consultant asks the consultee to describe the problem and, through questioning, prompts the consultee to repeat his or her description and perceptions.

Caplan delineates five categories of lack of objectivity that comprise most instances of consultee lack of objectivity. While these will be described in more detail in the following paragraphs, the categories are (1) direct personal involvement, (2) simple identification, (3) transference, (4) characterological distortion, and (5) theme interference.

The first type of lack of objectivity, *direct personal involvement*, occurs when the consultee's professional relationship with the client changes to one of personal involvement. For example, a physician may be attracted to a patient (Caplan, 1970), a childcare worker

may become so involved with a child in residential care that he or she considers adoption, or a teacher is unduly punitive with a child who possesses some characteristic that he or she finds objectionable.

Caplan (1970) suggests two interventions when the consultant suspects that direct personal involvement is clouding the consultee's judgment and blocking effective action. In both cases consultants indirectly attempt to influence consultees to resume their professional role with regard to the client. With the first technique, the client's role conflict with the consultee is used to indirectly illustrate the consultee's own role conflict, for example, by pointing out the importance of the client's learning to relate appropriately to persons in various social roles and distinguish appropriate from inappropriate behavior in varying social contexts. In our example of the childcare worker who becomes overinvolved with a child in a residential institution, the consultant might point out how the child seems to be relating to the child care worker as a parent.

With the second technique, the consultant serves as a role model to the consultee. For example, the consultant who suspects that a consultee is responding to a client on the basis of some personal bias, such as strong feelings against homosexuality when dealing with a homosexual client, can assist the consultee to see the client and his or her problems more objectively by appraising all aspects of the client's situation during consultation rather than focusing on a single characteristic of the client.

The second category, *simple identification*, occurs when consultees identify with clients or other persons involved with their clients and lose their neutral viewpoint regarding the clients' situation. A social worker who assumed custodial care for her elderly parents and experienced considerable conflict over the disruption of her own family's routines and lifestyle may feel strongly that a client in a similar situation should seek other alternatives. As in consultation cases involving direct personal involvement, the consultant models objectivity while examining the client's situation with the consultee to assist the consultee in seeing the case more objectively.

The third category of lack of objectivity, *transference*, is derived from the psychodynamic construct of transference in psychotherapy where the client transfers feelings and attitudes from other relationships onto the psychotherapeutic relationship. In transference cases encountered in consultation, the consultee imposes a pattern of roles and expectations onto the client's situation based on his or her own past experiences. Over time, this pattern is repeated with similar clients.

Caplan relates an example of transference in which a teacher requested consultation regarding an immature child. The teacher appeared hostile toward the child and through the teacher's description of the case, the consultant surmised that she viewed the problem as an instance of a youngest child who was spoiled and expected his or her own way. There were several cues that indicated this assessment might not be realistic, such as (1) the teacher's clearly negative view of the child, (2) her difficulty providing convincing examples to support her assessment, (3) the teacher's report that the child got along well with peers and did not have a history of problems in school, which conflicted with the teacher's negative description of the child, and (4) the consultant's recollection that a similar case had been presented by the same teacher earlier. The consultant hypothesized that the teacher may have been involved in some unresolved conflicts regarding a spoiled younger sister similar to those she perceived in the present case. The consultant attempted to reduce the

teacher's transference by asking her to observe the child more closely in hopes of prompting a more objective view of the child and describing the child's problem as one in which the child was seeing the teacher as an older sister and the teacher was to help the child differentiate the teacher from an older sister.

The fourth category, *characterological distortion*, is the most extreme example of consultee lack of objectivity. Here, some enduring aspect of the consultee's personality interferes with his or her professional functioning. For example, a consultee who works with delinquent boys and has not resolved issues surrounding his own relationship with authority figures may consistently overreact to normal adolescent challenges of his authority, and yet display some of the same noncompliant behavior and challenges to his supervisors.

Although the consultant probably cannot improve the long-term functioning of the consultee, Caplan maintains that the consultant can assist the consultee in keeping deep-seated personal issues from disrupting the consultee's functioning on a case-by-case basis. The consultant provides support to the consultee to relieve the anger and anxiety he or she may feel and models objectivity and understanding of the clients' behavior when discussing the case, hoping this will increase the consultee's distance and objectivity.

Theme Interference

Although theme interference is only one subcategory of consultee lack of objectivity, it is discussed here in a separate section because Caplan gives it a central place in his writing.

According to Caplan, a theme represents an unsolved problem or defeat that the consultee has experienced, which influences his or her expectations concerning a client. The theme often takes the form of syllogism, that is, the consultee sees an inevitable link between a situation and an undesirable outcome. In Caplan's words: "Statement A denotes a particular situation or condition that was characteristic of the original unsolved problem. Statement B denotes the unpleasant outcome. The syllogism takes the form, 'All A inevitably leads to B.' The implication is that whenever a person finds himself [*sic*] involved in situation or condition A, he is fated to suffer B; also that this generalization applies universally, that everyone who is involved in A inevitably suffers B" (Caplan & Caplan, 1993, pp. 122–123). For example, a consultee might believe that all boys who are raised in single-parent homes will have poor self-control and end up as school dropouts and juvenile delinquents. An eight-year-old boy from a single-parent home who is somewhat immature and overactive and encounters minor difficulties when moving to a new school might be seen by the consultee as fitting the initial situation of the theme (boys from single-parent homes) and consultation is sought to prevent the undesirable outcome (poor self-control, dropping out, and juvenile delinquency).

When a consultee experiences theme interference, he or she views the current situation as hopeless and may make a number of problem-solving attempts that are ill-conceived, hasty, and ineffectual. These actions confirm the consultee's feelings of hopelessness about the case.

In Caplan's conceptualization of theme interference, consultees manipulate the situation to fit their preconceived notions: "Unconsciously, his [*sic*] consolation is that this time the catastrophe will occur to a client and not to himself. At a deeper level, there may

also be the reassurance that he stage-managed and directed the whole drama by manipulating the actors to conform to his theme and so achieved some measure of mastery by this vicarious experience" (1970, p. 147).

Caplan believes that theme interference is a relatively frequent, but normal work impediment. However, themes do not always interfere with a consultee's functioning. Theme interference typically occurs when some other current circumstances make a particular theme more salient. (Again, this is an example of how Caplan links environment and intrapsychic causes of behavior.)

The consultant who encounters a case involving theme interference has two intervention options: (1) unlinking, which is only temporarily effective, or (2) theme interference reduction, which brings about a long-term improvement in the consultee. Unlinking occurs when the consultant influences the consultee to perceive the client differently, so that he or she no longer fits the initial situation of the theme. As the consultee begins to see the client more objectively, his or her usual problem-solving skills return. Caplan considers unlinking a cardinal error in consultation technique because it leaves the consultee's theme intact and theme interference may occur again. The preferred intervention for theme interference is theme interference reduction, which involves accepting the consultee's unconscious premise that the client's difficulty is a test case for his or her theme and then persuading the consultee that the outcome is not inevitable. This relieves the consultee's anxiety about the case, and he or she then is able to resolve his or her problem with the client. This successful experience also serves to invalidate the theme so that the consultee's personal conflict is reduced and future professional functioning is enhanced.

Four principal methods can be used by the consultant to accomplish theme interference reduction. In each case, the consultant tries to weaken the link between the consultee's initial situation and inevitable outcome. The four methods are (1) verbal focus on the client, (2) the parable, (3) nonverbal focus on the client, and (4) nonverbal focus on the relationship.

Verbal Focus on the Client

With this method of theme interference reduction, the consultant and consultee examine the client's case in detail and consider possible outcomes. The consultant does not deny that the inevitable outcome feared by the consultee is possible, but also brings out the possibility of less dismal outcomes. In the example of the boy from a single-parent family, the consultant would acknowledge that some males from single-parent families do encounter school difficulties, drop out, and have brushes with the law, and that there is reason to be concerned about this possibility in the present case. However, other possibilities would also be considered. For example, the client's difficulties in school are not serious at this time and the family has expressed interest in a tutor. Alternately, the child may have missed some basic skills when he moved from another school district that used a different curriculum.

The consultant's actions serve two purposes. First, the consultee is influenced to perceive the present situation more realistically through an objective examination of the facts. Second, his or her preconceived ideas about the outcome of similar situations are also questioned implicitly by their relation with this particular case. This questioning and the successful resolution of the present case then reduce the strength of the theme.

The Parable

With this technique, the consultant uses an example derived from his or her own experiences to illustrate that the inevitable outcome feared by the consultee does not always occur. The consultant relates a story that is similar in crucial details to the present situation confronting the consultee, but alters the nonessential details such as setting and age or sex of the main character. A consultant working with a welfare eligibility worker who fears that a client's decision to allow her husband to return to the home will inevitably lead to wife and child abuse might relate a story about another family in which the husband's return led to increased stability in the home.

Nonverbal Focus on the Case

The consultant also can communicate indirectly that the consultee's concerns about the client are overstated by modeling a more realistic attitude toward the case. The consultant discusses the feared outcome of the case in enough detail to reassure the consultee that he or she has not misinterpreted the case. But this discussion is done in a relaxed way and the consultant does not respond to the consultee's urgency and call for quick action.

Nonverbal Focus on the Consultation Relationship

In theme interference the consultee's feelings and perceptions concerning a personal issue have been displaced onto a case. Caplan notes that these perceptions and feelings also may be displaced onto the consultation relationship. If so, what occurs in the consultation relationship can be used to invalidate the consultee's theme or show that the consultee's expectations are not correct. To illustrate, a teacher sought assistance for a child who was noncompliant at home and school. When the consultant suggested that the teacher might speak to the parents about parent training at a community mental health center, the teacher vehemently objected, stating that she knew about their methods and they would only chastise the parents and provide no real help. The consultant noted that throughout the consultation interviews the consultee would frequently make antagonistic remarks about mental health personnel that seemed to invite confrontation since the consultant was a member of a mental health profession. The consultant consistently ignored these remarks or dealt with them in a friendly, nondefensive manner.

Caplan states that these four techniques can be used alone or in combination to invalidate the theme that causes theme interference and improve the consultee's objectivity and problem-solving capacity with reference to the present case. When these objectives have been accomplished, the consultant leaves the consultee to deal with the client's problem independently. The consultant's exit assures that the consultee plays an active role in handling the difficulty that he or she previously saw as unsolvable, further invalidating the theme.

Program-centered Administrative Consultation

Program-centered administrative consultation is similar to client-centered case consultation. The consultant is viewed as a specialist who is called in to study a problem and provide a set of recommendations for dealing with the problem. In client-centered case consultation, however, the consultant's assessment, diagnosis, and recommendations are concerned with

the problems of a particular client; in program-centered administrative consultation, the consultant is concerned with problems surrounding the development of a new program or some aspect of organizational functioning.

Unlike consultation concerning a case, organizational factors that are important in administrative consultation may be outside of the mental health professional's usual area of expertise. Caplan cautions that, in addition to their clinical skills, administrative consultants should have an understanding of organizational theory, planning, financial and personnel management, and administration. The primary goal of program-centered administrative consultation is the development of an action plan, usually in the form of a written report, that can be implemented by the consultee and his or her associates to resolve the administrative problem that prompted consultation. As such, it is important that both the consultant's formulation of the problem and subsequent recommendations are correct. Therefore, the consultant takes an active role in data collection rather than using the perceptions of the consultee as the sole source of information.

Program-centered administrative consultation is usually rapid paced, reaching completion in a matter of days or weeks. Typically, the consultation process begins with initial contacts from the organization to explore the possibility of consultation. The consultant uses these contacts to assess the match between his or her skills and the perceived problem, as well as to identify at what level of the organization sanction will be needed for consultation, and the person or persons with the authority to implement consultative recommendations. Unlike case-centered consultation, where a single consultee usually has primary responsibility for a client, the identity of the appropriate consultee who has responsibility for an organizational problem may not be readily discernible.

Assessment procedures include understanding the organizational context by reviewing written documentation concerning the history of the organization, its goals, functions, and formal organizational structure, as well as any memos or reports concerning the specific issues to be addressed by the consultant. The consultant may contact others who are familiar with the particular organization or the type of organization with which he or she will be consulting. On-site assessment generally takes the form of interviews with individual staff members and groups of employees. Here, sanction of the top administrator as well as confidentiality are important to assure that staff members feel comfortable sharing their perceptions. By gathering multiple views on the same problem, the consultant arrives at an independent formulation of the problem. The consultant may also observe the behavior and interactions of organizational members as part of assessment.

Caplan (1970) divides problem formulation into three phases—an initial definition of the problem, a period of confusion where the consultant considers multiple viewpoints and data that may reinforce or conflict with the original conceptualization of the problem, and finally, a "gestalt closure" (p. 241) where the consultant views the problem in a more complex way that allows him or her to make sense of the data that have been gathered.

From this problem definition the consultant develops recommendations. The consultee and other members of the organization play an active role in the formulation and refinement of recommendations. Caplan describes the development of recommendations as a process of accretion. That is, the consultant seeks staff reactions to tentative recommendations and uses these to modify and refine the recommendations. This collaborative procedure not only helps assure that recommendations are workable, but reflects the basic assumption that the

technical correctness of a recommendation is not the sole determinant of its adoption. Caplan states that "unless people are personally involved in collaborating with the consultant in developing a plan, they are less likely to accept it and work toward its implementation" (1970, p. 247).

As with other types of consultation, the consultant does not take an active role in the implementation of recommendations made in his or her report; the consultee is free to accept, modify, or reject the consultant's proposed plan. However, the consultant does indicate interest in what actions the organization takes.

Consultee-centered Administrative Consultation

The goal of consultee-centered administrative consultation is to improve the professional functioning of members of an administrative staff. Although consultee-centered administrative consultation may take many forms, such as consultation with the head of a program or with a particular group of administrators, much of Caplan's (1970) description of this type of consultation is based on a more broadly conceptualized role for the consultant.

The consultant agrees to work with an organization on a long-term basis. However, the specific focus of consultation and the particular consultees are not specified. Administrators at all levels may seek consultation. In addition, the consultant is allowed to move freely throughout the levels of the organization. This freedom gives the consultant a view of the total organization that cannot be obtained by consultees who have a more prescribed role in the organization. Therefore, the consultant does not restrict consultation to problems brought to his or her attention by consultees, but takes an active role in identifying organizational problems and approaching potential consultees to discuss these issues.

Although the consultant may deal with almost any issue within the organization, consultation is still a voluntary relationship and the consultant has no authority to determine the content of consultation or responsibility for identifying and implementing solutions. Instead, the consultant acts as a catalyst, identifying a salient issue, bringing it to the attention of consultees, and hoping they will want to discuss it and initiate their own problem-solving efforts.

Consultee-centered administrative consultation may grow out of other types of consultation, or an organization may initially request this type of consultation. In negotiating an initial agreement, the consultant seeks sanction from the highest level within the administrative unit to assure free movement through all levels of the organization, as well as freedom to contact any organizational members who might have relevant information. The consultant then works to build relationships with the staff and develop an understanding of how the organization functions.

Caplan comments that several difficulties may impair building relationships in consultee-centered administrative consultation. The consultant's unrestricted movement and freedom to inquire about all aspects of the organization may be threatening and disturbing to staff members who are used to their customary patterns of communication and operation. The consultant also may be perceived as a spy or agent of the director. The consultant works to dispel these fears and build trusting relationships with potential consultees by attending meetings, making efforts to meet consultees informally, giving consultees opportunities to determine topics and issues for consultation, and maintaining a coordinate relationship with consultees.

During this period the consultant also works to understand the consultees and their organization, looking for barriers to effective consultee functioning at many different levels. The consultant must be prepared to "appraise individual personality characteristics and problems among the key administrators, intragroup and intergroup relations in and among the various units of the enterprise, organizational patterns of role assignment and lines of communication and authority, leadership patterns and styles, vertical and horizontal communication, and traditions of participation in decision making" (Caplan, 1970, p. 280).

Over time, the consultant develops a broader network of consultees at many levels of the organization and a greater understanding of the contextual factors that affect administrators' functioning. Within this ongoing set of relationships, the consultant deals with a broad range of consultative issues on a short-term basis. For example, over the course of a year, a consultant to college campus administrators might deal with such topics as communication between admissions officers and individual departments, procedures for dealing with students caught cheating, lack of objectivity in a particular administrator in relation to a hiring decision, dealing with a depressed employee, and conducting more productive meetings.

Interventions in consultee-centered administrative consultation can be directed toward individuals, groups, or the organization as a whole. At the individual level, the consultant might try to broaden the range of factors a consultee considers when trying to understand subordinates' actions. Or, the consultant might work to increase a consultee's tolerance of negative feelings and confusion, so that he or she is less likely to avoid dealing with difficult work problems that arouse these feelings. At the group level, the consultant might work to improve communication between members of a group or between a supervisor and his or her staff members. The consultant also might work to improve the overall health of the organization. For example, the consultant could work to open up formal avenues within an organization for acknowledging and dealing with negative feelings, such as helping a high school develop a student transfer policy for dealing with student/teacher personality conflicts.

As in consultee-centered case consultation, the consultant intervenes only to increase the consultees' problem-solving capacity or to direct their attention to an organizational issue. It is assumed that the consultant does not have sufficient information about the organization to design appropriate interventions and that any action plans are the responsibility of the consultees. As in other types of mental health consultation, however, the consultant always indicates an interest in knowing the outcome of any problem-solving efforts.

Further Developments in the Mental Health Consultation Model

In the 20-plus years following publication of Caplan's landmark text, *The Theory and Practice of Mental Health Consultation* (Caplan, 1970), the field of consultation has taken many directions. Mental health consultation continues to be practiced in much the same form as originally described by Caplan (James, Kidder, Osberg, & Hunter, 1986) and a limited body of research has emerged to support its use (Medway & Updyke, 1985). Others have modified mental health consultation (Altrocchl, 1972; Meyers, 1981; 1989; Meyers et al., 1993; Meyers & Kundert, 1988; Meyers et al., 1979; Pryzwansky, 1974, 1977) to

fit particular settings or consultees. Finally, Caplan himself (Caplan, 1981, 1982, 1986; Caplan & Caplan, 1993; Caplan, LeBow, Gavarin, & Stelzer, 1981; Erchul, 1993) has modified some of his ideas about consultation and the use of consultation as a preventive technique.

In this section, several developments in mental health consultation will be discussed. First, research related to the mental health consultation model will be summarized. Second, three models that draw heavily from Caplan's model or were developed in response to Caplan's model will be described. Third, Caplan's reflections on mental health consultation and changes in the model will be summarized.

Research on the Mental Health Consultation Model

In a 1985 meta-analysis of consultation outcome studies, Medway and Updyke synthesized the results of 54 studies examining the effectiveness of mental health, behavioral or organizational development consultation. Meta-analysis is a quantitative technique for integrating findings across studies (Glass, 1976). With this technique, the results of individual studies are converted to a common metric, effect size. Although space does not permit a detailed description of how effect sizes are calculated and interpreted, the conversion of all study results to this common metric allows a reviewer to average results across studies. The reviewer can then make general statements about the effectiveness of a treatment and compare groups of studies that differ on important dimensions. For example, the average effect size of studies using one method of treatment for a particular problem can be compared to the average effect size of studies using a second method of treatment.

Averaging effect sizes over the 24 studies which examined mental health consultation, Medway and Updyke (1985) found that mental health consultation had a positive impact on both consultees and clients, although its effects were most pronounced on consultees. Looking at the relative effectiveness of the three models of consultation across consultants, consultees and clients, no differences were found in terms of effectiveness.

Recently, the mental health model of consultation has come under fire for the lack of research to support its effectiveness (Gresham & Kendell, 1987). Although consultation, in general, lacks a large data base of research supporting its use, the results of Medway and Updyke's (1985) meta-analysis support the effectiveness of the mental health consultation model, as well as other models of consultation.

Gutkin and Curtis (1990) have questioned whether the studies classified in the Medway and Updyke meta-analysis as using the mental health model were truly examples of mental health consultation. Because little consultation efficacy research has provided data documenting how consultation was actually implemented during the study (Gresham, 1989), this issue is not easily resolved. The difficulty in verifying what consultants did and how they did it in existing consultation research points to the importance of collecting treatment integrity data in future research concerning any consultation model.

Altrocchi's Approach to Mental Health Consultation

Altrocchi (1972) draws heavily from Caplan in his description of consultation. However, he differs with Caplan on several points. Altrocchi broadens Caplan's definition of consulta-

---

Student Learning Activity 2.3

Identify the type of consultation described in each example.

1 = client-centered case consultation
2 = consultee-centered case consultation
3 = program-centered administrative consultation
4 = consultee-centered administrative consultation

A psychologist assesses a first grader with poor social skills and recommends ways of increasing positive social interactions in the classroom.   _____

A social worker visits a rest home to help the staff develop a cost-effective way of monitoring and improving residents' psychological adjustment.   _____

A psychiatrist is available to a group of visiting nurses to discuss the psychological aspects of patients' illnesses.   _____

A school counselor works with a teacher to improve his or her classroom management skills.   _____

A counseling psychologist assists the on-campus housing director develop a plan for handling dorm residents who may be suicidal.   _____

The head of a large division meets on an ad hoc basis with a consultant to discuss personnel concerns.   _____

A psychiatrist assesses back pain patients before surgery to estimate the extent to which psychological and physical factors contribute to their back pain.   _____

---

tion by including nonprofessionals as consultees. He comments that the principles of consultation are essentially identical for both professionals and nonprofessionals. Several other writers have also extended the definition of consultation to include nonprofessionals, such as family members, students, and persons in the community (Brown, Wyne, Blackburn, & Powell, 1979; Conoley, 1981).

Altrocchi also explicitly includes group consultation within his definition of consultation and discusses the advantages and disadvantages of consultation with groups and individuals. In his early work, Caplan (1970) had expressed concern that consultation with groups of consultees could present problems, particularly in consultee-centered consultation. With a group approach, the consultant has more difficulty controlling verbal interaction and consultees might lose face with peers should someone point out their apparent emotional involvement in a case. In addition, Caplan expressed concern that group members would not benefit from discussion of another consultee's problem.

In contrast to Caplan's (1970) position Altrocchi comments that group consultation offers some advantages. For example, more hypotheses and perspectives are available to the consultees. Similar experiences by other consultees and their successful ways of dealing with the problem can be shared to provide support to consultees currently experiencing distress. In his later work, Caplan (1977; Caplan & Caplan, 1993) also acknowledges the importance and benefits of group consultation, commenting that his concerns about this approach had not been borne out in practice.

Altrocchi's final point of departure from Caplan concerns the use of direct techniques in dealing with consultee affect. Unlike Caplan, who maintains that consultee affect should be dealt with indirectly, Altrocchi (1972) maintains that both indirect and direct methods can be used to deal with consultee affect. Open discussion of affect, such as noting consultee affect and accepting expression of these feelings, can sometimes mobilize consultees into action. However, the consultant runs the risk of heightening consultees' anxiety and defensiveness or opening the door for discussion of personal issues, particularly in individual consultation. Two variables that are important in the consultant's choice to use direct or indirect methods are (1) the consultant's comfort in dealing directly with consultees' feelings, and (2) the use of individual or group consultation.

Mental Health Consultation in the Schools

Meyers and his colleagues (Meyers, 1981, 1986, 1989; Meyers et al., 1993; Meyers & Kundert, 1988; Meyers et al., 1979; Meyers & Parsons, 1984) have written extensively concerning how mental health consultation constructs can be applied in a school setting. They have modified many of Caplan's constructs specifically for the school setting, as well as introduced new content and activities to consultation that were not discussed by Caplan. These changes and new content will be summarized here.

Meyers defines consultation as a problem-solving process that occurs between a help giver (consultant) and help seeker (or consultee) who has responsibility for another person as part of his or her work. The goal of consultation is to help the consultee solve a current work problem and respond more effectively to similar problems in the future (Meyers, 1989). Similar to Caplan, consultation is considered a voluntary relationship that is non-hierarchical, but the consultant is not assumed to be from an external agency.

Meyers has replaced Caplan's four types of consultation with a typology that is specific to the school setting. Within this typology, there are three levels of service that vary in terms of how directly services are provided to the student by the consultant (Meyers, 1989; Meyers et al., 1988). Level I is a focus on the child, Level II, a focus on the teacher, and Level III, a focus on the system. For example, at Level I, a consultant might work with a teacher to develop a strategy for dealing with a specific child's reading problem. At Level II, the consultant would work with the teacher to modify class grouping and instructional strategies so that all children with reading problems in that classroom receive more effective instruction. At Level III, the consultant would help develop inservice and other staff development activities to improve the entire faculty's effectiveness with children who are experiencing reading difficulties. Like Caplan, Meyers characterizes consultation as often beginning with child-centered focus and assuming a more preventive focus as teachers and schools become more comfortable and confident with the consultant and consultation (Meyers et al., 1993).

Meyers has modified many other aspects of mental health consultation to better match the school environment and professionals' roles in that environment (Meyers, 1981, 1989; Meyers & Kundert, 1988; Meyers et al., 1979). Caplan's five types of objectivity have been reconceptualized as four common conflicts experienced by teachers:

1. *Authority conflicts*—teachers may have ambivalent feelings about their need to maintain control in the classroom versus being liked by students.

2. *Dependency*—teachers may require excessive dependence and obedience from students and relate to authority figures in the same manner.

3. *Anger and hostility*—teachers may experience feelings of anger and hostility toward students and also be disturbed by them because they believe these feelings should not occur in professionals.

4. *Identification*—teachers may identify with a student or someone else involved in a case and fail to see the situation objectively.

Like Altrocchi, Meyers and his colleagues maintain that consultee affect and conflicts, such as those described above, can be assessed and dealt with in consultation both in an indirect and a direct manner. Direct approaches include asking the consultees to express their feelings, relationship-building techniques that focus on bringing out consultees' views, and confrontation (Meyers, 1981; Meyers et al., 1993). Unlike Caplan, who uses only indirect methods of dealing with consultee affect, Meyers and his colleagues maintain that indirect methods may not have an impact on consultees, and do not credit consultees' ability to handle appropriate confrontation.

In his recent writings, Meyers has described how consultation and an assessment role for school psychologists can be integrated (Meyers & Kundert, 1988) by broadening school psychologists' testing role to focus on the interaction of child, task, and setting characteristics. This broadened focus would result in a more direct link between assessment, intervention, and consultation. Meyers (Meyers et al., 1993) also has written about the role of school-based mental health consultation in primary prevention and maintains that preventive efforts may be most effective when they focus on working to modify school routines to better support children and teachers (Meyers, 1988). Modifications might include the teaching of interpersonal cognitive problem-solving skills or coping skills by teachers, programs to ease common but stressful school transitions (e.g., moving from elementary to secondary school), or modifying teaching materials (e.g., reading tests) to be more relevant to children's own experiences and needs.

Collaboration or Consultation?

The final model to be considered modifies some of the basic aspects of consultation to fit the needs, conditions, and consultee expectations that prevail in many organizations where consultative services are provided. As Pryzwansky (1977) points out, there is often a poor conceptual fit between models of consultation and the realities encountered by human services professionals who engage in consultation. For example, the mental health consultation model assumes that consultation is oriented toward broadening the range of alternatives considered by the consultee to resolve a problem, that consultants are external to the organization in which consultation takes place, and that consultees possess most of the skills they need to function effectively on the job. However, these assumptions do not fit all consultative situations. In school-based consultation the consultant is often internal, such as a school psychologist or school counselor. Teachers may frequently request consultation because they lack the knowledge or skill needed to deal with a child's difficulty (Gutkin, 1981) and may look to the consultant for concrete suggestions rather than a discussion of alternatives (Pryzwansky, 1974). The ongoing contact between the consultant and the

school also may lead to expectations that the consultant will be involved in implementation and follow-up activities (Pryzwansky, 1974).

Pryzwansky (1974, 1977) has proposed an alternate model of consultative service delivery, which he terms collaboration. Within a collaborative model, the consultant and consultee assume joint responsibility for all aspects of the consultation process. Consultants and consultees agree upon the objectives for consultation, define the problem together, jointly develop an intervention plan, and share responsibility for implementation and evaluation of the outcome of their plan.

Within Caplan's approach, the consultee maintains complete responsibility and control over implementation. Caplan (1970) sees this as an important aspect of consultation because consultees will resist intrusion into their professional responsibilities. In several studies, however, potential consultees have indicated a preference for shared responsibility between consultant and consultee throughout the consultative process. Pryzwansky and White (1983) surveyed teachers and found that they preferred collaboration over the mental health model of consultation, as well as over two additional models of indirect service delivery. This preference was found regardless of respondents' years of experience or locus of control. Babcock and Pryzwansky (1983) also found that regular education teachers preferred the collaborative model and extended these findings to school principals and special education teachers. Wenger (1979) found that teachers who had received consultative services where a collaborative relationship was fostered were more satisfied with consultation than those who had received client-centered case consultation. Weller (1984) found that parents indicated a preference for collaboration when seeking psychoeducational consultation concerning their children. West (1985) and Schulte, Osborne, and Kauffman (1993) also have found a preference for collaboration over consultation in school settings. Although these results have not been extended to other consultation settings, they suggest that consultants should consider expectations and preferences for direct service to clients in school settings in selecting a consultation model particularly when consultants are internal to the organization.

It is important to note that collaboration differs sharply from traditional models of consultation in terms of the level of involvement of the specialist in assessment and intervention activities related to the client. Provision of some direct service to the client is an integral part of collaboration (Przwansky, 1974, 1977; West, 1990), but generally not a part of consultation.

Although some authors distinguish collaboration from consultation, others have discussed models of collaborative consultation (e.g., Graden, Casey, & Christenson, 1984; Graden, 1989, Idol, Paolucci-Whitcomb, & Nevin, 1986; Parsons & Meyers, 1984; Rosenfield, 1987). All of these models emphasize the importance of collaborative problem solving and a collegial relationship between the consultant and consultee. However, the models differ from collaboration in that direct service to the client by the specialist receives less emphasis. Given the wide range of meanings for the terms *collaboration* and *collaborative*, in the consultation literature (Schulte & Osborne, 1993), care should be taken that important distinctions between models of service delivery, such as the presence or absence of direct service to the client, are not masked by the use of the same terms by different authors when they are discussing distinctly different aspects of the consultation process or models.

Beyond Mental Health Consultation

As stated earlier, mental health consultation is a central component of Caplan's approach to the preventive psychiatry. Over time, Caplan has broadened his theory of prevention into support systems theory (Caplan, 1982; Caplan-Moskovich, 1982). Unlike his theory of prevention, which focuses on the role mental health professionals play in preventing mental illness, support systems theory places more emphasis on the role of informal caregivers and community support in prevention.

Caplan's increased emphasis on informal caregivers grew out of his work in consultation (Caplan-Moskovich 1982). In a project with the Episcopal church, Caplan taught senior bishops how to consult with their less experienced colleagues. The consultants began meeting with each other to provide support and later formally organized peer support programs where clergy alternated roles as consultant and consultee with each other (Richards, 1976). This development led Caplan to rethink his approach to community mental health to recognize how peers rather than mental health professionals could provide support and buffer the effects of acute or chronic stress (Caplan-Moscovich, 1982). Thus, much of today's emphasis on mutual help groups and peer support programs in community mental health can be seen as an outgrowth of consultation.

Caplan also recognized that the indirect nature of consultation presented limitations when the mental health aspects of a case were complex, or when more rapid change was desired. In Caplan's words,

> *a purely enabling role has not proved optimally effective. We have found that in order to achieve our preventive goals we must also take part in dealing directly with clients in a community facility, and we must accept a commitment and responsibility inside the institution to enlarge its mission and change its organization (Caplan, 1981, p. 4).*

To address this limitation of consultation, Caplan proposed two additional patterns of partnership between mental health and other human services professionals that complemented consultation (Caplan et al., 1981). One of the patterns proposed was *mental health collaboration*, an alternative similar to Pryzwansky's (1974) collaborative model of services for the schools. Unlike consultation where the consultee retains sole responsibility for the client, in collaboration the mental health professional accepts responsibility for the mental health aspects of a case and works directly to improve conditions seen as counter to positive mental health goals. The second alternative to consultation is *executive partnership*, where the mental health professional accepts a leadership role within an organization or administrative unit. For example, a psychiatrist and pediatrician might co-lead a hospital unit that treats the physical and psychosocial aspects of children's illnesses simultaneously.

Recently, Caplan and his daughter, Ruth B. Caplan, have updated and expanded the ideas and concepts originally detailed in his 1970 book. This new work, *Mental Health Consultation and Collaboration* (Caplan & Caplan, 1993), places collaboration alongside consultation as a major tool for mental health professionals to infuse psychological and preventive principles into diverse work settings. They maintain that when mental health professionals are internal to an organization (e.g., school counselors or social workers), many

aspects of their functioning fit poorly with mental health consultation. The professional has an established service role, has responsibility for aspects of clients' functioning, and is governed by the institution's policies. Under these circumstances, Caplan maintains that mental health collaboration represents a better fit with the professional's existing role.

On a continuum of direct to indirect service, the Caplans place testing and therapy on one extreme, where the professional has the greatest control and responsibility; mental health consultation is at the other extreme—the professional has minimal control, and the consultee retains responsibility for the client. Collaboration falls in the middle of this continuum, and combines direct and indirect roles. The professional accepts responsibility for the mental health aspects of a client (direct service) but also works to have others with whom he or she collaborates understand, and be more responsive to, the mental health aspects of their work with clients (indirect service).

In sum, Caplan's mental health consultation remains a well-accepted, preventive technique within community mental health. However, both mental health consultation and the theory in which it is embedded have evolved. Consultation no longer stands alone, but has spawned a range of techniques, such as mutual help groups and collaboration, that can be used to meet the mental health needs of a community.

Implications for Practice

Caplan's work in consultation has great historical significance. However, professionals-in-training who will be internal consultants or whose future practice will not incorporate psychodynamic perspective, may have difficulty seeing how Caplan's work on consultation applies to them.

The particular aspects of Caplan's work that apply to different settings and roles will vary. But enduring aspects of Caplan's work have been noted in a recent volume honoring Caplan's contributions to professional psychology (Erchul, 1993). Drawing from this work and others (e.g., Caplan & Caplan, 1993; Caplan, Caplan, & Erchul, *in press*), as well as our own experiences, we believe that some of the important points for practice that can be attributed to Caplan are

1. Recognition that the perceptions and feelings of consultees are important, and that they influence their interactions with clients.
2. Discussion of how a consultant can serve as a role model to consultees for systematic problem solving and broaden the consultee's view of a client and his or her problems.
3. Description of the dynamic process of entry into an organization and recognition of the importance of explicit contracting and administrative sanction for assuring lasting change in an organization.
4. Recognition of the importance of prompt, effective treatment for the mental health needs of clients, and a focus on maximizing the impact of mental health professionals rather than focusing on intensive treatment for a small number of clients.
5. Recognition of the importance of consultee involvement in problem solving for increasing the likelihood that the intervention will be carried out.
6. Recognition that working indirectly (i.e., as a consultant) requires different skills from direct intervention and, as such, requires additional training for the professional.

Summary

Mental health consultation was developed as part of a preventive approach to dealing with mental disorders and is primarily identified with Gerald Caplan. Consultation is viewed as a process of interaction between two professionals where the consultant assists the consultee in dealing with the psychological aspects of a current work problem and, most importantly, to deal more effectively with similar problems in the future. A fundamental aspect of mental health consultation is the coordinate, nonhierarchical relationship between the consultant and consultee.

Several assumptions that underlie mental health consultation are delineated. Among these are the importance of intrapsychic and environmental factors in explaining and changing behavior, the unique aspects of each profession that make it likely that consultees will adapt any recommendations made by consultants from another profession, and the importance of the consultee's attitudes and affect in consultation,

Caplan distinguishes between four types of consultation, client-centered case consultation, consultee-centered case consultation, program-centered administrative consultation, and consultee-centered administrative consultation. Of the four types of consultation, Caplan discusses consultee-centered case consultation in the most depth. Four major sources of consultee difficulty often encountered in consultee-centered consultation are: lack of knowledge, lack of skill, lack of confidence, and lack of objectivity. Of these, Caplan believes consultee lack of objectivity is most appropriately dealt with in consultation. He delineates five categories of lack of objectivity. Intervention techniques to deal with lack of objectivity include theme interference reduction, the parable, and modeling an objective approach to problem solving.

Variations of mental health consultation have been proposed by Altrocchi, Meyers, and Pryzwansky. Caplan has suggested that consultation be complemented by other preventive techniques that involve existing community supports or involve mental health professionals in more direct service roles.

Tips for the Practitioner

1. As discussed in more depth in Chapter Five, it is important to seek sanction for your work as a consultant from the highest level administrator in an organization.
2. Keep in mind that the consultant role often begins with success in a direct service role.
3. Model thoughtful deliberation and rational problem solving in your interactions with consultees.
4. Starting consultation by allowing consultees to relate the problem in their own words, with minimal interruptions, gives you an opportunity to assess how they are viewing the problem and the client, and consider how this should affect your approach to them and the problem.

Review Questions

1. What are some of the factors that led to the emergence of consultation as an intervention strategy?

2. How does Caplan's definition of consultation differ from the definition presented in Chapter One?

3. Why does Caplan believe that it is important for the consultee to retain responsibility for any action taken as a result of consultation?

4. How do client-centered case consultation and consultee-centered case consultation differ?

5. How do program-centered administrative consultation and consultee-centered administrative consultation differ?

6. Describe the four sources of consultee difficulty in consultee-centered case consultation.

7. Give an example of a Caplanian theme.

8. Why is theme interference reduction preferred to unlinking when dealing with theme interference?

9. How does the consultant serve as a catalyst in consultee-centered administrative consultation?

10. How does Altrocchi's approach to dealing with consultee affect differ from Caplan's?

11. Why is collaboration seen as more appropriate in some settings than consultation?

References

Alpert, J., & Silverstein, J. (1985). Mental health consultation: Historical, present, and future perspectives. In J. Bergan (Ed.), *School psychology in contemporary society* (pp. 281–315). Columbus, OH: Charles E Merrill.

Altrocchi, J. (1972). Mental health consultation. In S. E. Golann, & C. Eisdorfer (Eds.), *Handbook of community mental health* (pp. 477–508). New York: Appleton-Century-Crofts.

Babcock, N. L., & Pryzwansky, W. B. (1983). Models of consultation: Preferences of educational professionals at five stages of service. *Journal of School Psychology, 21,* 359–366.

Brown, D., Wyne, M. D., Blackburn, J. E, & Powell, W. C. (1979). *Consultation.* Boston: Allyn & Bacon.

Caplan, G. (1964). *Principles of preventive psychiatry.* New York: Basic Books.

Caplan, G. (1970). *The theory and practice of mental health consultation.* New York: Basic Books.

Caplan, G. (1974). *Support systems and community mental health.* New York: Behavioral Publications.

Caplan, G. (1977). Mental health consultation: Retrospect and prospect. In S. C. Plog & P. I. Ahmed (eds.), *Principles and techniques of mental health consultation* (pp. 9–21). New York: Plenum.

Caplan, G. (1981). Partnerships for prevention in the human services. *Journal of Primary Prevention, 2,* 3–5.

Caplan, G. (1982). Epilogue: Personal reflections by Gerald Caplan. In H. C. Schulberg, & M. Killilea (Eds.), *The modern practice of community mental health* (pp. 650–666). San Francisco: Jossey-Bass.

Caplan, G. (1986). Recent developments in crisis intervention and in the promotion of support services. In M. Kessler, & S. E. Goldston (Eds.), *A decade of progress in primary prevention* (pp. 235–260). Hanover, NH: University Press of New England.

Caplan, G., & Caplan, R. B. (1993). *Mental health con-sultation and collaboration.* San Francisco: Jossey-Bass.

Caplan, G., Caplan, R. B., & Erchul, W. P. (in press). A contemporary view of mental health consultation: Comments on "Types of Mental Health Consulta-tion" by Gerald Caplan (1963). *Journal of Educa-tional and Psychological Consultation.*

Caplan, G., LeBow, H., Gavarin, M., & Stelzer, J. (1981). Patterns of cooperation of child psychia-try with other departments in hospitals. *Journal of Primary Prevention, 4,* 96–106.

Caplan-Moskovich, R. B. (1982). Gerald Caplan: The man and his work. In H. C. Schulberg, & M. Killilea (Eds.), *The modern practice of community mental health* (pp. 1–39). San Francisco: Jossey-Bass.

Conoley, J. C. (Ed.), (1981). *Consultation in schools.* New York: Academic Press.

Erchul, W. P. (1993). *Consultation in community, school, and organizational practice: Gerald Caplan's contributions to professional psychology.* Washington, DC: Taylor & Francis.

Gallessich, J. (1982). *The profession and practice of consultation.* San Francisco: Jossey-Bass.

Glass, G. V. (1976). Primary, secondary, and meta-analy-sis of research. *Educational Researcher, 5*(10), 3–8.

Graden, J. L. (1989). Redefining "preferral" interven-tion as intervention assistance: Collaboration between general and special education. *Excep-tional Children, 56,* 227–231.

Graden, J. L., Casey, A., & Christenson, S. L. (1985). Implementing a preferral intervention system: Part I. The model. *Exceptional Children, 51,* 377–384.

Gresham, F. M. (1989). Assessment of treatment integrity in school consultation and prereferral intervention. *School Psychology Review, 18,* 37–50.

Gresham, F. M., & Kendell, G. K. (1987). School con-sultation research: Methodological critique and future research directions. *School Psychology Review, 16,* 306–316.

Gutkin, T. B. (1981). Relative frequency of consultee lack of knowledge, skills, confidence, and objec-tivity in school settings. *Journal of School Psy-chology, 19,* 57–61.

Gutkin, T. B., & Curtis, M. J. (1990). School-based con-sultation: Theory, techniques, and research. In T. B. Gutkin & C. R. Reynolds (Eds.), *The handbook of*

school psychology (2nd ed., pp. 577–611). New York: Wiley.

Idol, L., Paolucci-Whitcomb, P., & Nevin, A. (1986). *Collaborative consultation.* Rockvllle, MD: Aspen Systems.

James, B. E., Kidder, M. G., Osberg, J. W, & Hunter, W. B. (1986). Traditional mental health consulta-tion: The psychodynamic perspective. In F. V. Mannino, E. J. Trickett, M. F. Shore, M. G. Kidder, & G. Levin (Eds.), *Handbook of mental health consultation* (pp. 159–174). Washington, DC: U.S. Department of Health and Human Services.

Kelly, J. G. (1993). Gerald Caplan's paradigm: Bridging psychotherapy and public health practice. In W. P. Erchul (Ed.), *Consultation in community, school, and organizational practice: Gerald Caplan's con-tributions to professional psychology* (pp. 75–85). Washington, DC: Taylor & Francis.

Medway, F. J., & Updyke, J. F. (1985). Meta-analysis of consultation outcome studies. *American Journal of Community Psychology, 13,* 489–505.

Meyers, J. (1981). Mental health consultation. In J. C. Conoley (Ed.), *Consultation in schools* (pp. 35–58). New York: Academic Press.

Meyers, J. (1989). The practice of psychology in the schools for the primary prevention of learning and adjustment problems in children: A perspective from the field of education. In L. A. Bond & B. E. Compas (Eds.), *Primary prevention and promotion in the schools* (pp. 391–422). Newbury Park, CA: Sage.

Meyers, J., Brent, D., Faherty, E., & Modafferi, C. (1993). Caplan's contributions to the practice of psychology in schools. In W. P. Erchul (Ed.), *Con-sultation in community, school, and organizational practice: Gerald Caplan's contributions to profes-sional psychology* (pp. 99–122). Washington, DC: Taylor & Francis.

Meyers, J., & Kundert, D. (1988). Implementing process assessment. In J. L. Graden, J. E. Zins, & M. J. Curtis (Eds.), *Alternative educational deliv-ery systems: Enhancing instructional options for all students.* Washington, DC: National Associa-tion of School Psychologists.

Meyers, J., Parsons, R. D., & Martin, R. (1979). *Mental health consultation in the schools.* San Francisco: Jossey-Bass.

Parsons, R. D., & Meyers, J. (1984). *Developing con-sultation skills.* San Francisco: Jossey-Bass.

Pryzwansky, W. B (1974). A reconsideration of the consultation model for delivery of school-based psychological services. *American Journal of Orthopsychiatry, 44,* 579–583.

Pryzwansky, W. B. (1977). Collaboration or consultation: Is there a difference? *Journal of Special Education, 11,* 179–182.

Pryzwansky, W. B., & White, G. W. (1983). The influence of consultee characteristics on preferences for consultation approaches. *Professional Psychology, 14,* 457–461.

Reschly, D. J. (1976). School psychology consultation: "Frenzied, faddish, or fundamental?" *Journal of School Psychology, 14,* 105–113.

Richards, D. E. (1976). Peer consultation among clergy: A resource for professional development. In G. Caplan, & M. Killilea (Eds.), *Support systems and mutual help* (pp. 261–271). New York: Grune & Stratton.

Rosenfeld, J. M. & Caplan, G. (1954). Techniques of staff consultation in an immigrant children's organization in Israel. *American Journal of Orthopsychiatry, 24,* 42–62.

Rosenfield, S. A. (1987). *Instructional consultation.* Hillsdale, NJ: Erlbaum.

Sarason, I. G., & Sarason, B. R. (1984). *Abnormal psychology* (4th ed.). Englewood Cliffs, NJ: Prentice-Hall.

Schulte, A. C., & Osborne, S. S. (April, 1993). What is collaborative consultation? The eye of the beholder. In D. Fuchs (Chair), *Questioning popular beliefs about collaborative consultation.* Symposium presented at the annual meeting of the Council for Exceptional Children, San Antonio, TX.

Schulte, A. C., Osborne, S. S., & Kauffman, J. M. (1993). Teacher responses to two types of consultative special education services. *Journal of Educational and Psychological Consultation, 4,* 1–28.

Wenger, R. D. (1979). Teacher response to collaborative consultation. *Psychology in the Schools, 16,* 127–131.

Weiler, M. B. (1984). *The influence of contact and setting on the ratings of parents for models of consultation.* Unpublished masters thesis, North Carolina State University, Raleigh, NC.

West, J. F. (1985). *Regular and special educators' preferences for school-based consultation models: A statewide study* (Technical report No. 101). Austin, TX: Research and Training Institute on School Consultation, The University of Texas at Austin.

West, J. F. (1990). The nature of consultation vs. collaboration: An interview with Walter B. Pryzwansky. *The Consulting Edge, 2*(1), 1–2, 3.

Chapter *3*

Behavioral Approaches to Consultation

Goal of the Chapter

The goal of this chapter is to present two models of consultation, one growing primarily out of operant learning theory and the other out of cognitive-behavioral learning theory.

Chapter Preview

1. Bergan and Kratochwill's (1990) behavioral model of consultation, a four stage model that relies primarily upon operant learning theory for its intervention techniques, will be presented at the outset.
2. The Social Learning Theory Model (SLM) of consultation will be presented. Its distinguishing characteristics include a unique view of the interrelationships among the consultant, consultee, and client and the assessment procedures that are followed.

Five models of consultation have evolved to date that are based upon the principles of behavioral psychology. In 1969, Tharp and Wetzel articulated the first operant model of consultation that, although important from a historical perspective, concentrated more on behavior modification than it did on the consulting process. In 1977, Bergan presented the first fully developed model of consultation founded in operant learning theory. His model was complete with a discussion of the consulting relationship, protocols for consultation interviewing, a description of the intervention process, and a framework for evaluating consultation outcomes. In 1990, Bergan and Kratochwill revisited Bergan's work and extended and clarified it to some degree. Piersel (1985) presented a problem-solving consultation model based upon operant psychology that was not as well developed as Bergan's model.

Russell (1978) and Keller (1981) drew primarily from operant methodology, at least in the assessment area, and thus have presented behavioral-eclectic models with remarkably similar ideas to those of Bergan that draw upon a broader spectrum of learning theory for their foundation. Like many eclectic models, the relationship between the theoretical and action principles have not been made clear. Moreover, both Russell and Keller draw upon operant methodology for their assessment and intervention strategies, adding little to Bergan's work, and thus they will not be discussed here. Finally, a model developed by the authors that draws upon cognitive-behavioral psychology (Bandura, 1977a) will be presented. This model was partially articulated in the earlier edition of this book (Brown, Pryzwansky and Schulte (1987) and more fully elaborated by Brown and Schulte (1987). Reynolds, Gutkin, Elliot, and Witt (1984), in an independent effort, also have referred to a cognitive-behavioral approach to consultation, but a model will be fully elaborated here.

Bergan and Kratochwill's (1990) model and the Social Learning Theory Model share the scientific heritage of behavioral psychology and are therefore similar in a number of ways. The most obvious of these is that the consultation process reflects a systematic problem-solving paradigm (problem identification, data gathering. choosing an alternative, etc.) seen in all behavioral approaches, whether they be contingency management programs or behavioral counseling. Behaviorally oriented consultants draw upon behavioral techniques that have been empirically validated as the basis for their work and seek to extend that validation by systematically collecting data regarding the impact of consultation. As we shall see, however, there are also significant differences between the two models.

Behavioral-Operant Model

Bergan and Kratochwill (1977) set forth the tenets of their model of consultation in a meticulous presentation that deserves the attention of any serious student of consultation. They define consultation as an indirect, problem-solving service involving a collegial relationship between the consultant and consultee in which the consultant acquires and communicates psychological data germane to the consultee's problem as well as the psychological principles that will enable the consultee to utilize the data. Although the consultee may accept or reject the consultant's communication, Bergan and Kratochwill feel strongly that one of the consultant's primary tasks is to function in a manner that will increase the probability that the consultee will accept the consultant's recommendations. Perhaps the most controversial aspect of the model is that the consultant uses verbal structuring techniques, such as questions designed to elicit specific data, as well as systematic reinforcement to enhance compliance with the consultant's point of view (Gallessich, 1982; Henning-Stout, 1993). While this hints of manipulation, Bergan and Kratochwill make it clear that influencing the consultee is not a covert process. The consultant should clarify his or her role, including the intent to enhance consultee compliance, at the outset of the process.

The goals of consultation are three-fold according to Bergan and Kratochwill: to change the client's behavior, to alter the consultee's behavior, and to produce changes in organizations. The specific objectives of organizational change are to improve both communication and problem solving within the organization. They have not elaborated fully upon the organizational consultation aspect of their theory.

Although the consultation objectives in this model are similar to those of other consultants, the communications techniques utilized are quite different. As is the case with many behaviorists, Bergan and Kratochwill do not address the consulting relationship directly. They do discuss what they term *role relationships*, including "control" of the consultee by the consultant. As could be deduced from their definition of consultation, the consultant's major role is to provide psychological information and principles to the consultee. On the other hand, the consultee's roles within consultation include (1) describing the problem in specific terms, (2) deciding upon a plan to deal with the client's concerns, (3) implementing the plan decided upon, and (4) supervising the client's behavior.

Bergan and Kratochwill (1990) indicate that clients may participate in varying ways in the consultation process particularly when it is time to select interventions to correct their behavior. They believe that the decision-making skills of clients may be enhanced through participation in the process and the result may be a more self-directed individual.

Communication in Consultation

One of Bergan and Kratochwill's (1990) unique contributions to consultation is the model they developed to facilitate the verbal interaction between consultant and consultee. Although the importance of the verbal interchange in consultation is recognized by all consultants, they place more emphasis upon this area because they view the consultant's utterances as the key not only to eliciting the information required to assess the problem but to influencing consultee behavior as well.

Communication from the consultant is aimed primarily at eliciting a description of the background and current circumstances surrounding the client's problem and the difficulty that the consultee is having with that concern. The manner in which the consultant phrases consulting leads such as direct questions is the key to communication. Leads should be phrased so that they will elicit key information from the consultee that can be classified with regard to both process and content. Bergan has posited that information gained from the consultee can be classified into the following subcategories: (1) background-environmental, (2) the setting in which the client's behavior occurs, (3) the parameters of the client's behavior, (4) special characteristics of the client, (5) the nature of the observations made, (6) plans that have been tried or might be tried, and (7) types of additional data needed to solve the problem.

The *background-environment subcategory* involves remote as opposed to immediate environmental conditions that may influence the current functioning of the client, whether the client be an individual or an organization. For example, a question posed to parents about early childhood illnesses, or to an agency head about the purposes of an organization when it was founded would elicit responses in this category. The *behavior-setting subcategory* focuses on the immediate environment in which the problematic behavior occurs. Leads that elicit information about the antecedents of a particular behavior or event and the results or consequences of the behavior fall into this area. So do leads that are aimed at uncovering schedules of reinforcement. An example of this type of lead would be, "Tell me what happened beginning just before the problem behavior and running several minutes after it. Be sure to tell me what each person involved did."

The *behavior subcategory* of consultant-consultee verbal communication involves gaining a precise description of the problematic behaviors of the actors in objective terms. The incidence of the behavior (how often), its duration (how long), the intensity of the behavior (what effort is expended), and when the problematic behavior occurs are key concerns. These data may be elicited by leads such as "How often does this behavior occur?" or by examining records such as absenteeism reports that provide the needed information. Data about antecedent conditions (events that lead to a behavior) and the consequences of the behavior (punishment and reward) may be elicited at the same time. Finally, the consultant needs to discern whether a pattern of behavior has existed over time. Questions such as "When did this problem first arise?" may be helpful to gain this perspective.

Another subcategory of verbalizations, *special characteristics of the client* (for example, learning disabilities, neurological difficulties, organizational goals), should also be elicited by the consultant. This information is generally gained by asking specific questions aimed at determining these characteristics, such as "Does this child (or organization) have any unique features?" and grow increasingly specific, "What is the child's intellectual capacity?" or "Is the decision-making process primarily democratic or autocratic?"

Since not all psychological data needed for proper problem identification will be immediately available to the consultee, the consultant usually asks that *observational data* be collected. These data, once collected, are then elicited from the consultee through direct questions that either ask for the data collected (What did you observe in the staff meeting?) or request the sharing of graphs or charts that have been constructed (for example, the incidence of aggressive behavior by an inmate).

Another important subcategory of consultant-consultee verbalizations has to with *plans*. Information in this category involves what the consultee has already tried (What has worked or failed to work?), suggestions of interventions that might work (I believe this might work), and questions designed to elicit untried plans from the consultee (Are there some things you have been considering?). Ultimately the consultant and consultee must agree upon a plan of action. Generally, this is accomplished when the consultant poses a plan validation elicitor, such as, "Can we agree that the best approach to dealing with this concern is a behavioral contract?"

Finally, the seventh content subcategory of verbalizations exists, which they list simply as *other*. Much of the information in this subcategory may be incidental to the identification of the problem, such as routine illnesses that cause absenteeism, the wearing of a soiled piece of clothing, or an incidental interaction with a fellow worker or student. Any verbal content that does not fit into the first six subcategories listed would be placed in *other*.

Verbal Processes

The verbal content subcategories discussed in the previous section are relatively straightforward. Most consultants, regardless of orientation, look for historical facts that influence current functioning of the client, the interaction between the problematic concern and the current environment, and a specific description of the problematic behavior, although the emphasis upon the various areas would differ across models. However, Bergan and Kratochwill (1990) suggest further elaborations regarding the verbal interaction occurring between consultant and consultee. There are five verbal processes that occur within each

of the seven content subcategories: specification, evaluation, inference, summarization, and validation.

Specification is a process by which the consultant asks the consultee to provide increasingly specific data about the presenting problem. The objective of this process is to discern what historical and environmental factors are contributing to the problem, to define the problem in objective terms, and to reach agreement on a plan of action. This communication process generally moves from general (Tell me about the behavior) to precise (How often does the behavior occur?).

The second process, *evaluation*, involves forming opinions about the values and emotions of the consultee (Does he or she like the child, the organization or the plan that has been devised?). It also provides the basis for positive and negative feedback to the consultee by the consultant (You have done a good job).

The third consultation process involves drawing *inferences* or generalizing from the data. Both consultee and consultant engage in inferential behavior. Bergan and Kratochwill tell us that certain key phrases are utilized when people make inferences. These include: I assume, I think, I feel (I think client A is happy, sad, depressed). Statements such as these are inferences that involve synthesizing data and making psychologically relevant statements about the client.

Another vital verbal process in consultation is *summarization*. Consultants realize that the verbal interchange between consultant and consultee results in a mass of data. When either the consultant or the consultee summarize, they are attempting to include only the relevant data in describing the situation or problem at hand. They are also attempting to facilitate recall on the part of the consultee. For example, "On three different occasions you have mentioned conflicts between the nursing staff and the psychologists regarding the token economy system" would be summarizing.

The last communication process is termed *validation*, which involves the consultant and consultee reaching conclusions about the facts at hand. The result of this process must be consensus since consultation cannot proceed unless both parties agree upon the nature of the problem, the goals to be pursued, and the strategies to be employed in coping with the identified problem. If a consultant states, "I assume that the primary problem between the psychologists and nurses lies in the work produced by the token economy system" and receives a "Yes," validation has occurred.

Emitters and Elicitors

Bergan and Kratochwill believe that effective consultants recognize the subcategories of verbalizations, understand the process involved, and practice making verbalizations that will result in information that falls into the subcategories and reflects the vital communication processes needed to identify the problem and move toward intervention.

Consultant leads fall into two categories: elicitors and emitters. *Elicitors* are assumed to have a controlling effect upon a listener while *emitters* are not expected to have a controlling effect. Elicitors are generally either open-ended imperative statements (such as Tell me about . . .) or direct questions (What is the . . . ?). Emitters are statements of content and process. In counseling/therapy jargon, a reflection of feeling or content is an emitter. For example, in response to a consultee who has exclaimed how frustrated he or she is with the decision-making process in his or her organization, the consultant may say, "I can

see that you are angry about the way decisions are reached." While the consultee may respond, no specific reaction is dictated. Summaries of content and process are also viewed as emitters as are statements of facts, such as Janet is twenty-eight years old.

Elicitors are used by the consultant to control the flow of information within the subcategories of verbal content and to move through the verbal processes to specify the client's background, current behavior, personal characteristics and data in the other subcategories of verbal content that will clarify and define the client's problem. Elicitors are also used to control the verbal processes, by which Bergan and Kratochwill (1990) mean increasing the specificity of the data being received, providing feedback to the consultee, and summarizing the data about the attitudes of the consultee about various aspects of the client's problem. Emitters are also used to communicate the consultant's personal evaluation of the situation at hand or of the consultee's functioning.

Drawing inferences about data collected requires both elicitors and emitters. Elicitors focus on the conclusions drawn by the consultee while emitters capsulize the consultant's inferences. Similarly, emitters are used by the consultant to summarize what has occurred to a particular point in the consultation while elicitors are used to get the consultee's point of view. Bergan and Kratochwill (1990) indicate that elicitors are the primary verbalizations used in the validation process when agreement is being sought on any of the subcategories of verbal content. Examples of elicitors and emitters as they would be used to gain information in several of the subcategories of verbal content are shown in Table 3.1.

The Process of Consultation

Bergan and Kratochwill (1990) identify the major steps in the consultation process as problem identification, problem analysis, plan implementation, and problem evaluation.

Problem Identification
Problem identification begins with establishing the objectives to be accomplished in consultation. These objectives should identify the client: specify the outcomes (changes) in measurable terms; establish an objective level of performance, either an increase or decrease; identify the conditions where, when, and with whom the outcome is expected to occur; and establish a date by which the behavior is expected to be performed. In order to establish these kinds of objectives a great deal needs to be known about the current functioning of the client.

Information about the client may be gained from a number of sources including test data, work samples, observational data, and problem identification interviews. With regard to the latter, they distinguish between interviews aimed at identifying longer term developmental problems and those aimed at shorter term problems that often arise out of crisis situations. An outline of the format for each type of interview follows.

Developmental Interview (For non-crisis situations)

I. Establish general objectives
 A. What are your general concerns about client?
 B. What does client need to do to overcome your concerns?
 C. Can we be more specific about your concerns and goals?

TABLE 3.1   Illustrations of Bergan and Kratochwill's Communication Systems

Verbal Content Subcategory: Background-Environment	Type Lead/Process
1. Tell me more about the relationship between the mother and father.	Elicitor/Specification
2. How do you feel about the treatment plan that John was on in the mental hospital?	Elicitor/Evaluation
3. It seems to me that there is a degree of defensiveness in the way that Jerry has handled agency business in the past.	Emitter/Inference
4. I wonder if you could capsulize your thoughts about the influence of the last five years upon the current situation.	Elicitor/Summarization
5. Can we agree that the home environment is probably the most salient factor in the current problem?	Elicitor/Validation

Verbal Content Subcategory: Behavior	
1. It's pretty clear that the incidence of behavior is over 30 times per hour.	Emitter/Specification
2. Give me your reaction to the data we have collected.	Elicitor/Evaluation
3. Even though the child is out of his seat a lot and gets reprimanded for it, I think he's enjoying himself.	Emitter/Inference
4. We have identified three areas of problematic behavior. Which one appears to be of the greatest concern based upon what you have seen?	Elicitor/Summarization
5. I believe that the reading problem is the most serious concern. What do you think?	Elicitor/Validation

Verbal Content Subcategory: Plans	
1. You indicated that you tried a number of approaches to raising the morale of volunteers. Can you tell me more about those plans?	Elicitor/Specification
2. How did you feel about the plans you have tried?	Elicitor/Evaluation
3. Which plans seemed to work the best?	Elicitor/Inference
4. Can you summarize good and bad parts of each plan?	Elicitor/Summarization
5. It seems to me that we should go with a combination of two of the programs that you have tried, drawing on the strengths of both. What do you think?	Elicitor/Validation

   II. Establish relationships between general and specific objectives
      A. Categorize objectives into general or specific
      B. Reach agreement with consultee regarding content of objectives
  III. Generate performance objectives
      A. Establish priority areas for generating performance objectives
      B. Establish behavior to be attained, the conditions under which it is to occur, and the level of the expected behavior
      C. Make sure that there is agreement with consultee regarding performance objectives

IV. Establish assessment procedures for performance objective
   A. Generate alternatives for behavior recording procedures
   B. Establish agreement on recording procedures
 V. Make appointments for follow-up meetings

Problem-centered interview (For crisis situations)

  I. Determine problematic behaviors of client and strength (intensity, duration, frequency) of these behaviors
   A. Ask for a behavioral description of client's problem
   B. Ask for specification of the strength of the behavior
   C. Reach agreement (validate) regarding both the description of the behavior and its strength
 II. Assess the conditions under which the problematic behavior occurs
   A. Determine antecedent conditions
   B. Determine situational variable(s) that may elicit behavior
   C. Establish sequence of events, antecedents to behavior and consequences
   D. Summarize to make sure that validation (agreement) has occurred
III. Determine how the client's performance will be assessed
   A. Establish need for assessment
   B. Review recording procedures and confirm agreement regarding them
 IV. Schedule future meetings

As can be seen from the foregoing outlines, the problem-centered problem identification interview focuses on the immediate concern without reviewing what may be some more general goals for the client.

Problem Analysis

Problem analysis is used to assist the consultee in identifying variables that will lead to problem resolution. Bergan and Kratochwill suggest that there are two nonmutually exclusive means by which this can be accomplished. One is to focus on the setting and the intrapsychic variables of the client that may act to maintain the problem. The second is to identify the skills deficits of the client.

As has been suggested earlier in this chapter, analyzing problematic behavior involves identifying antecedent behaviors, either environmental or covert, that may cue a particular behavior, determining the consequences of a behavior (its rewards and punishments), and determining the sequential conditions or the cumulative impact of behavior over time. Much of this information will come from observational data, but information about covert processes will necessarily come from the client. Background information may be determined by interviewing peers and significant others in the client's life.

Skills analysis involves a variety of approaches, including analyzing work samples and reports from others, but observational data is important in most instances. Once skills deficits are identified, Bergan and Kratochwill suggest that prerequisite skills be identified as well. For example, a high school student who is failing algebra may need to develop a series of mathematics skills and concepts before mastering algebra. Similarly, a manager

who fails to communicate adequately with the staff may need work in assertiveness before becoming an effective communicator.

Plan Implementation

Once a problem has been completely analyzed, a plan must be designed to deal with the problem. Objectives must be established, interventions or strategies selected, practical constraints regarding the utilization of the strategies assessed, and assessment procedures outlined. Bergan and Kratochwill offer the following steps for this phase of consultation.

1. Make sure that consultee and consultant agree upon the nature of the problem.
2. Complete either the setting and intrapersonal analysis or the skills analysis.
3. Design a plan to deal with identified problem.
   a. Establish objectives
   b. Select interventions
   c. Consider barriers to implementation
   d. Select assessment procedures
4. Make arrangements for follow-up sessions with consultee.

As has already been noted, plans are typically implemented by the consultee in Bergan and Kratochwill's (1990) model with the consultant in a monitoring role. However in some situations, the consultee might train others to implement the plan. For example, in custodial care institutions such as nursing homes, psychiatric hospitals, or prisons and in institutions such as schools, paraprofessionals such as aides or attendants may implement behavior plans and, in self-managed behavioral programs, clients can implement their own plans.

The major tasks of the person who implements the plan are to systematically apply the techniques that have been devised and to observe and plot the behaviors that are the focus of the intervention. Usually the consultant assumes the role of developing implementation skills, that is, teaching the plan implementor the behavioral techniques (for example, systematic reinforcement of desired behavior or modeling techniques) and training the plan implementor to employ more systematic observations. Some of the common techniques utilized can be seen in Table 3.2.

A number of processes must occur during the plan implementation phase. The two most obvious of these are monitoring client progress and simultaneously monitoring plan implementation in order to ascertain that it is being carried out in the prescribed manner. Failure to conduct the latter procedure can result in a variety of consequences including worsening the client's inappropriate behavior by inadvertently introducing intermittent schedules of reinforcement. According to Bergan and Kratochwill (1990), the consultant and the consultee share the responsibility of monitoring the implementation process. Other vital processes that must occur during plan implementation include revising the plan as needed and developing skills in the consultee. For example, if contingency contracting is to be utilized, the consultee must acquire the ability to establish the procedure with the client. Monitoring both client process and plan implementation are the responsibility of the consultant.

TABLE 3.2   Behavioral Intervention Strategies

Technique	Description
Systematic positive reinforcement	Providing rewards for desired behavior.
Social reinforcers	Positive statements. Smiles, nods, facial expressions, etc.
Negative reinforcement	Removing aversive stimuli to increase desired behavior.
Extinction	Removal of positive reinforcer in order to reduce or eliminate the incidence of undesirable behavior.
Punishment	Either the removal of a positive reinforcer or the presentation of an aversive stimuli as means of reducing or eliminating undesirable behavior.
Cues	Environmental stimuli that prompt behavior are put into place.
Schedules of reinforcement	Patterns used to present reinforcers.
Fixed interval	Reinforcers delivered at specified times.
Variable interval	Reinforcers delivered at varying time intervals.
Fixed ratio	Reinforcement tied to performance and is delivered at predetermined ratios (e.g., 1:4).
Variable ratio (Intermittent)	Reinforcement provided at varying behavioral performances (1:2; 1:10; 1:5).
Shaping	The development of a behavior by reinforcing successive approximation of the desired behavior.
Chaining	The development of complex behaviors or behavioral repertoires by linking several less complex behaviors (e.g., teaching addition, subtraction, and multiplication as the basis for learning division).
Generalization of behavior	Assisting client to transfer knowledge gained in one setting to another.
Reinforcing incompatible behavior	Reducing the incidence of undesirable behavior by reinforcing desirable behavior in the same situation.
Premack principle	Using high probability behavior (e.g., listening to music) as reinforcer for low probability behavior (e.g., doing homework).
Fading	The removal of artificial cues or reinforcers that prompt or reward behavior so that natural environment will provide basis for desired behavior.
Contingency contracts	Systematic contracts managed by client, consultee, or others that specify behaviors to be performed and outcomes if behaviors are performed.
Behavior rehearsal	A process that begins with modeling appropriate behavior followed by practice with feedback.
Discrimination training	Helping client to link environmental cues with appropriate behavior.

Several factors may necessitate revision of the behavior change plan, including miscommunication between the consultant and consultee resulting in faulty plan design, the inability of plan implementors to properly carry out the plan due to faulty training or other deficits, contingencies operating on the plan implementor that preclude full implementation (for example, institution policies, peer group pressure), the influences of the client upon the plan implementor resulting in misimplementation, and the client's environmental conditions. An example of the latter situation occurred during a parent consultation. A mother was unable to implement a plan to help her daughter increase her school attendance because the plan quite naturally called for parental insistence upon and reinforcement for school attendance. Since the child was the only social contact for the parent, carrying out the plan meant being alone, a situation which the mother finally admitted was unbearable. In this case, another plan executor would have to be found or the problem would have to be redefined.

Once the source of the difficulty in plan implementation is found, the consultant must remedy the situation. The strategy selected will, of course, depend upon the nature of the problem. If miscommunication results in a faulty plan, communication must first be improved, primarily through the elicitations of the consultant, and the plan revised according to the new data. If the plan executor does not possess the necessary skills to implement the plan, then those skills must be developed through educational efforts or the plan must be altered to fit the current skills of the executor. Plans may also have to be altered to bring them into line with institutional norms (group contingencies) or the executor may need to be helped to cope more effectively with the contingencies that are operating. As was already mentioned, a new executor may have to be found in some instances. It is quite possible that the consultation objectives will need to be altered in other situations and a new plan devised that corresponds more closely to the client's situation as the consultant and consultee understand it at the time of the reassessment.

Problem Evaluation

The problem evaluation stage of consultation consists of a series of ongoing consultant-consultee interviews in which certain key issues are addressed. In this stage of consultation, the consultant and consultee meet to determine (1) whether the goals established for the client have been attained; (2) the overall effectiveness of the plan that was established to attain the goals, and (3) whether consultation should be continued or terminated (Bergan & Kratochwill, 1990). Data for making this determination come primarily from observations that began during the problem identification stage and continues throughout the consultation process. Bergan and Kratochwill (1990) suggest that intensive or case study designs (Kazdin, 1984) that focus on the individual rather than groups are probably most appropriate for this purpose. Intensive designs will be discussed in detail later.

Evaluation data may indicate, if the objectives have been achieved and no new objectives have evolved, that termination of the consulting relationship should occur. In this event, plans should be made with the consultee to fade the intervention so the client will not regress to earlier behavior. Such data may also indicate that a new plan should be devised and implemented, particularly if the intervention was unsuccessful. In some instances, consultation should be terminated in favor of other interventions. Student Learning Activity 3.1 illustrates how data may be used to evaluate consultation.

Student Learning Activity 3.1

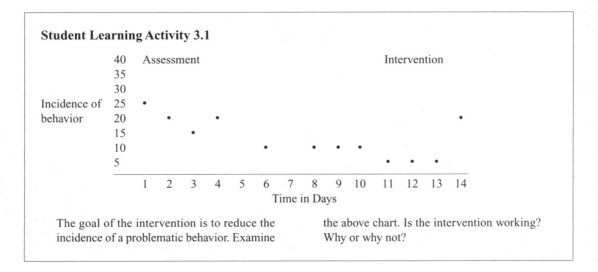

The goal of the intervention is to reduce the incidence of a problematic behavior. Examine the above chart. Is the intervention working? Why or why not?

Status

A number of authors have criticized operant learning approaches to consultation because of their deterministic philosophy (Heller & Monahan, 1977), the ethics involved in manipulating certain types of behavior (Winett & Winker, 1972), and the apparent assumption that the consultant takes responsibility for shaping the consultee's behavior (Gallessich, 1982). Bergan and Kratochwill's (1990) approach to consultation also can be criticized because it has as one of its basic assumptions that the consultee accepts operant principles and it tends to be rigidly theory bound.

While there have been frequent criticisms of behavioral consultation, the approach is not without support. Bergan and Tombari (1975, 1976) have produced data that suggest that consultee expectancies and behaviors can be influenced by the consultant and that this, in turn, increases the likelihood of consultation success. Medway (1979) reviewed the research on consultation between the years of 1972–1977 and concluded that with regard to empirical support, "Behavioral consultation, which has been subjected to some of the most stringent experimental controls, appears to be faring especially well" (p. 279). More recently, Kratochwill and Van Someren (1985) come to a similar conclusion and suggested that verbalizations "in the subcategories of behavior, behavior settings, observation, and plan message content" (p. 227) were linked to effective consultation.

Erchul (1987) explored an implicit dimension of Bergan's (1977) model, dominance of the consultant, and tentatively concluded that there is a positive relationship between consultant dominance and consultee perceptions of the consultant. Erchul also concluded that his research supported one of Bergan's basic assumptions: The consultant should control the consultation process. Subsequent research by Erchul & Chewning (1990) also appears to provide some support for this assumption although the data in this study suggests that the consultant appears to control the process less in later consultation sessions. It seems, as Conoley and Conoley (1992) conclude, that consultants who can influence the nature of the consultation process are more likely to be successful than those who cannot. However, it

remains to be seen whether the approach prescribed by Bergan and Kratochwill (1990) is the most efficacious approach to influencing this process (Henning-Stout, 1993).

A Social Learning Theory Model

Social Learning Constructs

The central construct underpinning the social learning theory model (SLM) of consultation is reciprocal determinism. Bandura (1977a, 1978, 1982a, & 1982b) posits that human functioning is the result of a dynamic interrelationship among behaviors, the environment, and certain cognitive variables, mainly appraisals and expectations of outcome. In some situations, behavior dominates and can be used to predict how a person will function. In others, the environment is the dominating variable, while cognitions will be the determining factor in human functioning in yet other situations.

Behavior can be defined as a repertoire of skills acquired primarily through direct experience and/or vicarious learning (Bandura, 1977a). Appraisals are situation specific and relate to the value that an individual places upon successful performance in a given situation. Expectations relate both to expected performance (self-efficacy) and outcomes (rewards and punishments), which may be either extrinsic or intrinsic. Bandura (1982b) has placed increasing emphasis on self-efficacy expectations in human functioning and this emphasis is reflected in the SLM.

While Bandura (1977a, 1978) recognizes that the environment may be the dominant variable in human functioning, he has not defined it in any great detail. In one instance (1978), he uses an illustration of a swimmer thrown into the water to show that the environment (water) can dictate human functioning. The environment is more difficult to define because it is made up of social and physical factors, but primarily, it is viewed as the collective expectations held by significant others and the sanctions associated with them in the situation at hand.

With these definitions in mind a restatement of reciprocal determinism might be as follows: Human functioning in a particular situation will be the result of the interactions among environmental expectations, the behavioral skills germane to performance in the situation in question, the importance attached to successful performance, the confidence that one can perform (self-efficacy) the task at hand, and expectations of outcome. In any given situation one or any combination of these factors may determine performance. In the SLM of consultation these constructs guide the process.

Assumptions and Values

Two assumptions underpin SLM. The first was derived directly from reciprocal determinism and suggests simply that "consultant, consultee, and client funding are the result of the interaction of behavior, internal personal factors (intrapsychic variables), and environmental factors" (Brown & Schulte, 1987, p. 283) and that understanding a consultee or a client requires that these factors be examined simultaneously. The second assumption, which

was derived logically from the first, suggests that the goal of the consultant is to change the homeostatic relationship that exists among the behavior, intrapsychic variables, and environmental variables that preclude the consultee from functioning effectively with the present client and similar future clients. The consultee role is to perform the same task with the client, that is, intervene in the dynamic relationship that exists among behavior, cognitions, and environment to effect change.

The values that guide consultation are primarily the traditional goals of our society. However, Brown and Schulte point out that the values that guide the process may have to be tempered to meet the demands of a situation. For example, aggressive behavior such as fighting is usually not condoned by our society, but a child living in some sections of our cities may need to fight to survive and, thus, the welfare of the client becomes the overriding consideration in the consultation process.

As noted at the outset, Bergan (1977), Russell, (1978), and Keller (1981) have all indicated that consultation moves through five distinct problem-solving stages: (1) defining the problem, (2) functional analysis of the problem, that is, determining the incidence and severity of the problem, (3) goal setting, (4) intervention, and (5) evaluation. Little mention has been made by these behavioral consultants of the relationship stage of consultation. In the 1950s and 1960s, operant learning theorists scoffed at the idea that a human relationship was needed in a helping process. However, research has linked the consultant's ability to develop a relationship characterized by empathy, warmth, and trust to satisfaction with consultation (Horton & Brown, 1990).

The Consultation Process

Role of the Consultant

In the broadest sense, the role of the SLM consultant is one of facilitator. In more concrete terms, this means that the consultant should fill those roles that will (a) motivate the consultee to develop self-regulatory behavior and (b) assist the consultee to establish behavioral standards. According to Bandura (1977b, 1982b), motivation grows out of anticipated positive outcomes, self-efficacy that one can perform the tasks demanded by the situation, and goals that correspond to personal standards. Behavioral standards develop as a result of direct instruction, feedback, and the observation of models evaluating their own behavior (Bandura, 1976, 1977b, 1978).

In order to develop motivation and behavioral standards, the consultant may suggest that, as a result of consultation, the consultee will be better able to cope with the client, help consultees explore their own standards of functioning and set goals for themselves in accordance with those standards, provide needed information (e.g., bibliotherapy), engage the consultee in situations (e.g., roleplaying) where they can practice new skills and evaluate their own performance, provide feedback to the consultee, and arrange for the consultee to observe appropriate models. Since performance enactments are the most effective means of enhancing self-efficacy, those situations which allow the consultee to experience the consequences of their own behavior should be emphasized (Bandura, 1976, 1977b, 1978).

The Process of SLM Consultation

Relationship

Bandura (1977a) has also suggested that warm, nurturant individuals seem to engender more imitative behavior, as do those perceived as competent. It has also been shown that models who are perceived as similar in some way may be imitated more often than those seen as vastly different.

What, then, are the implications of the foregoing for the consulting relationship? One rather clear implication is that the consultant needs to be genuine and communicate a sense of concern for the consultee. Another implication is that the consultant needs to indicate that he or she is competent, a task that is obviously more difficult for trainees than veteran consultants. However, it is quite likely that trainees who are enrolled in good preparatory programs and have confidence in their consulting abilities will have little difficulty in this area. Finally, the consultant and consultee need to find some common ground. This common ground might be leisure interests or past work experiences, but one commonality between the consultee and the consultant should always be the welfare of the client.

In addition to establishing a consulting relationship characterized by warmth and open communication, consultant and consultee expectations must be aired and agreed upon during the early stages of consultation. Those issues to be discussed include the goals of consultation (for example, working toward independence for the consultee), roles of each party (for example, power relationships, working with the client), confidentiality of communications, and time and length of meetings. These initial agreements are renegotiated in many instances and altered in others as consultation progresses. However, it is the expectations developed in the initial stages that provide the framework for the process.

Assessing the Problem

The SLM approach to consultation places a great deal of emphasis upon assessing cognitive processes and, in particular, those related to self-efficacy beliefs. However, it would be inconsistent with the premises of social learning theory (Bandura, 1977b, 1978) if, in the assessment process, behavioral skills and environmental variables were excluded.

Brown and Schulte (1987, p. 285) suggest that several questions need to be answered as the consultant and consultee simultaneously assess the consultee's and client's functioning. They also suggest some assessment strategies for answering these questions.

Questions Regarding the Consultee	*Method of Assessment*
1. Is the consultee motivated to solve the problem at hand? How important is it that he or she solve the problem (appraisal)?	1. In interview, have consultee rate motivation on a 1–10 scale. 2. By inference from statements.
2. How self-confident is the consultee that he or she can perform the tasks necessary to deal with the problem at hand.	1. Use self-efficacy rating of 1–10, with 1 being low and 10 being very high.

3. Has the consultee developed the skills necessary to deal with the problem at hand?

1. Observation of consultee.
2. Consultee's self-ratings.
3. Roleplaying to assess skill.

4. Are there powerful environmental constraints (e.g., informal norms, rules, traditions) that preclude or limit consultee action?

1. Interviews with others by consultant.
2. Consultee reports.
3. Questionnaires sent to powerful role senders.

Questions Regarding Client

1. Does the client have the skill to deal with his or her problem?

1. Observation (consultee).
2. Roleplaying (consultee and client).
3. Self-ratings.

2. What is the client's self-efficacy regarding her or his ability to deal with the problem at hand?

1. Consultee interview to gain self-ratings.

3. What is the client's perception of the importance of dealing with her or his problem (appraisal)?

1. Consultee interview to gain ratings of importance.

4. Are there powerful environmental variables such as a peer group or home and school that constrain the client from taking action?

1. Observations by consultee.
2. Consultee interviews.

　　The processes of client and consultee assessment are described in more detail in the pages that follow.

　　One point should be made prior to addressing the mechanics of the assessment process, which is aimed at assisting both the client and the consultee. In the latter case, the goal should be to help the consultee become independent of the consultant. This cannot be accomplished if the consultant takes sole responsibility for any phase of the consultation. Assessment should be a collaborative process between the consultant and consultee. The question of who actually performs what role, particularly in the assessment process, depends upon a variety of variables including expertise, access to clients, and time available. Perhaps the only assessment strategy to avoid is unilateral action by the consultant that would preclude the consultee from acquiring the skills to function independently.

Client Assessment　　Although client assessment may begin at any point, it is suggested that it start with the identification of behavioral strengths and deficits. The basic question to be answered is, Has the client acquired the behaviors needed to function in a given situation? If the client is a child in a classroom, an additional set of questions regarding physical problems, intellectual functioning, and learning disabilities may need to be posed. In instances where the "client" is a group, answering those questions becomes a bit more complex but the concerns are the same. For example, "Do the members of a problematic work group possess the necessary communication and/or problem-solving skills to deal with their concerns?"

In both the case of the child and the work group, the basic assessment strategy used is likely to be direct observation, although techniques such as validated assessment instruments, roleplaying, self-observation, and behavioral checklists can also be used to assess behavioral deficits.

Assessing cognitions is certainly more difficult but, as has already been noted, just as important. One area that should receive a great deal of attention is the client's perception of his or her ability to perform in a certain area, or perception of self-efficacy. Self-efficacy scales (Bandura, 1982a, 1982b; Keyser & Barling, 1981) can be used to collect such data, but self-efficacy perceptions regarding performance in a problem area can often be gained simply by asking clients how confident they feel about their performance in a given area.

The client's expectations of performance are normally assessed by the consultee. The preferred assessment strategy is likely to be an informal interview (Mischel, 1973; Meichenbaum, 1977). The foci of the interview(s) will be (1) determining the extent to which the client expects rewards and punishments from the environment, (2) ascertaining the degree to which the client will self-reinforce if he or she performs appropriately, (3) determining the importance the client attaches to performance in the situation being discussed, and (4) assessing self-efficacy. The following outline may be used as a format for an interview assessing cognitions.

    I. With client, identify the problematic behavior.
        A. Verbally describe or roleplay the behavior in question.
        B. Identify time, place, and circumstances under which behavior occurs.
        C. Identify any environmental cues and reinforcers.
    II. With client, identify appropriate behavior(s) for situation.
        A. Verbally describe or roleplay.
        B. Get feedback from client about his or her view of behavior.
    III. Assess cognitions.
        A. How confident is client that he or she can perform desired behavior? Consultee may ask client to rate on 1–10 scale with 1 being low confidence.
        B. What will be the outcome if the client performs appropriately?
            1. Environmental
            2. Personal rewards
        C. How important is it for the client to behave appropriately in situation?
    IV. Review your assessment with the client.

Traditionally, behaviorists have targeted immediate environmental contingencies in the assessment process. The SLM takes a much broader view of the environment. Since Bandura (1977a) has not specified the dimensions of the environment, the systems theory work of Brofenbrenner (1979) and others (Rogers-Warren, 1977; Wahler, Berland, Coe, & Leske, 1977) has been drawn on for terminology and conceptualizations of the environment.

The first step in environmental assessment is to examine relevant aspects of the client's microsystems (for example, classroom, family, peer group). As in Bergan and Kratochwill's (1990) consultation model, the variables to assess include the antecedents to the behavior

(cues), the positive and negative contingencies involved in the problem behavior, and a consideration of sequential conditions (that is, Is there a sequence of behaviors in which this problem behavior is a part?). Assessment should also examine the appropriateness of the client's social role with peers and other interpersonal relationships, such as those in the family. The primary question to be answered in environmental assessment deals with the extent to which positive reinforcement is available if the client exhibits the desired behaviors. If reinforcement exists, a supportive environment exists to some degree.

Aspects of the ecosystem total setting, which includes the various subsystems of the client, that might influence behavior should also be investigated. For example, a shortage of exercise equipment may lead to an increase in aggressive acts in a prison setting; so may overcrowding. Formal assessment strategies have been developed to assess classroom environments (Goodwin & Coates, 1977) and family situations (Moos, 1981), but it is quite likely that much of the work involving impact of subsystems will need to be done informally using interview or observational strategies.

The culmination of the client assessment process should be the development of a data base that enables the consultant and consultee to determine the relative importance of environmental, behavioral, and cognitive variables in the client's functioning.

Consultee Assessment   Caplan (1970) was the first to point out that the assessment of consultees and their environments is a crucial step in consultation. He provided a framework for understanding consultee difficulties, indicating four potential problems that may exist in the consultee: lack of knowledge, lack of skill, lack of self-confidence, and lack of objectivity.

The SLM of consultation extends many of Caplan's ideas in that the behaviors (skills), cognitions (for example, self-efficacy beliefs), and environment of the consultee are specifically examined for sources of difficulty. Assessing consultee behaviors normally involves making informal observations of consultee identified situations as the consultee works with the client. These observation sessions may involve formal quantification of target behaviors if there is reason to believe the consultee will not accept the informal observational data or if it is expected that these data will be useful or necessary in evaluating the outcomes of consultation.

As was the case with the cognitive assessment of clients, much of this work is done informally. The questions to be answered include: (1) How important is it to the consultee that he or she functions appropriately with the client? (2) How confident is the consultee that he or she can deal with the identified problem? (3) What is the expected outcome in terms of environmental rewards and punishments if he or she functions appropriately with the client? (4) To what extent would he or she self-reinforce upon solving the problem at hand?

The assessment of the consultee's environment, like that for the client, is somewhat complex. The consultant is certainly interested in discerning the norms of the organization or group of which the consultee is a part. A teacher may be violating those norms if he or she abandons strict traditional approaches to teaching for more scientifically based approaches. Similarly, a therapist may have difficulty adjusting to a more consultative-educational approach because of an implicit belief among his or her peer group that individual psychotherapy is the treatment of "choice."

Student Learning Activity 3.2

Your consultee is a resident assistant (RA) who has been accused of inconsistent behavior by the students on his floor. After two consultation sessions you have developed four hypotheses about the reasons for this behavior. These are

A. The RA is non-assertive. He puts up with the behavior until he cannot stand it anymore, then blows up.

B. The job is not important (low appraisal) and

thus he only responds when he has to and then does so in a harsh manner.

C. The norm among RAs is not to get concerned until an emergency occurs and then to *crack down*.

D. The RA has little confidence in his ability to handle the job.

Tell how you would confirm one of these hypotheses.

Physical environmental constraints can also be assessed. Noise may preclude all but the most rudimentary communication on some industrial sites. Office arrangements may deter staff members in human service agencies from engaging in the type of informal communication that will lead to higher levels of cohesiveness. These factors and others must be taken into consideration during the environmental assessment process.

The result of the consultee assessment process should be a mutually agreed upon set of target areas that, if strengthened, will enable the consultee to address problems similar to the one under discussion in the future.

Problem Statement and Goals

The assessment process should result in the identification of client and consultee problem areas. Then one set of goals must be identified for the consultee and a second set for the client. These goals should be written down and prioritized. The priorities placed on the consultee's goals are normally established by the consultee. However, the consultant should provide guidance in the process to ensure the goals are rank ordered in a manner that will maximize the consultee's chances for success when he or she attempts the new approach with the client. The consultee who has low self-efficacy regarding leading a staff meeting focusing on identifying solutions to agency problems could begin simply by discussing the approach with two esteemed friends in order to gain self-confidence before moving on to the next step. Similarly, teachers involved in designing a drop out prevention program may need to observe others engaged in the process in order to gain self-confidence.

It was once a dictum in behavioral psychology that "if you cannot see and measure it, it doesn't exist, or at least we cannot be concerned about it." This led to widespread agreement that goals need to be established in observable, measurable terms. The only variation of this guideline in the SLM is that outcomes of the goals should be observable *whenever possible* and always measurable. For example, one goal of consultation will often be to increase consultees' self-efficacy, which can be inferred via performance, but can also be directly measured simply by asking consultees to rate their ability to perform in a given area on a 1 to 10 scale.

Client Intervention Selection and Implementation

Several considerations should go into the selection of an intervention strategy. First, what are the consultee's wishes? Bergan and Kratochwill (1990) indicate that the ultimate decision for selecting an intervention should rest with the consultee. Within certain limits, this is certainly a worthwhile suggestion. However, the consultant will undoubtedly have a wide range of experiences with various interventions that should be considered in the selection process. Additionally, the consultant is much more likely to be familiar with the empirical literature pertaining to various interventions. Intervention selection, therefore, should be a collaborative process between the consultant and consultee that draws upon both the technical knowledge and experience of the consultant and the information consultees have about their own situation.

A common error among behavioral consultants has been to design interventions that require tremendous amounts of time to observe and record client and consultee behaviors. These interventions soon become aversive and are often abandoned after a relatively short period of time. Consultants must work with consultees to select interventions that are both effective and can be implemented without producing an overload of work. In determining the amount of work involved consideration should be given to (1) the amount of time needed to learn the intervention (the complexity dimension), (2) the time needed to design, implement, and monitor the intervention (the load dimension), (3) the amount of time the actual intervention will be in place before the natural environment and/or client assumes maintenance of the change (the efficiency dimension), and (4) the expected results (the effectiveness dimension).

An additional factor should be considered when selecting an intervention: the impact upon the system. For example, behavioral interventions in business and industry such as lotteries to reward punctual employees have produced complaints from other units because they did not have a similar program. Family consultants have often observed shifts in the behavior of other members of the family when a problematic individual begins to make progress. Behavioral consultants working with families have long been aware of the fact that an intervention with one individual produces a ripple effect, that is, changes in one person in a family result in changes in one or more others in the family. Anticipating these consequences is difficult but mandatory since it is the consultant's goal to solve problems, not create them. The selection of an intervention might proceed as follows.

1. Generate a list of all possible approaches to assisting the client.
2. List the positive and negative aspects of each.

   a. Consultant's point of view
   b. Consultee's point of view
   c. Client's point of view

3. Identify potential positive and negative consequences of intervention (outside immediate impact on client and consultee).
4. Select intervention based upon the assessment.

Readying a consultee to implement an intervention requires meticulous care. Selecting an intervention that the consultee accepts and has confidence in is only the first step. After

selection the consultant will often find it necessary to model and have the consultee rehearse the implementation strategy if the consultee is to effectively implement it. During rehearsal the consultant should actively coach the consultee regarding appropriate ways of functioning. Once the consultee and consultant are both confident that the consultee has mastered the strategy, then implementation with the client can occur.

Types of Interventions for Both Consultees and Clients

Many of the guidelines outlined for client intervention also apply to selecting interventions to address consultee concerns. Consultees should be active participants in selecting approaches to resolve their own deficiencies, and work overload should be avoided when choosing an intervention strategy. Finally, simplicity, effectiveness, and the potential impact upon the remainder of the system should be considered.

Behavioral psychology has been accused of being technique ridden by some of its critics. Indeed, the diagnostic table of contents from a book on behavioral counseling (Krumboltz & Thoreson, 1976) lists 34 behavioral techniques, many of which can be readily adapted for use in behavioral consultation. A number of behavioral interventions are listed in Table 3.3, but to be more complete the list would have to be expanded to include interventions that focus on cognitive changes as well as environmental restructuring. Space considerations do not permit a detailed discussion of all techniques, but references such as

TABLE 3.3   SLM Techniques

Technique	Description
Symbolic modeling	The presentation of desired behaviors via audio or videotape, through written material, or by observing another.
Performance enactments	A process of guided practice in which the consultant provides models of desired behaviors and then asks the consultee to rehearse the observed behaviors. Coaching and feedback are utilized as adjuncts.
Covert modeling	Consultee imagines a model performing the desired behaviors.
Cognitive modeling	Process by which thoughts engaged in while performing desired behavior are "talked through."
Cognitive restructuring	Involves identifying current thoughts that either precede, occur during, or follow a problem situation, and replacing them with more appropriate thoughts. The process relies upon cognitive modeling and feedback.
Systematic desensitization	Eliminating phobic responses either by pairing them with a neutral stimulus such as a relaxed physical state or by gradually exposing persons with phobias to the stimulus that prefaces the phobic response.
Self-monitoring	A procedure engaged in by an individual with problematic behavior for the purpose of (1) identifying the parameters of the difficulty, or (2) monitoring their progress toward some preset goal.

Bandura (1977), Kazdin (1984), and many others can be drawn on for fuller explanation of the procedures. A partial list of procedures can be seen in Table 3.3.

Interventions to be used in addressing self-efficacy problems come primarily from the work of Bandura (1977a, 1982b). The most effective means of producing increases in self-efficacy is performance accomplishments, that is, the successful performance of a particular behavior. In the example of the director of a human services agency who lacked the confidence to lead a staff meeting addressing the problems in the agency, successfully performing that behavior should increase his or her self-efficacy.

Self-efficacy can also be increased through vicarious experience involving the observation of esteemed models (Bandura, 1977a). Our agency director's self-efficacy can be enhanced by observing another administrator lead a problem-solving group. In some instances the same results can be achieved if the consultant models the behavior. However, vicarious learning need not occur only through the observation of live models. Videotapes, films, and even written material can provide modeling experience (Bandura, 1977a).

The third source of self-efficacy expectations outlined by Bandura (1977a, 1982b) involves verbal persuasion. Although this source is generally viewed as less powerful than either performance attainment or vicarious modeling (Bandura 1977a; 1982b), exhortations that one can succeed can produce positive changes in self-efficacy.

The final source of self-efficacy expectations is emotional or physiological arousal. Bandura (1977a) posits that we rely upon physiological arousal to provide cues to vulnerability. High emotional arousal usually results in lower self-efficacy. Thus, one means of increasing self-efficacy is to reduce the emotional arousal by introducing cognitive controls using techniques such as systematic desensitization. It should be stressed that this is viewed as the least powerful means of increasing self-efficacy.

Although performance enactments are viewed as the most powerful means of increasing self-efficacy, it is rarely the case in consultation that either the client or the consultee is asked to begin the process of increasing self-efficacy by actually performing a particular behavior. A more typical approach would be (1) assuring the consultee or client that they can perform a particular behavior (verbal persuasion), (2) having them observe another individual performing a particular behavior (vicarious learning), and then (3) after some carefully designed roleplaying experiences, having them perform the behavior (performance enactment). Techniques that address emotional arousal would only be employed if irrational fears about performing in a general area persist.

Appraisals relate to the importance attached to performance in a particular situation. Students often devalue learning and thus are unmotivated to function at a level that reflects their potential. Some teachers have similar problems regarding the instruction of certain groups of students, just as some administrators have difficulty getting motivated to handle various aspects of their jobs. Appraisals are inextricably linked to expectations of outcomes (Bandura, 1977a), particularly those associated with intrinsic and extrinsic rewards. Accordingly, interventions must be selected that simultaneously address both the importance attached to performance in a particular situation and expectations of outcomes.

In some instances, appraisals and expectations can be altered simply by providing information about the importance of an activity. The performance of routine chores may

---

Student Learning Activity 3.3

Earlier we discussed the RA who acted inconsis-   Describe your course of action with the consultee.
tently. You have confirmed that he is non-assertive.

---

be as essential to good administration as is the ability to make good decisions. Managers may not be aware that their failures to perform "administrivia" may result in lowered staff morale and the perception that they are ineffective administrators. Similarly, teachers may not associate their failure to individualize instruction for slow students to the discipline problems that occur in their classroom. Information can correct these appraisals in some instances. In other situations consultants need to go beyond providing information to where they help the consultee develop systematic problem-solving skills. These skills are then utilized by the consultee to investigate the nature of their current situation and to identify causal factors in their current dilemma.

Simply providing information and problem-solving skills works in only a few cases, as most consultants are aware. In other instances appraisals and expectations must be addressed through cognitive restructuring, self-management systems, modeling, and guided learning activities that enhance performance. The consultee that has a motivational problem may enlist the support of the consultant to provide systematic feedback, to help establish a self-monitoring system, or to help alter some of his or her current thinking using cognitive restructuring procedures. These and the other techniques listed in Table 3.3 may also be utilized with client concerns.

To illustrate the limitations of simply providing information, let us consider the problems encountered by a consultant hired to consult with some ineffective house parents in a home for emotionally disturbed adolescents. Both parents had completed high school but had no other formal training. They had taken this particular position because they "loved children" and because their own children were grown with families of their own. However, they soon found that the approaches they had employed with their own children were not effective with many of the adolescents. The consultant's first tasks were to help them become more familiar with emotional disturbance generally and to assist them in overcoming some of their biases about people who were "mentally ill." One pervasive problem was that both house parents equated mental illness with low intelligence. The information about mental illness helped somewhat, but cognitive restructuring aimed first at identifying pervasive thought patterns and then substituting more appropriate thoughts was used effectively to overcome biases. The result was that the parents began to perceive their job as other than custodial care since they were more optimistic about the futures of the adolescents who came through their facility.

Improving performance skills (behavior) should be the forte of most behavioral consultants. Direct training in such areas as problem solving, communication, decision making and the use of performance contracts, modeling and behavioral rehearsal, and bibliotherapy (assigned readings) have all been used successfully with both consultees and clients. These approaches, particularly when coupled with systematic feedback, can be powerful techniques in consultation.

Monitoring and Evaluating the Intervention

Bergan & Kratochwill (1990) have provided an elaborate scheme for monitoring behavioral interventions with students. For the most part, these ideas are acceptable in the SLM. However, as would be expected from much of the foregoing discussion, evaluation would focus on behavioral and cognitive changes in both the client and consultee. Changes in self-efficacy, appraisals, expectations of outcomes, and the ability to self-reinforce in both client and consultee would be among the variables studied in the evaluation plan.

Bergan and Kratochwill's (1990) suggestion that intensive design studies be utilized in evaluating the outcome of consultation is viewed as a viable alternative in evaluation, particularly if only one consultee and one client are involved. In group and in organizational consultation, evaluation procedures based upon traditional scientific paradigms (extensive designs) as well as some qualitative approaches would be employed. Each of these will be discussed more fully in Chapter Eleven.

Summary

Two behaviorally oriented models have been presented. Bergan and Kratochwill's model relies primarily upon operant learning theory for its underpinning while the SLM is based upon social learning theory. Bergan and Kratochwill's model relies upon a complex communications model to elicit the information needed for successful consultation and includes a series of specific recommendations regarding problem identification and resolution. The two models differ on two major issues. First, Bergan and Kratochwill view the consultant as an authority figure who assumes primary responsibility for the consulting relationship while the SLM model views the relationship as more egalitarian in nature. Second, Bergan and Kratochwill's model focuses primarily on changing behavior as contrasted with the SLM approach, which focuses on cognitions to a greater degree. Both models rely upon a problem-solving approach, accept the empirical tradition of behaviorism, and take a similar view on evaluation.

Tips for the Practitioner

1. Decide where you stand on the critical issue of controlling the consulting relationship.
2. Write out your definition of motivation. Does it include self-efficacy expectations and appraisals?
3. Make sure that the goals for consultation are established in measurable terms.
4. Determine the roles that consultant and consultee are to fill in the client assessment, goal setting, intervention, and evaluation phases of consultation.
5. Establish a plan for evaluating progress in consultation.

Review Questions

1. Identify the key communication processes in Bergan and Kratochwill's model of consultation.

2. How does the consultant influence the consultee from Bergan and Kratochwill's point of view?

3. Contrast behavioral-operant and social learning theories views of the relationship variables in consultation.

4. Outline the tenets of reciprocal determinism.

5. Contrast assessment in the SLM and the behavioral-operant approach.

6. How would a consultant using the SLM pursue the identification of an intervention with a consultee?

7. Compare the involvement of the client in the SLM and the behavioral-operant model.

8. Identify several techniques for correcting cognitive difficulties in the client and consultee.

References

Bandura, A. (1971). Psychotherapy based on modeling principles. In A. E. Bergin & S. L. Garfield (Eds.), *Handbook of psychotherapy and behavioral change: An empirical analysis* (pp. 653–708). New York: John Wiley & Sons.

Bandura, A. (1977a). Self-efficacy: Toward a unifying theory of behavior change. *Psychological Review, 84,* 191–215.

Bandura, A. (1977b) *Social learning theory.* Englewood Cliffs, NJ: Prentice-Hall.

Bandura, A. (1978). The self system in reciprocal determinism. *American Psychologist, 33,* 344–358.

Bandura, A. (1982a). The assessment and predictive generality of self-precepts of efficacy. *Journal of Behavior Therapy and Experimental Psychiatry, 13,* 195–199.

Bandura, A. (1982b). Self-efficacy mechanism in human agency. *American Psychologist, 37,* 122–147.

Bandura, D. (1976). Self-reinforcement: Theoretical and methodological considerations. *Behaviorism, 4,* 135–155.

Bergan, J. R. (1977). *Behavioral consultation.* Columbus, OH: Charles E. Merrill.

Bergan, J. R., & Kratochwill (1990). *Behavioral consultation and therapy.* New York: Plenum Press.

Bergan. J. R., & Tombari, M. L. (1975). The analysis of verbal interactions occurring during consultation. *Journal of School Psychology. 13,* 209–226.

Bergan, J. R., & Tombari, M. L. (1976). Consultant skill and efficiency and the implementation and outcomes of consultation. *Journal of School Psychology, 14,* 3–14.

Brofenbrenner, U. (1979). *The ecology of human development.* Cambridge, MA: Harvard University Press.

Brown, D., & Schulte, A. (1987). A social learning model of consultation. *Professional Psychology: Research and Practice, 18,* 283–287.

Brown, D., Pryzwansky, W. B., & Schulte, A. (1987). *Psychological consultation: Introduction to theory and practice.* Boston: Allyn & Bacon.

Caplan, G. (1970). *The theory and practice of mental health consultation.* New York: Basic Books.

Clarizio, H. F., & McCoy, G. F. (1976). *Behavior disorders in children,* New York: T. Y. Crowell.

Conoley, J. C., & Conoley, C. W. (1992). *School consultation: A guide to practice and training* (2nd ed.). New York: Macmillan.

Erchul, W. P. (1987). A relational communication analysis of control in school consultation. *Professional School Psychology, 2,* 113–124.

Erchul, W. P., & Chewning, T. G. (in press). Behavioral consultation from a request-centered relational

communication perspective. *School Psychology Quarterly, 5,* 1–20.

Gallessich, J. (1982). *The profession and practice of consultation.* San Francisco: Jossey-Bass.

Goodwin, D. L., & Coates, T. J. (1977). The teacher-pupil interaction scale: An empirical method for analyzing the interaction effects of teacher and pupil behavior. *Journal of School Psychology, 15,* 51–59.

Heller, K., & Monahan, J. (1977). *Psychology and community change.* Homewood, IL: Dorsey Press.

Henning-Stout, M. (1993). Theoretical and empirical bases of consultation. In J. E. Zins, T. R. Kratochwill, & S. N. Elliot (Eds.) *Handbook of Consultation Services for Children* (pp. 15–45). San Francisco: Jossey-Bass.

Hetherington, E. M. (1981). Children and divorce. In R. W. Henderson (Ed.), *Parent child interaction: Theory, research, and prospects* (pp. 33–55). New York: Academic Press.

Horton, E., & Brown, D. (1990). The role of interpersonal skills in consultee-centered consultation: A review. *Journal of Counseling and Development, 68,* 423–426.

Kazdin, A. E. (1984). *Behavior modification in applied settings* (2nd ed.). Homewood, IL: Dorsey Press.

Keller, H. R. (1981). Behavioral consultation. In J. C. Conoley (Ed.), *Consultation in schools: Theory, research, and practice* (pp. 59–99). New York: Academic Press.

Keyser, V., & Barling, J. (1981). Determinants of children's self-efficacy beliefs in an academic environment. *Cognitive Therapy and Research, 5,* 29–40.

Kratochwill, T. R., & Van Someren, K. R. (1985). Barriers to treatment success in behavioral consultation: Current limitations and future directions. *The Journal of School Psychology, 23,* 225–239.

Krumboltz, J. D., & Thoreson, C. E. (Eds.). (1976). *Behavioral counseling: Cases and techniques* (2nd ed.). New York: Holt, Rinehart & Winston.

Medway, F. J. (1979). How effective is school consultation? A review of recent research. *Journal of School Psychology, 17,* 275–282.

Meichenbaum, R. (1977). *Cognitive-behavior modification: An integrative approach.* New York: Plenum Press.

Mischel, W. (1973). Toward a cognitive social learning reconceptualization of personality. *Psychological Review, 80,* 252–283.

Moos, R. H. (1981). *Manual: Family environment scale.* Palo Alto, CA: Consulting Psychologists Press.

Piersel, W. C. (1985). Behavioral consultation: An approach to problem solving in educational settings. In J. R. Bergan (Ed.), *School psychology in contemporary society* (pp. 331–364). Columbus, OH: Charles E. Merrill.

Reynolds, C. R., Gutkin, T. B., Elliot, S. N, & Witt, J. C. (1984). *School psychology: Essentials of theory and practice.* New York: John Wiley & Sons.

Rogers-Warren, A. (1977). Planned change: Ecobehaviorally based interventions. In A. Rogers-Warren & S. F. Warren (Eds.), *Ecological perspectives in behavioral analysis* (pp. 197–210). Baltimore, MD: University Park Press.

Russell, J. L. (1978). Behavioral consultation: Theory & Process. *Personnel and Guidance Journal, 56,* 346–350.

Tombari, M. L., & Bergan, J. R. (1978). Consultant cues and teacher verbalizations, judgments, and expectations concerning children's adjustment problems. *Journal of School Psychology, 16,* 212–219.

Wahler, R. G., Berland, R. M., Coe, T. D., & Leske, G. (1977). Social systems analysis: Implementing and alternative behavioral model. In A. Rogers-Warren & S. F. Warren (Eds.), *Ecological perspective in behavior analysis* (pp. 211–228). Baltimore, MD: University Park Press.

Winett, R. A., & Winkler, R. (1972). Current behavior modification in the classroom. *Psychology, 5,* 499–504.

$$C \ h \ a \ p \ t \ e \ r \quad 4$$

Organizational Change through Consultation

Goals of the Chapter

The primary goal of this chapter is to present two models of organizational consultation and some illustrations of how they can be applied to changing organizational structure and/or processes. A second goal of the chapter is to present some general principles of organizational change.

Chapter Preview

1. The basic principles of systems theory are outlined at the outset.
2. A model of organizational consultation is presented that is rooted in systems theory.
3. Several practical considerations in bringing about change in organizations are discussed.

As has already been noted in Chapters Two and Three, both behavioral and mental health models have implications for organizational change. However, a number of other models of organizational consultation have evolved over the past 40 years that are not rooted in the mental health field. These models were developed by practitioners and theorists interested in helping businesses and industries adapt to shifting economic and social climates so that they could remain competitive in the marketplace. Probably because of the orientation of these consultants to productivity and the recognition that the various sections of a business or industry are related to productivity, the organization, or some subsystem of it, became the "client" in these models. This is a departure from the more individually- and program-oriented mental health and behavioral models.

Human services workers often find themselves involved in consultation with organizations. In some instances psychologists, social workers, and mental health counselors are employed to provide counseling and/or psychotherapy as well as consultation within an organization. Probably the most typical situation in which this occurs at present is in employee assistance programs in business and industry. Other human resource consultants work as external consultants to schools, businesses, halfway houses, custodial care institutions for the mentally retarded, hospitals, nursing homes, police departments, correctional institutions as a result of contracts between their employing agencies and other organizations to provide consultation services. Still others provide consultation to organizations as private practitioners.

Consulting with organizations has many similarities to, and some important differences from, consulting with individuals. The similarities include the triadic nature of the process, the steps and stages through which consultation moves the general goals of the process for the consultee and the client, some of the intervention strategies used, and ethical issues that manifest themselves. However, there are some important differences. One of the major factors that distinguishes organizational consultation from consulting with individuals is the complexity of the client. Individually-oriented consultation usually involves a single consultee, one or a few clients, and the respective environments of the consultee and the clients. Organizational consultation is more typically conducted with one or more consultees, usually persons charged with the management of an organization, and involves a *client system*, often comprised of dozens of people who have formed into subgroups that have their own norms and culture.

The so-called complexity factor in organizational consultation can only partially be accounted for by numbers. Certainly, because of sheer numbers, subsystems are more complex and the processes required to coordinate the activities of the subsystem multiply. However, the output processes of an organization are invariably aimed at producing tangible goods and services that require marketing to the suprasystem or environment. This is not to suggest that individuals do not have outputs since they obviously do. But it is the structuring of individuals and the processes engaged in that separates organizations from individuals. It is difficult for some to envision a school, correctional institution, or sheltered workshop producing a product, but they do just as surely as IBM or Chrysler do. The difference is that IBM and Chrysler produce durable goods and technology, while human resources agencies "produce" human beings whose functioning has been enhanced as a result of the "production" process. As a result of the emphasis upon production, the interaction between technology, individuals, and small groups involved in the production of the product often becomes an issue in consultation. In fact, it is usually the key issue. And because it is necessary for most organizations not only to produce products efficiently and effectively but to market those products to various groups, marketing or output may also become an issue. Requests for consultation often originate as a result of the realization that some aspect of the production/marketing process is ineffective. An example of this is when a university counseling center finds that its budget is about to be slashed and seeks assistance to market its services more efficiently and improve its production processes.

Because of the complexity of organizations, consultants need a broader framework for conducting the consulting process, a framework that will enable them to conceptualize

how organizations function and how successful change strategies can be designed and implemented to correct problems that arise within organizations.

Principles of Systems Theory

Whether implicitly or explicitly, current models of organizational consultation are based upon systems theory. Systems theory has its roots in the biological sciences, but has been adapted by a number of authors (Beer & Spector, 1993; Katz & Kahn, 1978; Kuhn & Beam, 1982; Morasky, 1982) for use in describing the functioning of organizations. Before the basic principles of systems theory are identified, it may be useful to distinguish between open systems and closed systems since human services organizations are characterized as the former. Open systems differ from closed systems in that they have permeable boundaries through which inputs are received from and outputs are made to the environment. The cell is the classic example of an open system: It takes raw material in the form of amino acids from the cytoplasm, transforms it to protein, and exports it. Water flowing through a pump to a garden fountain and back again would constitute a closed system. Nothing is taken in, transformed, or exported.

It is also important to distinguish between two types of open systems; those that exist in natural settings and organizations. The circulatory system of the human body is an open system in that it absorbs food and oxygen from the lungs and intestines, carries them to various parts of the body where it exchanges them for waste products, and deposits these wastes in other systems of the body. The circulatory system is thus an open system, but it differs from an organization *because it has no goal.* Morasky (1982) notes, organizations have goals or preferences that direct them, albeit in varying degrees. All descriptions of organizations as open systems stress that certain underlying principles can be used as the basis for understanding how organizations function.

Systems Principles and Organizational Functioning

Differentiation is a natural tendency within organizations. Two interacting people can make up a system (Kuhn & Beam, 1982). Even with two people (For example, a husband and wife), there is tendency toward role differentiation. When many people are involved, this tendency toward specialization normally results in a variety of structures or subsystems. These subsystems are depicted in Figure 4.1.

The *leadership* subsystem is that group of people who are the organizational decision makers. For the most part members of this subsystem hold formal positions of authority, but as Beer (1980) and others have noted, there is also an informal power structure within any organization that influences the decision-making process. Beer uses the term *dominant coalition* to describe this particular subsystem.

The *goals and values* subsystem has two components. One of these pertains to the products produced by an organization. Products may range from the number of clients helped by a community mental health center to the number of tons produced by a large steel mill. These productivity goals are established in terms of expected outputs to the organization's environment. The second type of goals relates to meeting the needs of the people

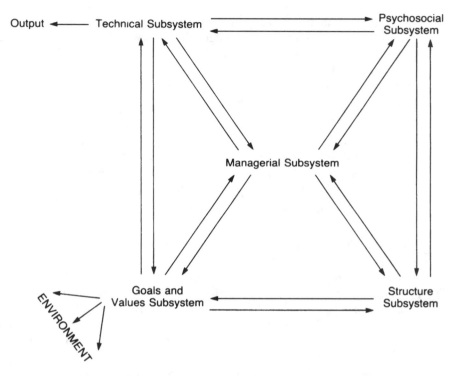

FIGURE 4.1   A Systems View of Organizational Functioning

within the organization. Lippitt (1982) classifies these needs into two areas: *personal life* and *personal fulfillment*. *Personal life needs* involve food, clothing, shelter, and security, while *personal fulfillment needs* relate to affiliation, achievement, recreation, work, and social support.

   Structure is that subsystem that has as its basic function the control of behavior within the organization. Reward systems, evaluation procedures, promotion policies, and formal policies aimed at regulating day-to-day behavior, such as attendance, are a part of the structure subsystem.

   The *technology* subsystem is usually aimed at increasing the effectiveness and efficiency of human processes within the organization (Lippitt, 1982). It involves those processes that at times operate somewhat independently from human processes (for example, automated assembly lines), but more typically interacts with them. There is an increasing awareness that the installation of technology without considering its impact upon human factors can have disastrous effects.

   The *psychosocial* subsystem consists of all the people in the organization, and, as Kurpius (1984) suggests, is an interaction of the knowledge held, beliefs about the organization, behavior, motivations, and emotions of the people. The result of this interaction is the creation of an organizational culture and certain human outputs, to paraphrase Beer (1980). It is the goal of any organization to socialize people in a manner that will enhance

the likelihood that organizational goals will be achieved. This is done through a variety of processes including recruitment, orientation, supervision, and rewards. However, much of the socialization process occurs through informal interaction and results in an inculcation of beliefs held widely in the organization.

The psychosocial subsystem can also be viewed as the culture of an organization. Schein (1990) defines organizational culture as

> *(a) a pattern of basic assumptions, (b) invented, discovered, or developed by a given group, (c) as it learns to cope with problems of external adaptation and internal integration, (d) that has worked well enough to be considered valid and, therefore, (e) is to be taught to new members as the (f) correct way to perceive, think, and feel in relation to those problems. (p. 111)*

His definition is not unlike the definition advanced above for psychosocial subsystem. However, essential to understanding culture is the idea of values or, as Schein termed them, *basic assumptions.* As an organization grows and develops, the people in it develop beliefs about how the organization can be successful and how they can be successful within the organization. These beliefs become institutionalized values. "Autocratic approaches are the best way to get things done" and "Consensus is the only approach to decision making" are values statements that have characterized some organizations from time to time. The question always is, Are they appropriate today? Unfortunately, as Beer and Spector (1993) note, the values that undergird culture are based upon experience and may become dysfunctional. Much of the work of organizational consultants is devoted to changing culture.

The subsystems of an organization are interrelated and interdependent. The process of differentiation creates a series of distinct entities within organizations. However, these structures are bound together in a dynamic fashion and a problem in one subsystem, for example, leadership, invariably causes reverberations in the other components of the organization. Beer (1980) reports that prior to systems thinking, organizational planners and consultants thought linearly, that is, in terms of a single cause for each problem, with a single solution, and a solitary outcome. The realization that the subsystems within an organization are interrelated requires us to consider the possibility of multiple causation. A problem in the accounting department of a hospital may result from (1) inadequate technology, (2) poor leadership, (3) inadequate communication, (4) low staff morale, (5) reduction in the number of patients, or (6) two or more of the above.

Just as the concept of interrelatedness requires that the possibility of multiple causation be considered, so must the multiple effects of interventions be anticipated. Installing a new computer may be an apparent solution to accounting's difficulty in billing customers on time. However, it may also require retraining of staff, introducing a personal touch in communicating with customers, and/or eliminating incompetent employees.

Because of the dynamic interrelatedness of organizational subsystems, there is no single solution to a particular problem. This postulate, usually referred to as the principle of *equifinality,* defies common sense thinking that there is one best solution for each problem. It also flies in the face of many current decision-making models that send the decision maker through a series of steps culminating in selecting the best alternative. Because of

the dynamic, dependent nature of organizations, it is assumed that there are many paths to a particular goal. If, for example, we wish to increase productivity, we may (1) improve our technology, (2) improve staff morale, (3) allow more overtime (change a part of the structure subsystem), and/or (4) change our supervision strategy to include quality circles. Problem solvers in organizations that produce services (as opposed to goods) also have multiple solutions available. Havelock and Hubermann (1978) note that one educator identified 20 ways to solve a particular problem. While this may not be typical, it is illustrative.

Organizations relate dynamically to their environments. As was noted earlier, organizations are open systems that interact beyond their boundaries with their environments to receive inputs and to produce outputs. Inputs come into the organization in the form of resources, such as people, raw materials, money, technology, and so forth. Outputs are marketed in the environment, and the extent to which an organization is successful is highly dependent upon this function. Marketing outputs is a function of all organizations, not just the so-called goods producing ones. Public schools must market their product, public education, since private schools vie for the resources needed for their operation. Even organizations such as the Salvation Army must market their programs in order to maintain a flow of donations.

Inputs and outputs are rather easily identified means of interaction between an organization and its environment. However, there are more subtle forms of interactions that occur. These relationships are to a large extent dependent on the values held in the social environment in which the organization functions. Practically speaking, these values are reflected in the policies and/or laws promulgated by various legislative groups that may influence the functioning of an organization. So-called "smoke stack" industries were for the most part unregulated with regard to sulphur emissions until a shift in societal values regarding air pollution resulted in a variety of statutes on air quality standards. Many organizations attempt to counter these environmental influences through advertising, public works programs, and direct lobbying with legislative groups.

Viable open systems can adapt to changing conditions within and without. Several key organizational processes and characteristics contribute to adaptability including sensing/communication, decision making and planning, organizational flexibility, and research and development. Perhaps none of these processes is so critical as the sensing/communication mechanisms, which are of two types (Kuhn & Beam, 1982; Morasky, 1982). The first of these has to do with (external) communication with the organization's environment. As already noted, there are three facets of the environment that are of concern: markets, technology, and societal values and norms (Beer, 1980). An organization that cannot anticipate the current economic and social trends and thus the demands for its products will probably not survive. For example, community mental health centers are greatly concerned about the demands for their products, which include direct services in the form of counseling and therapy, indirect services, or consultation, and educational programs, since this demand will ultimately be reflected in their funding base (Backer, Shifren-Levine, & Erchul, 1983).

Sensing devices must also be established that discern the impact of technology upon production and competitiveness in the marketplace as well as shifts in societal values and legislative programs that will influence markets and production. For example, congress currently seems determined to reduce expenditures for social programs, a trend that may reshape the delivery of various programs and services. Perhaps technologies such as the

videophone and computers will enable mental health programs to deliver certain kinds of services more efficiently.

Adaptable organizations also have sensing mechanisms that identify conflicts within the organization that may adversely affect the functioning of the organization. These mechanisms include routine needs assessments, structured and unstructured feedback sessions, and surveys of various types. Internal consultants are often employed to act as coordinators of these sensing mechanisms.

Sensing mechanisms are necessary, but communications of what is seen or heard is the key to organizational adaptability. Havelock and Hubermann (1978) have classified information flow into two types. Lateral communication involves communication between two equal units in an organization, for example, between research and development and production. Vertical communication involves communication between components of an organization that have differential status, such as the director of an agency and the staff. Bureaucratic organizations, such as public schools and the military, are organized primarily according to status and have notoriously poor internal communication, particularly from the bottom up. Both lateral and vertical, including top down and bottom up, information flow are necessary if organizations are to be adaptable.

Adaptable organizations avoid chaotic change and entropy. Chaotic change may destroy the basic harmony needed for organizational functioning. Entropy is a process of losing energy or momentum. Systems theory (Katz & Kahn, 1978) posits that entropy is a natural process in an open system. However, those organizations that produce products that are valued in the environment receive a constant supply of inputs from the environment in the form of raw material, workers and technology and avoid entropy.

Organizational Development Consultation

Organizational development consultation, as it currently exists, has been contributed to heavily by a number of theorists and social scientists, including Argyris (1970), Schein (1969), Bennis (1970) and Lippitt (1982). Kurt Lewin and Carl Rogers were particularly instrumental in the development of the philosophy of this approach. Lewin (1951) contributed to a field theory orientation, that is, a view that organizational problems must be solved in a manner that incorporates all individuals in the organization into the process because of the forces they bring to bear upon each other. Rogers (1951) postulated that the environment in which one works can either contribute to or detract from the self-actualization of the individual, and he set the tone for this approach to consultation.

A number of assumptions serve as the foundation for organizational development models of consultation. The first is that conflicts among individuals and groups are the basic barriers to effective and efficient organizational functioning. In this regard Bennis (1966) states: "These chronic conflicts probably dissipate more energy and money than any other single organizational disease" (p. 57). These conflicts are presumed to arise from several sources. Poor communication is viewed as a basic reason for group and individual conflict. It stems either from the fact that the individuals in the organization do not possess the skills to communicate properly or that the organization has not established appropriate communication devices. Other causes of conflict are individuals with inadequate personalities,

conflicting value systems among individuals and groups, lack of information, conflicting organizational objectives, and managers with decision-making skills (Baldridge, 1971; Chamley, McFarlane & Young, 1987; Huse, 1980; Lippitt, 1982).

These models also assume that organizations benefit whenever they place the psychological needs of their staff ahead of the bureaucratic concerns of the individuals (Bennis, 1970; Huse, 1980). Baldridge (1971) refers to this assumption as the "contented cows give more milk" theory. In short, when workers are able to meet their psychological needs, an organization becomes more productive and efficient. Another assumption underlying what has been termed a human relationship approach to consultation is that democratically governed organizations are more effective than those where managers use autocratic approaches (Beer, 1980; Lippitt, 1982). This is quite closely related to the concept that psychological well-being of individuals should be considered ahead of organizational goals. More precisely, individual need attainment is a prerequisite to organizational efficiency and effectiveness.

The Entry Process

Consultation passes through a series of stages, some of which are more distinct than others. Kurpius, Fuqua, and Rozecki (1993) identify six consultation stages: (1) preentry, (2) entry, problem exploration, and contracting, (3) information gathering, problem confirmation, and goal setting, (4) solution searching and intervention selection, (5) evaluation, and (6) termination (p. 601). The preentry phase is really not a phase at all for many internal consultants, but external consultants must make a reasoned decision about whether they have the time and expertise to tackle the problem presented to them. This phase is simply a go/no-go decision-making stage (Beer, 1980).

Contract setting actually begins in the preentry and concludes in the entry phase. Contract setting consists of both formal and informal processes. The consultant must establish that the resources and commitment needed to achieve the change goals are available or consultation should be terminated. Similarly, the consultant should ascertain that there will be an adequate source of valid data to provide a basis for problem identification or termination should occur. Finally, in the early stages the consultant must set an agenda and establish the relative roles the consultant and consultee will fill during consultation. This process is outlined in Table 4.1.

Step 4(b) in Table 4.1 indicates that part of the entry process is to establish acceptable role relationships between the consultant and the consultee. These relationships may take many forms, ranging from the consultant as expert on one hand to process consultant on the other.

In Schein's (1969, 1989, 1990) model of process consultation, which he defines as "a set of activities on the part of the consultant which helps the client to perceive, understand, and act upon process events which occur in the client's environment" (p. 9), the consultant assumes a role far different from the expert. In this model, the consultant generates data regarding the basic human processes, including communication, role interrelationships, leadership, decision making, group interaction, and normative structure of subsystems and the organization itself, shares these with the manager and encourages him or her to draw conclusions. Managers are also encouraged to make their own decisions about solutions to the problem at hand.

TABLE 4.1   The Entry Process of Organizational Consultation

Steps	No Go
Step 1. Generally survey the problems the organization and the goals that the organization wishes to pursue	a. Terminate if consultant views goals as unattainable
Step 2. Determine commitment to change	a. Commitment lacking
Step 3. Ascertain whether necessary resources (e.g., money, time, personnel) are available to complete desired change	a. Resources unavailable
Step 4. Establish a contract to continue the consultation	a. Timelines too severe b. Acceptable role relationships to accomplish task cannot be established

Consultants usually fill a number of roles at various times in the consultation process, sometimes filling roles and on other occasions becoming more of a process consultant. Perhaps the only advice that should be tendered to the prospective consultant is that both the formal contract and the informal agreements reached during entry should reflect the breadth and depth of roles that the consultant expects to fill.

Diagnosis—Some General Considerations

Diagnosis is the process of assessing the specific problem or problems being experienced by the organization and isolating causal factors associated with those problems. Although the consultant's clinical ability plays a role in this process, organizational development consultants view themselves as scientists at work, and thus diagnosis is a process of systemic data collection and synthesis. Four major data sources are tapped during the diagnosis phase (Beer, 1980; Huse, 1980; Lippitt, & Lippitt, 1986). Genetic data involve basic information such as goal statements and purposes and historical data such as minutes of meetings, year end reports, internal memoranda, and other similar data. Current descriptive data include organizational charts (how the organization is structured), personnel systems, reward structures, such as salary schedules, equipment/technology, and office arrangements. Process data would depict communications systems and devices, decision-making approaches, and other problem-solving related activities. The fourth type of data, interpretive data, consists of perceptions of the current functioning of the organization, attitudes and beliefs about the organization, and descriptions and/or perceptions of the informal relationships that exist within the organization.

The consultant must be prepared to utilize a number of data collection techniques to secure need information, including questionnaires, brainstorming sessions, analysis of records, interviews, systematic observation, and problem diagnosis sessions where various members of the organization focus their expertise on problem identification. Often these approaches to data collection focus on six problem areas: (1) inadequate goals have been established or goals have shifted without proper planning; (2) conflict is managed poorly

within the organization; (3) the division of labor (structure) is problematic; (4) leadership deficiencies exist; (5) methods used to direct and coordinate the organization have broken down, usually because of poor communication; and (6) the reward system is problematic because of internal or external discrepancies, that is rewards (for example, hourly wage) within or without are not relatively equal for persons filling approximately the same roles (Weisbord, (1976).

Diagnosis—A Systems Perspective

The systems principles outlined earlier provide a basis for diagnosing organizational problems. Beer (1980) believes that the starting points for a systems-based organizational analysis are three-fold: the efficiency of operation, the organization's effectiveness, and the health of the organization. An organization is operating efficiently when a minimum expenditure of energy and resources is required to keep people happy. When an organization is inefficient, absenteeism, grievances, and turnover are high.

Organizational effectiveness is equated with environmental compatibility. Profit statements and/or general community financial support, freedom from governmental regulations and/or societal sanctions, and keeping pace with technological advancement germane to the operation of the organization are indicators of organizational effectiveness.

Finally, organizational health refers to the ability of the organization to adapt to changing internal and external conditions. Indicators of health are the presence of structures that identify difficulties and a track record of reacting appropriately to both internal difficulties and external demands.

Beer's constructs of efficiency, effectiveness, and organizational health are certainly helpful as a consultant begins to think about the complex task of analyzing the dynamic operation of an organization. Morasky (1982) is even more concrete about how a systems analysis of an organization should occur. He suggests that the first step in the diagnostic process is to get a general picture of the organization. This process begins by describing the boundaries of the organization. This should be followed by an attempt to identify the general processes utilized within the organization and the general function of the organization.

The police department in a mid-sized community might serve as a case in point. Geographically, the boundaries of the department would be restricted to those accorded it by legal statute. Functionally, its boundaries would include traditional law enforcement responsibilities. However, many police departments have extended these boundaries to include education programs in the public schools, the organization of recreation leagues as prevention measures, public relations activities such as a speakers bureau, and other outreach efforts.

The general processes utilized by the department would parallel its functions (for example, surveillance, arrests, incarceration, monitoring, education, counseling, communication, etc.). Since the appropriate use of technology would be important in many of these processes, the analysis would also include a technology audit.

Finally, the function of the police department would include a description of its products such as number of arrests, convictions, crime rates in various categories, number of speeches, outcomes of prevention programs and so forth. The result of this preliminary analysis should be in a Who, What, Where, When and How description of the police department (Morasky,

1982). Who works in the police department? What do they do? When do they work? Where does the work occur? How does the work occur? Generally, how effective is it?

Once a general description of the organization is developed, the more specific analysis of the organization begins by determining what goals were established when the organization began (or when the last analysis occurred) and what goals are in effect at this time. Questions to be answered are: Is there a discrepancy between these two set of goals? If a discrepancy exists, is the discrepancy the result of planned or unplanned change? Are the current goals appropriate? Organizational goals are a major subsystem in that they determine the direction and/or preferences of the organization. Without a clearly articulated set of goals, the other subsystems of the organization are likely to be in conflict.

Goal identification should be followed by the delineation of input/output boundaries (Morasky, 1982). Input boundaries for some organizations, such as schools, are easily identified. Children come from a community area set forth by school board regulations. Technology comes from a few publishing companies, and for some subgroups in the school, such as school psychologists or counselors, the source of technology is even more limited. Similarly, staff inputs are from rather specific sources, colleges and universities that prepare professionals in a given area.

Outputs in schools are also easily defined. But input and outputs are a great deal more difficult to define for our aforementioned police department, a public health department, or a department of social services. Several days may actually be required to construct this type of audit.

The next step in organizational analysis is identifying specific target groups within the environment (Morasky, 1982). In some instances, these groups are defined by law, for example, school psychologists must serve certain classes of handicapped students. In other instances community agencies are influenced both by law (for example, the department of social services must investigate child abuse complaints) and policies that originate both within and outside the agency. For example, a community mental health agency might decide that it will target a 65 and over population, unwed mothers, or some other group that the staff considers in need of services. In the organizational analysis these target groups must not only be identified, but some determination of how they can be reached must be made as well.

The external support network of the organization must also be described (Morasky, 1982). This process involves answering a number of specific questions. Are there environmental factors such as laws or governmental regulations that impinge on the organization? Are there environmental trends such as outmigration of the population that will affect the source of personnel (inputs)? Do local factors such as a poor educational system or a high tax rate influence the recruitment process? Is the overall environment friendly or unfriendly? Basically, the consultant must generate a clear picture of the interaction of the environment with the organization.

The production process, whether it be for goods or services, is the essence of the organization. Morasky (1982) suggests that it is necessary to understand the components of this process, the subsystems, and how they relate to inputs and outputs. Let us consider a small counseling center at a prestigious eastern university. The production processes include (1) individual counseling, (2) group counseling, (3) assessment, (4) outreach/education, and (5) consultation. Inputs into these processes come from the student body, the faculty, and the staff of the university. Outputs are better adjusted students.

Questions to be answered regarding inputs include the following.

1. How are workers selected?
2. Are selection criteria appropriate?
3. Is the reward system appropriate for new workers?
4. What attitudes develop as workers are socialized?
5. Are these at variance with the expectations held when the workers enter the organization?
6. How do management processes facilitate/retard the input processes that are involved in production?

Questions that need answers regarding the production process related to productive use of technology, quality of product, cost/price considerations, and, in some instances, competitiveness with other agencies (counseling center versus student mental health center).

Questions regarding the relationship of production to marketing (output) must also be posed and answered. Is our program effective? Do we have the most effective form of advertising? Is our sales program having the desired impact?

The sixth set of questions have to do with feedback mechanisms (Morasky, 1982). Essentially, these sensing mechanisms are the basis for adjustments to external conditions and internal difficulties. An analysis of these mechanisms requires that we (1) describe the input-output sensing mechanisms, (2) determine how valuable the information is that comes from these sensors, and (3) evaluate the mechanics (for example, the frequency with which data are collected) of the systems.

The final set of questions that should be answered in our organizational analysis has to do with the overall constraints on the organization. Is the personnel supply adequate? What is the morale level of the staff? What is the financial picture? What economic trends may retard development? Has the management team been forward looking? What community and societal trends need to be countered? What internal problems pose a threat to growth? Are there geographic factors that preclude or diminish functioning in a given area or areas? The result of this series of questions should be a compilation of organizational constraints. These steps are summarized in Table 4.2.

Student Learning Activity 4.1: Applying Morasky's Principles

Analyze the organization of which you are currently a part by completing the following questions.

1. What are the goals of the organization?
2. Are the current goals clear? Appropriate?
3. What are the input boundaries?
4. What are the output boundaries?
5. What are the target groups of the organization?
6. What is the external support network of the organization?
7. Are the input and output processes well integrated?
8. What are the chief marketing strategies employed?
9. What are the major constraints placed on the organization at this time?

TABLE 4.2   Conducting a Systems Analysis of an Organization

Step 1. Conduct a general review of the organization	a. Define geographic and functional boundaries b. Identify production processes c. Identify products
Step 2. Identify input-output boundaries	a. List input/output boundaries
Step 3. Identify the goals of the organization	a. State goals operationally b. Relate these to input/output boundaries
Step 4. Identify target groups	a. List target groups in terms of priorities
Step 5. Describe external support	a. List environmental factors that interact with organization (e.g., laws, availability of personnel, etc.)
Step 6. Describe production processes	a. Relate each aspect of the process to input/output
Step 7. Identify feedback mechanisms	a. List external sensing mechanisms b. List internal feedback mechanisms
Step 8. List organizational constraints	a. List external constraints b. Identify internal constraints by subsystem

Beer and Spector (1993), like Morasky, view data collection as the first step in the diagnosis. The critical step is ascertaining which of a myriad factors are limiting the function of the organization. They label this critical step the *discovery process*, which occurs when top-level managers begin to assimilate and discuss the implications of the data that have been collected. Beer and Spector also suggest that the discovery process can be enhanced if the data are analyzed and interpreted in a systemic framework such as the one developed by Waterman, Peters, and Phillips (1980).

In this framework the 7-Ss are examined. In other words the data should be used to answer the following questions:

1. Are the management *strategies* employed appropriate, given the nature of our organizational pattern, the relationship we are trying to establish between processes and outcomes, and how we hope to have the organization interface with our environments?
2. Does our organizational *structure* allow us to accomplish our goals in an efficient manner?
3. Are the reward and communications *systems* synchronized with our goals? Does our personnel *system* produce the types of leaders we need?
4. Do our managers have the *skills* they need to facilitate the processes that have been set into place?
5. Do we have the *staff* we need to accomplish the tasks to be performed?
6. Is the management *style* appropriate?
7. Are the *shared values* appropriate given the goals of the organization, the structure, the processes, and our need to interact with our environment?

Perhaps the oldest and most useful tool for synthesizing data is the force field analysis (Lewin, 1951). The beginning of this process is to identify the major problem(s) that exists

in the environment. For example, a problem that arose in an outpatient drug rehabilitation agency pertained to staff burnout and turnover. The problem, generally stated, was as follows: How can we reduce staff stress and its resultant impact upon staff attrition?

The second step in the force field analysis is to identify driving forces, that is, forces that exert pressure to, or support for, solving the problem. This is followed by listing restraining forces, or forces that retard problem resolution.

The force field analysis developed for the aforementioned drug rehabilitation program appeared as follows.

1. Driving Forces
   a. Absenteeism due to stress
   b. Low staff morale
   c. Staff turnover
   d. Lowered program effectiveness
   e. Cost of recruiting/ retraining

2. Restraining Forces
   a. Heavy caseload results in little time for change activities
   b. State level bureaucracy
   c. State level policies/laws/regulations
   d. Judges that sentence all offenders to drug rehabilitation programs
   e. Recruitment policies (e.g., don't get best trained personnel

Once driving and restraining forces are identified, an attempt should be made to rank order them in terms of what appears to be their degree of contribution to the problem. Turnover may be the result of recruitment and orientation mechanisms, supervisory practices, and/or compensation. However, in this case it is clear that the primary problem is stress evolving out of the treatment program. Thus, focusing on approaches that both reduce the case load (for example, group treatment, educating judges about use of rehabilitation services) and those that reduce stress (for example, stress management training) received the highest priority in this situation.

After ranking forces that are related to the problem, alternate solutions to the problem should be considered. Each potential solution needs to be examined not only for its potential for solving the identified problem but for unintended negative consequences as well (Huse 1980).

Goal Setting and Intervention

Diagnosis is followed by goal setting and intervention. At the outset, agreement regarding the nature of the problem should be established along with the hoped for outcomes of problem resolution. Beer (1980) and Huse (1980), as well as others, believe that goal setting and intervention begin during the diagnosis phase, since the result of this process is a heightened awareness of the problem and reposturing to cope with the difficulty. Although it can certainly be argued that intervention begins during problem identification, the formal process of intervention does not begin until after specific objectives are established and measures designed to achieve these objectives are implemented. These steps can be illustrated by returning to our hypothetical drug rehabilitation program.

In our force field analysis, six forces were identified as driving the program staff toward problem resolution including absenteeism due to stress, low staff morale, high staff

turnover, lowered program effectiveness, and the added costs of recruiting and retraining new staff. Some obvious goals might be: (1) to reduce absenteeism growing out of staff burnout by 75 percent; (2) to increase staff morale as indicated by survey instruments developed to measure that aspect of functioning; (3) to reduce staff turnover by 25 percent; and (4) to decrease the client recidivism rate by 30 percent.

The restraining forces could also be used to develop similar objectives, such as decreasing the caseload by educating judges regarding the types of clients that could most benefit from the program being offered.

Once goals are set, intervention strategies must be selected. Kurpius (1985) indicates that "Choosing an intervention is not a matter of imposing a favorite technique, but rather entails an approach that will address specific needs and concerns" (p. 373). He goes on to indicate that there are four factors that should influence the choice of an intervention: (1) the diagnosed need, (2) the context in which the intervention is to be used; (3) the target group with which it is to be employed, and (4) the consultant's match of values and skills with the interventions being selected. Beer (1980) earlier identified some additional criteria to be used in the selection of an intervention. For example, he suggests interventions should be utilized that (1) reduce costs, including money, time, and energy, (2) speed the change, (3) minimize psychological and organizational strains, and (4) maximize the likelihood that goals will be attained.

In summary, there are three general considerations when selecting an intervention. One of these is the consultant's values and knowledge. Another is the context in which the intervention will be applied. The third is the nature of the intervention itself (for example, amount of strain it will produce).

Organizational development consultants have generated vast numbers of intervention strategies, which have in turn been classified using a number of systems (Blake & Mouton, 1976; French & Bell, 1973; Beer, 1980; Lippitt, 1982; Kurpius 1985). Perhaps the most parsimonious classification system has been one developed by French and Bell (1973). Their system begins with individual or intrapersonal interventions and progresses through relatively simple interpersonal interventions (dyads) to more complex interpersonal situations, including groups, intergroup relationships, and the total organization.

Individual Interventions

The class of interventions is aimed at enhancing the functioning of organizations by improving the performance of key individuals within the organization. Coaching and counseling activities aimed at skills development or attitudinal change (Blake & Mouton, 1976; French & Bell, 1973) are examples of individual interventions as are life and career interventions (French & Bell, 1973; Kurpius, 1985) aimed at having persons intensify or redirect their career-related energies. The administrator- (consultee-) centered approaches identified by Caplan are also individually oriented interventions.

Group Interventions

Process consultation, mediation, and conflict management strategies are utilized by organizational development consultants as means of enhancing the functioning of dyads or triads. Group goal setting and group building techniques aimed at enhancing group communication and cohesiveness are techniques often employed when groups within orga-

nizations are having difficulties (French & Bell, 1973). Quality circles, which Kurpius (1985) depicts as primarily small problem-solving groups, are also increasingly used as a means of helping work groups function more effectively. Training groups, involving intact work groups that focus on a variety of factors including valid communication, decision making, and leadership skills, can also be useful in dealing with group problems.

Intergroup Organizations

The techniques employed with intergroup problems are somewhat the same as those employed when dyadic or triadic interpersonal problems are encountered. Process consultation, mediation, conflict resolution, and providing data gained from surveys regarding the problems being experienced are examples of these techniques (French & Bell, 1973; Lippitt, 1982).

Total Organization

Interventions involving the total organization include surveys and questionnaires regarding the problems being experienced, large group meetings where people are allowed to air their concerns, examining basic processes such as communications and decision making, culture building focused on developing a new normative structure, strategic planning, job enrichment and redesign, and utilizing management by objective procedures (Beer, 1980; Kurpius, 1985; Lippitt, 1982). These are perhaps the most complex of the interventions and may need some additional clarification.

All of these procedures grow out of the philosophy that by placing the welfare of the individual first the organization will benefit. Accordingly, techniques aimed at assessing organizational functioning, such as surveys, would focus on the extent to which human needs are being met. Analysis of basic processes would be conducted to determine the degree to which open and valid communication characterizes the organization and the extent to which participatory decision-making procedures are employed. Culture development would be largely undertaken in small groups and would focus primarily on the degree to which organizational development philosophy, that is, meeting the needs of individuals, first, is being espoused and practiced. Job enrichment and redesign flows from the same philosophy and attention would be given to whether the job is meeting the needs of the individual. Specific attention is paid to the extent to which the employee has personal responsibility for his or her own function and whether or not the task performed contains enough variety and importance to satisfy the worker's needs in this area. In job redesign an attempt is made to determine the degree to which the worker receives verbal feedback from supervisors and, if there is a deficit in this area, corrections are made in this process as well (Hackman & Oldham, 1980).

Strategic planning (Fuqua & Kurpius, 1993) and management by objectives (MBO), which came not so much out of organizational development philosophy but from scientific management, is now widely used by organizational consultants. MBO is a management scheme that attempts to establish a series of objectives that will serve as the basis for decision making in the company. (See Figure 4.2.) Strategic planning attempts to help managers develop an awareness of the relationship between their values and the choices they make and encourage creative decision making by focusing on an unknown future and the organization's functioning in that unknown future. Managers are taught to identify the knowl-

---

FIGURE 4.2   Strategic Planning in Organizations

---

1. What are our beliefs about ourselves? . . . . VALUES STATEMENT
    A. What is our culture?
    B. Are we focused on the past or the future?

2. Where do we wish to go? . . . . VISION STATEMENT
    A. What is our overall goal?
    B. What is our specific objective?

3. What are our internal strengths and weaknesses in . . . . SELF AUDIT STATEMENT
    relationship to our mission?
    A. Will our culture support our new mission?
    B. What is the nature of our staff and other resources?

4. What are the immediate opportunities and barriers in . . . . ENVIRONMENTAL
    our environment?   ASSESSMENT STATEMENT
    A. What is the competition?
    B. How will factors like governmental regulation influence
        us in the short term?

5. What "futures" might we encounter in route to our mission? . . . FORECASTING STATEMENT
    A. Where can we find information about our futures?
    B. What scenarios do these sources suggest?

6. What policies and strategies do we need to negotiate . . . . STRATEGIC PLANNING
    alternative futures?   STATEMENT
    A. What policies regarding management and the allocation
        of resources do we need to put into place to cope with
        alternative futures so we can adapt as change occurs?

7. Who is responsible for monitoring our progress toward . . . . MONITORING STATEMENT
    our mission?
    A. What person or persons is responsible for monitoring
        our progress?
    B. Who has the authority to make changes?

8. How do we revise our strategic plan? . . . . RECYCLING STATEMENT

---

edge bases required for making decisions; to establish procedures, such as environmental scanning, to generate that data; and to learn systematic problem-solving skills needed to utilize the data at hand (Kurpius, 1985).

The French and Bell (1973) system of classifying interventions is the most parsimonious, but Blake and Mouton's (1976) scheme is the most comprehensive. They have attempted to classify interventions as they related to the four general types of problems found in organizations: power/authority, morale/cohesion, norms/standards, and goals and objectives. These problems may reside within individuals, groups, among groups (intergroup), in the total organization, within the larger social system of which the organization is a part, or in a number of these components simultaneously. In order to deal with these problems the consultant may choose from among five interventions, which Blake and Mouton label acceptant, catalytic, confrontation, prescriptive, and theory or principles.

Acceptant interventions are similar in nature to Rogers' (1951) client-centered therapy in that consultants (1) rely upon listening and empathy as basic tools, (2) restate, clar-

ify, and accept the feelings of the consultee, and (3) use encouraging leads such as, "Tell me more." Consultees are also encouraged to diagnose their own problems through direct questions such as, "What do you believe the problem to be?" Finally, the consultant not only expects self-growth and progress toward problem resolution but states this belief.

Catalytic interventions are most nearly related to acceptant reactions, but are designed to speed problem resolution and thus the consultant tends to be somewhat more active. The consultant suggests processes for collecting data about the problems once consultees have defined them; once data are collected, the consultant encourages consultees to rethink and possibly redefine the problem in light of this new information. As was the case with acceptant interventions, the consultant encourages consultees to make their own decisions and avoids making specific suggestions regarding the problem. This intervention approach is analogous to Schein's (1989) process consultation.

Consultants who use confrontational interventions take nothing for granted. They assume that the consultee will rationalize about the problem at hand, and they act in a manner that will force the consultee to face the facts of the situation. Consultants employing this strategy do not hesitate to ask probing questions designed to stimulate insight into the problem and to share their thinking with the consultee, openly challenging the consultee's assumptions, values, and conclusions. The utilization of this intervention strategy requires the consultant to interact genuinely, but not to be so abrasive as to make consultees feel attacked. If a consultee becomes defensive, the consultant should solidify the relationship before continuing.

Prescriptive interventions are based upon the assumption that the consultant is an expert or authority in the area under scrutiny. These consultants collect data needed to solve the problem, draw conclusions, provide the best solution, and turn it over to the consultee to· implement. Resistance is attacked logically, and if consultees do not proceed to solve the problem along prescribed lines, the consultation is terminated. Blake and Mouton (1976) note that this approach is most effective when a consultee has exhausted all possible alternatives and is in a state of desperation.

Theory/principle interventions are based upon validated models (for example, communication process) drawn from the social sciences. The assumption of this set of interventions is that intuition, trial-and-error learning, and common sense approaches to problem solving are less effective than theory based approaches because the latter are more systematic and can be easily tested. The goal of the consultant using this intervention strategy is not only to introduce theory based interventions, but to have the consultee internalize the theory that is introduced. In order to accomplish this, the consultee is asked first to describe the problem and state how he or she has attempted to solve it. Then the consultant introduces a theory, for example, one regarding job satisfaction, that pertains to the situation at hand. The consultee is then asked to redefine the problem using the theory that has been introduced, and the consultant gives feedback about the consultee's understanding of the problem. Once the theory is understood by the consultee, the consultant asks him or her to develop strategies for its application through discussions, roleplaying, and simulations. The theory based solution is then implemented and evaluated by the consultee. The consultant monitors the process and provides feedback. Blake and Mouton (1976) believe that theory based interventions can be used to make changes in the consultee's values, perspective, approach to communication, motivation, creativity, and autonomy.

Selecting an Approach

Given these five intervention strategies or styles, which one should a consultant use? Blake and Mouton (1976) suggest that personality style may dictate consulting style. They posit that some consultants, because of their personality, may be overly concerned about people and thus rely too heavily upon acceptant interventions. Others may focus more on products and thus become more content, or prescriptive, oriented.

Blake and Mouton (1976) believe that it is an error to over rely upon a single intervention strategy and suggest that the approach be governed by the shifting dynamics of the consulting relationship. For example, they have observed that when power and authority issues are involved and the consultant is dealing with individuals in the organization who are not in authority positions, the acceptant intervention strategy is most useful and confrontational approaches are least useful. Catalytic interventions are the second most used strategy in this situation; theory based interventions rank third; prescriptive interventions, fourth. Thus, in consulting situations it is incumbent upon the consultant to make decisions based not only on the focus of the intervention and the nature of the problematic situation, but upon the characteristics of the consultee as well.

Evaluation and Termination

These two phases often occur simultaneously, particularly if the goals that were established at the outset have been accomplished. Evaluation, then, is the process of systematically measuring the impact of the intervention that was selected when the problem was identified. If this is the case, termination is a natural culmination of the consulting process. (Approaches to evaluation will be discussed in a later chapter.) If the evaluation reveals that the established goals have not been reached, the consultant and consultee have two choices: reevaluate the intervention and perhaps modify it or select another or terminate the consulting relationship. Often the decision is to continue the relationship. Termination can be initiated by either the consultant or the consultee independently, or they can arrive at a conclusion to terminate jointly. Kurpius, Fuqua, and Rozecki (1993) recommend that, if the intervention has failed to produce the desired result, the consultant and consultee make every attempt to understand why the failure occurred prior to termination.

Student Learning Activity 4.2:
Consulting Case: What Would You Do?

Your agency has sent you to work with a local school that is experiencing an inordinate amount of vandalism, the source of which, they believe, is their own students. The principal describes himself as "being from the old school" and runs a tight ship. Little input is sought from teachers or pupils and everyone in the school is expected to follow the rules as set forth in the policy manuals for teachers and students. You have made successful entry into the school and have agreed with the principal that some changes are needed. Which one of Blake and Mouton's approaches would you expect to be the most successful? Why?

Principles of Organizational Change

Ultimately, the consultant is concerned with planned change. Although this process can be viewed from a variety of theoretical perspectives, consultants must take the knowledge they possess and apply it in a real life setting. This section is devoted to identifying certain principles of organizational change. One cautionary note is warranted. For the most part these principles are based more upon the observations of organizational consultants than they are upon empirical data.

Principle One: Organizational Variables

Certain organizational variables will influence the change process and must be accommodated if a change effort is to be successful. Probably the organizational variable that has the greatest relevance to the change process is the power structure (Chin & Benne, 1976; Hage & Aiken, 1970; Huse, 1980). Most observers of organizational change agree that not only must the change process begin with the managers, but it must be tailored to their style. Autocratic leaders are more likely to endorse coercive approaches to change while democratic managers may be more likely to endorse participative strategies.

Hage and Aiken (1970) and Fuqua & Kurpius (1993) go so far as to suggest that the authority structure of an organization may be the major factor in determining potential for organizational change. They indicate that decentralized organizations are more open to change. Perhaps this is true since centralized or autocratic organizations can only change from the top down. However, the key issue may be an organization's flexibility (Huse, 1980). Flexibility relates both to power/authority issues and to the number of rules, regulations, policies, and so forth, in place. Rigidity (centralization of authority and high degree of rules, regulations, etc.) retards change.

The clarity of organizational goals is also a major factor in the ability of an organization to undergo change. Goals should be examined for clarity and completeness early in the consultation process (Seiber, 1975; Beer, 1980; Huse, 1980; Lippitt, 1982; Lippitt & Lippitt, 1986). It is difficult for organizations with diffuse goals to plan and to be productive, and it is equally difficult for these organizations to change since new directions cannot be clearly established.

A related issue that sometimes occurs involves hidden agendas in the goal-setting process. For example, the public relations value of announcing certain programs may be more important to an organization than the realization of actual results from the programs. A university, having received much unfavorable publicity following the death of a student driving under the influence of alcohol, announced the creation of a program to address the complex problem of substance abuse on campus. Much favorable publicity followed, although the university allocated resources for only one year. In a similar vein, a university athletic department initiated a drug education program for its student athletes. Although not overtly stated, one of the prime reasons for the program was to counteract the negative publicity that had followed the arrest of a student athlete on drug charges. Both these examples demonstrate that consultants, internal or external, must be aware of unstated organizational goals. The achievement of truly successful long-term outcomes requires candor

between both parties. Consultants should include an examination of possible hidden agendas in their assessment process.

Organizations that are particularly susceptible to societal pressures are also problematic so far as planned change efforts are concerned (Seiber, 1975). Public schools are an excellent example of organizations that embark upon change programs only to have their efforts interrupted, stalled, or diverted by societal trends. This is not to suggest that planning and change in these organizations is impossible—Havelock and Huberman (1978) and Schmuck (1982) have attested to the potential for change in public schools—only that it is more difficult. The potential for interference from the environment must always be considered when initiating change in these institutions.

Finally, organizations that focus on efficiency as a primary survival mechanism may have trouble changing (Huse, 1980). This may be partially because change requires resources and these types of organizations can be reluctant to underwrite any effort that requires lowering efficiency, even in the short term. However, it is more likely that organizations that focus on efficiency may develop fairly rigid policies and practices. These, in turn, lower the potential for change.

Principle Two: Intervention Design

The design of the intervention will be a major determiner of the outcome of the change effort. Interventions aimed at change must be tailored to the institution, particularly the power structure. What follows are some general characteristics of interventions that seem to make them more or less acceptable.

Interventions that cost less, increase some aspect of the worker's comfort, such as decreasing workload (Havelock, 1973), do not threaten traditional roles (Kurpius, 1976; Lippitt, 1982), and can be easily communicated (Lin & Zaltman, 1973) are likely to be more successful than those not so designed.

Cost in this context refers not so much to total cost as relative cost, that is expenditure versus outcomes. Most consultants have observed that managers will quickly embrace a suggestion that results in increased production. In fact, managers may adopt suggestions too quickly in some instances without considering the long-term consequences. However, the relative cost of an intervention when considered against all possible outcomes is a reasonable criterion to use in selecting change strategies.

Little resistance will result from innovations that reduce workload or increase compensation. (A more comprehensive treatment of resistance will appear in Chapter Six.) However, resistance may be fostered by change strategies that increase workload *and* compensation, for example, requiring after hours work for pay. Designing acceptable interventions requires constant attention be paid to the personal load and compensation of those involved. Similarly, innovations that threaten traditional roles may be problematic.

Finally, interventions that can be communicated easily, which are usually less complex and thus require fewer actual changes in the organization, are more readily acceptable than innovations that are increasingly complex. A new word processing system that has easily understood documentation will be more readily accepted than one that has poor or complex documentation.

Principle Three: Managing Resistance

Managing resistance is one of the keys to successful interventions. It should be noted at the outset that resistance to change is a natural phenomenon and is to a large degree adaptive. Organizations maintain their homeostasis by resisting change. The presence of resistance illustrates the stability of an organization. But resistance can be counterproductive, particularly when it retards necessary adaptation processes.

Managing resistance requires first that we recognize the sources of resistance. Kurpius (1985) and Wickstrom and Witt (1993) identified four explanations of resistance: normal coping behavior because of fear of the unknown, satisfaction with the status quo, concern about the consequences of change, and concern about loss of freedom. Certainly resistance may stem from irrational concerns (for example, the inadequate personality) as well as rational sources of resistance. These sources of resistance might actually be subsumed under anxiety or fears based upon real threats and those based upon imagined threats, which may or may not have their basis in reality.

Real threats involve the potential loss of livelihood, status, interpersonal support, or self-esteem. Changes that eliminate jobs, destroy existing social networks, reduce the status of persons within the organization, or diminish the importance of the person (for example, automation) are sources of real threats. Much resistance, however, is based upon imagined threats to livelihood, self-esteem, social support, and status.

Communication is an obvious key to managing resistance. As far as possible, the precise nature of the need for the change, the design of change strategies, and the implications of the change for the people involved should be accurately conveyed. However, without the presence of other factors, such as trust among those initiating the change and those who will be affected most by the process, accuracy of communication may not be sufficient to forestall resistance. Even in those situations where trust is great, if the magnitude of the change is also great, resistance is likely to be substantial (Huse, 1980).

Perhaps the best approach in dealing with resistance is to assume first of all that it will be present and conflict will result. Conflict management requires that all parties involved bargain in good faith, working in an atmosphere of mutual respect where motives and feelings are clearly identified. It may also involve the use of systematic problem-solving procedures (for example, force field analysis), negotiation involving arbitrators or mediators, and at times will undoubtedly be based upon legal-judicial solutions such as union contracts or court decisions.

Principle Four: Locus of Consultant

The consultant may operate from either inside or outside the organization. It is clearly the bias of many organizational development consultants that the change agent be external to the organization (Beer, 1980; Huse, 1980). Others (Havelock & Huberman, 1978; Steele, 1982) present arguments and data supporting the idea that consultants may function from within the organization. In an early study, Jones (1969) found that successful consultants in business and industry come from both outside and inside the organization.

The argument for the consultant coming from outside the organization rests on a number of factors, not the least of which is that an external change agent will have a higher

degree of objectivity than will one from inside the organization (Beer, 1980; Huse, 1980). Others argue that change cannot emanate from within because of institutionalized norms and because persons in authority positions will not risk their status to initiate change (Schaller, 1972). However, if the internal consultant can avoid potential entanglements that lead to concerns about objectivity and can overcome institutionalized resistance, several benefits can accrue from being internal to the organization. Among these are knowledge of the informal power structure, ready access to the sources of data that may reflect the need for change, and familiarity with the vital decision-making and communication processes of the organization.

Schmuck (1982) has advocated that organizations should establish a cadre of consultants in order to maximize their effectiveness. This is in keeping with the systems perspective that effective organizations maintain sensing mechanisms and other structures that will allow them to anticipate the need for change and to act expeditiously. However, there are undoubtedly times when an organization will need an external change agent, either because it has failed to establish its own change team or because conditions within the organization have rendered the change team ineffective.

Principle Five: Role of Leadership

Change efforts require not only the approval of persons in leadership positions, but their active support as well. Organizational leaders are vested with certain prerogatives inducing goal setting, policy-making authority, and coercive powers, including the ability to provide extrinsic rewards and make personnel changes. Because of this unique status, it is important that organizational leaders endorse and support the change process.

Beer (1980) identified three general strategies that can be employed by leaders to facilitate change: setting expectations, inducing new behaviors, and reinforcing desired behaviors. Employee expectations arise primarily out of (1) the public goals the organization has established and (2) the informal norms that develop and are transmitted as an employee is socialized by the organization. A leader can obviously initiate efforts aimed at clarifying or altering existing goals. A leader can also affect the socialization process by influencing the recruitment and orientation structures within the organization. Leaders also influence the informal norms of the organization by their actions. For example, a leader who follows established policies in decision making reinforces an informal norm that is consistent with formal policy.

Inducing new behaviors can be done in a variety of ways (Beer, 1980; Fuqua & Kurpius, 1993). However, it is probably true that setting clear expectations and then reinforcing actions consistent with those expectations is the most effective means of developing new behaviors or maintaining those in place. In a change process leaders must develop clear statements regarding expected ways of functioning and then reinforce them.

It is possible, theoretically at least, for change to also emanate from the bottom of the organization. Furthermore, the normative-reductive approach, which essentially involves the recreation of a new normative system within the organization, requires that all parties involved in the change process be involved at each step. There is a relationship between the degree of support needed from leaders and the bureaucratic structure of the organization (Chin & Benne, 1976), with more bureaucratic organizations needing more administrative

support if change efforts are to be successful. But, practically speaking, leader support is necessary if any change effort is to be highly successful.

Principle Six: Reinforcement

Change requires constant reinforcement. To a degree this principle is related to Principle Five in that leader support is required for innovative efforts because leaders are an important source of reinforcement for new behaviors. However, reinforcement comes not just from leaders. There are also intrinsic rewards from peers. Therefore, the entire group must be involved so that peers will be a source of support and reinforcement. Additionally, the change effort should be planned so as to maximize the possibility of success since this is an important source of intrinsic rewards. Because sustaining motivation relies upon all of these sources of motivation, change strategies must be planned accordingly.

Principle Seven: Systems Perspective

A number of authors (Chin, 1976; Chin & Benne, 1976) have commented on the importance of a systems perspective in the planned change process. Collectively, they have set forth a number of systems principles that must be considered in organizational innovation. Chin (1976), for example, has commented that if we are to change an organization we need to consider the interface of the organization with its environment and "change either the internal characteristics of the system such as its awareness, perceptions, and images of the environment, or its internal responsiveness to the changing environment" (p. 111). Stated more simply, organizational members must either develop a new awareness of the environment or, if current perceptions are accurate, change to meet the demands of the environment.

Chin and Benne (1976) are more specific. They suggest that changes must be initiated in subsystems within an organization that interact with the target subsystem to reinforce the innovation. Unless this is done, the change will either not be initiated or not endure if it is initiated. This principle suggests that the change process must consider the dynamics of organizations, particularly the interrelatedness of subsystems and the influence of the environment upon the organization.

With this we have come full circle, from a consideration of systems principle to the relationship of those principles to planned change. As has been demonstrated, organizational consultants need to arm themselves with a thorough understanding of the systems perspective.

Summary

Three areas of concern to organizational consultants have been addressed in this chapter: systems theory, models of consultation, and principles of planned change. Systems theory provides a viable means of understanding the functioning of organizations and should be viewed as the point of departure when considering organizational consultation. Human resource consultants need to be particularly aware of the interrelationship between an

organization and its environment and the problem of the permeability of the boundaries of human resource agencies.

A model of organizational consultation was also presented. The essence of this model is that the goals of meeting human needs and productivity are interlinked. It was also posited that the principle of systems theory—the interdependence of individuals, groups, and subsystems—should provide the basis for the work of the organizational consultant.

Finally, some principles of changing organizations were presented. These are, for the most part, common sense principles that have been generated by practicing consultants.

Tips for the Practitioner

1. Analyze your family or current living arrangement using systems principles.

   A. What roles do people play? (Differentiation)
   B. How are decisions reached? (Leadership)
   C. Are family goals well articulated? Are there conflicts in goals?
   D. What is the basic reward system in the family?
   E. What technology is used to enhance family functioning? Is any of the use of technology counterproductive?
   F. What are the values of the family? How are these communicated? Enforced?
   G. Identify problems that could be solved in several ways.
   H. How does the family adapt to changing conditions?

2. Now use these same principles to analyze a simple organization. Get permission to observe the organization for a day or two. Do not interact with the people. After you have made your observations, test them with the head of the organization to determine their accuracy.

3. Volunteer to help a consultant who works with organizations.

Review Questions

1. Identify instances in which linear thinking has produced undesirable consequences in organizations.
2. How can human resources agencies make their boundaries less permeable? Take a specific agency (school, counseling center, health department, etc.) and outline a plan.

3. Identify a problem of concern to you. Using the force field analysis approach, generate a problem-solving approach to deal with the concern.

4. What are the assumptions underlying the human relations model of consultation?

5. Contrast the human relations and process models of consultation.

6. Do you agree with Schein's recommendations on the consultant's role regarding the content of consultation? Why or why not?

7. Identify specific situations in which acceptant, catalytic, confrontational, prescriptive, and theory based interventions could be used. Generate rules for determining what you would use.

8. What organizational factors are likely to impinge upon the change process?

9. How would you manage resistance in a change process starting with entry and ending with completion of the intervention?

References

Alpin, J. C. (1978). Structural change versus behavior change. *Personnel and Guidance Journal, 56,* 407.

Argyris, C. (1970). *Integrating the individual and the organization.* New York: John Wiley & Sons.

Backer, T. E., Shifren-Levin, I., & Erchul, W. P. (1983). *Consultation and educational activities in mental health programs.* Los Angeles: Human Interaction Research Institute.

Baldridge J. V. (1971). *The analysis of organizational change: A human relations strategy versus a political systems strategy.* Palo Alto, CA; Stanford Center for Research and Development in Teaching and Research, Memorandum No. 75.

Bandura, A. (1977). Self system: Toward a unifying theory of behavioral change. *Psychological Review, 84,* 191–215.

Beer, M. (1980). *Organizational change and development: A systems view.* Santa Monica, CA: Goodyear.

Beer, M., & Spector, B. (1993). Organizational diagnosis: Its role in organizational learning. *Journal of Counseling and Development, 71,* 642–650.

Bennis, W. (1970). *Beyond bureaucracy.* New York: McGraw-Hill.

Blake, R. R., & Mouton, J. S. (1976). *Consultation.* Reading, MA: Addison-Wesley.

Caplan, G. (1970). *Mental health consultation.* New York: Basic Books.

Chamley, J. D., McFarlane, I. R., & Young, R. L. (1987). Counselor-consultant: A complex imperative. *CACD Journal, 8,* 13–18.

Chin, R. (1976). The utility of systems models and developmental models for practitioners. In W. G. Bennis, K. D. Benne, R. Chin, & K. D. Corey (Eds.), *The planning of change* (3rd ed.) (pp. 22–45). New York: Holt, Rinehart & Winston.

Chin, R., & Benne, K. D. (1976). General strategies for effecting changes in human systems. In W. G. Bennis, K. D. Benne, R. Chin, & K. D. Corey (Eds.), *The planning of change* (3rd ed.) (pp. 45–63). New York: Holt, Rinehart & Winston.

French, W. L., & Bell, C. H. (1973). *Organizational development: Behavioral science interventions for organizational improvement.* Englewood Cliffs, NJ: Prentice-Hall.

Fuqua, D. R., & Kurpius, D. J. (1993). Conceptual models in organizational consultation. *Journal of Counseling and Development, 71,* 607–618.

Gardner, L. C. (1971). The therapeutic relationship under varying conditions of race. *Psychotherapy: Theory, Research and Practice, 8,* 78–87.

Gardner, N., & McGill, M. E. (1970). *Guidance for the training of professional and technical personnel in the administration and management of developmental functions.* New York: Public Administration Division, Department of Economic and Social Affairs, United Nations.

Goodstein, L. D. (1978). *Consulting with human services systems.* Reading, MA: Addison-Wesley.

Hackman, J. R., & Oldham, G. R. (1980). *Work redesign.* Reading, MA: Addison-Wesley.

Hage, J., & Aiken, M. (1970). *Social change in complex organizations.* New York: Random House.

Havelock, R. G. (1973). *The change agent's guide to innovation.* Englewood Cliffs, NJ: Educational Technology Publications.

Havelock, R. G., & Hubermann, A. M. (1978). *Solving educational problems: The theory and reality of innovation in developing countries.* New York: Praeger.

Huse, E. F. (1980). *Organizational development and change* (2nd ed.). St. Paul, MN: West Publishing.

Jones, G. N. (1969). *Planned organizational change*. New York: Praeger.

Katz, D., & Kahn, R. L. (1978). *The social psychology of organizations*. New York: John Wiley & Sons.

Kotter, J. (1980). *Organizational dynamics: Diagnosis and intervention* (2nd ed.). Reading, MA: Addison-Wesley.

Kuhn, A., & Beam, R. D. (1982). *The logic of organization*. San Francisco: Jossey-Bass.

Kurpius, D. J. (1976). Organizational development: An overview. *National Society for Performance and Instructional Journal*, 15(7), 24–28.

Kurpius, D. J. (1984). Quality of worklife: Preparing consultants to work with the total organization. Paper presented at Annual Conference of the American Association for Counseling and Development, Houston, TX (March 18–21).

Kurpius, D. J. (1985). Consultation interventions: Success, failures and proposals. *The Counseling Psychologist*, 13, 368–389.

Kurpius, D. J., Fuqua, D. R., & Rozecki, T. (1993). The Consulting process: A multidimensional approach. *Journal of Counseling and Development*, 71, 601–606.

Lawler, E. E., & Rhode, J. G. (1976). *Information and controls in organizations*. Santa Monica, CA: Goodyear.

Lawrence, P. R., & Lorsch, J. W. (1976). The differentiation-and-integrated model. In W. G. Bennis, K. D. Benne, R. Chin, & K. D. Corey (Eds.), *The planning of change* (3rd ed.) (pp. 112–117). New York: Holt, Rinehart & Winston.

Lewin, K. (1951). *Field theory in social science*. New York: Harper & Row.

Lin, N. & Zaltman, G. (1973). Dimensions of innovations. In G. Zaltman (Ed.), *Processes and phenomena of social change* (pp. 93–115). New York: John Wiley & Sons.

Lippitt, G. L. (1982). *Organizational renewal* (2nd ed.) Englewood Cliffs, NJ: Prentice-Hall.

Lippitt, G. L. & Lippitt, R. (1986). *The consulting process in action* (2nd ed.). San Diego. CA: University Associates.

McLean, A. J., Sims, D., Mangham, B. P., & Tuffeld, D. C. (1982). *Organizational development in transition*. New York: John Wiley & Sons.

Morasky, R. L. (1982) *Behavioral systems*. New York: Praeger.

Ostlund, L. (1969). The role of the product perceptions in innovative behavior. Proceeding: Fall Conference of the American Marketing Association, Chicago: American Marketing Association.

Rogers, C. R. (1951). *Client-centered therapy*. Boston: Houghton Mifflin.

Schaller, L. E. (1972). *The change agent*. New York: Abingdon Press.

Schein, E. H. (1969). *Process consultation: Its role in organizational development*. Reading, MA: Addison-Wesley.

Schein, L. E. (1970). *Organizational psychology* (2nd ed.). Englewood Cliffs, NJ: Prentice-Hall.

Schein, E. H. (1989). Process consultation as a general model of helping. *Consulting Psychology Bulletin*, 41, 3–15.

Schein, E. H. (1990). Organizational culture. *American Psychologist*, 45, 109–119.

Schmuck, R. A. (1982). Organizational development in the schools. In C. R. Reynold & T. B. Gutkin (Eds.), *Handbook of social psychology* (pp. 829–857). New York: John Wiley & Sons.

Seiber, D. (1975). Organizational influences on a demonstrative role. In J. R. Baldridge & T. E. Deal (Eds.), *Managing change in educational organizations* (pp. 95–105). Berkeley, CA: McCutcheon Publishing.

Steele, F. (1982). *The role of the internal consultant*. Boston: CBI Publishing.

Waterman, R. H., Peters, T. J., & Phillips, J. R. (1980). Structure is not organization. *Business Horizon*, 23, 14–26.

Weisbord, M. (1976). Organizational diagnosis: Six places to look for trouble without a theory. *Group and Organizational Studies*, 1, 430.

Wickstrom, K. F., & Witt, J. C. (1993). Resistance with school-based consultation. In J. E. Zins, T. R. Kratochwill, & S. N. Elliot (Eds.) *Handbook of Consultation Services for Children* (pp. 159–178). San Francisco: Jossey-Bass.

Zaltman, G., Duncan, R., & Hobek, J. (1973). *Innovation and organizations*. New York: John Wiley & Sons.

Consultation Stages and Processes I

Goal of the Chapter

The goal of this chapter is to provide a description of the consulting process and some illustrations of the communication skills needed by the consultant.

Chapter Preview

1. Two views of the consultation process are provided: a description of the stages of consultation that details the activities that comprise consultation and a description of the interpersonal processes that contribute to effective problem solving in consultation.

2. Eight stages of consultation are identified and illustrated: entry, initiation of a consulting relationship, assessment, problem definition and goal setting, strategy selection, strategy implementation, evaluation, and termination.

3. An overview of the different issues faced by internal and external consultants, particularly in the early stages of consultation, is provided.

4. Carkhuff's model of helping is extended to consultation.

5. Research and concepts from the consultation literature are discussed in relation to Carkhuff's model and its application to consultation.

Traditionally the process of consultation has been conceptualized in two distinct, although not necessarily contradictory, ways. In the first of these approaches, consultation is viewed as an activity that consists of stages in which each stage involves qualitatively different activities. In the second, the relationship between the consultant and consultee is examined

within an interpersonal framework (Meade, Hamilton, & Yuen, 1982). The stage approach is primarily descriptive: It details activities that occur in most instances of consultation. The process approach focuses upon the consultant-consultee dyad and how consultant behavior influences subsequent consultee behavior and attitudes. Both approaches are useful in understanding what goes on in consultation and in linking specific aspects of consultation with desired outcomes. This chapter begins with a description of consultation, dividing it into eight stages. In the second half, interaction between the consultant and consultee will be discussed in depth.

Stages of Consultation

In broadest terms, consultation is a process by which a consultant and consultee seek to change a problem situation. Therefore, it is not surprising to find that most stage models of consultation (e.g., Bergan, 1977; Bergan & Kratochwill, 1990; Gibb, 1959; Hansen, Himes & Meier, 1990; Havelock, 1973; Kurpius, 1978; Lippitt & Lippitt, 1978; Meyers, Parsons & Martin, 1979) portray consultation as a problem-solving process in which the consultant and consultee work together to define a problem and bring about its resolution. The stages common to problem-solving models in many disciplines (assessment, problem definition, strategy selection, implementation, and evaluation) are also present in stage models of consultation. In the following discussion consultation has been divided into eight stages: (1) entry into an organization, (2) initiation of a consulting relationship, (3) assessment, (4) problem definition and goal setting, (5) strategy selection, (6) strategy implementation, (7) evaluation, and (8) termination.

When a complex process is described in stages, a lock-step sequence that must take place in all instances of the process is often implied (such as the stages of human development described by Piaget). The term "stages" is not used in that sense when applied to consultation. Rather, the stages described here reflect the activities that typically occur in consultation and their usual sequence. In many instances of consultation one or more stages will not be present, or activities within different stages may overlap. For example, entry into the consultee's setting, initiation of a relationship with the consultee, and assessment of factors relevant to the presenting problem are often described as separate stages in consultation, yet these activities often occur simultaneously. In other instances, consultation is initiated when a consultee approaches a consultant with a description of his or her concerns and the consultant responds with pertinent questions. Thus, assessment of the problem has begun and entry and relationship building as separate, preceding stages have been bypassed. However, as interaction between the consultant and consultee progresses, a positive working relationship must be established or consultation is likely to be aborted.

The division of consultation into stages also does not imply that consultation occurs in an invariant sequence; consultants and consultees may recycle through earlier stages of consultation if new information arises that calls for reinterpretation of information from a prior stage (Bergan, 1977; Gutkin & Curtis, 1990). For instance, if a strategy developed in consultation does not bring about problem resolution, the consultant and consultee may decide that more assessment is needed in order to develop a workable solution, and the focus of consultation would return to assessment.

The purpose of the following sections is to describe a common core of activities and issues that characterize consultation, regardless of the model of consultation that is employed or the setting in which consultation takes place. In some cases the activities of internal and external consultants will be discussed separately; particularly in the early stages of consultation the issues faced by each type differ. Further discussion of the different issues faced by internal and external consultants is contained in Chapter Six.

Entry into the Organization

Entry refers to the consultant's crossing of organizational boundaries into a system or work setting. As such, entry issues are most relevant for consultants who are external to the organization in which consultation takes place. In this section, issues pertinent to the external consultant will be discussed first, followed by a discussion of issues pertinent to entry for internal consultants.

There are two distinct components to entry—formal entry, or sanctioning of the consultant's activities by persons in authority positions within the organization, and informal acceptance or acceptance of the consultant by organizational members who will be consultees. Both aspects of entry are crucial in setting the stage for successful consultation.

Formal Entry

Gallessich (1982) has delineated several substeps in formal entry. For the external consultant, entry usually begins with a preliminary exploration of the match between organizational needs and the consultant's skills. Generally, this exploration takes the form of one or more preliminary meetings where the consultant and a member (or members of the organization) exchange information. Topics included in these preliminary discussions may include basic descriptive information about the organizations, perceived needs of the organization and desired outcomes, information regarding the consultant's skills and working style, and a formulation of how consultation might be implemented in that particular work setting. Fees and a time frame may be discussed. Such a meeting also provides an opportunity for both the consultant and members of the organization to assess each other and form judgments about the potential for a productive working relationship.

Prior to reaching a formal agreement, the consultant may want to consider why the organization chose to ask for consultation at this particular time and for this particular problem, as well as why he or she was approached rather than another consultant (Pipes, 1981). Several factors playing into this decision could have a profound effect on the course and outcome of consultation. For example, the choice of a consultant with a particular area of expertise, such as increasing productivity or school-wide discipline programs, tells the consultant how the organization has conceptualized the problem. Should the consultant conceptualize the problem differently, he or she may meet with resistance. There also may be hidden agendas in the request for consultative services. A supervisor may have pressured a manager to seek help, or an organization may be looking to gather evidence to scapegoat someone for a particular problem. Also, more than one consultant has found that they are expected to legitimatize a decision that has already been made by the director of an agency, such as the dismissal of certain personnel or the discontinuation of a service. The consultant who carefully considers the questions Why me? and Why now? not only has begun the

assessment process, but may anticipate and avoid many difficult consultative dilemmas (Pipes, 1981).

Provided the consultant and the representative(s) of the organization can reach agreement about some potential ways the consultant can be of use to the organization, they move onto the second step of formal entry, contracting. *Contracting* refers to negotiation and agreement between the consultant and the organization regarding the nature of consultation. Although contracting may not involve a formal written contract, particularly when internal consultants are involved, the outcome of the activity is the same as that of negotiating a written contract—clear understanding and agreement by both parties of the other's responsibilities. Although contracting is typically carried out at several levels of an organization to assure understanding of consultation by all those involved, sanction from the highest-level administrator is especially important to assure that subordinates participate in the consultation process (Caplan, 1970; Caplan & Caplan, 1993; Kelly, 1993; Meyers et al., 1979). Without this sanction, it may be unclear to employees how participation in consulting activities will be viewed and what the potential consequences of participation might be.

Although Chapter Twelve discusses the components of a consulting contract in depth, it is relevant here to list some of the topics typically discussed in contracting:

- goals or intended outcomes of consultation
- identity of consultees
- confidentiality of service and the limits of this confidentiality
- time frame—how long will the service be provided to the organization? to the individual consultee?
- times the consultant will be available
- procedure for requesting to work with the consultant
- space for consultant
- how to contact the consultant if needed
- possibility of contract renegotiation if change is needed
- fees, if relevant
- consultant's access to different sources and types of information within the organization
- person to whom the consultant is responsible

At times, a formal contract will not be drawn up and contracting will take the form of discussion between the consultant and a representative of the organization. In this case, the consultant may wish to write a letter to the administrative head of the organization, summarizing his or her understanding of their agreement and asking that the consultee organization bring any points of disagreement up for further discussion. This letter can serve as a written document to which both parties can refer should any question arise about the consultant's activities and also prevent problems where the consultant and the consultee organization have perceived the nature of their agreement differently.

The third step in formal entry is the actual physical entry of the consultant into the workplace (Gallessich, 1982). Often the external consultant's entry into the organization takes the form of a formal introduction of the consultant to consultees and other staff of the organization. It is often beneficial for the external consultant to arrange to be introduced

in a staff meeting where he or she is also given a few minutes to summarize the types of services to be provided and answer any questions potential consultees may have. This procedure has several advantages. Introduction at a staff meeting is one way of communicating that the consultant's activities have been formally recognized and sanctioned and also communicates the consultant's interest in meeting with prospective consultees and answering their questions. This procedure also gives the consultant control over how his or her services are represented. When no introduction takes place, or consultation is introduced in a less formal or systematic manner, misunderstanding or distortion of the consultant's role is more likely to occur. For example, a formal meeting where confidentiality of consultation is discussed and endorsed by the administrative head of the organization may dissipate the notion that the consultant is a "spy" for the administration who will report on consultees' weaknesses and failures. Finally, such a formal introduction assures that all consultees have had a preliminary introduction to both consultation and the consultant in a nonthreatening manner. Consultees are more likely to approach the consultant if their uncertainty about the consultant's role and interpersonal style has been reduced prior to individual contact.

Informal Acceptance

After formal contracting and introduction to the staff have been accomplished, the consultant enters the organization. Even though the consultant now may begin work with individual consultees, there is generally a transition time where the external consultant has entered the workplace, but has not been entirely accepted by staff members. During this time, consultation may be hindered by lack of trust, lack of cooperation, or consultee reluctance to share information (Gallessich, 1982). An inexperienced consultant may be frustrated by this period of what, on the surface, appears to be largely wasted time. However, this transition period should be expected, and in many ways, it serves a useful function for both the consultant and consultees.

Consultees' wariness in accepting the consultant can serve as a protective mechanism: It allows consultees an opportunity to evaluate the consultant, his or her skills, operating style, and potential value to the organization, and assess the risks (for example, loss of time, adverse organizational consequences) that may be associated with consultation, before engaging in consultation. For the consultant, this time period provides an opportunity to go beyond a surface level understanding of the organization and gain information important in functioning successfully as a consultant. The consultant may become aware of subtle, but critical, aspects of organizational functioning, such as interpersonal schisms, formal and informal networks within the organization, and organizational taboos and norms, as he or she observes and participates in the day-to-day activities of the organization. An example follows.

> *A psychologist provided consultation at an elementary school to teachers who requested help in dealing with individual children in their classrooms. The school also had a committee of school personnel whose role was to make placement decisions for special education services. Since the consultant and a teacher sometimes decided to refer a student for special education services as a result of consultation, the consultant began to sit in on these meetings. At one of the first meetings he attended, he was asked to sign a sheet indicating who had been present when a*

particular child's case was discussed. The consultant inadvertently signed the form with a red pen. This precipitated an immediate crisis, as one of the district-level persons present objected to any color ink but dark blue or black. All discussion ceased as two teachers searched for cover-up liquid so that the offending ink could be masked. The committee's reaction provided valuable insight about the school's priorities and power dynamics within the committee. It was clear the committee operated in fear of the district-level person and that the person held considerable power over the committee. This information was important to the consultant's functioning, as the district-level person's opinions were likely to influence place-ment decisions on any child whom the consultant and a consultee might refer. In addition, this knowledge suggested a new avenue for consultative involvement that might be negotiated later: effective group decision making.

The consultant who acts too quickly, without gaining acceptance or taking time to fully understand the organization, may find that he or she has misdiagnosed the problem, ignored factors important in the design of successful interventions, or failed to gain the coopera-tion of consultees.

Although all external consultants can expect a period of time between formal entry into the organization and acceptance by organizational members, the time required for accep-tance can vary as a function of several factors. Many times, characteristics of the consultant can impede or facilitate acceptance. For example, similarity to organizational members in background, training, or outside interests can sometimes aid informal acceptance. Another factor that can facilitate acceptance is a reputation based on previous consultation work or expertise in a particular field. Both may enhance the consultant's status and consultee will-ingness to participate in consultation.

In addition to characteristics of the consultant, such as similarity to consultees or rep-utation, characteristics of the organization and critical incidents that take place during the entry phase can also have an impact on informal acceptance of the consultee. With regard to characteristics of the organization, some organizations may be more open to new ideas and more readily accepting of the consultant. This attitude may grow out of an administra-tor's consistent rewarding of innovative subordinates or an organizational history of suc-cessful innovations. Another organizational factor that can facilitate acceptance is crisis (Caplan, 1970). As it becomes clear that some action is needed to alleviate a crisis situation, organizational resistance to change may be lowered, allowing the consultant to progress more quickly from entry to problem solving.

Student Learning Activity 5.1

If you are entering a new training placement, keep a journal where you record your impressions of the organization, leaders, leadership style, communica-tion patterns, and the common concerns and issues that you observe among staff members. Also record the basis of your impressions. At the close of your placement, look back at your journal. How has your perspective changed? What misconceptions did you have? In what areas were your impressions on tar-get? Also note how staff perceptions of you have changed over time.

Often a critical incident can have a substantial impact on the consultant's acceptance, such as a successful instance of direct service that makes the consultant more credible. For example, a consultant worked in a school for several months and achieved only minimal entry, working largely with one teacher and on relatively trivial problems. One day, in passing, the teacher mentioned difficulty with several fourth graders who had failed to master their times tables. The consultant volunteered to work with them for a brief period each day and discovered that the students were overwhelmed by the task and had no idea where to begin on a task so large. The consultant brought in some index cards and taught the children to make flashcards, to break down the memorizing into small units, and how to rehearse. After a few sessions, the children had made substantial progress with their multiplication tables. Within a few weeks, the consultant experienced a dramatic leap in the number of teachers seeking her services and later learned that the fourth grade teacher had told several teachers of the consultant's work and its effectiveness. This successful instance of direct service had provided the staff with evidence of the consultant's credibility in dealing with classroom problems. In another situation, a counseling psychologist worked with police officers on stress management and also consulted with community groups regarding the design of drug prevention programs. The success of his direct service to police officers in the stress management area resulted in numerous referrals from officers for consultation with community groups interested in drug prevention programs.

Consultees' apprehension about the consultant also can be decreased by interactions that provide a means for the consultant and consultee to get to know one another prior to consultation (Caplan, 1970). For example, the consultant may give a lecture or workshop for potential consultees and, afterwards, talk informally with the group. The consultant might attend organizational social events or have lunch in the staff lounge and initiate conversation with potential consultees. These contacts can help assure consultees that the consultant is friendly and interested in the organization and its members. Also, concerns about consultation may be breached informally by consultees and the consultant can clarify any misconceptions about himself or herself or consultation.

To summarize, entry for the external consultant is not a single step, but an ongoing process that has both formal and informal components. Successful entry is characterized by a progressively deeper understanding of the organization on the part of the consultant, increased trust and acceptance of the consultant by members of the consultee organizations, and a clear, mutual understanding of the objectives, methods, and procedural details of consultation by both parties.

Internal Consultants

Many models of consultation assume that the consultant is from outside the organization in which he or she is consulting. However, it is not unusual for a professional with specialized skills in an organization to be asked to act as an internal consultant. For example, a psychologist in a university counseling center might be asked to provide consultation to residence hall directors about student matters or a child psychiatrist might be asked to consult in the pediatric surgery department about children's reactions to surgery.

In one sense the consultants described in these examples have already accomplished entry because they are members of the organization in which they consult. However, ignoring entry issues completely and moving immediately into the problem-solving aspects of

consultation can lead to difficulties. Several aspects of both formal and informal entry are of special concern to the internal consultant.

With regard to formal entry, administrators may be less likely to question aspects of consultation before making a commitment because they are familiar with the consultant, although in another role. Thus, expectations on the part of the consultant and the organization may not be clearly defined, leading to misunderstandings later. Even if such detail is not called for by members of the organization, the internal consultant should delineate his or her role and clarify administrative expectations (Fine, Grantham, & Wright, 1979).

The formal introduction of the consultant to staff members also should not be ignored. Although internal consultants usually are known by their colleagues, their particular role as a consultant in a particular situation may not be understood. For example, a counseling psychologist who is assigned to the student development and counseling center may be acquainted with most of the persons in the student service organization. However, a formal explanation that this individual is to assume a consulting role with housing staff members to assist in resolving a vandalism problem may need to be made by the director of housing. This introduction provides the necessary sanction for consultation from the head of an agency, just as an announcement by the principal at a faculty meeting that a school counselor has been asked to provide consultation assistance to teachers as a part of a dropout prevention program legitimizes that activity.

Another issue to be dealt with during formal entry is the confidentiality of consultation. The internal consultant will be with an organization much longer than the external consultant and is more likely to interact with other individuals and groups within the organization (Pipes, 1981). This situation makes confidentiality concerns more acute. The internal consultant should take steps to assure that administrators understand that information remains confidential in consultation and also try to anticipate confidentiality issues that could place the consultant or consultee in uncomfortable positions or present conflicts of interest. For example, a school psychologist who has acted as a consultant to a teacher with classroom discipline problems may find that confidential information obtained while consulting is relevant to decision making about a child referred to special education services from that classroom, or the principal may ask for information to be used in evaluating that teacher. Formal entry into the consultation process is an opportunity to deal with confidentiality issues before critical situations arise.

Like formal entry, informal acceptance also is more easily achieved by the internal consultant. He or she may already know consultees or, at the least, is perceived as similar to the consultee in an important way. However, this advantage is gained at the loss of role clarity (Lippitt & Lippitt, 1978). It is important that internal consultants spend time clarifying their role as a consultant and distinguishing it from their role within the organization, particularly when the other role(s) involve direct service. For example, when a school counselor or school psychologist acts as a consultant, there may be the expectation that he or she eventually will take responsibility for the problem by providing counseling or testing the child.

Initiation of a Consulting Relationship

A central premise of consultation is that two professionals with different areas of expertise can engage in more effective problem solving than would be possible if either worked alone.

However, a productive working relationship is not a given in consultation. One of the earliest activities in working with a new consultee should be the establishment of a positive working relationship. The components of this relationship have been identified in Chapter One—an egalitarian relationship characterized by open communication between the consultant and consultee, collaboration between the consultant and consultee at each phase of consultation, and confidentiality of all communication.

The first step in initiating a productive working relationship is a discussion of the roles the consultant and consultee will take in consultation. This procedure assures that the consultee has an opportunity to express his or her preferences and that the consultant and consultee understand and agree on the basic parameters of consultation (Parsons & Meyers, 1984). This open discussion of their working relationship, initiated by the consultant, also provides a model to the consultee of the clear, open communication that should characterize later consultative communication.

As part of this initial discussion and structuring of role relationships, the consultant should explicitly recognize the importance of a coordinate, nonhierarchical relationship between the consultant and consultee. Despite the consultant's lack of formal power, the consultee may ascribe power to the consultant on the basis of perceived expertise and competence (Caplan & Caplan, 1993; Gaupp, 1966). When consultees do not perceive themselves as equals, they may take a less active role in developing a problem solution, may feel more easily threatened or defensive, and may not freely express disagreement or reservations when problem solving begins.

A second important component of role structuring involves establishing an agreement for action. Consultation is aimed at altering a problem situation, resulting in change, which requires action on the part of *both* the consultant and consultee. As mentioned earlier, there may be the unspoken expectation that eventually the consultant will assume responsibility for the problem and its solution. Agreement regarding the extent of consultant involvement in implementation and the expectation for action on the part of the consultee should be established early.

Finally, development of the initial relationship should take place in such a way that termination is an expected result. Although it may seem somewhat strange to talk of termination in the initial phase, it is important to immediately recognize the goal of developing a fully functioning, independent consultee.

Efforts at role structuring can prevent unspoken expectations from blocking successful consultation. For example, the consultant may assume that the consultee understands that he or she is to take an active role in problem solving, while the consultee perceives the consultant as an expert who is to solve the problem. Similarly, the consultant may assume that the consultee understands the importance of being open with the consultant, yet the consultee may be hesitant to be entirely truthful, especially when he or she believes that what is said may not be pleasing to the consultant.

Another source of misunderstanding is the consultee's experiences working with other consultants who operated differently. The consultee may assume that all consultants operate in the same manner and this can be a source of conflict that retards the consultation process.

Structuring role relationships also includes a discussion of ethical concerns, such as the confidentiality of communication and data collected within consultation. Consultees may have concerns that seeking consultation services is an admission of weakness, or they may

feel that information divulged to the consultant will be passed on to their supervisors. Assurances that the content of consultation is confidential are seen as central to the free exchange of information and opinions that determines successful consultation. Agreements about the confidentiality of data collected through surveys, observations, and other assessment strategies also need to be reached.

Structuring role relationships and discussing confidentiality concerns are part of establishing a relationship with the consultee. So is providing an atmosphere in which the consultee feels accepted and comfortable. Because consultation involves interaction between consultant and consultee, consultants who are able to use their interpersonal skills to make such interactions rewarding for consultees will be more successful. The consultee who perceives the consultant as genuinely interested in him or her and the problem at hand is more likely to accept consultant help and ideas. Facilitative characteristics of the consultant and their role in consultation are discussed in more depth in the second half of the chapter.

Internal Consultants

Initiation of a consulting relationship presents special concerns for the internal consultant. As with informal acceptance by staff members, the initiation of consultation with individuals may be easier for the internal consultant because of prior interactions with staff members. However, despite efforts during entry to distinguish the consulting role from other roles the human services professional plays in the organization, consultees may still fail to understand the nature of consultation. The internal consultant should not bypass a discussion of the parameters of consultation and the role structuring steps outlined above because of familiarity with the consultee.

The following excerpts illustrate the use of role structuring by two consultants to clarify expectations about consultation. The first excerpt is part of a consultation session between a psychologist and a visiting nurse, and represents an example of role structuring by an external consultant. The second excerpt is from a consultation session between a school counselor and elementary school teacher. In this case, the consultant is internal to the consultee's organization and known to the consultee, but only in his or her role of providing counseling services to students. Both excerpts begin after the consultee has briefly described the problem.

Excerpt One, External

Consultant: I can see why you're concerned. Mr. Tuttle's failure to follow his dietary restrictions and occasional refusal to use insulin can have some serious consequences. But before we go any further, let's talk about some ways we can work together. There are two ways I think I can be of help. First, I can provide you with some information about the psychological aspects of diabetes in the elderly. Also, we can work together to come up with some ideas about how to help Mr. Tuttle take more responsibility for his self care.

Consultee: I really hope you can tell me what to do. I've tried everything I can think of.

Consultant: I know how much thought and effort you've put into this already. I sure wish I had some magic answer for you. But, it's really a matter of us working together to come up with some alternatives.

Consultee: Well, OK, but as I said, I'm pretty much out of ideas.

Consultant: You know Mr. Tuttle better than I do, and I want the ideas we come up with to be ones that you feel comfortable with. What I can do is tell you some of the things that have been successful with other patients, and some of the general principles to keep in mind when dealing with noncompliant patients. But we'll need to work together to see how these ideas might apply in Mr. Tuttle's case.

Consultee: Do you think it would be helpful if you talked to Mr. Tuttle?

Consultant: I'm not sure that would be helpful. From what you've said, Mr. Tuttle doesn't even see that there's a problem. It's unlikely that he would agree to see a psychologist. But he seems to respect you and look forward to your visits. At this point, I'd say you were in the best position to make a difference with Mr. Tuttle.

Consultee: I guess you're right. He really does seem to be happy to see me when I come. Sometimes he'll have a newspaper article to show me or a card from his grand-child.

Consultant: So, are you comfortable with trying a few new things with Mr. Tuttle?

Excerpt Two

Consultee: So that's my problem with Bobby. I know how to deal with his learning diffi-culties; it's his behavior that I have trouble handling. He sees how much further ahead all the other children are in reading and it frustrates him. He's the class clown. He'll do anything to get a reaction out of the other children.

Consultant: You've really touched on an important aspect of working with students with learning disabilities. You've got to deal with the children's feelings about themselves as well as the academics. Not all teachers recognize that.

Consultee: The other children avoid him. Of course, that just makes him do even sillier things to get their attention.

Consultant: I think we could help Bobby learn a few more positive ways to get attention in your class. Would you be interested in working together on that?

Consultee: I'd like that.

Consultant: What I had in mind was two or three sessions, each lasting about 20 minutes or so, where we try to come up with some strategies for you to use to help Bobby.

Consultee: That's fine, as long as the plans don't take too much of my time during teach-ing.

Consultant: It's important that we devise something that will work for you. That's why I suggested we work together. I don't know the details of how you manage your classroom, you're the expert in that area. Your input about the amount of time a plan would require and how the plan fits with your classroom is important.

Consultee: Oh, I'd let you know if a plan took too much time.

Consultant: Well, I'd want you to tell me. There's no point in coming up with ideas that are unworkable.

Consultee: Sometimes it's easy to forget that there are 25 kids who need my time.

Consultant: I know you take your commitment to your children seriously. Turning back to how we might work together, does that sound like a workable plan? Two or three sessions to brainstorm some ideas?

Consultee: Yeah, I can use part of my planning period, if you're available during third period.

Consultant: That would work out. I'm hoping that we can come up with a fairly specific plan in those sessions. There also might be some ways I can help you carry it out in the classroom. For example, cover your class if you need time to explain the plan to Bobby or meet with his parents.

Consultee: Thanks, I'll keep that in mind.

Consultant: One last thing about working together. I guess it goes without saying that our work together is confidential. Sometimes that aspect helps teachers feel more comfortable about having me in the class to observe or help carry out a plan.

Consultee: Oh, that doesn't worry me. I've been teaching too many years to be worried about what people say about my classroom.

Assessment

The primary activity that takes place during the assessment stage is an examination of factors relevant to the problem that the consultee brings to consultation. Another type of appraisal that can be considered part of assessment, the consultant's and consultee's assessment of each other, also plays an important role in consultation. Both aspects of assessment are discussed in this section.

With regard to assessment of the presenting problem, consultation models vary in terms of what is assessed. These differences are largely attributable to underlying assumptions within each of the models, discussed in earlier chapters, regarding the causes of human behavior and how people change. Figure 5.1 divides potential causes or maintaining factors in human behavior in terms of three major domains of assessment. These major domains are *consultee characteristics*, *environmental characteristics*, and *client characteristics*. Models of consultation differ in terms of the particular domain(s) assumed to be important in the change process, as well as the particular variables that are emphasized within a domain. For example, within operant learning theory, human behavior is explained largely in terms of changes in the immediate environment, particularly consequences following a given behavior. Working within a consultation model that draws heavily from operant learning theory, such as Bergan (1977; Bergan & Kratochwill, 1990), the consultant would be likely to focus assessment and intervention on aspects of the immediate environment, such as schedules of reinforcement. Alternately, a consultant working with the Caplanian model would focus assessment on the attitudes, feelings, and skills of the con-

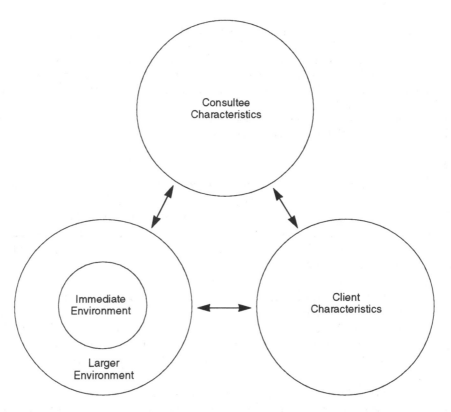

FIGURE 5.1   Domains in Which Consultation Problems May Be Conceptualized

sultee, because they are seen as the most important factors in problem resolution within this model. A consultant with a systems or ecobehavioral orientation (Gutkin, 1993) might focus on both the immediate environment and how that environment is affected by events in the larger environment.

The domains and factors within a domain that will be the focus of assessment represent a major choice in consultation. The choice of what factors are to be examined during the assessment phase has a major impact on subsequent stages of problem solving. Variables that are ignored during assessment most likely will not be considered in defining a problem and developing a solution. If a consultant and consultee assume that a problem lies in the client and design a problem solution based on that assumption, consultee actions or aspects of the environment that contribute to the problem will not be addressed, jeopardizing problem resolution. Or the consultant and consultee may ignore system-level factors important to problem resolution. To illustrate, a consultant began working with the classroom teacher in a children's psychiatric facility who had requested help in developing a social skills curriculum. Since the children in the classroom spent much of their time in the care of psychiatric nurses on the ward, the consultant and consultee planned to request assistance from the nurses to assure that skills taught in the classroom were reinforced on the ward. However, in developing the program, the consultant failed to consider the ideological differences

---

Student Learning Activity 5.2

With a partner, formulate a problem situation that you might encounter in consultation. Tape record a five minute roleplay where one of you is a consultant, and ask the consultee about various aspects of the problem situation. Listen to your session. What domains did you touch upon in your assessment? What domains and factors within domains did you ignore? Discuss the same problem situation with others and ask what types of information they would ask for from a consultee when assessing a similar situation.

---

between the teacher, who used a behavioral approach, and the nurses, who worked within a psychoanalytic framework. The program failed to gain the backing of the nurses once it was implemented and the children's gains were minimal. Another consultant found that her efforts to assist a school district to mainstream behavior disordered students failed because she had not considered teachers' reluctance to accept disruptive students when a district-wide teacher observation system had been implemented and linked to merit pay.

Because a wide range of factors may have an impact on a problem situation, the consultant and consultee should begin assessment with a broad consideration of all factors that might be important in correctly designating the problem and designing its solution. *A priori* rejection of a domain of assessment, or potentially important variables, on the basis of the consultant's or consultee's preconceived notion of the problem and what contributes to it will lower the probability of a correct solution. As in counseling (Ivey, 1983), one possible goal of consultation is to help the consultee view the problem in a more complex way than would be possible without the consultant (Caplan & Caplan, 1993). Table 5.1 provides examples of factors that might be considered in each of the three domains of assessment.

While the consultant and consultee assess factors relevant to the problem situation, another type of assessment is also taking place—the consultant and consultee are learning more about each other. As the consultee describes the problem for which he or she is seeking consultation, the consultant is assessing aspects of the consultee that will influence the consultation process. For example, does the consultee perceive a child's misbehavior as a result of poor parental control or as a result of poor classroom management? Does the agency manager seeking help in increasing employee morale view the problem as the employees'; or as a result of his overcontrol of their duties? Have previous interventions the consultee describes been simplistic or do they show a high skill level on the part of the consultee? In each case, the consultant's assessment may result in changes in his or her interactions with the consultee. In some instances, the consultant and consultee may spend additional time on problem definition and client assessment if their perceptions of the problem differ. The consultant who works with a less-skilled consultee may use more examples and explanations when outlining a proposed intervention plan or may provide more support to the consultee during implementation.

The consultee also assesses and forms judgments during this phase about the consultant, his or her style, the probability that the consultant will be able to aid in solving the problem, and what the consultant wants. These judgments can influence the process and outcome of consultation. Tombari and Bergan (1978) found that consultant questions consistent with a medical or behavioral model of consultation elicit consultee definitions of the

TABLE 5.1 Examples of Concerns within Each of the Three Domains of Assessment in Consultation

Client Characteristics

- What client behaviors are of concern?
- How are client cognitions contributing to the problem?
- If the client is a child, are there developmental issues that must be considered?
- How does the client perceive the consultee?

Consultee Characteristics

- Is the problem one of lack of knowledge, skill, objectivity and/or confidence?
- How does the consultee view the problem?
- What are the consultee's expectations for self and client?
- What intervention skills does the consultee possess?
- What types of treatment are acceptable to the consultee?

Environmental Characteristics
Immediate Environment

- What aspects of the environment are reinforcing or maintaining the client's behavior?
- What resources are available that could be used in resolving the problem?
- What constraints in the immediate environment must be considered?

Larger Environment

- Are there structural aspects of the environment that are contributing to the problem?
- Are there factors outside of the immediate environment that are affecting client behavior?
- Are the changes proposed for the client or consultee consistent with organizational norms and expectations?

problem that are consistent with that viewpoint and also affect consultees' estimate of how effective they will be in resolving the problem. For example, consultant questions that focus on the client's behavior and the consultee's actions in relation to the client's behavior elicit definitions of the problem that focus on the client's behavior and lead the consultee to view the problem as more likely to be solved.

Problem Definition and Goal Setting

As the consultant and consultee examine variables that might be relevant to the presented problem, a more complex conceptualization of the problem should emerge. Both research and theoretical works characterize this stage as crucial in consultation. Bergan and Tombari (1976) found the best predictor of behavioral consultation outcome was definition of the problem as a discrepancy between desired and actual behavior in the client. Research by Curtis and Watson (1980) suggests that less skilled consultants differ from highly skilled consultants in the amount of time spent clarifying and defining the problem. Less skilled consultants appear to focus more quickly on planning a strategy to cope with what may be an ill-defined problem.

In order to enhance the problem definition process, consultants might wish to consider some of the aspects of problem solving laid forth in policy analysis. According to Dunn (1981), the most crucial and least understood aspect of policy analysis is problem structuring, where the analyst considers which conceptual framework best fits a particular problem and will produce a successful solution. Professionals who deal with complex problems involving multiple levels of a system run a high risk of a "Type III error" as described by decision theorist Howard Raiffia (1968):

> *One of the most popular paradigms in . . . mathematics describes the case in which a researcher has either to accept or reject a so-called null hypothesis. In a first course in statistics the student learns that he [sic] must constantly balance between making an error of the first kind (that is, rejecting the null hypothesis when it is true) and an error of the second kind (that is, accepting the null hypothesis when it is false) . . . practitioners all too often make errors of a third kind: solving the wrong problem (p. 264).*

Two examples illustrate the notion of solving the wrong problem. A consultant was called in to assist a teacher in a sheltered workshop for adults with mental retardation. One of the clients had recently started to ask for soft drinks almost incessantly during the workday. The consultant and consultee developed a plan to use reinforcement and response cost to decrease the client's requests for drinks. Only later did the consultant and consultee discover the true problem—the client had recently been placed on a medication whose side effects included increased thirst. Once the client's medication was changed, the drink requests decreased dramatically. In another consultation case, a consultant assisted an organization in implementing a mandatory drug testing policy for all employees to cut down on absences and increase productivity. Although the program identified a few substance abusing employees, it did not achieve its intended effects on absenteeism and productivity. When another consultant reconceptualized the problem as one of low employee morale due to an authoritarian management style and the boring, repetitive nature of most employees' jobs, the organization initiated quality circles and other programs designed to allow employees more control over their work. Absenteeism decreased and productivity showed a marked increase.

How does the consultant avoid a Type III error? As suggested by Dunn (1981) and others who have studied change (e.g., Watzlawick, Weakland, & Fisch, 1974), this may be the least understood aspect of problem solving. One key factor in successful problem definition may be a broad based assessment in which the consultant and consultee spend sufficient time on assessment to consider how a broad range of factors may be related to the problem. A second factor is a clear and specific statement of the problem definition and objectives for resolving it. Such a statement, developed through consultation, can facilitate successful problem solving in several ways: (1) it assures that all parties involved have a clear understanding of what is viewed as the problem and what objectives they are working toward, (2) such specificity suggests techniques for measurement, which facilitates development of an evaluation strategy, and (3) an explicit statement of objectives assures the consultant that the consultee's expectations regarding change are realistic. Two sample statements that provide a problem definition, state the focus of interventions to resolve the problem, and give specific objectives relevant to the interventions follow. Both are statements of the problem that might be developed by a consultant and used to assure that the

consultant, consultees, and other organizational members agree on the specifics of a problem and plans to resolve it. The first example refers to a situation where a consultant is asked to help determine the cause of a high turnover rate in volunteers and assist the organization in developing a program to reduce the turnover rate. In the second example, a consultant was called in to help develop a more effective school suspension program. However, after meetings with several administrators and teachers, the consultant and consultees redefined the problem as one of school-wide difficulty with classroom management that resulted in a high referral rate for inschool suspension.

Problem #1　　Services to adults with mental retardation have been disrupted because of a 60 percent turnover among sheltered workshop volunteers. This turnover appears to be due to:

1. Selection of volunteers who are unaware of the behavior, mannerisms, and problems of adults with mental retardation.
2. Poor communication between professional staff and volunteers.
3. Lack of a support network for volunteers, including no systematic program for providing positive feedback and recognition.

Interventions will focus on reducing volunteer turnover.

Objectives

1. To alter the volunteer orientation process so that volunteers develop an understanding of the functioning of adults with mental retardation to facilitate volunteer self-screening.
2. To develop and implement a communications skill development program for volunteers and staff members.
3. To develop a budget for providing recognition lunches, plaques, certificates, etc. to volunteers by soliciting funds from local businesses, industries, and service organizations.

Problem #2　　Teacher referrals have overloaded the inschool suspension program because of:

1. Lack of understanding by staff of the changing cultural values in the community served by the school.
2. Need for different classroom management strategies that are more effective with the population now served by the school.

Interventions will focus on reducing the rate of inschool suspension referrals.

Objectives

1. Teachers will be made aware of the values of the students in their classrooms as a result of a comprehensive program including speakers, workshops, and films addressing this concern.

2. Teachers will be systematically exposed to a classroom management program that includes individualizing classroom instruction, managing learning activities to reduce disruption, and empirically-based principles of classroom management.

Strategy Selection

When the problem has been defined and a goal selected, the next step is the selection of a means for reaching the goal. Just as models of consultation vary in terms of their domains of assessment, the type of strategy typically employed also represents a major point of divergence among models. However, some general comments about strategy selection can be made.

First, one of the major premises of systems theory is *equifinality* (Katz & Kahn, 1978), that is, within a system, there are multiple means of achieving the same goal. The consultant should explore several strategies with the consultee and aid him or her in making a considered choice among alternatives. Increasing the ability of the consultee to develop alternatives and choose among them leads to more adaptive functioning on the part of the consultee and is an important aspect of the preventive nature of consultation. Another important aspect of the preventive nature of consultation is helping consultees identify and use resources that exist within the system that have not been previously utilized.

Two additional important factors are strategy integrity (Reynolds, Gutkin, Elliott, & Witt, 1984) and strategy acceptability to the consultee (Witt, Elliott, & Martens, 1984). Interventions vary in how much they can be adapted or changed without an impact on their effectiveness. The consultant should consider the level of understanding and skill of the consultee, as well as the ease of implementing particular intervention strategies in the consultee's work setting. Some interventions may be changed so much by the consultee to fit his or her skill level and environment that the treatment is no longer effective (Fuchs, Fuchs, Bahr, Fernstrom, & Stecker, 1990). For example, an employee incentive program that rewards productivity with increases in salary might be effective in one workplace where considerable money is available for merit pay, but ineffective in a setting where the amount of money available for merit increases is so small that the raises are meaningless. Similarly, a classroom teacher who has little training or experience in behavior modification may not implement a behavioral treatment effectively because he or she does not understand the importance of providing reinforcement only when the desired behavior is displayed and providing specific rather than general praise.

Several researchers also have proposed that the acceptability of a particular intervention to the treatment agent plays an important role in whether or not the treatment is implemented (Kazdin, 1984; Reimers, Wacker & Koeppl, 1987; Witt & Elliott, 1985). Based on this premise, a sizable body of research has emerged concerning the acceptability of various treatments and the factors that affect persons' judgments of treatment acceptability. Much of this research has involved teachers' judgments about the acceptability of behavioral treatments for school children (Elliott, 1988) and, therefore, has important implications for consultants working in the schools. However, a portion of the research has focused on the acceptability of various treatments to parents (Frentz & Kelley, 1986; McMahon & Forehand, 1983), children themselves (Elliott, Witt, Galvin & Moe, 1986; Shapiro & Goldberg, 1986), or psychiatric staff (Kazdin, French & Sherick, 1981).

Several variables have been found to affect teachers' judgments about the acceptability of a particular intervention strategy or treatment. Elliott (1988) has divided these into four categories: consultant, consultee, treatment, and client variables. *Consultant variables* include how the consultant describes the intervention and the rationale given for treatment. For example, Witt, Moe, Gutkin and Andrews (1984) found that teachers rated an intervention more highly when it was described in pragmatic terms rather than humanistic or behavioral terms (e.g., describing staying in from recess as a logical consequence of not doing work vs. an intervention important to the child's development, or as punishment to decrease inappropriate behavior). Other researchers have found that behavioral jargon can increase the acceptability of some interventions (Hyatt & Tingstrom, 1993). In a recent study, Conoley, Conoley, Ivey, and Scheel (1991) found that rationales that were individually formulated to match each consultee's perspective on a referral problem and its causes increased consultee ratings of treatment acceptability. *Consultee variables* that have been found to affect judgments of treatment acceptability include the consultee's years of experience, knowledge of behavioral techniques, and feelings of self-efficacy in their jobs (DeForest & Hughes, 1992). Interestingly, experience has been found to be negatively related to judgments of treatment acceptability (Witt et al., 1984). *Client variables* thought to influence treatment acceptability include types of problems, such as acting out versus withdrawn behavior, and problem severity.

Treatment variables that have been found to be related to teachers' judgments of acceptability include the time required, type of treatment, and reported effectiveness in the research literature. Of these, the time required and type of treatment seem to have the strongest effects. Teachers predictably prefer interventions that require less time, but are more willing to accept larger treatment time commitments for problems they consider severe (Elliott, 1988). Teachers also prefer treatments that involve positive rather than negative treatment procedures (Witt, Elliott, & Martens, 1984). In one large scale study of general and special education teachers' perception of a wide range of school-based interventions (Martens, Peterson, Witt, & Cirone, 1986), two categories of treatments were rated as most effective, easiest, and most frequently used. These were redirection of the student to appropriate behavior (e.g., telling the student to get back to work) and manipulating material rewards (e.g., behavior contract).

The above discussion gives some sense of the variables that may influence the consultees' judgments of treatment acceptability. But the consultant should not depend on research to determine what interventions are acceptable to a particular consultee. As noted by Elliott (1988) and Rosenfield (1987), there is considerable individual variability in consultees' reactions to a particular treatment. Consultants should be sensitive to consultees' beliefs about the causes of a problem and how behavior changes and should try to match treatment rationales to these beliefs (Conoley et al., 1991). In addition, the early stages of strategy selection should include a discussion with consultees about the types of interventions they have found to be successful and that they would be willing to implement. As the consultant and consultee begin to discuss the specifics of a particular strategy, the consultant also should specifically inquire about the consultees' comfort level with the interventions that are considered. Some examples of how the consultant might discuss treatment acceptability issues with a consultee are presented in the following dialogues.

Excerpt One

Consultant: So we both agree that the major focus of our work should be to decrease the amount of time that Sally spends off task, particularly settling down to her work once you've given an assignment.

Consultee: Yes. Once she starts a task, she seems to be OK, but she has difficulty getting started. Sometimes, I'm amazed. I'll check on her 10 minutes after seatwork time has started and she's just put her name on the paper.

Consultant: Yes, I saw that when I observed her during math. Before we discuss any strategies to get Sally started, I want to be sure that what we decide on is comfortable for you. If I've learned one thing through the years, it's that if an idea doesn't fit with a teacher's style and classroom, it won't work. So please, be sure and tell me if any of the ideas we come up with are unrealistic, or don't fit with your classroom.

Consultee: I guess the most important issue for me is time. The kids do seatwork while I'm with a reading group, so I can't be running over to Sally to check on her work every few minutes. I'd disrupt the reading groups.

Consultant: OK, so an important aspect of devising a plan is that it can't involve much of your time.

Excerpt Two

Consultant: If we're seeing eye to eye here, a major concern for the bank is turnover in teller positions. Training is a considerable expense and even decreasing turnover in these positions by a small amount would save a lot of money. Plus, it's good for public relations if customers see familiar faces at the counter. Also, experienced tellers make less errors, so you've got another savings factor there.

Consultee: That about sums it up. Tellers have the highest turnover rate of any position at the bank.

Consultant: Good. I'm glad we have agreement on the problem. Now, what to do about it? Other banks have tried a number of ideas, such as longevity pay, increased flexibility in hours, more teller involvement in decision making about their jobs, contests, and team building experiences. But I need to have some ideas about what would be acceptable here and would fit your resources and management philosophy. Can you tell me a little bit about what you've considered in trying to address this problem in the past?

Consultee: We tried a contest where customers could nominate tellers who had done an exceptional job. We called it the "Teller of the Month." I didn't like the program. I didn't like the idea that only one teller could win. We weren't recognizing everyone that did a good job.

Consultant: Good. That gives me some ideas about what you want. You don't want a program that only lets one person get recognition or some kind of reward. But you do feel comfortable with a reward program?

Consultee: Yes, but we've really got limited funds for that kind of thing. Also, I'm not sure that a simplistic solution like that will get the results we want.

Consultant: It sounds like a program that involves more than just one facet would be acceptable to you. For example, we could work on having tellers feel that their jobs are more integral to the bank and also have some kind of incentive program. But you don't have a lot of money to play with. How do you feel about allowing employees extra time at lunch or breaks?

Consultee: That's an idea, or maybe even just trying to make breaks more pleasant. Our lounge is pretty dismal.

Some Practical Guidelines for Strategy Selection

We close this section by paraphrasing the guidelines offered by Zins and Erchul (*in press*) for selecting and implementing interventions in consultation. Although the original guidelines were formulated for school-based consultants, these general guidelines are useful in a variety of settings.

1. In general, implement positive intervention approaches before resorting to behavior suppression or reduction techniques.
2. Choose the least complex and intrusive intervention possible. Modifying existing practices rather than learning new skills is generally easier for consultees.
3. When a new skill must be learned by the consultee, design it to fit into current organizational structure and routines as much as possible.
4. Promote interventions that require less time, are not ecologically intrusive, and are seen by consultees as effective.
5. As a long-term strategy, help consultees access existing resources or develop new ones in their own organizations.
6. Focus intervention efforts on promoting change at the highest organizational level possible.

Implementation

In many ways plan implementation is the moment of truth in consultation. Most of the other stages of consultation involve only the consultant-consultee dyad, but this stage involves the enactment of an action plan in a complex environment. No matter how thorough strategy selection and planning have been, it is likely that the plan derived during consultation will be in need of adaptation and adjustment to meet unanticipated problems. For example, one consultant had worked for several weeks with a teacher to develop a token economy for her class. During implementation, the teacher contacted the consultant and was quite upset. Small plastic chips had been used as tokens, and one child had become quite adept at pilfering others' tokens without detection. The intervention ran smoothly after the consultant and consultee decided to switch to checks on name cards in place of tokens. In another instance, a consultant from a community mental health center had to revise a plan for collegial governance in a small religious order when the bishop vetoed the idea. Consultees should be aware that unanticipated problems may occur and that such problems are not unusual or a sign of failure.

Frequent contact between the consultee and consultant can help assure that a plan is implemented successfully. It also provides support to the consultee at a time when the extra effort and alteration in routines and habits involved in change may lead the consultee to abandon the plan (Zins & Erchul, *in press*). Some consultants have found that frequent telephone calls can effectively replace more time consuming face-to-face contacts at this stage.

Evaluation

For any procedure to be self-correcting, some indication of the match between desired and actual outcomes must be obtained. Within social science, the formal mechanism for this feedback is often termed evaluation. Two types of evaluation are important in consultation: formative evaluation and summative evaluation. *Formative evaluation* takes place during plan implementation; *summative evaluation* takes place after consultation has been completed.

Formative evaluation is often less formal than summative evaluation. Information is sought regarding how well the plan is working and whether adjustments must be made to the plan. One outcome of formative evaluation might be a decision to return to an earlier stage of consultation. The consultant and consultee might decide that the plan they had developed is unworkable and return to the strategy selection phase, or a consultee might decide that the original conceptualization of the problem as a lack of motivation on the part of the client was incorrect and that the client lacks the skills necessary to complete his or her work. In this case, the consultant and consultee might return to the problem definition stage.

Summative evaluation is generally more formal. Although one purpose of summative evaluation often is to provide corrective feedback, it is often associated with questions of overall effectiveness. What is important in summative evaluation depends on who desires the feedback. Consultees and organizations that hire a consultant will desire different information about consultation than consultants. Consultees are likely to be interested in the effectiveness of consultation to individual consultees and the overall organization, its benefits relative to its costs, and the satisfaction of consultees and clients. Consultants will be interested in these aspects of consultation, but may also desire additional feedback to help them understand processes or aspects of consultation that are of less interest to the consultee. For instance, was the consultant effective in establishing trust, transmitting an understanding of consultation to consultees, or working with particular types of consultees?

As Gallessich (1982) comments, many organizations may be resistant to evaluation of consultation interventions because of the cost and difficulty. However, by planning for evaluation early in the consultation process, by addressing issues of interest to both the consultant and consultee, and by defining goals of consultation precisely enough to allow measurement, information valuable to the consultant and consultee can often be gained through evaluation. Specific strategies for evaluation of consultation are discussed in depth in Chapter Seven.

Termination

Termination refers to the cessation of consultation. Although termination generally takes place when the consultee and consultant agree that the problem that prompted consultation has been resolved, earlier termination is also an option. Two major reasons for early termi-

nation are discussed in literature. Caplan (1970) discusses instances where a more direct intervention strategy may be mandated by the seriousness of the problem or the need to act quickly. For instance, a client who is threatening suicide may necessitate direct intervention by the consultant rather than consultative services. Gallessich (1982) discusses the possibility of early termination when consultation is not progressing. She comments that in some instances termination may serve as a stimulus to both the consultant and consultee to define their values and professional goals.

As discussed earlier, termination should be addressed early in consultation. Gallessich (1982) offers several additional guidelines for consultants to prevent termination difficulties. First, consultants may gradually transfer responsibilities to the consultees. This transfer of responsibility signals the consultant's exit and also prevents an abrupt change upon departure of the consultant that can be disruptive to consultees. Second, a disengagement period where the consultant reduces his or her involvement on a trial basis may give consultees a chance to see if the problem is resolved or if he or she can make needed changes without consultant input. Lastly, rituals, such as a summary conference, a request that the consultee fill out an evaluation form, or a formal review of a case, can help signal or remind consultees that the end of consultation is imminent.

Interpersonal Processes

To date, no comprehensive model of the interpersonal processes in consultation and their relation to different consultative stages has been proposed, although some models of consultation, such as the mental health and collaborative models, have emphasized the importance of interpersonal variables in consultation. The small amount of research that has been concerned with interpersonal processes in consultation reflects a variety of approaches and perspectives and often focuses on an isolated aspect of consultation (Meyers et al., 1979). In the present discussion, consultation is treated as a particular instance of the more general process of helping, and the model of helping developed by Carkhuff (Carkhuff, 1969a, 1969b, 1983; Carkhuff & Anthony, 1979; Carkhuff & Berenson, 1977) is extended to consultation. Although the application of this model to consultation has not been empirically validated, aspects of the model have been extended to consultation previously (Brown, Wyne, Blackburn & Powell, 1979; Conoley & Conoley, 1982; Meyers, 1981; Meyers et al., 1979), and both the relationship and problem-solving skills emphasized in the model have been related to consultation outcome (Bergan & Tombari, 1976; Maitland, Fine, & Tracy, 1985; Schowengerdt, Fine, & Poggio, 1976).

Overview of Carkhuff's Model of Helping

Carkhuff has proposed a generic model of helping that describes phases a helpee (person seeking assistance) progresses through in resolving a problem or achieving meaningful change. Also included in the model are helper (person providing assistance) actions that facilitate the helpee's progression through these phases.

In Carkhuff's model, providing assistance or information to a person will only be effective in bringing about change when the person (1) feels that the helper has understood the

problem, (2) perceives the need for action on his or her part, and (3) receives assistance in carrying out the desired change. Therefore, the effective helper not only has expertise in the particular content area in which he or she is offering assistance, but also has the interpersonal skills to facilitate action on the part of the helpee (Carkhuff, 1983).

Two types of interpersonal skills are important—responsive skills and initiating skills. Responsive skills include empathy, warmth, respect, and concreteness. Initiating skills include advanced levels of empathy and genuineness, as well as self disclosure, confrontation, and immediacy. The next section will define these terms and illustrate how they might be used in consultation. However, a brief overview of Carkhuff's phases of helping is provided here as an advanced organizer.

Figure 5.2 depicts helpee phases in resolving a problem and helper actions that facilitate the helpee's progression through these phases. Initially, a helpee must be willing to devote time and energy to change. He or she must recognize that an undesirable situation exists and believe that there is some possibility of resolving it. The helpee must also believe the helper is capable of providing some assistance and be willing to share his or her experiences with the helper. In this prehelping phase, the helper's role is to respond in a way that promotes involvement on the part of the helpee. The helper is polite and pleasant and listens carefully to the helpee. He or she tries to see the problem from the point of view of the helpee and withholds judgment.

These actions lead the helpee to feel "listened to" and accepted by the helper. In turn, the helpee feels free to examine the problem in depth. During this exploration phase, the helper's role is to reflect the content, feeling, and meaning of the helpee's statements, and to prompt the helpee to be specific about his or her concerns.

After the helpee has fully explored the problem, the helper uses initiating skills to assist the helpee in viewing the problem in a more objective manner (Egan, 1975) and to establish a direction for problem solving. In this stage, the helper continues to respond empathetically to the helpee, but also uses self disclosure, confrontation, and immediacy to assist the helpee in personalizing the problem or understanding what aspects of the problem are within his or her control. The helper also prompts the helpee to formulate specific goals based on the personalized problem definition.

In the final stage, acting, the helpee develops and carries out plans to achieve these goals. Here, at last, the content area skills of the helper become important. The helper

PHASES OF HELPING

	PRE-HELPING	I	II	III
HELPER SKILLS	Attending ———	Responding	Personalizing	Initiating
HELPEE LEARNING		Exploring	Understanding	Acting

assures that the helpee's plans are sound and assists the helpee in implementing them. Recycling occurs once the helpee has acted. The helper and helpee evaluate the results of the helpee's actions by recycling through the exploring, understanding and acting phases. They explore the results of the new course of action, develop new goals, or try new ways to achieve the original goals.

The preceding paragraphs provided only a brief overview of Carkhuff's model. In the following sections, Carkhuff's model is offered as a heuristic tool for understanding and discussing the role of consultant-consultee interaction in facilitating consultee problem solving. The discussion will be organized around three issues that reflect Carkhuff's model of helping: establishing the consultation relationship, facilitating consultee understanding of the problem, and facilitating action. For each of these topics, Carkhuff's model will be applied to consultation.

Establishing the Consultation Relationship

Consultation culminates in goal-directed action on the part of the consultee. In order for goal definition, strategy selection, and action to take place, the consultee first must be willing to commit time and energy to identifying and resolving the problem. The problem situation must be explored in sufficient depth that the consultant and consultee understand the nature of the problem and reach agreement regarding the aspects of the problem that can be addressed through consultation. These preconditions for effective action are facilitated through the establishment of a good working relationship between the consultant and consultee.

The consultant's function at this point is to use the responsive skills of warmth, empathy, respect, and concreteness to facilitate the establishment of this relationship. Warmth refers to skill in communicating to the consultee that the consultant cares for and is committed to the consultee. It is conveyed by paying attention to the consultee and clearly showing interest in what he or she has to say. Empathy, or accurate understanding, is communicated primarily through restatements of the consultee's verbalizations. By restating the consultee's concerns, the consultant shows that he or she has grasped the verbal and affective content the consultee is trying to convey. It is also important for the consultant to convey respect for the consultee by suspending judgment and communicating that the consultee is valued despite any perceived self-deficits.

Warmth, personal respect, and empathetic understanding also are communicated through the consultant's nonverbal behavior. Egan (1994) uses the acronym SOLER to describe the attending behaviors that communicate concern for and interest in the consultee:

> S—face the other person SQUARELY
> O—adopt an OPEN posture
> L—LEAN toward the other
> E—keep good EYE contact
> R—try to be "at home" or relatively RELAXED in the position

Finally, nonverbal and verbal demonstrations of warmth, personal respect, and empathetic understanding must be coupled with concreteness. In the early phases of consultation,

concreteness refers to skill in eliciting descriptions of specific experiences and feelings from the consultee rather than vague abstractions (Gazda, 1973).

To illustrate the foregoing ideas, let us consider a first-year junior high teacher who came to a consultant with some grave concerns about her teaching ability. Although the teacher discussed her problems very openly, it was still necessary to establish a basic relationship along the lines that Carkhuff describes. The consultant began simply by listening attentively and restating (empathic understanding), as is illustrated in the following excerpt.

T: I just became aware that you were working in a school this year as a consultant to teachers. Believe me, I could use some consultation or I'm going to need my own counselor full time.

C: Sounds like things aren't going well for you this year and you're kind of happy to have someone like me around.

T: Yeah . . . I'm a first-year teacher and to say the least things aren't going as planned. If they don't get better in a hurry I may go back to working in a bank.

C: At this point, things have already gone so badly you're beginning to think about getting out . . . going back to the bank?

T: Well, I really don't want to do that. What I want to do is teach. But I didn't know that schools could be such a zoo. The kids here are horrible.

C: You want to teach . . . but the kids are really getting to you.

(Later in the same session.)

T: There are times when I think I shouldn't be in this school. I feel so different.

C: How, specifically, do you feel different?

T: My ideas about teaching and my students seem to be different from other teachers in this school.

C: You feel a little odd because your views are different from the other teachers', but they are uniquely yours and that seems important to me.

T: Well I'm glad to hear you say that . . . I get the feeling that nobody else around here cares whether I have any opinions or not.

In the opening statements, the consultant responds empathetically to the consultee and merely listens. In response, the consultee continues talking, providing more information and bringing out another aspect of the problem, his or her disillusionment about teaching. In the later statements, the consultant uses concreteness to clarify the consultee's statements. Following the clarification, the consultant's demonstration of respect serves to increase consultee involvement and bolster the consultee's own self-respect.

At this point, the consultant's verbalizations have primarily served to establish a relationship between the consultant and consultee. By withholding judgment and reflecting

the content of the consultee's verbalizations, the consultee feels "listened to" and free to discuss his or her own concerns. But in later phases of helping, movement toward problem resolution becomes important. The relationship between the consultant and consultee changes—the consultant becomes more genuine in his or her own actions and uses responsive skills to foster consultee understanding of the problem.

Concepts from the Consultation Literature

Several authors within consultation have suggested that relationship-building skills play an important part in consultation (Brown et al., 1979; Conoley & Conoley, 1982; Gutkin & Curtis, 1990; Meyers, 1981). In one of the few research studies on this topic within consultation, Schowengerdt et al. (1976) found that the facilitative characteristics of school-based consultants accounted for a major portion (44 percent) of the variance in consultee satisfaction. The consultant who exhibited warmth, understanding, and empathy when interacting with the consultee was more likely to have had a significant impact. This finding was confirmed by Maitland et al. (1985), who also found that consultant facilitativeness was related to problem resolution in consultation.

Another concept that has been discussed in the context of establishing a consultative relationship is interpersonal or social power. Generally, a nonhierarchical relationship between the consultant and consultee is seen as one of the cornerstones of the consulting relationship (e.g., Caplan, 1970; Gutkin & Curtis, 1990; Meyers, Brent, Faherty, & Modafferi, 1993; Meyers et al., 1979) for several reasons. First, it assures the free exchange of ideas and opinions. When the consultee is hesitant to express his or her own views of the problem situation, is inhibited in suggesting how principles and ideas brought up by the consultant might apply in a particular situation, or does not share his or her reservations with the consultant, it is unlikely that an effective plan will be designed and carried out. Second, when the consultee takes an active role in understanding the problem and developing a solution, it is more likely that he or she will feel some ownership for the problem and its solution. By minimizing feelings of coercion through collaborative problem solving, the consultee is more likely to carry out whatever action plan is developed during consultation. Finally, active participation is seen as a means of increasing the probability that the consultee will generalize techniques used in consultation to similar situations in the future.

Despite the fact that the consultant has no supervisory or formal power over the consultee, other types of power have potential impact on the consulting relationship. The social bases of power proposed by French and Raven (1959) provide a useful framework for understanding how power and influence operate in the consulting relationship (Martin, 1978).

French and Raven (1959) identify five forms of social power that are operative in interpersonal relationships. These are reward power, coercive power, legitimate power, expert power, and referent power. *Reward power* refers to person B's perception that person A is capable of giving him or her access to desired or needed resources contingent on some desired behavior. *Coercive power* includes and extends beyond reward power and is based on the perception that person A can reward or punish B. *Legitimate power* is exercised when person B allows person A to influence him or her because of a belief by person B that person A has a legitimate right to control his or her actions. These three sources of power, reward power, coercive power, and legitimate power, form the basis for supervisory or line authority in our society (Martin, 1978). As such, they are not available to the consultant.

However, the remaining two sources of power, expert and referent power, as well as a third source of power, informational power (Raven, 1965), are potentially available to the consultant (Erchul, 1984).

Expert power is person B's perception that person A has certain knowledge or skills that are necessary for person B to accomplish his or her goals. *Referent power* is based on person B's perception that A possesses characteristics similar to B or that B would like to possess. When a consultant possesses referent power, the consultee identifies with the consultant and is more likely to internalize the consultant's beliefs, attitudes, and actions as his or her own. A final source of power that is also available to consultants is *informational power*. This source of power was added by Raven (1965) and is somewhat similar to expert power. Unlike expert power, informational power is not a characteristic of the person, but a characteristic of the information presented. When the consultant is able to offer information that is perceived as relevant by the consultee, regardless of whether or not the consultant is perceived as an expert, he or she gains additional influence.

Although he did not use French and Raven's conceptual framework, Caplan (1970) recognized that sources of power other than formal, supervisory power could be operative in consultation. In general, Caplan discussed these informal sources of power in terms of consultee perceptions of the consultant that were potential impediments to the coordinate, nonhierarchical relationship needed for successful consultation. For example, Caplan offered techniques for decreasing the influence of the consultant when the consultee showed undue deference or appeared to be trying to please the consultant. Caplan also maintained that consultants were to avoid giving precise, direct recommendations since such recommendations put the consultant in an expert, rather than coordinate, role. Chapter Two provides a more comprehensive discussion of Caplan's approach to establishing a coordinate relationship.

Caplan's techniques are based on the premise that control is largely unidirectional in the consulting relationship and that consultees will often assume a subservient role despite efforts by the consultant to establish a coordinate relationship. Equalizing power in the consultation relationship can only be achieved by decreasing the consultant's power. An alternate view of power within consultation is offered by Martin (1978) who suggests that power is bidirectional and that informal sources of power or influence are available and should be exercised by *both* the consultant and consultee. In this framework, the consultant is viewed as an expert in human behavior and as a result has access to information unavailable to the consultee. However, the consultee also has expert power because he or she is more familiar with the work setting and the client and has sole access to his or her own feelings about the problem situation and the acceptability of various intervention plans. Since all of these are important in understanding the problem and implementing a successful problem solution, the consultee can also be viewed as possessing expert and informational power. In addition, the consultee also may have accrued some referent power in his or her relationship with the consultant.

Within this framework, equalizing power does not necessarily mean that the consultant must take steps to reduce his or her power. An alternate means of equalizing power is making the consultee aware of his or her own expert power or developing the consulting relationship to increase consultee referent power. By acknowledging that consultees have sources of influence open to them, it becomes more acceptable for the consultant to exercise influence because these may be offset by consultee influence and the balance of power

maintained. Martin (1978) proposes that the optimal relationship between consultant and consultee is one in which referent and expert power are exerted equally by both the consultant and consultee.

The notion that both the consultant and consultee have sources of power or influence available to them within the consultative relationship does not mean that power issues can be ignored in consultation. As suggested by Caplan (1970), consultees may assume a deferential or lower status with regard to the consultant because of feelings of incompetency due to their request for assistance or to test the consultant's adherence to his or her claim of equal status. In addition, consultees may not be aware of their own sources of power and may therefore perceive the consultant as more powerful. Likewise, some consultants may be more comfortable in an expert role and be uncomfortable when consultees are reluctant to accept advice or interpretations. Power issues should be addressed at the outset of consultation through consultant explanations of consultation and role structuring. Consultants may want to remind consultees of their sources of power and remain sensitive to the balance of power throughout the course of consultation to assure that the consultee maintains an active role.

Facilitating Consultee Understanding

The issues discussed in the previous section were concerned with facilitating consultee involvement and exploration of the problem. But merely involving the consultee in consultation does not bring about change, as pointed out by Carkhuff and Berenson (1977):

> *Responding only to what is presented by the helpee is not enough. The helper must be able to organize the resulting helping exploration to give the helping process direction. More specifically, the helper must make the process goal directed. The helper's ability to appropriately* initiate *may be even more important than his or her ability to respond, in the sense that without initiating the helpee never gets to where he or she needs to be . . . The determination of goals concerning where the helpee needs or wants to be, and getting there, wait upon helper initiatives (p. 153).*

Once a basic relationship has been established with the consultee, the nature of consultant-consultee interaction changes. The consultant's verbalizations move the consultee toward understanding his or her degree of personal control and responsibility in the problem situation. A personalized understanding or definition of the problem is necessary if the consultee is to perceive a role for himself or herself in problem resolution. This point is particularly important in consultation. Because the problem involves a client, or third party, consultees may focus on the problem as it relates to the client, rather than focusing on the aspect of the problem that they can control. When the focus of problem exploration is on aspects of the problem the consultee cannot control and no connection is drawn between the actions of the consultee and problem resolution, it is unlikely the consultee will perceive a need for action.

To achieve this personalized understanding, a shift in focus takes place. Initially, consultant verbalizations reflect the consultee's frame of reference. Once a basic relationship has been established, the consultant helps the consultee to achieve a more objective view of the problem, one that suggests constructive action (Egan, 1975b). This change is accomplished through the consultant's use of the initiating skills of advanced accurate empathy,

---

Student Learning Activity 5.3

Consider the following two consultant responses to a consultee verbalization occurring early in the consultative relationship:

Consultee: This job is so stressful. I never imagined that managing a staff of seven could be so draining. Everyone has different agendas, no one seems to realize that I can't please everyone all the time.

Consultant One: It sounds like you feel a lot of pressure to keep everyone happy and no one seems to realize how hard it is.

Consultant Two: You know, just from talking to you for 10 minutes, I can see that you're not assertive enough and your employees have lost respect for you. I think one goal of our work together could be to help you become more assertive.

Within Carkhuff's framework, what type of response has Consultant One made? What errors has Consultant Two made? Why is Consultant One's response more likely to facilitate consultation?

---

facilitative genuineness, self-disclosure, confrontation, and immediacy (Carkhuff, 1983; Egan, 1975b) to stimulate further exploration by the consultee and help him or her see the larger picture. Also important in seeing the larger picture are summaries of what has been discussed in consultation by either the consultant or consultee.

With the introduction of facilitative genuineness, self-disclosure, confrontation, and immediacy, the consultant shares more of himself or herself as a person with the consultee. The consultant's feelings and concerns are disclosed to the consultee, hoping that this will lead to greater self-disclosure from the consultee. Early self-disclosures might simply be the consultant's attitudes and ideas that are germane to the consultee's situation. Later, genuineness involves responding authentically to the consultee in both a negative and positive manner (Carkhuff, 1969b). The following excerpts illustrate some of these ideas using the example of the junior high school teacher presented earlier.

Self-disclosure

T: I have some doubts about my ability to deal with eighth graders. They are much more complex than I ever suspected.

C: You are experiencing some of the same self-doubts that I and others have felt.

Later

T: Things just aren't what they should be. Schools aren't doing what they should be for students!

C: I get a little angry about the inadequacies of this school, too.

Genuineness, Excerpt One

T: I just want to pick up every kid that misbehaves and shake them until something comes loose. I actually hate some of those students.

C: Your anger turns into pure hate at times and you just want to get some of those kids, to really hurt them, but that doesn't seem like a very good idea to me . . . There must be a better way.

T: You're right, but the anger builds anyway and I do want to learn some ways of coping with the students.

Excerpt Two

T: We've talked three times now and things just aren't going as I had hoped. I'm disappointed.

C: You're feeling a little down because your situation hasn't cleared up as quickly as you would like. Actually, I think things have gone pretty well and that you are making good progress.

T: That surprises me. I thought you expected me to become a super teacher just by talking to me.

C: I'm sorry that I've conveyed that type of expectation.

Note that in the foregoing excerpts the consultant felt free to express his or her own feelings, both positive and negative. The initiating skill of confrontation requires that the consultant express ideas and opinions. Technically, a confrontation is an incident in which the consultant points out discrepancies between consultee verbalizations and behavior, underlying affect and cognitive content, or consultant and consultee experiences (Carkhuff, 1969b). Confrontation is used only when the consultant feels that it will lead the consultee to understand the problem more fully.

The following excerpts are examples of confrontations.

Confrontation, Excerpt One

C: We've been talking about your classroom for the past several sessions, and the last two times we talked about specific courses of action. On both occasions you have not taken any action and I am wondering what is going on.

T: Well to be honest, I'm scared to death to try some of the ideas. I'm afraid I'll fall on my face.

Excerpt Two

C: You've told me repeatedly that the parents in this school encourage their children to run wild, and that they don't care. My experiences have been quite the opposite. I have found most of the parents to be extremely cooperative.

T: (Defensively) Well, try talking to some that I have talked to and besides you don't have to deal with them like I do.

C: You got pretty uptight about what I said and you think I'm being unfair because my experiences are different.

T: That's right! (more calmly) I have to deal with them when there is some problem . . . I suppose you have to do that, too.

In addition to genuineness and confrontation, immediacy can be used to facilitate consultee understanding. *Immediacy* refers to the ability to discuss directly and openly with the consultee what is happening in the here-and-now of an interpersonal relationship (Egan, 1975b) and generally involves focusing on the inability of the consultee to communicate some aspects of his or her concerns. Carkhuff (1969b) views this inability as indicative of a difficulty that transcends the helping situation, relating to a deficiency in self-understanding and self-acceptance. However, he recommends that the problem be interpreted within the context of the helping relationship. The immediate relationship between the consultant and the consultee can be used to assist the consultee to perceive reality if the consultant can discern and focus upon the inability of the consultee to communicate adequately. The following excerpts help clarify the concept of immediacy.

Immediacy, Excerpt One

T: Well . . . I am sure you are going to think I'm silly, but I just can't get going before the second period and my first period class suffers.

C: You seem to be afraid of what I'll think about your inability to get started in the morning. Perhaps we should take a look at that.

Excerpt Two

T: I really do apologize for smoking. It's a nervous habit that I just can't seem to break.

C: That's the third time you've apologized after I assured you that it was perfectly OK to smoke. You seem awfully jumpy about my reaction to you.

Excerpt Three

T: I would like to tell you one personal thing about myself but . . . oh, forget it.

C: That's happened before. I am beginning to wonder if you trust me.

Immediacy, then, is focusing upon the consultant-consultee relationship in the hope of deepening the intensity of the relationship and facilitating self-understanding on the part of the consultee.

The final initiating skill is advanced accurate empathy. Like primary level empathy, the consultant still reflects the content of the consultee's verbalizations, but communicates a deeper understanding of the consultee's statements by expressing what is implied, summarizing material that is fragmented, and identifying themes. By making interpretations of the

consultee's statements, the consultant assists him or her in adopting a more objective and focused view of the problem and what action is needed.

This approach is demonstrated in the following excerpt.

C: Things haven't been going well for you this year and, in fact, they are extremely frustrating. Thus far in our session you've raised questions about your choice of a school, your skills in dealing with students, and underlying the whole thing has been your concern about your competency as a person in all areas.

T: That's right. You know it's all so overwhelming. Things just couldn't be worse. (sigh)

C: Things seem pretty bad now . . . hopeless.

T: Yeah, if I could just get on top of something, particularly my classroom.

C: So right now your classroom discipline seems to be the most important thing to you.

By summarizing and specifying the parameters of the situation, the consultant causes the teacher to focus upon the global nature of the problem. Then, out of this series of communications emerges a primary concern: classroom discipline. The consultee is now ready for goal setting, strategy selection, and action.

Concepts from the Consultation Literature

Consultant skills in assisting the consultee to see a role for himself or herself in resolving whatever problem is brought to consultation, although a critical part of consultation, have not been discussed extensively in the literature. However, the results of three studies (Bergan, Byrnes, & Kratochwill, 1979; Cleven & Gutkin, 1988; Tombari & Bergan, 1978) suggest that the content of consultant verbalizations can affect both the way that consultees conceptualize problems and their expectancies for solving problems.

Bergan and Tombari (1978) and Bergan, Byrnes, and Kratochwill (1979) found that when consultants focused on events and actions controllable by the consultee (for example, the client's behavior and environmental variables affecting it), consultees were more likely to focus on these aspects in their definition of the problem and see the problem as more likely to be solved. Cleven and Gutkin's (1988) study suggests that this effect can be enhanced when consultants make explicit references to the process they are using in assisting the consultee to define the problem. For example, a consultant working with a teacher concerned about an inattentive student might state, "In helping Robin, it's important that we specify very precisely the types of problems you are seeing in the classroom."

Facilitating Action

The skills emphasized in the two previous sections have focused primarily on involving the consultee and assisting him or her in "owning" the problem or seeing a need to act. Only when both of these conditions have been met is the consultee ready for action. At this time, the consultant continues to use responsive skills to maintain and deepen consultee involvement and understanding, but also uses skills in his or her particular content area to

assist the consultee in developing and implementing a workable solution to the problem (Carkhuff, 1983).

This process begins with assisting the consultee in defining his or her goal in objective and measurable terms and assuring that the goal is achievable (Carkhuff & Berenson, 1977). One way this task can be accomplished is to ask questions that prompt the consultee to focus on specific aspects of his or her goal, such as who, what, where, when, and how. Next, the consultant assists the consultee in exploring alternatives for reaching the goal by prompting the consultee for alternatives or suggesting alternatives when the consultee is unable to provide them. Finally, the consultant assists the consultee in choosing between alternatives on the basis of how each alternative fits with the consultee's values (Carkhuff & Anthony, 1979). This process is illustrated in the following interchange between a consultant and staff at a drug treatment center.

Consultant: We have pretty much agreed that the current program of treating offenders referred to the center just isn't getting the job done; the recidivism rate is just too high.

Staff Member One: Yeah! And we aren't doing a thing to prevent the problem in this community either. But given our mission, I suppose that prevention programs are out of the question.

Director: Perhaps not. But for now, let's focus on getting a more effective treatment program together.

Staff Member Two: That would be a big step. I get tired of seeing some of these people walk through the door. It's frustrating . . . just makes me think we are spinning our wheels.

Staff Member Three: We do have some successes though. I think our first job is to determine who benefits from what we're doing right now. I don't want to throw the baby out with the bath water.

Consultant: That's a good point! It's a good idea to retain what you are doing right and I agree that some people are being helped, but a lot aren't. Based upon the data we have collected, the younger offenders seem to be returning the most often. However, some of those over 21 are getting back into drug abuse and being sent here as well. Maybe the best plan of action is to work with one group or the other.

Director: Well, I opt for the younger group at this time. I think that there are some alternatives to our current individual and group therapy programs that may be helpful to this group, such as family therapy and working with school personnel.

Staff Member Two: I'd like to see us try to establish some support groups in the schools as well. I've found that a lot of the kids don't have many friends and they either use drugs and alcohol to be one of the gang or to escape the reality of their loneliness.

Consultant: There seems to be some consensus based upon the nodding heads that the younger group of offenders should be the target group, at least at first. That doesn't preclude focusing on the older group later, but I believe that you should take one group at a time. Now there is a matter of which path to take in reducing recidivism among the 16 to 21 year olds who come to the center. First, let's try to establish some realistic expectations about

how much this problem can be reduced and then select some alternatives for pursuing that objective. Two have already been suggested.

When a particular action plan has been selected, the consultant then assists the consultee in operationalizing the goal by developing steps to meet the goal. The consultant and consultee discuss each step and the consultant monitors the consultee to see that he or she fully understands each step and has the skills needed to complete it. This monitoring and adjustment of each step is accomplished by reviewing, rehearsing, and revising each step of the program with the consultee prior to implementation. At the completion of each step, "recycling" begins as the consultant again uses responsive skills to help the consultee assess the action taken.

Concepts from the Consultation Literature

This last set of skills described by Carkhuff is similar to the problem-solving skills included in several models of consultations. For instance, Kurpius (1978) includes problem definition, exploration of alternatives, and planning effective behavior change programs as skills for the consultant.

Bergan's (1977) model of behavioral consultation discusses in some detail how the consultant can assist the consultee in setting measurable, objective goals and developing a plan through questions and summary statements covering specific topic areas. Bergan and Tombari (1976), working within this model, have identified several factors that are related to facilitating consultee plan implementation. Using multiple regression, they examined the contribution of three general classes of consultant variables (consultant efficiency, flexibility in applying psychological principles, and interviewing skill) to the occurrence of problem identification, plan implementation, and problem solution in school-based behavioral consultation. The authors found that consultant variables had their greatest impact on the problem-solving process at the problem identification stage. Problem identification was more likely to occur with consultants who were efficient, that is, who had a small time lag between a request for assistance and the initial interview and who were flexible in applying psychological principles. Flexibility was determined by examining the range of plans formulated by consultants over all cases. Presumably, the consultant with a narrow set of intervention techniques, who fit the case to the technique, rather than fit the intervention technique to unique variables in the case, was less likely to be successful.

One indicator of interviewing skill, message control, also contributed significantly to problem identification. Message control was defined as the proportion of elicitors (generally questions) to emitters (or statements). It appeared that effective consultants used a higher rate of elicitors, which served to direct the consultee to various topics relevant to consultation.

The extent to which consultants should direct and structure consultative problem solving has emerged as one of the more controversial topics in recent consultation research and writing. Gutkin and Curtis (1990) maintain that consultants must be experts on how to go about solving problems and that "the major responsibility of the consultant during consultation is to maintain and direct the collaborative problem solving process" (Gutkin & Curtis, 1990, p. 585). In keeping with this view, Erchul and his colleagues (1987; Erchul & Chewning, 1990; Erchul & Schulte, 1990) have found that behavioral consultants tend to structure and control verbal interaction and that higher levels of structure and control of ver-

bal processes are associated with more positive perceptions of the consultant by consultees. Fuchs (Fuchs & Fuchs, 1989; Fuchs et al., 1990) also found that school-based behavioral consultation was more likely to lead to changes in target student behavior when prescriptive instructions were used to guide both consultant and consultee through the consultation process.

These findings seem to contradict the research pointing to the importance of interpersonal skills and support of the consultee in consultation (Hughes & DeForest, 1993; Schowengerdt et al., 1976). However, this contradiction is probably more apparent than real, because it assumes that a consultant must choose between structuring consultation and establishing a positive, supportive relationship with consultee (Erchul, 1992). In fact, the research by Maitland et al. (1985) suggests the extent to which consultants use a problem-solving process that integrates behavioral problem solving *and* interpersonal facilitativeness predicts consultee satisfaction and professional growth, as well as problem resolution.

Summary

Several authors have described consultation as an activity comprised of particular stages (Meade et al., 1982). Though these descriptions of consultation vary in terms of the number and order of stages, they all conceptualize consultation within a problem-solving framework. Drawing from several descriptions of the stages of consultation, the activities of consultation include: (1) entry into an organization, (2) initiation of a consulting relationship, (3) assessment, (4) problem definition, (5) strategy selection, (6) strategy implementation, (7) evaluation, and (8) termination.

Another means of understanding the "how" of consultation is to examine the interaction of the consultant and consultee and its role in facilitating consultee action. No comprehensive model of interpersonal processes in consultation has been proposed. Therefore, Carkhuff's (1969a, 1969b, 1983) model of helping, which emphasizes the role of relationship building, initiating skills, and problem-solving skills in facilitating constructive action, was proposed as a general framework for understanding and interpreting consultant-consultee interaction and its role in consultation outcome.

Tips for the Practitioner

1. Ask experienced consultants to share materials, such as letters of agreement, intervention plans, and evaluation materials with you. It is generally easier to modify materials that have been successful to fit your situation than to devise new materials on your own.
2. If you are new and inexperienced at consultation, using treatment manuals such as the ones developed in the Fuchs' studies (Fuchs, Fuchs, Reeder, Gilman, Fernstrom, Bahr, & Moore, 1989) to guide consultation problem solving may increase the effectiveness of your intervention plans.

3. Ask consultees if you can record your interviews. Then transcribe them and look for examples of relationship building, facilitating action, and problem solving in your interactions.

4. Be sure to ask consultees what they have tried previously when consulting. Proposing an already-tried intervention is often frustrating to the consultee.

Review Questions

1. How does the concept of stages of consultation differ from the concept of stages in child development?

2. What is contracting? Why is it important in consultation?

3. How can direct service by the consultant facilitate entry?

4. What special difficulties does the internal consultant face when trying to insure that the administrative head of an organization and staff members understand consultation?

5. What are the three major domains of assessment? Give an example of a problem that might be presented to you in consultation and list several factors within each domain that might be relevant in understanding the problem and developing a solution.

6. Distinguish between formative and summative evaluation.

7. Briefly describe the three phases of Carkhuff's model of helping.

8. Describe the nonverbal and verbal components of relationship building. Why is relationship building important to the subsequent problem solving and action components of consultation?

9. Give two views of the role of social power in consultation.

10. What is a personalized understanding of a consultation problem?

11. Develop an action plan for a problem you might deal with as a consultant, specifying a goal and steps to meet that goal.

References

Bergan, J. R. (1977). *Behavioral consultation*. Columbus, OH: Charles Merrill.

Bergan, J. R., Byrnes, I. M., & Kratochwill, T. R. (1979). Effects of behavioral and medical models of consultation on teacher expectancies and instruction of a hypothetical child. *Journal of School Psychology, 17*, 307–316.

Bergan, J. R., & Kratochwill, T. R. (1990). *Behavioral consultation and therapy*. New York: Plenum.

Bergan, J. R., & Neumann, A. J. (1980). The identification of resources and constraints influencing plan design in consultation. *Journal of School Psychology, 18*, 317–323.

Bergan, J. R., & Tombari, M. L. (1975). The analysis of verbal interactions occurring during consultation. *Journal of School Psychology, 13*, 209–226.

Bergan, J. R., & Tombari, M. L. (1976). Consultant skill and efficiency and the implementation and out-

comes of consultation. *Journal of School Psychology*, *14*, 3–13.

Brown, D., Wyne, M. D., Blackburn, J. E., & Powell, W. C. (1979). *Consultation*. Boston: Allyn & Bacon.

Caplan, G. (1970). *The theory and practice of mental health consultation*. New York: Basic Books.

Caplan, G., & Caplan, R. B. (1993). *Mental health consultation and collaboration*. San Francisco: Jossey-Bass.

Carkhuff, R. R. (1969a). *Helping and human relations, Vol. 1: Selection and training*. New York: Holt, Rinehart & Winston.

Carkhuff, R. R. (1969b). *Helping and human relations, Vol. 2: Practice and research*. New York: Holt, Rinehart & Winston.

Carkhuff, R. R. (1983). *The art of helping* (5th ed.) Amherst, MA: Human Resource Development Press.

Carkhuff, R. R., & Anthony, W. A. (1979). *The skills of helping*. Amherst, MA: Human Resource Development Press.

Carkhuff, R. R., & Berenson, B. G. (1977). *Beyond counseling and therapy* (2nd ed.). New York: Holt, Rinehart & Winston.

Cleven, C. A., & Gutkin, T. B. (1988). Cognitive modeling of consultation processes: A means for improving consultees' problem definition skills. *Journal of School Psychology*, *26*, 379–389.

Conoley, J. C., & Conoley, C. W. (1982). *School consultation*. New York: Pergamon.

Conoley, C. W., Conoley, J. C., Ivey, D. C., & Scheel, M. J. (1991). Enhancing consultation by matching the consultee's perspective. *Journal of Counseling and Development*, *69*, 546–549.

Curtis, M. J., & Watson, K. L. (1980). Changes in consultee problem clarification skills following consultation. *Journal of School Psychology*, *18*, 210–221.

DeForest, P. A., & Hughes, J. N. (1992). Effect of teacher involvement and teacher self-efficacy on ratings of consultant effectiveness and intervention acceptability. *Journal of Educational and Psychological Consultation*, *3*, 301–316.

Dunn, W. N. (1981). *Public policy analysis: An introduction*. Englewood Cliffs, NJ: Prentice-Hall.

Egan, G. (1975). *The skilled helper*. Monterey, CA: Brooks/Cole.

Egan, G. (1994). *The skilled helper* (5th ed.). Pacific Grove, CA: Brooks/Cole.

Elliott, S. N. (1988). Acceptability of behavioral treatments: Review of variables that influence treatment selection. *Professional Psychology: Research and Practice*, *19*, 68–80.

Elliott, S. N., Witt, J. C., Galvin, G. A., & Moe, G. L. (1986). Children's involvement in intervention selection: Acceptability of interventions for misbehaving peers. *Professional Psychology: Research and Practice*, *17*, 235–241.

Erchul, W. P. (1984). *A relational communication analysis of control in the consultant-consultee dyad across three interviews*. Unpublished doctoral dissertation, University of Texas.

Erchul, W. P. (1987). A relational communication analysis of control in school consultation. *Professional School Psychology*, *2*, 113–124.

Erchul, W. P. (1992). On dominance, cooperation, teamwork, and collaboration in school-based consultation. *Journal of Educational and Psychological Consultation*, *3*, 363–366.

Erchul, W. P., & Chewning, T. G. (1990). Behavioral consultation from a request-centered relational communication perspective. *School Psychology Quarterly*, *5*, 1–20.

Erchul, W. P., & Schulte, A. C. (1990). The coding of consultation verbalizations: How much is enough? *School Psychology Quarterly*, *5*, 256–264.

Fine, M. J., Grantham, V. L., & Wright, J. G. (1979). Personal variables that facilitate or impede consultation. *Psychology in the Schools*, *16*, 533–539.

French, J. R. P., & Raven, B. H. (1959). The bases of social power. In D. Cartwright (Ed.), *Studies in social power* (pp. 150–167). Ann Arbor, MI: University of Michigan Institute of Social Research.

Frentz, C., & Kelley, M. L. (1986). Parents' acceptance of reductive treatment methods: The influence of problem severity and perception of child behavior. *Behavior Therapy*, *17*, 75–81.

Fuchs, D., & Fuchs, L. (1989). Exploring effective and efficient prereferral interventions: A component analysis of behavioral consultation. *School Psychology Review*, *28*, 260–283.

Fuchs, D., Fuchs, L. S., Bahr, M. W., Fernstrom, P., & Stecker, P. M. (1990). Prereferral intervention: A prescriptive approach. *Exceptional Children*, *56*, 493–513.

Fuchs, D., Fuchs, L., Reeder, P., Gilman, S., Fernstrom, P., Bahr, M., & Moore, P. (1989). *Mainstream*

assistance teams: A handbook on prereferral intervention. Nashville, TN: Department of Special Education, Peabody College of Vanderbilt University.

Gallessich, J. (1982). *The profession and practice of consultation.* San Francisco: Jossey-Bass.

Gaupp, P. G. (1966). Authority, influence and control in consultation. *Community Mental Health Journal, 2,* 205–210.

Gazda, G. M. (1973). *Human relations development: A manual for educators.* Boston: Allyn & Bacon.

Gibb, J. K. (1959). The role of the consultant. *Journal of Social Issues, 2,* 1–4.

Gutkin, T B., & Curtis, M. J. (1982). School-based consultation: Theory and techniques. In C. R. Reynolds & T. B. Gutkin (Eds.), *The handbook of school psychology* (pp. 796–828). New York: John Wiley & Sons.

Gutkin, T. B. (1993). Moving from behavioral to ecobehavioral consultation: What's in a name? *Journal of Educational and Psychological Consultation, 4,* 95–99.

Gutkin, T. B., & Curtis, M. J. (1990). School-based consultation: Theory, techniques, and research. In T. B. Gutkin & C. R. Reynolds (Eds.), *The handbook of school psychology* (pp. 577–611). New York: Wiley.

Hansen, J. C., Himes, B. S., & Meier, S. (1990). *Consultation: Concepts and practices.* Englewood Cliffs, NJ: Prentice-Hall.

Havelock, R. G. (1973). *The change agent's guide to innovation in education.* Englewood Cliffs, NJ: Educational Technology Publications.

Hughes, J. N., & DeForest, P. A. (1993). Consultant directiveness and support as predictors of consultation outcomes. *Journal of School Psychology, 31,* 355–373.

Hyatt, S. P., & Tingstrom, D. H. (1993). Consultants' use of jargon during intervention presentation: An evaluation of presentation modality and type of intervention. *School Psychology Quarterly, 8,* 99–109.

Ivey, A. E. (1983). *Intentional interviewing and counseling.* Monterey, CA: Brooks/Cole.

Katz, D, & Kahn, R. L. (1978). *The social psychology of organizations.* New York: John Wiley & Sons.

Kazdin, A. E. (1984). *Behavior modification in applied settings* (3rd ed.). Homewood, IL: Dorsey.

Kazdin, A. E, French, N. H., & Sherick, R. B. (1981). Acceptability of alternative treatments for chil-

dren: Evaluations by inpatient children, parents, and staff. *Journal of Consulting and Clinical Psychology, 49,* 900–907.

Kelly, J. G. (1993). Gerald Caplan's paradigm: Bridging psychotherapy and public health practice. In W. P. Erchul (Ed.), *Consultation in community, school, and organizational practice: Gerald Caplan's contributions to professional psychology* (pp. 75–85). Washington, DC: Taylor & Francis.

Kurpius, D. (1978). Consultation theory and process: An integrated model. *Personnel and Guidance Journal, 56,* 18–21.

Lippitt, G. & Lippitt, R. (1978). *The consulting process in action.* San Diego, CA: University Associates.

Maitland, R. E., Fine, M. J., & Tracy, D. B. (1985). The effects of an interpersonally based problem-solving process on consultation outcomes. *Journal of School Psychology, 23,* 337–345.

Martens, B. K., Peterson, R. L., Witt, J. C., & Cirone, S. (1986). Teacher perceptions of school-based interventions. *Exceptional Children, 53,* 213–223.

Martin, R. (1978). Expert and referent power: A framework for understanding and maximizing consultation effectiveness. *Journal of School Psychology, 16,* 49–55.

McMahon, R. J., & Forehand, R. L. (1983). Consumer satisfaction in behavioral treatment of children: Types, issues, and recommendations. *Behavior Therapy, 14,* 209–225.

Meade, C. J., Hamilton, M. K., & Yuen, R. K. (1982). Consultation research: The time has come, the walrus said. *Counseling Psychologist, 10,* 39–51.

Meyers, J. (1981). Mental health consultation. In J. C. Conoley (Ed.), *Consultation in schools* (pp. 35–58). New York: Academic Press.

Meyers, J., Brent, D., Faherty, E., & Modafferi, C. (1993). Caplan's contributions to the practice of psychology in the schools. In W. P. Erchul (Ed.), *Consultation in community, school, and organizational practice: Gerald Caplan's contributions to professional psychology* (pp. 99–122). Washington, DC: Taylor & Francis.

Meyers, J., Parsons, R. D., & Martin, R. (1979). *Mental health consultation in the schools.* San Francisco: Jossey-Bass.

Parsons, R. D., & Meyers, J. (1984). *Developing consultation skills.* San Francisco: Jossey-Bass.

Pipes, R. B. (1981). Consulting in organizations: The entry problem. In J. C. Conoley (Ed.). *Consulta-*

tions in schools (pp. 11–33). New York: Academic Press.

Raiffia, H. (1968). *Decision analysis*. Reading, MA: Addison-Wesley.

Raven, B. H. (1965). Social influence and power. In I. D. Steiner & M. Fishbein (Eds.), *Current studies in social psychology* (pp. 371–382). New York: Holt, Rinehart & Winston.

Reimers, T. M., Wacker, D. P., & Koeppl, G. (1987). Acceptability of behavioral treatments: A review of the literature. *School Psychology Review, 16*, 212–227.

Reynolds, C. R., Gutkin, T. B., Elliott, S. N., & Witt, J. C. (1984). *School psychology: Essentials of theory and practice*. New York: John Wiley & Sons.

Rosenfield, S. A. (1987). *Instructional consultation*. Hillsdale, NJ: Erlbaum.

Schowengerdt, R. V., Fine, M. J., & Poggio, J. P. (1976). An examination of some bases of teacher satisfaction with school psychological services. *Psychology in the Schools, 13*, 269–275.

Shapiro, E. S. (1987). Intervention research methodology in school psychology. *School Psychology Review, 16*, 290–305.

Shapiro, E. S., & Goldberg, R. (1986). A comparison of group contingencies for increasing spelling performance among sixth grade students. *School Psychology Review, 15*, 546–557.

Tombari, M. L. & Bergan, J. R. (1978). Consultant cues and teacher verbalizations, judgments, and expectancies concerning children's adjustment problems. *Journal of School Psychology, 16*, 212–219.

Watzlawick, P., Weakland, J., & Fisch, R. (1974). *Change*. New York: W. W. Norton.

Witt, J. C., & Elliott, S. N. (1985). Acceptability of classroom management strategies. In T. R. Kratochwill (Ed.), *Advances in school psychology* (pp. 251–288). Hillsdale, NJ: Erlbaum.

Witt, J. C., Elliott, S. N., & Martens, B. K. (1984). Acceptability of behavioral interventions used in classrooms: The influence of amount of teacher time, severity of behavior problem, and type of intervention. *Behavioral Disorders, 9*, 95–104.

Witt, J. C., Moe, G., Gutkin, T. B., & Andrews, L. (1984). The effect of saying the same thing in different ways: The problem of language and jargon in school-based consultation. *Journal of School Psychology, 22*, 361–367.

Zins, J. E., & Erchul, W. P. (in press). Best practices in school consultation. In A. Thomas & J. Grimes (Eds.), *Best practices in school psychology—III*. Washington, DC: National Association of School Psychologists.

Consultation Stages and Processes II

Goals of the Chapter

The primary goal of this chapter is to present five variables that pose special complications for consultation. The second goal is to provide some suggestions for diagnosing and dealing with problems in these areas whenever they arise.

Chapter Preview

1. The various roles of the consultant will be discussed and a scheme for classifying them developed.
2. The strengths and weaknesses of the internal and external consultant will be presented. An argument will be advanced that internal and external consultants usually do not fall into dichotomous categories.
3. Several models of resistance will be presented.
4. A brief discussion of the cross cultural consultation process will be presented.
5. Organizational variables that may influence the consultation process will be identified and means for offsetting their influence discussed where possible.

In the foregoing chapter, the consultation process was presented and illustrated. In this chapter and the one that follows some special process concerns will be discussed. One of these concerns deals with the roles that consultants fill during the consultation process. Unlike therapy or teaching, which require the therapist or educator to function in a single role, consultation demands that the consultant function within a number of roles over the

course of consultation. The skilled consultant must be able to discern when each of the various roles is appropriate and act accordingly. As has been stressed since the outset, the relationship of the consultant to the organization, whether internal or external, is also an important variable within the consultation process and as such will be discussed in some detail. Resistance to consultation will also be discussed since recognizing and managing resistance is a key element in consultation, whether it be individual or organizational. Finally, environmental factors and their influence on consultation are considered.

Roles of the Consultant

Most authorities recognize that consultants do not fill a single role. Some, like Caplan (1970), have not discussed these roles directly, but have alluded to them in their writings. For example, in client-centered consultation the consultant assumes the role of expert. Gallessich (1982) posited that consultants fill a limited number of roles such as technical adviser or healer. A more common approach is to depict the consultant as filling multiple roles (Blake & Mouton, 1976; Lippitt & Lippitt, 1986). Stryker's (1982) position on roles is, if not illustrative, interesting. He identified seven basic roles that a consultant may fill: (1) doctor, (2) marketer, (3) scientist, (4) detective, (5) technical expert, (6) broker, and (7) sanitary engineer.

Roles within consultation may be tied to two different variables: the model chosen by the consultant and the stage of the consultation. For example, an individual operating within Caplan's framework doing case consultation would assume the roles of doctor (diagnose, prescribe) and technical expert. Schein's (1969, 1989) process consultant is certainly acting as a scientist and a detective in that he or she is using scientific and observational procedures to identify the problem (culprit). In other models a consultant might very well be involved in linking persons to ideas or persons to persons and thus fill the broker role. Cleaning up messy problems (sanitary engineer) is also not an uncommon role for consultants.

Although certain models of consultation dictate certain roles, consultants assume various roles regardless of the model followed. Within the collaborative model, the consultant would definitely assume the scientist's role in the assessment and evaluation stages, might serve as technical assistant in the intervention design stage, and would at times be a marketer and broker. Certainly all consultants occasionally fill the roles of doctor and technical expert, particularly when there is an emergency situation.

Lippitt and Lippitt (1986) have developed a helpful model for conceptualizing the roles that consultants may fill. Their approach to defining consultant roles is tied to the degree of activity of the consultant. For example, the objective observer-reflector is somewhat analogous to Schein's (1969, 1989) process consultant, in that it is a somewhat passive role. In this role, the consultant observes basic processes engaged in by the consultees and asks questions designed to help consultees develop an understanding of their own problems. The consultant is least directive in this role and is minimally involved in providing technical assistance.

The process counselor, also similar in some ways to Schein's process consultant, observes key organizational processes as well as engages in joint diagnosis of process prob-

lems confronted by the organization. The consultant acting in this role also collects data about the organizational processes through means such as surveys and observations and shares them with the consultee. As can be seen, the activity level and utilization of technical expertise increases when the consultant functioning as process counselor is compared to the one functioning as observer-reflector.

The fact finder, a third role identified by Lippitt and Lippitt, must be able to develop methods of generating data and providing feedback to the consultee. Five basic approaches are utilized in the fact-finding process: interviews, questionnaires, observations, analysis of records and documents, and the administration and analysis of appropriate tests. This role deviates from the first two described in that the consultant interprets the data collected and attempts to stimulate thinking about its meaning. This is one step removed from the role of identifier of alternatives and resource linker, which requires more activity and use of technical expertise. In this role the consultant is an active participant in problem identification and problem resolution. The joint problem solver, another of Lippitt and Lippitt's roles, is a full partner in problem identification and in the task of solving the problem.

The trainer/educator brings a set of skills to the consultation process that involve both the technical expertise related to the problem being experienced by the consultee and the ability to impart that knowledge to the consultee. This role is closely akin to another role, that of information specialist in which the consultant acts as a technical expert to the consultee. Lippitt and Lippitt (1986) suggest that no consultant should rely upon this role of information specialist exclusively because the organization's problem-solving skills could become dysfunctional and the quality of problem solving reduced if the consultant becomes the problem solver for the organization. The likelihood that a consultant has the knowledge needed to act as decision maker for others is remote.

The final role identified by Lippitt and Lippitt (1986) is that of advocate. They posit that the consultant may be either a process or a content advocate, that is, the consultant may promote either an approach or a method of problem solving. In the role of content advocate the consultant encourages the consultee to accept a certain set of goals, presumably goals predicated on the values held by the consultant. As was noted in Chapter One, advocacy and consultation are somewhat antithetical. However, it is probably impossible for consultants to remain totally value free in their work and some degree of advocacy regarding both content and process may be inevitable. One risk in this role is pushing one's values onto a consultee. As Abidin (1982) forcefully indicates, the "zenith of stupidity" in consultation may be pushing one's own ideas on a reluctant consultee.

Earlier, Margullies and Raia (1972) provided a useful scheme for conceptualizing the roles of the consultants, one that is somewhat analogous to the model just presented. Their position is that the role assumed by the consultant depends upon whether they are oriented to task (technical expert) or process (process facilitator).

It is clear at this juncture that the potential roles of a consultant can be classified in various ways. The most obvious one is on a content/process dimension. The second is the degree to which the consultant "intrudes" into the change process, which Lippitt and Lippitt characterize as an activity dimension, although it is actually more than activity. It is a dimension that reflects, to some degree, the extent to which consultants introject their own values into consultation. Process consultants focus on those areas most valued—human processes in organizations—yet are less intrusive than other consultants. On the other hand,

the technical expert is often employed to apply not only technical expertise but a set of values to the problem-solving process. Consultants may also be hired because of their views on organizational processes and asked to help implement their values system within the processes of the organization. Similarly, consultants to individuals, such as teachers, may be contacted because of their technical expertise on learning disabilities or their views on instructional processes. They may also be asked to function as process observers to "help me get a handle on things."

Therefore, the conclusion reached here is that a number of basic consultant roles can be identified that relate to the process/content and intrusiveness dimensions. These are:

1. Process Observer	Values owned by consultant, but focus is on helping consultee identify key process variables.
2. Process Collaborator	Values owned by consultant and consultee. Focus on process variables. Emphasis on joint problem identification and problem resolution.
3. Content Collaborator	Values owned by consultant and consultee. Focus on content or technology. Emphasis upon joint problem identification and problem resolution.
4. Content/Process Collaborator	Values owned by consultant and consultee. Both process and content viewed as potentially important. Focus on joint problem identification and resolution.
5. Process Expert	Values of consultant dominant. Emphasis upon diagnosing and resolving process problems by the consultant.
6. Content Expert	Values of consultant dominant. Emphasis upon diagnosing and resolving the technical problems by the consultant.
7. Content/Process Expert	Values of consultant dominant. Emphasis on diagnosing and resolving process and content problems by the consultant.

Role Taking

The orientation to the process and content and expected involvement in problem solving will, in large part, determine the role the consultant assumes. However, the final determination of the consultant's role is influenced by a number of factors. Lippitt and Lippitt (1986) suggest that the nature of the consultation contract, the values of the consultant and consultee, the skills of the consultant, the locus of the consultant (internal versus external), and what has worked in the past for the consultant influence role taking. To this list should be added the degree of crisis involved in the presenting problem because an immediate crisis may force either the consultant or consultee to abandon traditional role expectations

(Bergan, 1977; Bergan & Kratochwill, 1990). It is also true that the consultation model adopted by the consultant will influence the roles assumed.

Contracts, whether explicit or implicit, establish a set of expectations about the functioning of the consultant and consultee. If an external consultant is employed to provide case consultation to the staff of a community mental health center, the explicit expectation, unless otherwise specified, is that the consultation will provide technical assistance in dealing with certain types of cases. However, consultation contracts are rarely this specific and thus role definitions may evolve out of the process rather than being specified in advance.

The values of the consultee and consultant are also important considerations in role selection. What does the consultee believe is needed? How does the consultant perceive the consultation process? What are the basic beliefs of both about help giving and help receiving? The interaction of the consultant and consultee will probably lead to mutual role expectations if consultation is successful. In some instances this agreement will differ from that established in the contracting stage. Thus, consultants must be willing to alter role expectations as the consultation process progresses.

The skills of consultants may limit the roles they can assume. School psychologists or school counselors who are asked to function as process consultants in their respective schools may not have been thoroughly grounded in either the theory or techniques of process consultation. Human resource consultants often find that they lack technical expertise in areas such as cost accounting, production processes, or marketing strategies. These deficits may preclude their functioning as an expert in these areas and may dictate that they assume other roles in the consultation process, such as resource linker. It is unethical for consultants to assume roles for which they are unqualified, but it is typical for consultants to identify the source of the needed expertise and develop the linkages that will result in problem solving.

As detailed in a subsequent section, a host of environmental variables related to institutional history, norms, and personnel will tend to preclude the consultant from assuming certain types of roles and make other roles attractive. For example, autocratically oriented institutions may expect consultants to fill certain types of roles, such as technical assistant, while democratically oriented institutions may be more inclined toward process observer/facilitator types of roles.

Consultants may develop a preference for certain roles (for example, process collaborator) simply because they have worked in previous situations (Lippitt & Lippitt, 1986). However, stereotyping of the consultees and their situations should be avoided unless the consultant rather carefully discerns whether or not the circumstances that resulted in an effective consultation in a prior situation exist in the current setting.

The degree to which crisis exists will undoubtedly determine the extent to which a consultant assumes a particular role. The physician who is called in to consult on a case involving a patient who has severe burns over most of his body cannot afford the luxury of collaborative approaches. Neither can the psychologist who is asked to provide consultation regarding a potentially suicidal client. In both situations, the consultant is likely to assume the role of a content expert. However, few situations within human resource agencies dictate this role.

As discussed in earlier chapters, certain models of consultation dictate role taking. Bergan and Kratochwill's (1990) behavioral model requires that the consultant control the

---

Student Learning Activity 6.1

What follows is a list of situations into which a consultant might enter. Select from the list of roles a consultant might fill in the right hand column and match them to the situations.

Situations

a. A residential treatment home for adolescents who are educably, mentally retarded has had a number of runaways.
b. A third grade classroom is out of control.
c. Staff morale at a mental health center has fallen to an all time low.
d. The agency director confides that the staff is very anxious about employment of a consultant.
e. A teacher expresses a need for help, but wants to do things her way.
f. The outreach program at a university counseling center has ceased to function.
g. Tests used in the placement of students in a community college aren't doing the job.

Roles

1. Process Observer
2. Process Collaborator
3. Content Collaborator
4. Content/Process Collaborator
5. Process Expert
6. Content Expert
7. Content/Process Expert

---

topics discussed in consultation and be an expert in the application of learning theory principles, which places the consultant squarely in the role of process/content expert. Caplan's client-centered case consultation dictates that the consultant function as a technical expert. And, as has been mentioned throughout, Schein's (1969, 1989) process consultants suspend their values while focusing on process, thus functioning in the process observer role.

Finally, it is quite likely that human resource workers will be involved in many roles as they function as consultants. It is difficult to envision a consultant who does not shift roles as he or she moves from consultation to consultation and consultee to consultee. For the most part, role taking in consultation grows out of a dynamic set of circumstances involving the consultant, the consultee, the client, and the environment in which the consultation occurs.

Resistance

Wickstrom and Witt (1993) suggest that there are at least five explanations of resistance that they define as "anything that impedes problem solving or plan implementation and ultimately problem resolution" (p. 160). One of these explanations grew out of Caplan's theory of mental health consultation, and although Wickstrom and Witt assert that Caplan (1970) never used the term *resistance* in his writing, both they and Mendoza (1993) agree that the concept was implicit in his writing. Caplan did suggest that when resistance to plan implementation is met the consultant needs to be aware of four sources of this resistance: realistic perceptions that the plan might not work, lack of information about how to implement the plan, inadequate skills to implement the plan, and resistance based on lack of objectivity (Mendoza, 1993). Except for lack of objectivity, the consultant deals

with resistance by reconceptualizing the plan or linking the consultee to resources from which they can gain more information or skills. When there is lack of objectivity, which is most often caused by theme interference according to Caplan (1970), the consultant uses the strategies discussed in Chapter Two to deal with the resistance. The primary focus of the consultant's efforts to reduce resistance is to correct the faulty logic system by using indirect strategies. These strategies may focus solely on the client in the verbal exchange by inserting statements that are contrary to the consultees' beliefs (while not being confrontive), by using parables that indirectly take issue with the consultees' beliefs, and by indirect modeling by discussing the client and possible outcomes that are at odds with the consultees' expectations.

Second (as was discussed in Chapter Four), organizational development consultants tend to focus on organizational or systemic variables that may impede the change process. To be sure, individual barriers such as fear of the unknown, loss of status, or loss of self-esteem play a role in resistance. However, the culture of the organization, including the values, the characteristic ways of behaving, the myths about success in the organization, and the socialization, are viewed as major contributors to resistance. Not unexpectedly, organizational development consultants focus on leadership, communication, and cultural changes as ways of overcoming resistance.

Third, Gross (1980) defined resistance to change in the consultation process "as a normal coping behavior having as its purpose the preservation of the organism rather than the obstruction of change" (p. 1). Gross (1978, 1980) sees faulty consulting relationships as giving rise to resistance. He also suggests that there are relatively easy means of diagnosing the presence of resistance. If the consultee blames others such as parents or administrators for the problem, tries to suggest that the client's problem is insoluble because it falls into a specific category, becomes dependent upon the consultant, thus relinquishing responsibility for the problem-solving process, or becomes defensive and tries to justify strategies that have been used with the client, resistance is occurring.

Not unexpectedly, Gross (1980) suggests that, to overcome resistance, one should begin by examining the consulting relationship. This perusal should begin with consultants' analyzing their own behavior and attitudes. Consultants who blame consultees for clients' problems may be inadvertently communicating that belief to the consultees, thus giving rise to defensiveness. Consultants who experience resistance should also take a hard look at their own consulting style and techniques to determine whether they are functioning in the most effective manner (Wickstrom & Witt, 1993).

Gross (1980), like Caplan (1970), recommends against direct, confrontive approaches to dealing with consultee resistance, at least until the precise source of the resistance is identified. It is suggested by the authors that if confrontation is to be used to deal with resistance that it be "soft confrontation." Soft confrontation comes in the form of questions instead of statements. Contrast the following approaches.

A: It seems to me that you are saying that because the child has an attention deficit disorder the situation is hopeless.

B: Is it possible that you think that because the child has been labeled as having an attention deficit disorder you feel it is an impossible situation?

Fourth, resistance can be conceptualized as being based upon the loss of rewards or the anticipation of unpleasant or aversive outcomes. This conceptualization can be attributed to Bergan (1977, 1985) and the problem-solving literature according to Wickstrom and Witt (1993). This model of resistance is the classic behavioral model and relates to changes in the consultee's reward system that may occur if the consultee changes his/her functioning. Wickstrom and Witt suggest that in order to overcome resistance the consultant must understand the antecedents of the consultee's behavior, the consequences of current behavior, and the possible outcomes if the consultee alters her/his functioning. They also suggest the consultant needs to have control over some of the contingencies if resistance is to be dealt with effectively.

Fifth, Wickstrom and Witt (1993) identify psychological reactance, the reaction of people to experiences that take away their freedom to behave as they want in specific areas such as the work setting (Brehm, 1966). People react to this abridgement of their "freedom" either aggressively or through passive-aggressive means. The intent of both of these approaches is to maintain the status quo. Intuitively psychological reactance makes sense as a source of at least some of the resistance that consultants experience. Changes in organizations inevitably result in modifying the manner in which people in those organizations behave. Consultation with individuals such as teachers may have the same result. Probably the best approach to avoiding psychological reactance is to establish a co-equal relationship, adopt a collaborative decision-making style, and always recognize that the consultee has the power to reject any and all portions of the consultant's recommendations.

In summary, when taking all of the conceptualizations of resistance together it seems clear that resistance can be the result of normal reactions to change as Brehm (1966) and Gross (1980) suggest, psychological deficits as Caplan (1970) suggests, the fear of the consequences of the change as Bergan (1977, 1985) has posited, or systemic variables as a number of organizational development specialists (e.g., Schein, 1989) have suggested. The consultant's job is to minimize resistance to enhance the likelihood of change.

Factors That Increase Resistance

While it is incumbent upon the consultant to recognize and deal with resistance that stems from psychological deficits, resistance arising from either threats to role competence or concerns about needs being met can be anticipated and prevented to some degree. The following factors appear to stimulate "normal" resistance and should thus be avoided or taken into consideration during the process of consultation.

Ambiguity
Randolph and Graun (1988) suggest that at times consultees may request counseling or therapy or that there may be incongruence between the expectations of the consultee and the consultant. One possible explanation for both of these occurrences is that insufficient structure has been introduced into the consultation process with the result being that the consultee does not fully understand the nature of the process. Ambiguity can be avoided by carefully reviewing consultant-consultee roles and the goals of consultation at the outset and revisiting these occasionally as the process continues.

Overwork

Consultants sometimes forget that their consultees are involved in a variety of activities and either take too much of their time or design interventions that require great amounts of work. In either case, the result may be resistance simply because consultation has resulted in role overload. By careful scheduling and the use of the least time consuming interventions, resistance can be reduced.

The question is, how can one determine when resistance stems from psychological deficits and when it is the normal process of maintaining one's equilibrium in the face of perceived threats? Certainly one indicator that resistance grows out of psychological deficits is when either bias or self-confidence problems persist in the face of objective data that contradicts the bias or when successful experiences do not ameliorate self-confidence problems. However, a more general rule of thumb relates to the degree to which there is a discrepancy between "objective reality" and the consultee's subjective perceptions of the situation that exists. Zaltman and Duncan (1977) suggest that selective perception is one indication of resistance in the consultation process. However, it is the degree to which this occurs and its persistence that provides the clue to its source. A consultee that persists in his claim that premature termination of minority counseling clients is due to their lack of motivation would be exhibiting perceptual difficulties. So would a consultee/teacher that blamed her out-of-control classroom solely on lack of administrative support.

Complexity of the Intervention

Lin and Zaltman (1973) suggested that the more complex the intervention the more likely it is that resistance will occur in consultees. Complex interventions are more difficult to communicate and to implement. Kast and Rosenzweig (1974) tied resistance to the ability of change agents to accurately communicate the nature of the interventions to consultees. Havelock (1973) linked increased workload to the same problem. It may well be that when complex programs are used as interventions in consultation, concerns about role competency increase because the interventions are not fully understood and the time required to learn and implement them is great, thus lowering the consultee's effectiveness temporarily. Both situations could create performance anxiety.

Tradition or Habit

Individuals, groups, and organizations develop traditions or habitual ways of functioning. For the most part these traditions develop because the practice is both comfortable and successful. They may also be maintained even when they are no longer successful because of a concern that new practices may worsen matters (Kaufman, 1971). New approaches threaten tradition and call for changes in habitual ways of behaving. Changes in traditional patterns of functioning apparently create ambiguity and fear related to role competence.

Sunk Costs

Sunk costs is a business term used to denote time, energy, and money required to establish existing practices or programs (Kast & Rosenzweig, 1974). An analogous term for individuals is psychic costs (Kaufman, 1971). A suggestion that change occur, particularly when psychic or sunk costs are high, will probably result in resistance. More than one consultant has been confronted by the statement, "We spent hundreds of hours developing our

current approach and now you want to change it." Sunk costs and tradition are to some degree interrelated as is the first construct introduced, complexity of intervention. However, resistance growing out of sunk costs and tradition may be the positive force identified by Watson (1967) and Chin (1976), that is, a force related to the equilibrium of the system. It may also be related to job/role complexity.

Upsetting the Power or Status Balance

Loss of perceived or real status by an individual or group will inevitably cause resistance in consultation. Loss of status may occur because an individual or individuals actually lose power or prestige because of an organizational change. For example, one school district took their deans of students out of the administrative category and placed them in the pupil personnel services category, thus reducing their actual power. Changes in job titles (for example, educational assessment specialist to school psychologist) may mean no actual job change, but may result in perceptions of a change in status.

Power shifts can also occur because of perceived and real losses in expertise. Many organizations have installed computer assisted systems ranging from test scoring services and computer assisted counseling to complex scheduling systems for institutions of higher learning. Practitioners who had, or could quickly develop, the expertise associated with these innovations gained in status while those who did not possess them lost status and/or power. Certainly, concerns about role competency and having needs met arise whenever status and power changes occur.

To summarize briefly, two situations seem to raise normal resistance in consultation: introducing novelty and need competition. Both raise concerns about role competency (Gross, 1980). In some instances, these concerns have a legitimate basis and thus are indicators that the suggested changes are inappropriate. In other cases, they grow more out of concern for self than maintaining the organization or solving the problem.

Overcoming Resistance

Although resistance is viewed as a positive process by which consultees cope with changes growing out of consultation, it is nevertheless the case that one objective of the consultant must be to overcome or at least to reduce resistance. Although it is possible in many situations to coerce the consultee into conformity by enlisting the aid of authority figures, this violates the spirit and intent of consultation. Rather, it is incumbent upon the consultant to find positive means of reducing resistance.

Reducing the Threat

Consultation should be planned and conducted in a manner that minimizes threat. Unquestionably the most often recommended procedure for reducing threat is through collaboration where the consultant and consultee are co-equals (e.g., Firestone, 1977; Klein, 1976; Lippitt, 1982). Firestone (1977) adds a cautionary note, however. Involvement is not enough! Consultees must be permitted to participate as full partners in the entire process including the choice of strategies for ameliorating problems or the outcome will be heightened resistance.

Gross (1980) also suggests that the consultant must be prepared to work through all the aspects of consultation that arouse the threat to competence. Communicating support for the consultee and being receptive to the consultee's ideas are key elements in dealing with the threat. However, he also indicates that once consultants identify the source of the resistance they may need to confront the consultee with the difficulty. The outcome of the "working through" process should be change in the consultee's perceptions of the situations that aroused the threat (Gross, 1980).

Support from status leaders and informal leaders has also been viewed as a means of reducing threat (Gray, 1984; Huse, 1980; Lippitt, 1982). The process of change produces ambiguity. Will I be more or less valued if I adopt a new procedure or attitudes? Will I be as successful? Reassurance from leaders that things will be "alright" can provide the support necessary to have consultees persevere in the face of ambiguity.

Other common sense approaches such as open communication (Gray, 1984) and providing training to provide the skills needed in the change process (Kast & Rosenzweig, 1974) can be useful means of reducing threat and thus resistance. There are undoubtedly others. What is essential is that the consultant take all possible steps to reduce any temporary feeling of loss of competence that may occur.

Developing Positive Expectations

Positive expectations grow out of the consultee's perception that, once an innovation is adopted, the identified problem will either be eliminated or reduced. In other words, the alternative approach to the current situation must have a perceived advantage to the current situation (Lin & Zaltman, 1973). How can this perception be developed? It may come in those situations where a highly credible consultant generates an alternative that is immediately acceptable by the consultee. Most consultations are rarely this simple.

Developing positive expectations is done in a number of ways. One useful way utilized by the authors is to have consultees visit individuals, groups, or organizations who have had similar concerns but have adopted new ways of coping with them. These visitations can both illustrate the problems involved in changing and prepare the consultee for these problems to some degree. More important, consultees will see people who have gained the skills necessary to cope with a problematic situation similar to that which they are experiencing.

Reports of research and evaluation outcomes, reading case studies, and attending presentations dealing with the current problems can all be used to develop expectations that change will result in desired outcomes. Regardless of the technique utilized, at some point a particular consultee must begin to believe that change will produce the desired results. If this expectation does not develop, the consultee is likely to end up in hopeless frustration.

Incentives

If incentives are offered to consultees to make incentive changes (for example, from individual to group therapy) then incentives are one way of developing positive expectations and would rightly be placed in the foregoing section. However, in this context we are talking of providing incentives to people who participate in consultation. One school district has added one item to its evaluation check list for teachers: makes use of available consultation sources. Incentives such as this can encourage initiating and continued involvement

---

Student Learning Activity 6.2

After several sessions the following conversation occurred between a consultant and consultee.

Consultant: How did the intervention go this week?

Consultee: About the same I guess. I really don't think that it's going to work. I have followed every suggestion you have made to the letter. I'm beginning to think that we are never going to improve this situation.

Consultant: Don't give up. I have several other tricks up my sleeve.

Tell how the consultant has inadvertently contributed to the consultee's concerns about maintaining his or her competence.

---

in consultation. Other types of incentives can also be offered that encourage consultees to participate in consultation. Providing released time to complete needed training programs is one form of incentive. So is recognition through formal communications organs such as newsletters. Individuals, groups, or subsystems that have completed successful consultation can be highlighted in featured news stories. Individual recognition can also serve as an incentive. Supervisors should make it a point to recognize successful involvement in consultations in their day-to-day associations. Through these formal and informal mechanisms organizations can clearly communicate that involvement with available consultants is a valued activity within the organization.

Establish a Clear Contract
This point will not be belabored since it has been discussed elsewhere. However, the clarity of the consultation contract should be reflected in the congruence of consultant-consultee expectations about consultation (Kurpius, Fuqua, & Rozecki, 1993). The greater the clarity of expectations, the lower the consultee resistance should be.

Reduce the Consultee's Effort
Sensitivity to the consultee's schedule and workload must pervade the consultant's attitudes. This sensitivity should translate operationally to consultation sessions that correspond to the consultee's schedule and to consultation activities that do not result in role overload.

Internal versus External Consultants

Before the issues regarding the locus of the consultant are addressed, it should be noted that there are times when consultants may have to consciously consider whether they are functioning internally or externally or, as Alpert and Silverstein (1985) suggest, somewhere on the continuum between the two. For example, school psychologists are employed by school districts partially to provide consulting services, but they are often not assigned to a particular building. Traditionally, school psychologists functioning in this manner have been viewed as internal consultants because they are paid by the school district. However, most school psychologists/consultants realize that their status may vary as they function in vari-

ous schools within the educational system. Counselors and counseling psychologists working in college counseling centers have a similar problem when they become involved as consultants with housing officials, career planning and placement workers, and other personnel within the college or university. The point here is a simple one: Actual employment on a full-time basis may not be the only variable that determines whether a professional is functioning as an internal or external consultant. The perceptions of the consultee are also important in this regard. These perceptions are probably shaped by the consultant's identity with the situation in which the consultation occurs, feelings of territoriality, and the consultant's and consultee's feelings regarding the internal-external division (Alpert & Silverstein, 1985).

Technically "an external consultant is administratively and legally independent of the organization for which he (sic) works" (Kubr, 1978, p. 12). Perhaps the key word in the foregoing sentence is "technically," since external consultants, particularly those who work within an organization for a long period of time, may begin to take on some of the same characteristics of the internal consultant. However, the constructs of internality and externality have real meaning within the consulting process and it is up to the consultants to identify where they are on the internal-external (I-E) continuum.

Lippitt and Lippitt (1986) provide an interesting and useful summary of the relative advantages of the internal and external consultants. How a particular consultant fares in each of these areas can be an indicator of how he or she is viewed on the I-E continuum. A summary of the advantages and disadvantages is presented in Table 6.1.

From Lippitt and Lippitt's (1986) point of view, the major advantages of internal consultants is their proximity to the problem, their access to data both in the problem identification and evaluation stages, and their ability to make judgments about the potential for change in the system. External consultants are viewed as being accorded more status, freer to make demands upon personnel (particularly authority figures), having a broader perspective, and arousing less defensiveness generally.

Steele (1982) has provided some support, albeit non-empirical, for the Lippitt and Lippitt position regarding the internal consultant. Steele notes that internal consultants are often confronted with situations where they have no legitimate power and thus must rely upon personal influence and power derived from expertise as the basis for their functioning. Additionally, there are few performance measures by which consultants can be judged, there are conflicting demands upon their time, and, as already noted, they often have less credibility than outside consultants. To Steele's list should be added the fact that most human resource consultants provide other services such as assessment, counseling, therapy, and supervision. The result of all of these factors, according to Steele, is role conflict and ambiguity.

Internal consultants limit their own effectiveness in a number of ways. For example, Steele (1982) recommends that internal consultants begin to consciously define their functioning within an organization in order to maximize their effectiveness. When one's expertise is spread too thin, there may be little input in the planning process and thus less influence. Certain consultants also limit their effectiveness by engaging in certain behavior patterns. Making it difficult to schedule meetings, being unable to perceive the perceptions of the consultee about the time needed to complete a consultation, and assuming inappropriate authority are examples of these patterns.

TABLE 6.1 Advantages and Disadvantages of Being an Internal and an External Consultant

Stage	Advantages Internal	Disadvantages Internal	Advantages External	Disadvantages External
Entry/Early	1. More aware of problem 2. Better prepared to clarify problem because of experience	1. Harder for peers to admit need for help 2. May cause defensiveness 3. Defensiveness may hinder establishing collaborative relationship 4. May stereotype people because of experience in organization	1. Easier to share problem with outsider 2. Accord more expertise 3. Can openly test readiness for change 4. Better able to determine resources available for change	1. Less actual knowledge (e.g., history)
Entry/Contract Setting	1. Better able to assess feasibility of consultation	1. Individuals may be hesitant to enter into contracts because of concern about withdrawing from them 2. Less able to make demands if immediate superior involved	1. Brings greater perspective	
Assessment/ Diagnosis	1. Closer to data flow 2. Familiar with internal data sources		1. May be better able to get commitment for evaluation	1. Dependent upon insiders for information
Goal Setting	(No differences identified)			
Intervention	1. More aware of potential consultee(s) 2. Better able to discern linkages to be established	1. Less able to involve power figures	1. Better able make demands on power figures 2. More leverage generally regarding participation	
Evaluation	1. Better able to assess outcomes on a continuous basis	1. Consultees may "hide" data because of defensiveness		

Student Learning Activity 6.3

Examine Table 6.1, which is abstracted from Lippitt & Lippitt's (1986) work. Do you agree with each of the conclusions they have reached about the relative advantages and disadvantages of the internal consultant? Place a (/) by those you agree with and an (X) by those you disagree with.

Coping with role ambiguity can enhance one's effectiveness as an internal consultant but it requires a host of actions. Role definitions that legitimize consultation are one useful means of clarifying the consultant's role, although they will not solve the problem totally. Separating consultants from other employees and managers in distance and perhaps formally through organizational redefinition can give consultants more status and remove them from the situation of having to consult with superiors. This redefinition also allows consultants to have input into the consultative planning process as well. Finally, defining workloads more realistically can reduce the demands upon consultants' time and thus keep them from spreading their expertise too thin.

Stylistic concerns that hinder the functioning of the internal consultant are more easily managed. Establishing a time perspective similar to that of the consultee regarding the length of the consultation makes good common sense as does arranging one's own schedule to meet that of the consultee. Assuming inappropriate authority is always to be avoided as well.

In terms of formal definitions of internal and external consultants, it is easy to distinguish between the two, but in reality the distinction may not be so simple, as has been shown. A school counselor assigned to a single school is an internal consultant. A clinical psychologist who works with the police department in riot control as a part of his or her responsibilities in a mental health center is serving as an external consultant. But what of the earlier mentioned school psychologist who works out of the central administrative offices of the school district or the counseling psychologist who works out of a counseling center on a university campus? Are they internal or external consultants when they work with other parts of the organization that employs them? Quite simply, they are both.

A counseling psychologist who works with a residence hall staff may not be accorded the same status that an external consultant would be, but would not be placed in the situation of consulting with a superior, could probably withdraw from consultation with relative ease should the consultation not progress as expected, and would probably not raise the defensiveness that Lippitt and Lippitt (1986) think is a likely companion to consultation between a consultee and an internal consultant. The best advice that can be tendered to consultants in these roles is to make few assumptions about the influence of your location. Rather, try to discern how you are being perceived as the consultation progresses.

Cross-Cultural Consultation

The paucity of empirical literature dealing with cross-cultural consultation suggests that this area has not received serious consideration in the field. However, literature dealing with cross-cultural helping relationships such as counseling and therapy indicates that similar

ethnic and socioeconomic backgrounds lead to great exploration in the early stages of therapy (Carkhuff & Pierce, 1975) and that dissimilar cultural backgrounds may lead to premature termination (Sue, 1977) and negative feelings toward therapy and the therapist (Sager, Brayboy, & Waxenburg, 1972). Therefore, consultants working in cross-cultural situations should consider that cultural variations between the consultant and consultee may raise barriers to the successful conclusion of consultation and act accordingly.

Models of Cross-Cultural Consultation

Two authors, Pinto (1981) and Gibbs (1980), have offered models of cross-cultural consultation that may be useful. Since Gibbs's model focuses on differences in African American and white consultees, it will be discussed in Chapter Eight. Pinto's model, which focuses more on the general parameters of the consultation process, is presented here. Pinto makes two assumptions. The first is that consultants come to a consultation with an explicit set of technologies and strategies regarding consultation, that is, a mental health consultation approach, as well as an espoused view of the cross-cultural consultee. The second assumption is that the consultant holds a set of implicit values and perceptions regarding consultation and the culturally different consultee. The latter, according to Pinto, is the actual or in-use perspective of the consultant and may vary greatly from the explicit or espoused point of view presented by the consultant. To be more specific, according to Pinto, consultants' values and norms (in-use perspective) and the model of consultation they have adopted will govern their consultation behavior.

Pinto's (1981) position is that successful consultation requires the consultant to be culturally empathic. To some degree, cultural empathy requires a rational understanding of cultural differences. It also requires that the consultant appreciate the culture of consultees, view the problem as they do, and vary both style and techniques to the cultural perspective of the consultee.

Pinto (1981) has identified four cross-cultural consultation styles, only one of which is effective. In the first style, *Self-Centered Anti-Adaptive*, consultants implicitly view the culture of the consultee as less developed and therefore inferior. The consultant's inability to adapt to the cross-cultural context of the consultee renders him or her incapable of devising workable strategies for helping the consultee.

In the *Technique-Centered Non-Adaptive* style, consultants are able to explicitly voice a congruence between their position and that of the consultee and are implicitly more congruent than the persons exhibiting the Self-Centered Anti-Adaptive style. Consultants employing the Technique-Centered Non-Adaptive style are able to be culturally empathic, but because they are not aware of the need for adaptation of their techniques to meet the cultural variations of the consultee, they are ineffective. The approach of these consultants is to use the techniques employed in their own culture and, because the techniques are not adapted to the cross-cultural situation, they fail.

In the *Client-Centered Adaptive* style consultants recognize the cultural variations of their consultees, recognize that these variations differ from their own values and norms, and adapt to the particular demands of the situation. As a result, the techniques and technologies employed in consultation are geared to the values and norms of the consultee and are more likely to be effective.

In the fourth style, *Contract-Centered Flexible*, consultants explicitly honor the terms of the contract established at the outset without regard to the unique needs of the consultee. In this style consultants suspend their own judgment. Thus, professional opinions and perceptions, cultural context, and models of consultation become irrelevant. The result is that solutions to consultee problems that result from the consultation may not fit the cultural perspective into which they must be placed. Pinto portrays this model as the antithesis of the Technique-Centered Non-Adaptive model of cross-cultural consultation.

The essence of Pinto's (1981) position is that effective cross-cultural consultants have (1) awareness of their own personal values, (2) a well-developed awareness of their personal consultation paradigm, (3) cultural empathy, and (4) the ability to make appropriate adaptations according to the needs of the consultee.

Organizational Variables and the Consultation Process

The setting in which a consultation takes place greatly affects the consultation process (Illbeck & Zins, 1993). For example, consultants working with organizations with little turnover, high morale, and adequate personnel and fiscal resources can expect to face very different issues than those who work with an organization with high turnover, budgetary problems, and an overworked consultee. However, no comprehensive model relating system, resource, and personnel variables has yet been set forth. The content of this section, therefore, is based largely on suppositions drawn from systems thinking, some authoritative thinking in the consultation field, and a modicum of research on this issue (Sarason, 1982; Huse, 1980; Chin & Benne, 1976). Some of the commentaries available in the literature regarding the problems of applying behavior modification techniques in natural settings without regard to systems variables also stimulated some of the thinking found in this section (e.g., Abidin, 1982; Reppucci & Saunders, 1974). However, none of these sources attempts to describe the intrusion of organizational variables into the consultation process per se.

Conoley (1981) and Sarason (1982) have each provided a partial listing of organizational characteristics that are intervening variables in the life of an organization and thus the consultation process. These can be divided into *extra system variables*, such as legislatures, local governmental bodies, political and economic climate, unions, advocacy groups, accrediting bodies, and existing laws, and *intrasystem variables*. The latter group includes the power structure, the overall characteristics of the people involved, the normative structure of the organization, role clarity, decision-making patterns, and communications systems.

Accrediting bodies influence a variety of organizations including training programs, hospitals, counseling centers, public schools, and colleges and universities. Accrediting organizations set forth regulations regarding qualification of staff, physical facilities, and administrative procedures. They may also influence variables such as the size and diversity of the library, the qualifications and geographic origin of students, the demographic characteristics of students in the case of training programs, or the manner in which services are delivered in the case of hospitals or counseling centers. Often consultants are told at the outset that these programs, policies, or procedures are untouchable because they are required for certification or accreditation. This inability to change existing policies or practices is

often the source of problems. For example, a number of teacher preparation institutions have attempted to ignore the accreditation standards of the National Council for the Accreditation of Teacher Education only to find that their graduates were hampered in the certification and employment process. Unaccredited hospitals are ineligible to receive certain payments including those from Medicare. Consultants working within institutions operating under the auspices of accrediting agencies would be well advised to determine the impact of the agency regulations upon individual and organization behavior prior to initiating consultation.

Union agreements influence an organization and the individuals in it in much the same way as accrediting bodies, although the influence is much more likely to be felt at the level of the individual worker. For example, many consultants have been frustrated in their efforts by the seniority rules included in many contracts. Tenure laws in public schools and universities have a similar impact. This is particularly problematic in situations such as public schools and civil service agencies when principals or other managers attain tenure and are virtually guaranteed a position regardless of how they perform on the job.

For the most part, accrediting standards, union rules, and tenure laws are relatively well-known influences and can therefore be anticipated by the consultant and consultee. However, there are more subtle external factors that are just as influential but much more difficult to anticipate. Delicate racial/ethnic relationships may suddenly present themselves during the course of a consultation, particularly when public institutions are the settings for consultation. More than one consultation has been disrupted because those in authority positions informed the consultant and consultee that a certain individual's approach cannot be altered because of a real or presumed concern within an ethnic or racial group. Political power blocks provide similar problems.

Institutional norms loom as one of the most potent of the internal variables that will intervene in the consultation. Norms are implicit standards that regulate to some degree the behavior of the members of a particular group. An obvious indicator of norms is the manner in which employees, students, or other organizational members dress. Unfortunately, not all organizational norms are as easy to discern as the "dress code."

Norms exist in most institutions and are evident in a variety of functions including communication patterns, interaction with peers and superiors, standards of performance, and a host of other variables. Of these, normatively based perceptions regarding performance appear to pose the greatest problem for the consultant. For example, if the norm has developed that Fridays after one o'clock are to be "happy hours" for the employees, productivity and quality of product will suffer. A norm that dictates that students pass whether they have learned the subject matter or not has developed in some public schools; this influences both teacher and student behavior. Some correctional agencies have abandoned rehabilitation programs and reverted to being custodial institutions, or, to use a more popular term, warehousing. The internal consultant is particularly at risk in these kinds of situations because consultees may very well be acculturated with the result being that their view of the situation follows the "party line." The external consultant may be frustrated because the consultee seems unwilling or unable to deal with the problems that are presented. Finally, a client, such as a student in the aforementioned school, may not respond to the efforts of a single teacher because implicit communications within the school support the notion that effort is not needed to succeed.

Norms regarding communication patterns can also present problems for a consultant. For example, most bureaucratic organizations like schools and many businesses expect communication to flow through the formal chain of command, an expectation that is rarely realized. However, if a norm develops that significant figures such as principals or agency heads are routinely bypassed by their subordinates, these principals or agency heads are cut off from much needed information about the working of the organization that they supposedly direct. These patterns must be altered in order to restore authentic communication.

The power structure has been identified by many as the key to change in any institution. This structure can be divided into two components: formal and informal. The formal power structure consists of those designated individuals vested with coercive/reward power. The principal, an agency head, a dean, and a plan manager are all formal power authority figures. As was stated earlier, these authority figures need to endorse and continuously reinforce change efforts if these are to be successful (Beer & Spector, 1993). A prior requirement is that they endorse the concept of consultation and reinforce participation in it (see Chapter Four).

The informal power structure is to a large degree related to the normative structure. It is discussed here as a separate entity because it can be and often is as influential as the status leaders in determining the success of consultation. The informal power structure consists of an individual or, more likely, a group of individuals who have acquired the ability to influence others because of their expertise, tenure in the position, control of a key process, or some external factor such as their social position in the community. Secretaries acquire power because they control, to some degree, access to status leaders. Very proficient teachers, clinicians, and other workers also acquire power because of their ability to function in the work setting. Particularly in the case of the latter group, these proficient workers become role senders. That is, they establish norms regarding organizational performance. If consultation is not an "appropriate" role for the counseling psychologist who heads the Employee Assistance Program, resistance to consultation may occur. Or if consultation with an individual not greatly influenced by the informal power structure requires the assistance of those who are a part of that structure, the consultant and consultee may not be able to tap into the resources they need. For example, a school psychologist finds that other teachers will not cooperate in helping a consultee who has largely ignored the normative structure in the school.

Lack of clarity in organizational goals has confounded consultation in many instances (Morasky, 1982; Sarason, 1982). These problems perhaps arise more often in consultation within public schools primarily because goals are often ill defined and may shift as the political winds variously place pressure on the schools to stress fundamentals, prepare individuals for the labor market, drop humanistic education because of its "godless nature," and so forth. However, consultants in public schools are not the only ones to run aground in the shoals of goal ambiguity. Most human resource agencies have a number of goals, some of which have not been articulated clearly, but more often the goals of the agency have not been clearly prioritized. Another problem is that resource expenditures may not follow stated goals, a problem that often exists when an agency places a high priority on prevention of crime, problem pregnancies, mental health problems, or family violence. It is a truism that primary prevention efforts are not supported to the same degree that secondary and tertiary prevention efforts are by most agencies.

Morasky (1982) recommends that the place to begin in organizational consultation is in goals clarification. This could be paraphrased to include all types of consultations whether they be aimed at individuals, groups, subsystems, or the total system. "What are the goals of the organization and how do these influence the consultant and the consultee?" is the question to be asked and answered.

Role clarity may impinge upon both the consultant and consultee. As was mentioned earlier, internal consultants may be particularly susceptible to ambiguity regarding their roles if they have assignments other than consultation. Some managers, division heads, principals, and others in authority positions are jealous of their prerogatives in the area of leadership and change, and see themselves as the "consultant." In these situations, the consultant is viewed as usurping the role of the status leader, and consultation as a function becomes problematic. In other instances, the status leader may hold only a few areas sacred (for example, personnel relations), but may not communicate this well. Consultants need, in so far as is possible, to clarify these territorial problems prior to beginning consultation.

External consultants who carefully define their roles may be less inclined to encounter problems of role ambiguity until, as it often does, the presenting problem shifts to broader areas. At this juncture, role redefinition is required.

Consultees are often concerned about violating their role boundaries as a consultation continues. It is probably true that the greater the specialization within an agency, the greater the likelihood that this problem will arise (Sarason, 1982). Whenever a concern arises about consultee role, the consultant and consultee should clarify the concern by seeking input from the agency head and others whose role boundaries might be violated prior to proceeding.

The time commitment required in a particular occupational role as well as the job description will influence the extent of involvement by a consultee and may influence the model of consultation utilized by a consultant. For example, job descriptions of personnel employed in many human services agencies allow a great deal of control over one's time. In other cases, the description specifies extensive time commitment to the job, thus limiting the amount of time available for consultation. Secondary school teachers are often given only one free period per day and that is supposed to be devoted to class preparation. Understandably, consultation is difficult to initiate. In these situations, the consultant will have to consider the time required by various consultation models and roles and choose accordingly. In some instances, job descriptions limit the extent to which consultees can alter their functioning, and the focus of the consultation may have to shift to the program or organizational level prior to working with individuals.

The characteristics of the consultee also influence the nature of consultation. This topic will be considered in detail in Chapter Eight.

The following lists are a summary of external and internal organizational variables that influence consultation.

External Variables

1. Accrediting bodies
2. Union agreements
3. Legislation

Student Learning Activity 6.4

Examine the categories of organizational variables identified in the list just above. Then match the type of organizational problem to the consultant and con- sultee statements that follow. *A problem may have more than one source.*

Situation One   ***Probable Source of Problem***

Consultant: We've been considering two or three potential solutions to reorganizing this unit so that the patients will receive better services.

_____

Consultee: (Response one) I'm just not sure where we should go next. Neither of us may have the authority to carry out the changes we have been discussing.

_____

Consultee: (Response two) I'm just not sure any of the ideas we've generated would fly in our community.

_____

Consultee: (Response three) You know that we are going to catch a bunch of flak from everyone involved in this effort even though there is tacit agreement that something thing has to be done.

_____

Situation Two

Consultant: The handicapped students in this classroom just aren't getting what they need. We have both agreed on that.

_____

Consultee: (Response one) Yes, we have. But you know we really prefer the self-contained classroom to this new mainstream approach.

_____

Consultee: (Response two) Yes, we have. And I know that there is a lot of pressure to do something from the outside, but our principal thinks that the old way was better.

_____

Consultee: (Response three) The special education teacher should be dealing with this situation.

_____

Situation Three

Consultant: The attrition rate from this dormitory is higher than any other on campus. Demographic variables certainly don't explain what is happening.

_____

Consultee: (Response one) Our major concern is to provide a pleasant environment for students to live in.

_____

Consultee: (Response two) Other residence hall directors are running pretty much the same type of program that we are.

_____

Consultee: (Response three) I'm going to be meeting with the dean to discuss these issues.

_____

4. Community pressure groups
5. Community political organizations
6. Tenure laws
7. Civil service regulations

Internal Variables

1. Group norms
2. Formal power structure
3. Informal power structure
4. Clarity of organizational goals
5. Prioritization of organizational goals
6. Role clarity
7. Consultee's characteristics
8. Job description

Summary

Five rather diverse issues relating to the consulting process have been addressed in this chapter: consultant roles, resistance, locus of the consultant, the cross-cultural consultation process, and organizational variables in consultation. In the first section on roles, consultation was depicted not as a single role, but as an interrelated set of roles. However, the roles actually assumed will vary with the model of consultation adopted and will also be affected by variables such as the consultee's expectations and the consultant's training.

Resistance is an adaptive process by which consultees attempt to maintain their equilibrium. Some resistance grows out of psychological deficits, but the consultant's ability to deal with this type of problem is minimal because of the nature of the consultation process. However, dealing with adaptive resistance requires the consultant to possess and utilize a variety of interpersonal skills as well as to develop programs and approaches that will reduce the concern.

The long held view that consultants should be external to the organization has given way to the view that consultants may function effectively from within or may be brought in from the outside. Internal consultants have certain advantages such as familiarity with the situation at hand and the ability to make ongoing observations with greater ease. The external consultant may be accorded more status and may be able to make greater demands on the system. Recognizing one's limitations as the result of being internal to the organization or external to it should be a prime concern to consultants.

Cross-cultural consultation was briefly considered and will be discussed in more detail in Chapter Eight. However, the model discussed indicates that successful cross-cultural consultation is based upon cultural empathy, personal awareness, and the ability to adjust one's own consulting model to the culture of the consultee.

Finally, a number of variables related to the functioning of an organization were discussed. These were divided into those variables outside and inside of an organization that influence its functioning and, as a result, may intervene in consultation.

Tips for the Practitioner

1. Write out your own definition of resistance.
2. Identify an intervention that you might use with a consultee. Develop a written description of it. Then identify the potential sources of resistance to the intervention you have developed. Redesign the intervention to reduce or eliminate the resistance you have described.
3. Which of the roles consultants assume are you ready to assume?

    A. Technical expert (list areas of expertise)
    B. Trainer
    C. Process observer
    D. Scientist
    E. Other

4. Depending on whether you expect to function as an internal or external consultant, identify the barriers you will need to overcome.

Review Questions

1. Identify the various roles engaged in by the typical human resource consultant functioning as an external consultant. Then, do the same thing for the internal consultant. Are there any differences?

2. List and explain the variables that influence the roles consultants fill.

3. Contrast the position taken in this chapter regarding resistance with that posited by Caplan (Chapter Two). Then compare the way that a consultant deals with each form. Which is the most realistic conceptualization of resistance for the psychological consultant? Why?

4. Identify three to five concrete ways that you as a consultant would identify resistance growing out of a "psychological deficit."

5. Many human resource workers function as internal consultants in hospitals, community mental health services, schools, and universities. Take an institution with which you are familiar and identify personnel and institutional factors that enhance or hinder the work of the consultant in this setting.

6. As a new internal consultant, how would you attempt to structure your work setting so as to enhance your consultation role?

7. Could cross-cultural differences be mistaken for resistance? Could it be a *legitimate* source of resistance? Explain both your answers.

8. Identify strategies for overcoming problems that may arise in the consultation process as a result of extra- and intraorganizational variables.

References

Abidin, R. R. (1982). A psychosocial look at consultation and behavior modification. *Psychology in the Schools, 9,* 358–364.

Alpert, J., & Silverstein, J. (1985). Mental health consultation: Historical, present, and future perspectives. In J. R. Bergan (Ed.), *School psychology in contemporary society* (pp. 121–138). Columbus, OH: Charles E. Merrill.

Beer, M., & Spector, B. (1993). Organizational diagnosis: Its role in organizational consultation. *Journal of Counseling and Development, 71,* 642–650.

Bergan, J. R. (1977). *Behavioral consultation.* Columbus, OH: Charles E. Merrill.

Bergan, J. R. (1985). *School psychology in contemporary society: An introduction.* Columbus, OH: Merrill.

Blake, R. R., & Mouton, J. S. (1976). *Consultation.* Reading, MA: Addison-Wesley.

Brehm, J. W. (1966). *A theory of psychological reactance.* San Diego: Academic Press.

Brown, D., & Schulte, A. (1987). A social learning model of consultation. *Professional Psychology: Research and Practice, 18,* 283–287.

Brown, D., Pryzwansky, W. B., & Schulte, A. (1987). *Psychological consultation: Introduction to theory and practice.* Boston: Allyn & Bacon.

Caplan, G. (1970). *The theory and practice of mental health consultation.* New York: Basic Books.

Carkhuff, R. R., & Pierce, R. M. (1975). *The art of helping—Trainer's guide.* Amherst, MA: Human Resources Development Press.

Chin, R. (1976). The utility of systems models and developmental models for practitioners. In W. G. Bennis, K. D. Benne, R. Chin, & K. E. Corey (Eds.), *The planning of change* (pp. 90–102). New York: Holt, Rinehart & Winston.

Chin, R., & Benne, K. D. (1976). General strategies for effecting changes in human systems. In W. G. Bennis, K. D. Benne, R. Chin, & K. E. Corey (Eds.), *The planning of change* (pp. 45–63). New York: Holt, Rinehart & Winston.

Clarizio, H. F., & McCoy, G. F. (1976). *Behavior disorders in children.* New York: T. Y. Crowell.

Conoley, J. C. (1981). Emergent training issues in consultation. In J. C. Conoley (Ed.), *Consultation in schools: Theory, research, and procedures* (pp. 223–263). New York: Academic Press.

Conoley, J. C., & Conoley, C. W. (1992). *School consultation: A guide to practice and training* (2nd ed.). New York: Macmillan.

Erchul, W. P. (1987). A relational communication analysis of control in school consultation. *Professional School Psychology, 2,* 113–124.

Erchul, W. P. & Chewning, T. G. (In Press). Behavioral consultation from a request-centered relational communication perspective. *School Psychology Quarterly.*

Firestone, W. A. (1977). Participation and influence in the planning of educational change. *Journal of Applied Behavioral Science, 13,* 167–183.

Gallessich, J. (1982). *The profession and practice of consultation.* San Francisco: Jossey-Bass.

Gibbs, J. T. (1980). The interpersonal orientation in mental health consultation: Toward a model of ethnic variations in consultations. *Journal of Community Psychology, 8,* 195–207.

Gibbs, J. T. (1985). Consultant training and supervision: Can we continue to be color-blind and classbound. *The Counseling Psychologist, 13,* 426–435.

Goodwin, D. L., & Coates, T. J. (1977). The teacher-pupil interaction scale: An empirical method for analyzing the interaction effects of teacher and pupil behavior. *Journal of School Psychology, 15,* 51–59.

Gray, J. L. (1984). *Supervision: An applied behavioral science approach to managing people.* Boston: Kent Publishers.

Gross, S. J. (1978). *A basis for direct methods in consultee-centered consultation.* Unpublished manuscript, Indiana University, Bloomington.

Havelock, R. G. (1973). *The change agent's guide to innovation in education.* Englewood Cliffs, NJ: Educational Technology Publications.

Heller, K. & Monahan, J. (1977). *Psychology and community change.* Homewood, IL: Dorsey Press.

Hetherington, E. M. (1981). Children and divorce. In R. W. Henderson (Ed.), *Parent child interaction: Theory, research, and prospects* (pp. 33–55). New York: Academic Press.

Huse, E. F. (1980). *Organization development and change* (2nd ed.). St. Paul, MI: West Publishing.

Illbeck, R. J., & Zins, J. E. (1993). Organizational perspectives in child consultation. In J. E. Zins, T. R.

Kratochwill, & S. N. Elliot (Eds.) *Handbook of Consultation Services for Children* (pp. 87–109). San Francisco: Jossey-Bass.

Kast, F. Z., & Rosenzweig, J. E. (1974). *Organization and management: A systems approach* (2nd ed.). New York: McGraw-Hill.

Kaufman, H. (1971). *The limits of organizational change*. Tuscaloosa, AL: University of Alabama Press.

Klein, D. (1976). Some notes on the dynamics of resistance to change: The defender role. In W. G. Bennis, K. D. Benne, R. Chin, & K. E. Corey (Eds.), *The planning of change* (3rd ed.) (pp. 117–124). New York: Holt, Rinehart & Winston.

Kratochwill, T. R., & Bergan, J. R. (1990). *Behavioral consultation in individual settings: An individual guide*. New York: Plenum Press.

Kubr, M. (1978). *Management consulting: A guide to the profession*. Geneva, Switzerland: International Labour Offices.

Kurpius, D. J., Faqua, D. R., & Rozecki, T. (1993). The consulting process: A multidimensional model. *Journal of Counseling and Development, 71,* 601–606.

Lin, N., & Zaltman, G. (1973). Dimensions of innovations. In G. Zaltman (Ed.), *Process and phenomenons of social change* (pp. 93–115). New York: John Wiley & Sons.

Lippitt, G. L. (1982). *Organizational renewal: A holistic approach to organizational development* (2nd ed.). Englewood Cliffs, NJ: Prentice-Hall.

Lippitt, G., & Lippitt, R. (1986). *The consulting process in action* (2nd ed.). San Diego, CA: University Associates.

Margullies, N., & Raia, A. (1972). *Organization development: Values, processes, and technology*. New York: McGraw Hill.

Martens, B. K., Lewandowski, L. J., & Howk, J. L. (In Press). A correlational analysis of interactions during the consultative interview and subsequent consultee perceptions. *Professional Psychology: Research & Practice.*

Mendoza, D. W. (1993). A review of Gerald Caplan's *Theory and Practice of Mental Health Consultation. Journal of Counseling and Development, 71,* 629–635.

Morasky, R. L. (1982). *Behavioral systems*. New York: Praeger.

Pinto, R. F. (1981). Consultant orientations and client system perceptions: Styles of cross cultural consultation. In R. Lippitt, & G. Lippitt (Eds.), *Systems thinking: A resource for organization diagnosis and intervention*. Washington, DC: International Consultants Foundation.

Randolph, D. L., & Graun, K. (1988). Resistance to consultation: A synthesis for counselor-consultants. *Journal of Counseling and Development, 67,* 182–184.

Reppucci, N. D., & Saunders, J. T. (1974). Social psychology of behavior modification: Problems of implementation in natural settings. *American Psychologist 5,* 649–660.

Sager, G., Brayboy, T., & Waxenberg, B. (1972). Black patient-white therapist. *American Journal of Orthopsychiatry, 42,* 415–423.

Sarason, S. B. (1982). *The culture of the school and the problem of change* (2nd ed.). Boston: Allyn & Bacon.

Schaller, L. E. (1972). *The change agent*. New York: Abingdon Press.

Schein, E. H. (1969). *Process consultation: Its roles in organizational development*. Reading, MA: Addison-Wesley.

Schein, E. H. (1989). Process consultation as a general model of helping. *Consulting Psychology Bulletin, 41,* 3–15.

Steele, F. (1975). *Consulting for organizational change*. Amherst, MA: University of Massachusetts Press.

Steele, F. (1982). *The role of the internal consultant*. Boston: CBI Publishing.

Stryker, S. C. (1982). *Principles and practices of professional consulting*. Glenelg, MD: Bernard Books, Inc.

Sue, S. (1977). Community mental health services to minority groups. *American Psychologist, 32,* 616–624.

Wickstrom, K. F., & Witt, J. C. (1993). Resistance within school-based consultation. In J. E. Zins, T. R. Kratochwill, & S. N. Elliot (pp. 159–178). San Francisco: Jossey-Bass.

Zaltman, G., & Duncan, R. (1977). *Strategies for planned change*. New York: John Wiley & Sons.

Chapter 7

The Skills and Characteristics of the Consultant

Goal of the Chapter

The goal of this chapter is to examine the skills and characteristics needed by effective consultants.

Chapter Preview

1. The characteristics of the effective consultant will be reviewed.
2. The skills needed by organizational and human resources consultants will be presented.
3. Recommendations for research regarding both the skills and characteristics of consultants will be made.

The skills needed by the effective consultant have been discussed at great length by a number of authors (e.g., Brown, 1993; Idol & West, 1987; Kratochwill, VanSomeren, & Sheridan, 1989). Conversely the characteristics of effective consultants have received little attention by authors of texts and even less attention by researchers even though few would doubt that the characteristics of the consultant are important. This lack of attention may be because consultants are not a separate professional group and thus have not concerned themselves with the qualities needed by effective practitioners. Consultation is a role assumed by counselors, psychologists, social workers, and others, a role that is perhaps secondary in nature to the primary roles of counseling, therapy, and assessment. It is interesting to note that literally thousands of studies have focused on the characteristics of effective counselors and therapists (Herman, 1993) and only a handful have addressed the traits

needed by consultants (Horton & Brown, 1990). A few studies have addressed this topic indirectly (e.g., Erchul, 1987). In the section that follows the literature on the characteristics of the effective consultant will be discussed and examined along with the speculation about these characteristics. This section will be followed by a look at the skills needed by consultants. However, the position taken here, which is in accordance with Dougherty (1990), is that the effective consultant must have certain personal characteristics along with the knowledge and consulting skills to be effective.

Characteristics of the Consultant

It is widely recognized that one of the essential characteristics of the consultant is a high level of awareness of his or her values (e.g., Caplan, 1970; Conoley & Conoley, 1992; Dougherty, 1990). Consultants and consultees deal with values-laden issues that can result in conflicts. A consultant may value democracy in the classroom. A teacher may value order and discipline based upon autocratic methods. A consultant may value the sharing of ideas and opinions in the workplace. A manager may believe that his or her ideas are the only important ones. By recognizing their values, consultants can anticipate potential conflicts and work to avoid them. Recognition of their values is also essential if consultants are to avoid ethical problems. This topic will be taken up in more detail in Chapter Twelve.

Another characteristic that the consultant must possess is the ability to solve problems (Henning-Stout, 1993). Every definition of consultation from Caplan's (1970) to a recent one posed by Kurpius and Fuqua (1993) emphasizes the problem-solving nature of consultation. Salmon and Lehrer (1989), in an analogue study, investigated the problem-solving behavior of two consultants and found that their interpretation of problems was influenced by the beliefs held by the consultee (teacher) about the client (student), the consultee's involvement with the client, and their own beliefs about the child. Not unexpectedly, the background and experience of the consultants were also instrumental in the way they viewed both the consulting process and the manner in which problems are to be resolved.

The fact is that we know little about the characteristics of effective problem solvers in the context of consultation. Varney (1985) suggests that consultants need to have the ability to engage in high levels of moral reasoning. He also suggests, along with Hunsaker (1985), that consultants need to be able to analyze problems from many perspectives. Bushe and Gibbs (1990) termed this quality *tactical flexibility* and suggested that this trait, along with a strong self-concept, are essential to success in consultation.

Bushe and Gibbs (1990) tried to carry their suppositions about the characteristics needed by effective consultants one step further. They tried to develop a predictive model of success in consultation as determined by trainer and peer evaluations. They found that intuition as measured by the Myers-Briggs Type Indicator (MBTI) and level of ego development (Loevinger, 1976) were in fact predictors of consultation success, with level of ego development being the better predictor. Their work supports not only their own hypotheses about the characteristics needed by consultants but also those of others already cited. With higher levels of ego development come increasing self-awareness, reliance on self-generated standards, levels of moral reasoning, ability to accept ambiguity, and ability to accept the paradoxes that occur within the consulting situation.

Earlier, in a study of internal organizational development (OD) consultants, Bushe and Gibb (1989) found that only when consultants reached what Loevinger (1976) terms the *conscientious stage* do they adopt consulting styles that were in accord with OD philosophy. Also in an earlier study, Hamilton (1988) found that intuition as measured by the MBTI is related to trainers' rating of competence. However, Hamilton did not study the levels of ego development.

Another essential characteristic of consultants is that they can establish working alliances. One aspect of establishing working alliances is the proper use of skills, some of which were outlined in Chapter Five. They will be revisited briefly in the section to follow. However, there is widespread agreement that people who can establish effective working relationships possess certain key characteristics, namely empathy, genuineness, and positive regard (Horton & Brown, 1990; Kupius & Rozecki, 1993). Empathy is the ability to perceive the internal frame of reference of another while maintaining one's objectivity. Positive regard involves prizing others even when they are quite different from oneself. Genuineness involves understanding oneself to be capable of freely interacting with others in an honest, spontaneous manner.

The aforementioned characteristics of empathy, genuineness, and positive regard were derived from the literature on effective therapeutic alliances. This list of traits needed to establish working alliances is probably not extensive enough to cover the complexity of the consulting relationship. To the list should be added the willingness to take interpersonal risks. Consultants are often required to initiate the consulting relationship, act as models as they help consultees acquire new skills, and to give opinions and advice based upon their expertise. These all require risk-taking behavior. Maher (1993), when discussing the characteristics of the organizational consultant, termed this risk-taking quality *entrepreneurship*, which he defined as "the ability to create value by recognizing new professional opportunities, managing risk associated with those opportunities, and following through with value-added services" (p. 319). While the human services consultant may not be entrepreneurial in the way Maher suggests, they are just as involved in risk taking.

Maher (1993) identified some additional characteristics of effective consultants that, although they have not been widely discussed as some of those already mentioned, would

---

Student Learning Activity 7.1

Will you be a good consultant? Rate your consultation characteristics using the following scale:

1 = not like me
2 = somewhat like me
3 = very much like me

A. Self-confident. A risk taker. _____

B. Empathic. Can see others' points of view. _____

C. Genuine. Not afraid to be myself. _____

D. Value others even if they hold values different from mine. _____

E. A good model. Willing to use my own behavior to instruct others. _____

F. Highly motivated. Want to help consultees and clients. _____

G. An achiever. I get things done. _____

probably be accepted by most people. He suggests that effective consultants possess commitment, determination and persistence, desire to achieve, and a desire to continuously enhance their effectiveness through feedback about their services. He also suggests that, in addition to being risk takers, effective consultants may be risk seekers, which is consistent with his concept of the consultant as an entrepreneur. Perhaps this "package" of characteristics can be more succinctly labeled as "motivated to succeed," because without a high level of motivation a consultant will certainly be discouraged by the inevitable failures that occur in the consultation process.

Skills of the Consultant

The objective of this section is to identify a minimum set of competencies needed to be effective in consultation. Unfortunately at this juncture in the development of consultation, we cannot base this discussion solely upon research for two reasons. First, the skills of the consultant have not been extensively studied and, thus, the data base is limited. Second, the research that has been produced has produced mixed results, partially because of inadequate procedures. Consequently, this discussion will be based partially upon research findings and to a larger degree upon the opinions of experts in the field.

Prerelationship/Preentry and Entry

Organizational consultants such as Kurpius et al. (1993) emphasize the importance of the preentry phase of the consulting process. They stress that, in this phase, consultants need two essential competencies: the ability to do realistic self estimates of their characteristics and skills and to communicate these skills to potential consultees. The human resources consultant needs the same types of skills, although entry and preentry are probably misnomers for this group because they are typically internal consultants and thus have theoretically entered the consulting arena. However, having a firm understanding of self and one's consulting skills is essential to effective, ethical practice. Being able to communicate the nature of these skills is also essential because, without some understanding of the benefits that can be derived from consultation, potential consultees will not avail themselves of the services. External consultants call this skill *marketing*. Internal consultants are in no less a need of marketing skills than are external consultants, although they rarely think in terms of the need to market their services. To summarize, the essential skills required in the preentry/prerelationship phase are:

1. Capacity to analyze one's own strengths and weaknesses.
2. The ability to identify consulting skills and make estimates of how these can help consultees.
3. Marketing skills, that is, the ability to persuade others that they can benefit from consultation.

Entry is that point in the consulting relationship at which consultant and consultee make contact and begin to negotiate a working agreement. This latter aspect of consulting

is called *contracting*. A contract may be a complex legal document or may be an informal agreement to work together to solve a problem. The consultant needs a basic understanding of the legal aspects of developing contracts but will probably need to consult with a lawyer for verification that the contract does in fact constitute a workable document (Remley, 1993). If the contractual agreement is informal, as it often is, the consultant needs to be able to explain the nature of consultation to the consultee, identify the roles each is to play in the process, and to reach accord on the dimensions of the process and the roles.

Consultants need to be able to ascertain, on a preliminary basis at least, whether consultation is feasible. By *feasibility* is meant that the consultee has the motivation and resources needed for success (Kurpius et al., 1993). They also need to consider whether they have the skills needed to proceed, because to proceed without the necessary competencies to bring the consultation process to successful fruition is unethical (ACA, 1988; APA, 1992).

To reiterate, consultants need skills to:

1. Make preliminary estimates of the likelihood of success if the consultation process is joined.
2. Make accurate estimates of their own ability as consultants.
3. Draw up preliminary formal contracts and develop informal consulting contracts.
4. Explain the nature of consultation to consultees.

Relationship Skills

Research has consistently shown that consultants who have the skills (and characteristics) needed to establish good interpersonal relationships are more favorably perceived by consultees than those who do not (Hansen & Himes, 1977; Maitland, Fine, & Tracy, 1985; Weissenberg, Fine, & Poggio, 1982). Paskewicz and Clark (1984) looked at a different dimension of the consulting relationship: language structural errors. They found that, when abstract rather than concrete words were used, the child rather than the child's behavior became the topic of consulting behavior, and when words were used that suggest that actions should be taken, consulting became less effective. Hansen & Himes (1977) also looked at the nonverbal dimension of the relationship and, not surprisingly, found that teachers thought that attending (e.g., eye contact) and minimizing nonverbal distractions were effective consulting behavior.

One area of controversy regarding the verbal skills needed by the consultant is in the area of controlling the counseling conversation. Bergan (1977) was the first to suggest that, to be effective, consultants needed to have the skills to control the consulting conversation. To that end he elaborated an extensive list of skills that were set forth in Chapter Three. Early research (Bergan & Tombari, 1976) generally supported Bergan's propositions, as has some recent research by Erchul (1987) and Erchul & Chewning (1990). However, as Henning-Stout (1993) reports, "there is ample evidence that consultees resist being told what to do" (p. 18). The basis of this argument is whether the consultant needs the skills to establish what have variously been termed *coordinate*, *collegial*, and *collaborative* relationships or the skills needed to skillfully elicit the responses needed to dominate the consulting relationship. Few would disagree that consultants be prepared to elicit responses that

will lead to problem identification and goal setting. However, with a few exceptions such as Erchul and Chewning (1990) and Witt (1990), most consultants believe that the skills needed by the consultants lie in the area of establishing coordinate, not dominant, relationships (Henning-Stout, 1993).

What conclusions can be drawn from this conflicting information? Most consultants would agree that consultants need the active listening skills required to establish basic human relationships (Horton & Brown, 1990; Idol & West, 1987; Parsons & Meyers, 1984; Randolph, 1985). These basic skills would include attending (including maintaining appropriate eye contact and other nonverbal behavior) and communicating to the consultee that both the verbal message and the affective content of the message have been heard using the skill known as *reflection*. Additional active listening skills include clarifying both the content of the consultee's communication, using questions and synthesizing a series of communications in summaries, and soliciting information by asking both open-ended (What can you tell me about the client?) and closed (What grade is the student in?) questions. In building consultation relationships, consultants will also need to use "soft" confrontations that gently point out discrepancies in consultees' communications and leads that focus on the consulting relationships in an effort to repair problems that have developed or flush out problems that lie beneath the surface (Kurpius & Rozecki, 1993).

Veteran consultants will attest to the fact that consultants need to be able to avoid being drawn into therapy-like discussions with consultees. In order to avoid this possibility, consultants need to master a strategy termed *supportive refocus* (Randolph, 1985). This technique is used to return the focus of the consultation relationship to the client when consultees have inadvertently started to talk about their own problems. The use of supportive refocus involves responding empathetically to the consultee's concerns (e.g., You're very upset about what is happening in your classroom and to a certain extent it makes you feel inadequate.) and returning the focus to the client (And John seems to be a major part of the problem because of the way he acts.). Pursuing the teacher's feeling of inadequacy is inappropriate in this context and probably unethical since the consultation was probably initiated to deal with John.

To summarize, the consultant needs:

1. Active listening skills.
2. Skills such as those involved in conflict resolution (e.g., confrontation) that will allow the consultant to deal with complex problems such as resistance.
3. The ability to maintain the focus of the consultation process on the client thus avoiding incidental therapy.

Consultants as Problem Solvers: General Considerations

Consultants are problem finders in that they "probe beneath the surface of a dilemma or a conflict in order to isolate the essential question, then attack it" (McPherson, Crowson, & Pitner, 1986, p. 271). Several writers have likened the role of the consultant to that of a detective (Kolb, 1983; Sandoval, Lambert, & Davis, 1977) probing for clues and information while gathering ideas to develop their hunches. Preliminary data indicate that experts in various fields analyze and deal with problem situations in ways that novices do not. Problem-

solving studies have been in the subject matter domains of physics, geometry, art, and the social sciences. Given the fact that the social sciences typically deal with problems that do not have well-established, generally agreed upon solutions in the manner of the physical sciences, the focus of this discussion will be on the studies from the social sciences area.

In their studies Voss, Tyler, and Yengo (1983) compared the strategy used in solving social science problems (for example, a hypothetical Russian agricultural problem) by experts in the field (faculty members whose expertise was the Soviet Union) and novices (undergraduates taking a course on Russian domestic policy). Given the similarity of problem solving in social science domains, their findings might begin to help us better understand this aspect of the consultation process. What they found was that experts spent a relatively large proportion of their time in developing a representation of the problem they encountered. That is, the expert took time to consider the "givens" of the problem and the goal. Constraints of the situation that impede solutions and knowledge of past solution attempts also contributed to the problem orientation being drawn up.

By contrast, novices spent little time in developing problem representations. In fact, any representations were included in a strategy of isolating possible causes of the problem. The causes are quite specific and the proposed solutions are stated in relation to the specific causes. Novices began discussing possible solutions to the problem without any consideration of constraints on or orientations to the solutions proposed. In summary then, novices represented the problem only as a set of specific causes requiring solutions. Interestingly, when experts from another discipline had their problem-solving approach to this problem analyzed they resembled the novices to a great degree.

In terms of solutions, the experts proposed one or a few proposals that were usually abstract. Much of the solution activity then went into justifying and examining what was proposed. The development of arguments may have been done for several reasons: (1) to justify a solution and in doing so show that it can be achieved; (2) to consider problems that may arise from the solutions and examine how those may be solved; (3) to evaluate the solution in terms of the problem representations; (4) to elaborate on the solution and; (5) to contribute to the possibility that new information may be retrieved that may suggest even more solutions. By contrast novices tended to do little in the way of such argument development.

Only a few studies have applied the findings from the cognitive psychology literature to the consultation process. In the exploratory study comparing the think-aloud protocols of school psychology graduate students with practitioners in response to an audiotape of an actual consultation session, definitive and some parallel observations to the novice-expert differences noted above were reported (Pryzwansky & Vatz, 1988). Essentially three levels of problem representation were evident with the highest level characterized by a problem definition and solution reflecting abstract- and theoretically-based information. In contrast to the lowest level, this group critically examined the premises and evidence used by the consultees in defining the problem and were more global in their assessment versus the lowest group's acceptance of the problem and restricted child focus. Equally important was the observation that the highest level group used what was labeled an "orientating mechanism" and defined as metastatements regarding the consultation process. Examples of orientating mechanisms include the consultants questioning of himself or herself, the role he or she was being asked to play, and the perceived expectations of the consultee. In this study seven out of 32 subjects reflected this level of problem finding and six of those were from the prac-

titioner group, although there was no relationship with years of experience and consultation coursework. In two subsequent studies (Vatz & Pryzwansky, 1987; Pryzwansky & Vatz, 1988) repeating the study with nominated expert consultants from the school psychology field (practitioners and trainers), the three levels were again reflected in the protocols with the highest group similar in approach to those in the previous study but made up primarily of trainers; problem finding level was not related to years of experience or coursework. Also, 90 percent of the interventions proposed by the highest level were focused *within* the session while 69 percent of the interventions proposed by the lowest level were externally based (class discussion, student interview, parent consultation). Interestingly, in all these studies the number of problems and categories of intervention strategies proposed by the different levels may not differ, but clearly the lowest level offered nearly double the number of strategies; perhaps they were more concerned with the challenge of what to do versus identifying the problem. Perhaps the biggest surprise was the finding that five out of 17 nominated experts were similar to the lowest group in the manner of representing the problem, including only a limited use of orientating mechanisms. Finally, a study of novice (graduate students in counseling) problem solving approaches reported that as a group they adopted the literal givens of a presented problem whether it was appropriate or not (Pryzwansky & Schulte, 1989). Similarly, their interventions were client focused, even if no clear cut client problem had been identified. Also their problem solving did not differ in response to changes in the nature of the problem or the consultant's approach which was being employed.

What are the implications of these findings for consultation? For one, it suggests that consultants and consultees may go about a problem-solving activity in very different ways, such as how they perceive the problem and what may be necessary to their thinking before closure on a solution is achieved. The above description suggests that the consultant (expert) will want to spend more time on problem definition and to focus on abstract material. By contrast, the consultee may be reminded of the role expertise differences and become either intimidated or put off by this questioning and abstract emphasis. Descriptions of consultation as a collaborative effort between equals may be seen as misrepresentations, and the potential for failure in this aspect of the consultation process is understandable. The consultant is advised to remain sensitive to the problem-solving differences and even consider utilizing techniques that promote the functioning of the consultee during the early stages of problem solving.

Consultant and consultee should agree:

1. To take stock of the situation together either as a review or refinement task.
2. That the consultant should evaluate the quality of the information provided by the consultee.
3. That the consultant needs to consider the expectations the consultee holds for the consultant.
4. That the consultant and consultee should collaboratively collect data in a systematic manner.
5. To conduct a process analysis of the problem. (Do contributing variables, identified problems, and problematic outcomes relate logically?)
6. To identify a (or several) competing hypothesis.
7. To consider the constraints affecting a problem solution.

Problem Identification and Goal Setting

Research has shown that, when consultants' verbal skills can be instrumental in problem identification (Bergan & Tombari, 1975) and when the consultant is unable to quickly help the consultee identify the problem, the process is more likely to fail (Bergan & Tombari, 1976). As has already been noted, Bergan (1977) and, more recently, Bergan and Kratochwill (1990) have set forth a set of skills that, if mastered, will allow the consultant to identify the problems from a behavioral perspective.

Idol and West (1987), Parsons and Meyers (1984), and many others have suggested that consultants need a host of assessment skills that will allow them not only to assess the consultees' problems, but also will guide the process of identifying the clients' problems as well. The organizational consultant quite obviously needs the skills to diagnose a wide range of problems from maladaptive aspects of the culture to managerial style problems. The human resources manager working in the school needs to be able to assess instructional and classroom management deficiencies. Consultants working with parents must be able to determine whether parents are engaging in child-rearing techniques that are facilitating or retarding the child's psychological and educational development. Quite obviously there are many ways to assess organizational, instructional, and parenting problems, many of which are discussed in this book.

Once consultee and client problems are identified, consultants need to help clients establish attainable goals. Kurpius, Fuqua, and Rozecki (1993) suggest that, after problem identification and prior to goal setting, it is essential that ownership of the problem be established. They go on to suggest that if the consultee "blames" the client it will be difficult to establish meaningful goals. Once ownership of the problem is established, it becomes the consultant's responsibility to collaboratively establish goals in measurable terms although, as has been suggested elsewhere in this book, it may be a mistake to persevere too long on writing well-defined objectives if the goal is actually consultee satisfaction.

Kurpius et al. (1993), drawing upon the work of McClelland (1989), suggest that the primary reason that interventions fail is because problems are not adequately diagnosed. The primary skills needed to properly diagnose problems and establish a course of action in consultation are:

1. Understanding theories of individual/organizational behavior and the ability to use that information to conceptualize problems.
2. Using various information-gathering strategies including the interview and questionnaires to collect valid information about the problem.
3. Communicating the nature of the problem in a manner that is readily understood by the consultee.
4. Developing ownership of the problem.
5. Establishing attainable goals.

Intervention Selection and Implementation

Kurpius and his colleagues (1993) suggest another set of reasons why consultation failures can be linked to intervention selection. As has been said repeatedly, consultation is a prob-

lem-solving process. The crux of this process is changing problematic practices in a manner that will be acceptable to the consultee and will have the desired impact on the client. Often it is the consultant's role to identify the intervention, explain it to the consultee, and then teach it to the consultee (Zins, 1993). This process presupposes that the consultant has a considerable knowledge of the duties of the consultee and the forces that impinge on those duties. In earlier chapters some of the interventions used by various types of consultants were listed and they will not be repeated here.

Consultants will, for the most part, use interventions that are tied to their theoretical orientation, that is, behavioral consultants will use behavioral contracts and cost-response interventions, and consultants following a Social Learning Model will use modeling strategies in conjunction with cognitively oriented interventions. Staying within a single theoretical framework may be an error (Brown, 1985; Carlson & Tombari, 1986), particularly if that theoretical framework is incompatible with that of the consultee or does not adequately consider factors such as cross-cultural concerns. Unless the consultant is flexible and knowledgeable enough to adapt to consultee and contextual variables, the consulting process is likely to fail.

What then are the key skills needed in the all-important intervention selection process? Some of these are:

1. Assessing consultees' values and theoretical perspective to determine which types of intervention are likely to be most acceptable.
2. Having a working knowledge of numerous interventions related to the problems that the consultant is likely to encounter.
3. Being able to communicate the nature of an intervention as it relates to consultees'/ clients' problems and, if necessary, teaching the intervention to the consultee.
4. With the consultee, monitoring the efficacy of the intervention and redesigning it as necessary.

Evaluation and Termination

Evaluation may not lead to termination, particularly if the data suggest that the intervention has been ineffective. However, if the evaluation is not supportive, intervention redesign (one of the techniques mentioned above) will be needed. If it is supportive then termination should be the result.

Termination can occur under circumstances other than success and often does. If the consultant and consultee develop a disagreement about the goals that should be pursued or the strategies that should be employed, termination of the process should occur unless these differences can be resolved. Also, in human resources consultation, the process should be terminated if the consultee consistently fails to follow through or if the resistance cannot be eliminated.

The skills required at this stage of consultation are:

1. Ability to evaluate the extent to which the consultation intervention is achieving the goals that have been established.

2. Communications skills needed to explain the outcomes that are being observed.
3. Ability to identify factors in the consultation that prevent it from being untenable and terminating the relationship for cause.
4. Skills for terminating consultation processes that have been successful, that is, when goals have been attained.

Student Learning Activity 7.2

Rate your consultation skills using the following scale.

1 = inadequate in this area at this time
2 = somewhat skilled but need additional work
3 = very skilled; feel totally competent

1 2 3   1. Analyze my personal strengths and weaknesses.

1 2 3   2. Identify my areas of competency as a consultant.

1 2 3   3. Market my consultation skills.

1 2 3   4. Forecast the likelihood that consultation will be successful.

1 2 3   5. Develop formal consulting contracts.

1 2 3   6. Establish informal consulting contracts.

1 2 3   7. Explain the consulting process in easily understood terms.

1 2 3   8. Listen and understand both the affective message as well as the verbal content of the consultee's communication.

1 2 3   9. Respond sensitively to consultees who have a cultural perspective different from my own.

1 2 3   10. Clarify the consultee's communication using various techniques such as open-ended questions.

1 2 3   11. Identify the points of conflict and resolve them before they impair the consulting relationship.

1 2 3   12. Have sufficient knowledge of individual behavior, including educational and psychological concerns, so that I can conceptualize problems and communicate them in easily understandable terms.

1 2 3   13. Have sufficient knowledge of organizational functioning so that I can conceptualize problems and communicate them in easily understandable terms.

1 2 3   14. Can conceptualize family problems and communicate them in a manner that is easily understood.

1 2 3   15. Can conduct a fact-finding interview that will yield valid data about the individual, the organization, or the family.

1 2 3   16. Can assist consultee in developing ownership of the problem once it is identified.

1 2 3   17. Can help consultee identify and prioritize attainable goals.

1 2 3   18. Can use supportive refocus to maintain focus on client and avoid therapy.

1 2 3   19. Can assess consultee's values prior to intervention selection.

1 2 3   20. Can design interventions based on at least two divergent theoretical perspectives and communicate these in understandable terms.

1 2 3   21. Establish monitoring system to determine intervention effectiveness.

1 2 3   22. Design evaluations that will establish efficacy of intervention.

1 2 3   23. Determine whether resistance is interfering with consultation progress and either terminate or ameliorate resistance.

1 2 3   24. Communicate the outcomes of consultation and explain reasons for success or failure.

1 2 3   25. Terminate successful consultations.

Needed Research

In a review of the empirical foundations of consultation, Henning-Stout (1993) noted several gaps in our knowledge base about consultation. Interestingly, she did not mention the fact that we know relatively little about the characteristics of the effective consultant. As mentioned earlier, it is particularly odd that hundreds of studies have focused on the characteristics of the effective therapist, but the traits of the consultant have been ignored by researchers. Perhaps this is because much of the research on consultation has been conducted by behaviorally oriented consultants who have paid more attention to the technology employed by the consultant than they have to the characteristics of the person employing the technology. This oversight stands as a major gap in the consultation research literature, particularly when the literature suggests, but does not confirm, that certain characteristics such as warmth and empathy seem to be important to consultees (Horton & Brown, 1990) when rating consultants.

The skills of the consultant have been studied much more extensively than the characteristics, but much of this research has been conducted from a behavioral perspective. Some of this research (Erchul, 1987; Erchul & Chewning, 1990) has led to a current debate about whether the consulting relationship should be collegial/coequal or dominated by the consultant. Consultants need very different skills if they are to dominate the counseling relationship as opposed to acting as a coequal. Henning-Stout (1993) marshals support for both sides of this argument, but, nevertheless, considerable research is needed in this area. This research should focus on the goals of consultation, which are to reduce or eliminate current mental health and/or educational problems and prevent future problems from occurring by empowering the consultee with new perspectives and skills.

We also need additional research on the process of consultation as it relates to the skills of the consultant. Henning-Stout and Conoley (1987) found that counseling and consultation are procedurally divergent, which was not unexpected. But the questions of how best to establish consulting relationships in what is often a brief process, assess consultee values and skills, and deal with issues such as resistance remain unanswered.

Finally the area of multicultural consultation has gone unaddressed by researchers. It is tempting to generalize from the counseling literature (e.g., Ponterotto & Casas, 1991) and suggest that there will be a host of problems in these cross-cultural consultation interactions. However, whether there will be problems and what the nature of these problems will be remains to be established. Perhaps more important, the skills needed to handle problems (if they exist as expected) need to be developed and validated.

Summary

In this chapter the skills and characteristics of the consultant have been addressed in some detail. Admittedly, there are few answers to the questions, "What are the characteristics of the effective consultant?" and "What basic skills must a consultant have to be effective?" However, we do have some preliminary information that can guide our training. It is up to the researchers to expand our knowledge base so that our selection and training processes can be more effective.

Tips for the Practitioner

1. After you have completed the checklist shown in Student Learning Activity 7.2, formulate a plan for developing the skills you need to overcome your deficiencies.
2. Follow a consultant for a day, trying to ascertain the characteristics that make them effective or ineffective. Can you identify areas that need improvement? Can you identify any personal deficits that may need remediation.
3. Interview several consultants to ascertain what traits and skills they believe are essential to success in consultation.

Review Questions

1. List five traits that seem to be essential to success in consultation. Which of these has the greatest support empirically?
2. List the essential skills needed at each phase of the consulting relationship based on what we know at this time.
3. Identify areas of needed research pertaining to skills and characteristics. Which of these is most essential? Defend your choice.
4. Discuss the pros and cons of the consultant's controlling the consulting relationship. What skills would be most useful if the consultant does wish to control the consultation process?
5. What would be the essential skills if the consultant wants to establish a coequal consulting relationship?

References

ACA (1988). *Ethical Standards*. Alexandria, VA: Author.

APA (1992). Ethical principles of psychologists and code of conduct. *American Psychologist, 47,* 1597–1611.

Bergan, J. R., & Tombari, M. L. (1975). The analysis of verbal interaction occurring during consultation. *Journal of School Psychology, 13,* 209–226.

Bergan, J. R. (1977). *Behavioral consultation.* Columbus, OH: Merrill.

Bergan, J. R., & Kratochwill, T. R. (1990). *Behavioral consultation and therapy.* New York: Plenum Press.

Bergan, J. R., & Tombari, M. L. (1976). Consultant skill and efficiency and the implementation of out-

comes in consultation. *Journal of School Psychology, 14,* 3–14.

Bushe, G. R., & Gibbs, B. W. (1989). *Ego development, role enactment, and corporate staff behavior: A field study.* Paper presented at the annual meeting of the Academy of Management, Washington, DC.

Bushe, G. R., & Gibbs, B. W. (1990). Predicting organizational development consulting competence from Myers-Briggs Type Indicator and stage of ego development. *Journal of Applied Behavioral Science, 26,* 337–357.

Brown, D. The preservice training and supervision of consultants. *The Counseling Psychologist, 13,* 410–425.

Brown, D. (1993). Training consultants: A call to action. *Journal of Counseling and Development, 72,* 139–143.

Caplan, G. (1970). *The theory and practice of mental health consultation.* New York: Academic Press.

Carlson, C. I., & Tombari, M. L. (1986). Multilevel school consultation training: A preliminary analysis. *Professional School Psychology, 1,* 89–104.

Conoley, J. C., & Conoley, C. W. (1992). *School consultation: A guide to practice and training* (2nd ed.) New York: Macmillan.

Doughtery, A. M. (1990). *Consultation: Practice and Perspectives.* Pacific Grove, CA: Brooks/Cole.

Erchul, W. P. (1987). A relational communications analysis of control in school consultation. *Professional School Psychology, 2,* 113–124.

Erchul, W. P., & Chewning, T. G. (1990). Behavioral consultation from a request-centered relational communication perspective. *School Psychology Quarterly, 5,* 1–20.

Hamilton, E. (1988) The facilitation of organizational change: An empirical study of the factors predicting agents' effectiveness. *Journal of Applied Behavioral Science, 24,* 37–59.

Hanson, J., & Himes, B. (1977). Critical incidents in consultation. *Elementary School Guidance and Counseling, 22,* 291–295.

Henning-Stout, M. (1993). Theoretical and empirical bases of consultation. In J. E. Zins, T. R. Kratochwill, and S. W. Witt (eds.) *Handbook of Consultation Services for Children* (pp. 15–45) San Francisco, CA: Jossey-Bass.

Henning-Stout, M., & Conoley, J. C. (1987). Consultation and counseling as procedurally divergent: Analysis of verbal behavior. *Professional Psychology: Research and Practice, 18,* 124–127.

Herman, K. C. (1993). Reassessing predictors of therapist competence. *Journal of Counseling and Development, 72,* 29–32.

Horton, G. E., & Brown, D. (1990). The importance of interpersonal skills in consultee-centered consultation. *Journal of Counseling and Development, 68,* 423–426.

Hunsaker, P. L. (1985). Strategies for organizational change: Role of the inside change agent. In D. D. Warrick (ed.) *Contemporary Organizational Development* (pp. 123–137) Glenview, IL: Scott, Foresman.

Idol, L., & West, J. F. (1987). Consultation in special education: Training and practice (Part II). *Journal of Special Education, 20,* 474–497.

Kolb, D. A. (1983). Problem solving management: Learning from experience. In S. Srvasta (ed.) *The Executive Mind* (pp. 109–143) San Francisco: Jossey-Bass.

Kratochwill, T. R., VanSomeren, K. R., & Sheridan, S. M. (1990). Training behavioral consultants: A competency-based model to teach interview skills. *Professional Psychology: Research and Practice, 4,* 41–58.

Kurpius, D. J., Fuqua, D. R., & Rozecki, T. (1993). The consulting process: A multidimensional approach. *Journal of Counseling and Development, 71,* 601–606.

Kurpius, D. J., & Fuqua, D. R. (1993). Fundamental issues in defining consultation. *Journal of Counseling and Development, 71,* 607–618.

Kurpius, D. J., & Rozecki, T. G. (1993). Strategies for improving interpersonal communication. In J. E. Zins, T. R. Kratochwill, and S. N. Witt (eds.) *Handbook of Consultation Services for Children* (pp. 137–158) San Francisco, CA: Jossey-Bass.

Loevinger, L. *Ego development.* San Francisco: Jossey-Bass.

Maher, C. A. (1993). Providing consultation services in business settings. In J. E. Zins, T. R. Kratochwill, and S. N. Witt (eds.) *Handbook of Consultation Services for Children* (pp. 317–328) San Francisco, CA: Jossey-Bass.

Maitland, R. E., Fine, M. J., & Tracy, D. B. (1985). The effects of an interpersonally-based problem-solving process on consultation outcomes. *Journal of School Psychology, 23,* 337–345.

McClelland, D. C. (1989) How do self-attributed and implicit motives differ? *Psychological Review, 96,* 201–210.

Parsons, R. D., & Myers, J. (1984). *Developing consultation skills.* San Francisco: Jossey-Bass.

Paskewicz, C. W., & Clark, C. D. (1984, April). *When behavioral consultation fails.* Paper presented at the annual convention of the National Association of School Psychologists. Philadelphia, PA.

Ponterotto, J. G., & Casas, J. M. (1991). *Handbook of racial/ethnic minority counseling research.* Springfield, IL: Charles Thomas.

Pryzwansky, W. B., & Schulte, A. (1989). *Novices responses to two types of problems and consulta-*

tion approaches. Paper presented at annual meeting of the American Psychological Association.

Pryzwansky, W. B., & Vatz, B. C. (1988, April). *School psychologists solutions to a consultation problem: Do experts agree?* Paper presented at annual convention of the National Association of School Psychologists, Boston, MA.

Randolph, D. L. (1985). *Microconsulting: Basic psychological consultation skills for helping professionals*. Johnson City, TN: Institute of Social Sciences and Art.

Remley, T. P., Jr. Consultation contracts. *Journal of Counseling and Development, 72*, 157–159.

Sandoval, J., Lambert, N. M., & Davis, J. M. (1977). Consultation from the consultee's perspective. *Journal of School Psychology, 15*, 334–342.

Varney, G. H. (1985). OD professionals: The route to becoming a professional. In D. D. Warrick (ed.) *Contemporary Organizational Development* (pp. 49–56) Glenview, IL: Scott, Foresman.

Vatz, B. C., & Pryzwansky, W. B. (1987, April). *The problem solving style of expert consultants in school psychology*. Paper presented at annual convention of the National Association of School Psychologists, Boston, MA.

Voss, J. F., Tyler, U., & Yengo, L. A. (1983). Individual differences in solving of social science problems. In D. F. Dillon & R. R. Snack (eds.) *Individual Differences in Cognition, Vol I* (pp. 205–223) New York: Academic Press.

Weissenberg, J., Fine, M., & Poggio, J. (1982). Factors influencing the outcomes of consultation. *Journal of School Psychology, 20*, 263–270.

Witt, S. N. (1990). Collaboration in school based consultation: Myth in need of data. *Journal of Educational and Psychological Consultation, 1*, 367–370.

Zins, J. E. (1993). Enhancing consultee problem-solving skills in consultative interactions. *Journal of Counseling and Development, 72*, 185–190.

Chapter *8*

The Consultee as a Variable

Goal of the Chapter

The goal of this chapter is to present the perspective and characteristics of consultees as potential factors influencing the process and outcome of consultation.

Chapter Preview

1. Consultee expectations and preferences for consultation services as reflected in research findings are presented.
2. Characteristics of consultees such as experience, personality, problem-solving style, ethnic background, and affect are examined in terms of their impact.
3. The preparation of consultees for this role both during preservice training programs as well as the consultation process, itself, are discussed.

As late as the mid-1970s, writers in the consultation area were noting with concern the lack of attention directed toward the consultee as a variable affecting the process or outcome of consultation (Bardon, 1977; Mannino & Shore, 1975). A more recent review by Piersel (1985) suggests that the situation is changing and some progress is being made in our appreciation of the consultee's impact, although not at the pace and with the breadth of coverage one would expect. For example, of the 87 doctoral dissertations reported since 1978, only 10 percent dealt with this influence (Duncan & Pryzwansky, 1988). Although the emerging knowledge is still fragmentary overall, the available research should be of assistance to consultants and particularly trainees as they attempt to understand and practice consultation.

This chapter has as its primary goal the development of our awareness that the characteristics of the consultee are a major influence in the consultation process. Specifically, the characteristics of the consultee that appear to influence the consultant-consultee interaction

will be discussed. Special emphasis is placed on the cultural variations that have recently been hypothesized to affect the consultation relationship and the interference they may cause in the problem-solving task. The possibility of consultee training is explored as a way of enhancing their use of consultation and contributing to the eventual outcome. Some suggested approaches for training of this type are also offered.

Initially, the discussion will be centered on what is known about consultees' expectations when they consider the consultation service. As will be pointed out, expectations are different from their stated preferences for what should take place. These two consultees' views represent the emphasis of research in the past few years, and although our information is still limited, some important glimpses into the "consumers'" priorities are emerging.

Expectations and Preferences of the Consultee

It is important to distinguish between what consultees *prefer* to happen when they request consultation and actually *expect* to happen in consultation. The work that has been done in the counseling field suggests that this distinction reveals differences on the part of clients that were important to take into account.

Expectations refer to those preconceived notions regarding anticipated occurrences. They can include notions about the consultant's role and degree of involvement throughout the process, the stereotypical behavior pattern that should be displayed by the consultant, the nature of the process itself, and the probability of success resulting from this professional contact. *Preferences*, on the other hand, are quite separate considerations for they represent what the consultee would like to experience rather than what they believe will be experienced. It is logical to hypothesize that a smoother, more productive consultation will result when congruence exists between the expectations and preferences of the consultee and what actually transpires, although that relationship has yet to be demonstrated empirically. At the very least, we can assume that the "set" (that is, expectations and preferences) of the consultee serves to influence the process. Thus, conscious awareness on the part of the consultant of the influence of the consultee's preferences and expectations is as important as the data regarding the consultation problem.

Expectations

A somewhat dated study provides some tentative, but nevertheless provocative, data in this area. Macarov (1968), in a follow-up evaluation of consultation projects involving two consultants and 40 consultees, reported that consultees questioned and even rejected the term "consultation" as a descriptor for the experience. Rather, they described the contact as an informal experience that resulted in the sharing of information. To a larger degree, consultees tended to see consultants as resource persons versus any other role. Macarov later speculated that the consultee's conceptualization of what had taken place reflected negative associations with the term "consultation" in that the term suggested that help was needed and given. Consultees apparently had trouble asking for help, taking help, or admitting they needed help. This subject is explored further in Chapter 13, but for now it is sufficient to recognize the reactions of one group of consultees to the term. This finding suggests that

at a minimum we reconsider the intent of our service (that is, is it to give help?) as well as the manner in which it is described.

Yet another study found significant discrepancies between the expectations for service and the service actually provided or recommended by the consultant (Noy, DeNour, & Moses, 1966). In spite of a common professional background, referring physicians and psychiatric consultants tended to be caught up in the intricacies and idiosyncrasies of their particular doctor-patient relationship. In one sense the professionals were alike in their personal motivation to become a physician and help, even cure, patients. Yet each was committed to a view of the patient and illness that tended to exclude the other's point of view according to Noy et al.; psychiatrists placed considerably more emphasis on emotional factors in diagnosis and treatment than did physicians. Similar relationships can be experienced in other fields, such as education where classroom teachers and special education teachers work together or where either of those instructional staff members interact with other resource personnel such as the school counselor or school psychologist. One of the book's authors annually documents the existence and power of preconceptions in the consultation relationship. For example, it has been observed over several years that when students from school counseling and school psychology programs view a mental health consultation film during their initial consultation course they bemoan the lack of directness and intellectual assertiveness in the consultant's style, for example, "He (consultant) never told her what to do." Both groups of students are completing a first year of training in which direct service has been emphasized and have an obvious expectation about the consultant's role in consultation.

One additional study in this area has suggested that teachers' expectations for consultation are influenced by a variety of factors such as work experience and position in the system. For example, Gilmore & Chandy (1973) found that teachers with four or more contacts per year with a school psychologist are more likely than the other teachers to consider the psychologist as a consultant rather than simply as a test administrator. The less experienced teachers (four or fewer years teaching) were more likely to expect the psychologist to function in the traditional role of assessment versus consultation. However, psychologists and principals are more likely to view the psychologist as a consultant than are teachers. A related finding from this same study supports the premise that consultation is reserved for rare instances. As a group, teachers were of the opinion that problems should be of a relatively serious nature before a psychologist becomes involved. If such a criterion should influence consultation contacts, it could suggest to the consultee that a variety of interventions may be warranted including immediate, direct client intervention. Furthermore, any potential preventative benefit derived from stressing the consultation model of service delivery is defeated.

Preferences

Some limited data are available to support the preferences for consultation services, but for only one setting. In an early set of studies, Gutkin (1980), Roberts (1970), and Waters (1973) found that teachers do indeed prefer that the school psychologist place more emphasis on the consultant role, particularly versus psychometric services. In a sense, this preference is somewhat inconsistent with their expectations regarding consultation as we have just discussed.

Generally, when we think of preferences we assume that there has been some experience with all the choices from which one is to make a selection. In the absence of any experience with consultation, then, it actually may be unreasonable to be asking consultees to state their preferences for receiving this type of service. Such a dilemma makes the Waters (1973) and Gutkin (1980) findings all the more interesting. In the Waters study, data were collected six months after the psychological services department had shifted from a psychometric model to a consultant model. While a Hawthorne effect (that is, any change brings about initial enthusiasm for the change) could be postulated as an explanation for the results, these teachers did experience at least one other service delivery model and therefore had some comparisons on which to base their ratings. In the Gutkin study (1980) using 12 student consultants over a period of 14 weeks, 69 percent of the teachers responding to the questionnaire indicated they found consultation services to be more effective than the traditional testing role of the school psychologist. Here again, there may have been strong extenuating circumstances influencing the teachers' ratings. For example, if they felt that a positive rating would increase the likelihood of continuing university services that were somewhat helpful, they might be tempted to provide supporting feedback.

By contrast, we know much more about consultees' ideas of how they would like to be worked with, that is, their preference for consultation models or approaches. This information has been almost exclusively gained from studies that ask consultees to choose between written descriptions of two or more models. For example, there is some indication that teachers prefer collaborative problem-solving relationships with consultants. In studies by Coleman (1976) and Wenger (1979) that compared collaborative consultation with conventional or expert-oriented consultation, all but one of the teachers expressed a preference for the collaborative model. Similarly, teachers and other school staff chose the collaborative model over three other models (Behavioral, Expert, Mental Health) whether descriptions of the four models were provided to them and they were asked to rank them, or the consultant-consultee responsibilities at five stages of consultation in each model were described separately (Babcock & Pryzwansky, 1983; White & Pryzwansky, 1982). Weiler (1984) reported the preference of parents, regardless of the setting in which they served as consultees (community or school), was for the collaborative approach over three other models. The active involvement of the consultee in the collaborative consultation approach may be a critical feature of the model that influenced the choice. Indeed, Gutkin (1983) found that teachers believe that their involvement in the development of remedial programs for students is very important. Schulte, Osborne, and Kauffman (1993) studied the preferences of regular classroom teachers over time as they received consultation from special education teachers. They found a marked preference for the collaborative model before and after receiving services that involved solely consultation or a combination of consultation and direct instruction with the child. These authors considered teacher-time as a key factor for the teachers' preference of the collaborative model. Similarly, based on survey results of teachers from a study of the status of "consultant teacher service in special education," Gold and Hollander (1992) recommended revised nomenclature and suggested "collaborating teacher" may be more palatable than "consultant." Not only did it appear to authors that the former term would be less likely to elicit antagonism from mainstream teachers but it would more accurately describe the relationship.

Although there is also some evidence that teachers as a whole prefer nondirective consultants to behavioral or direct consultants (Miller, 1974), the findings are not conclusive. For example, in a study using simulated consultation videotapes teachers rated the behavioral consultant as generally more effective on three of the six effectiveness dimensions; no preference determination was reported (Medway & Forman, 1980). Blesser, Fine, & Tracy (1990) replicated aspects of the Medway and Forman study and found both the mental health and behavioral consultants were viewed as being about equally "facilitative" overall, although higher consultation outcome scores were given to the behavioral consultant. In addition, Clark (1979) reported that teachers in a behavior modification training program did not make differential judgments between consultants who elicited an intervention plan and those who told the teachers what to do. On the other hand, Gutkin (1980) reported that 96 percent of the teachers in his sample indicated that it was "quite" or "very" important for them to be involved in the development of remedial plans for their students who were experiencing difficulties.

Finally, Mischley (1973) had teachers express their preference between the Caplanian approaches of consultee-centered consultation (Mental Health) and client-centered consultation (Medical/Expert) and found relatively equal numbers preferring each model. Furthermore, when offered one of those consultation approaches under either a group or individual format, equal numbers of teachers chose among the four conditions. Thus, Mischley's study raises an important consideration where the consultee's preferences are involved. Not only should consultants take into account the consultee's preferences by, at the very least, acknowledging them, but some attention would be well spent on recognizing the conditions under which the consultation is offered.

Several additional points should be addressed to aid in interpreting the relevance of the studies' findings. In most of the research mentioned, the consultee was not helped to adopt any "set" toward the choices, that is, asked to identify what they would *ideally* like to experience or what is the *best* they can hope for. Consequently, it can be argued that the choices we have just reported might be dictated by ideal versus reality considerations. Secondly, preferences of individuals reflect a cognitive behavior; it is not possible to predict what the consultee's preferences will be once they experience a particular consultation approach. Third, constraints on their role in the organization may be a more important factor influencing their thinking than what they would like. For example, Sarason (1971) has effectively described the demands placed on teachers and the lack of school flexibility in accommodating anything but an instructional role. The teacher role, and the organizational structure of schools, do not allow for collegial input from consultants; teachers simply cannot function in that way. The time required for certain consultation relationships such as collaboration may simply not be available. Similarly, there may not be administrative sanction to support such professional interchange. Given the current emphasis directed to increasing instructional time-on-task there may be even less inclination to disrupt the teacher's primary responsibility—instruction.

As indicated, consultee preferences and expectations can be confounding variables in the consultation relationship. Although in the truly collaborative relationship the consultant and consultee engage in a process of determining the preferences and expectations of the other, it seems likely that in most situations this responsibility will rest on the consultant's shoulders. A suggested set of techniques for accomplishing this task, therefore, is presented in Table 8.1.

TABLE 8.1   Consultation Techniques for Determining Consultee Preferences and Expectations

Consultant Technique	Message to Consultee
Model expected behavior by sharing one's own expectations and preferences	I've shared my attitudes with you, now tell me yours
Direct questions such as "What do you expect from a consultant?", or use of questionnaire (see Chapter 11)	I'm interested in your input regarding my functioning
Relay stories of failed consultations due to misperceptions of consultee	It is important that we agree
Informal contracting: "Let's agree on what our roles will be"	Commitment to models of functioning is important to our success

There are other facets of the consultee that need to be taken into account by the consultant. Some of them are obvious, such as the amount of experience the consultee has in his or her position and in general, that is, how old the consultee is. The ethnic background of the consultee is another seemingly obvious factor to take into account, but surprisingly has only recently been considered with some unexpected results. The personality of consultees and their reaction to characteristics of the consultant also play a part in the nature and amount of involvement invested in the consultation relationship. Some tentative findings of other investigations into personality variables of consultees should also be noted. Mischley (1973) reported a relationship between personality characteristics and model of consultation preferred: consultees who reflected a general authoritarianism preferred a client-centered model while more introspective consultees preferred a consultee-centered model. Finally, some relatively new ideas regarding the problem-solving ability of consultees and the degree to which their affective state may influence consultation outcome represent other characteristics that should not be overlooked. The next section examines what is known about these characteristics and suggests ways of dealing with them.

Consultee Characteristics Affecting Process

Experience

This variable, professional experience, has received considerable attention but only when a teacher is identified as the consultee and even this research is somewhat contradictory. In an early study, young professionals were found to be the segment of the school staff taking advantage of consultation services (Iscoe, Pierce-Jones, Friedman, & McGehearty, 1967). It could be argued that the novice is most eager for support and reassurance and also more idealistic in terms of the anticipated outcome. But Baker (1965) and Gilmore and Chandy (1973) found a positive correlation between years of experience and use of consultants. Each of these studies isolated the experience factor. As is the case in other areas of consultation research, studying variables in isolation from one another may not lead us any further

toward understanding the process but only lead to simplistic answers. Consider, for example, the multivariate study where overall experience along with years of teaching at the current school were taken into account to answer this question. It was found that the longer teachers have taught in a school was related to a tendency to use consultation; just the opposite is true when simply number of years teaching is considered (Gutkin & Bossard, 1984). If nothing else, these studies illustrate how careful the consultant must be in making judgments about a consultee from only one bit of information.

Teachers with more teaching experience gave higher ratings to both a mental health and behavioral consultation tape they viewed than did their less-experienced counterparts, when the consultation experience was viewed as educational and leading to better problem solving in the future (Slesser, Fine, & Tracy, 1990). Also, these teachers were more satisfied with the mental health approach than were the less-experienced teachers. On the other hand, it has been reported that, in considering twelve vignettes describing classroom problems, experienced teachers selected referral over consultation more often than less-experienced teachers; however, it was noted that 89% of all the teachers reported using consultation services in their schools at least once a year (Hughes, Barker, Kemenoff, & Hart, 1993).

Perceptions of Consultants' Styles

We probably know less about this factor, with the exception of the degree to which consultees want to be involved as an equal in the process. The notion of receiving help may hold some negative connotation for the person who is helped. For example, in organizations such as schools, where the ideas of teaming, mentoring relationships, and consultation are positively received, the pressure on the teacher and administrator to handle all problems in their domain is still the prevalent expectation. In the one study of this phenomenon, consultees who were professionals in community volunteer agencies were found to be able to accept "help" if it took place as a sharing experience or an informational exchange (Macarov, 1968). Thus, the informal context of consultation seemed to be an element that intervened to make it acceptable as a valuable experience. By contrast, these same consultees (professionals in community volunteer agencies) seemed to reject both the word "consultation" and the concept. Thus, there was a clear preference for information over advice, in that it was easier to ask for and admit having received.

On a more theoretical level, the manner in which responsibility for both a problem and its solution are assumed by the consultee could be related to a style of coping/helping (Brickman, Rabinowitz, Karuza, Coates, Cohn, & Kidder, 1982). Brickman et al. identified four models of coping/helping: (1) moral—people are responsible for problems and solutions, (2) compensatory—people are not responsible for problems but are responsible for solutions, (3) medical—people are not responsible for problems or solutions, and (4) enlightenment—people are not responsible for solutions but are responsible for problems. Each position has an influence on the consultees' assumptions toward any problem-solving situation. Consultees should be listened to carefully in terms of the conditions under which they can accept resources. Consultants must also be careful how they describe their services and what assumptions they make regarding the helping orientation of the consultee.

Ethnic Background

The consultee characteristic that can have the most significant impact on the consultation process is their sociocultural background. This factor has potential for affecting not only the consultation and the quality of the relationship that is established, but the value placed on consultation itself. The impact of cultural background differences has been explored in a number of areas, such as counseling relationships (Sue & Sue, 1977), organizational development (Pinto, 1981), schooling activities (e.g., Brady & Schneider, 1973; Bronkowski, 1968), consultation efforts (e.g., Morrison, 1970), and therapist-patient relationships (e.g., Sager, Brayboy, & Waxenberg, 1972).

The literature has noted issues involving communication barriers, negative self-attributions and feelings engendered on the part of the recipients of the service, differences in priorities in the relationship, and the potent effect of the interaction between explicit and implicit themes of change and values. Yet little has been done to address these observations in a systemic manner that could help facilitate the consultant-consultee relationship and the efficacy of the consultation contact. For the most part, consultants rely on their own sensitivity to the impact of cultural differences in their work with consultees. In addition, their training and experience, which impact on a theory of consultation, their value orientations, and their perception of the client/systems' value orientation (Pinto, 1981) play a role.

A theoretical model that emphasizes an interpersonal orientation in mental health consultation and directly addresses the ethnic question has been proposed by Gibbs (1980). She has formulated the following three propositions: "(a) there are ethnic (e.g., black-white) differences in the initial orientation to the consultant-consultee relationship; (b) these differences are along the dimension of interpersonal *versus* instrumental competence; and (c) these differences have significant implications for the implementation of the consultation process and its outcome" (p. 195). Using both a historical/sociological perspective and a data based literature review, stages in the consultees' behavior during entry and themes in the relationship between the consultant and black consultees during the entry phase of consultation are then delineated. Gibbs's model, which she considers tentative but nevertheless worthy of consideration at the training and practice levels, rests on the premise that black consultees focus on the "interpersonal competence" (process rather than content) of the consultant, while whites tend to focus on the "instrumental competence" (goal/task-related aspects) of the consultant. Interpersonal competence then, is defined as "a measure of the ability of the individual to evoke positive attitudes and to obtain favorable responses to his actions" (p. 199). On the other hand, instrumental competence is considered to be "a measure of the degree of effectiveness with which a goal or task is accomplished by the individual" (p. 199).

She presents a predictable sequence of five stages that the interactions between the consultants and the consultees will follow during the entry phase of a consultation, modified of course by the perceived degree of ethnic and social class similarities between consultant and consultee. Those stages include an appraisal stage, investigation stage, involvement stage, commitment stage, and an engagement stage.

During the appraisal stage, the black consultee is seen as evaluating the consultant's personal authenticity and consequently remains aloof and reserved. The consultant's genuineness is gauged. The white consultee meanwhile is judged to be evaluating the overall consultation project and the professional skills of the consultant. In the second stage, inves-

tigation, black consultees shift from sizing up the consultant to making inquiries about the consultant's personal life, background, opinions, and values. Judgments are made regarding the ways the consultant relates to people of similar and different backgrounds. White consultees, by contrast, "will inquire about the details of the consultant project, not about the consultant's personal life" (p. 199).

The third stage, involvement, is characterized by the black consultee's attempt to establish a more personal relationship through exchange of personal information, personal favors, and quasi-social interactions such as lunch or a coffee break. Thus the consultant's degree of identification with others different in background is gauged. It is interesting to note that Gibbs argues that reciprocation by the consultant is crucial if the black consultee is to accept the consultant's expertise. Yet much of the consultation literature tends to argue against such an involvement with a few exceptions (Altrocchi, 1972). The white consultee during this stage maintains the consultation relationship on a formal professional level.

A transition from personal support to program support in terms of loyalty and personal regard for the consultant by the black consultee takes place during the fourth stage, commitment. Interest is shifted to the consultation task. During this stage, white consultees "will express their commitment in terms of the goals to be accomplished" (p. 200). The final stage has both consultee groups committed to participation (task involvement). Black consultees' commitment is "the result of their evaluation of interpersonal competence of the consultant; the white consultee's commitment is made [as a result] of the instrumental competence of the consultant through the preceding stages" (p. 200).

Gibbs reports that these stages exist for both white and black consultants. Similarly, comparisons were the same whether the consultees were black or white. She also hypothesizes that the concept of an interpersonal orientation in consultation can be generalized to other ethnic minority groups sharing similar societal experiences with blacks. However, it would seem prudent to consider the two orienting mechanisms, interpersonal and instrumental, as operating within the general population and reflecting value systems of the consultee regardless of race. Thus, such relationship needs may be triggered whenever external consultants, such as was the case in the experiences that served as the basis for Gibbs's conceptualization, enter a system wherein consultees exhibit a high level of protectionism toward their clients and/or project (for example, a school for handicapped children, an inner city project, a center for abused women).

Beyond such obvious conditions that indicate careful review of the consultant's style, personality factors of individuals may result in their responding in varying degrees along the interpersonal-instrumental continuum wherein consultation and/or change experiences are involved. The priorities that were hypothesized by Gibbs are likely to be expressed in less obvious ways and consequently be less apparent to the consultant. The result would be that some premature closure would take place during the entry phase only to have interpersonal issues arise later. For example, a white student consultant and a white consultee worked jointly to complete consultation preference scales. The consultant then discussed reading from the scales with the consultee pertaining to working together, along with ideas on intervention strategies. As they met to develop an intervention plan they began to share common working experiences. The discussion precipitated a crying spell on the consultee's part and the revelation of her real reasons for requesting consultation. In another situation, a white consultant to a community was told by a black consultee after a year that he

was the first white person he had ever trusted. After that revelation the flow of information changed both in terms of quantity and content. It also became possible for them to engage in more collaborative problem solving.

In an extension of Gibbs's ideas, 124 black female elementary teachers with a median 10 years of experience were asked to give their preference of black and white consultants observed on a videotape and to rate their effectiveness (Duncan & Pryzwansky, 1993). No significant preferences were noted for either a same (or opposite) race consultant, although the teachers preferred the instrumentally oriented consultant. In terms of this latter finding, it is important to recognize not only the experience level of the teachers but the fact that they fell at the highest stage of a racial identity development scale suggesting they felt comfortable about their own racial identity.

Consultees' Perceptions of Consultants

Every "young" consultant has experienced the consultee's implicit competence check by having to answer questions such as "How long have you been a social worker?", "Do you have any teaching experience?", or even less tactful inquiries relating to age or marital status. The importance of these variables during the entry stage of consultation, let alone later stages, is unclear. Age, gender, race, assertiveness, personality, and so forth are all consultant characteristics that may affect the consultees' perception of the consultation process and their commitment to and prognosis for the success of the activity. Yet, little is known about these relationships, a fact that may either reflect their perceived importance for consultants or a significant oversight. One study (Gutkin, 1983) reported that the consultee's perception of both the consultant's communication and content skills were consistently related to the consultee's perceptions of outcomes, that is, the utility of the programs or ideas generated as a result of consultation. Likewise, the consultee's perception of the consultant's interest and enthusiasm was seen as an important element related to the outcome of the consultation process. Finally, the nature of the written language used to describe an intervention has marked impact on teachers' perceptions of its acceptability. Pragmatic descriptions, for example, were judged to be more acceptable than humanistic or behavioral descriptions (Witt, Moe, Gutkin, & Andrews, 1984).

Questions about the consultant's background and training are best handled in a direct, factual manner. Subtle, nonconfrontational follow-ups concerning the consultee's reasons for asking the questions can lead to some important "baring of the soul" by the consultee. Once expressed and confronted, consultation can proceed. Similarly, asking for feedback and/or identifying the presence of indices of involvement help the consultant make judgments relevant to this area.

The Consultee as Problem Solver

As consultation is increasingly defined in terms of a problem-solving activity in which the active participation of the consultee is expected, the focus on the unique skills of the consultee required to function in this way will need to be addressed.

One basic observation about the implications of the problem-solving approaches of the consultant and consultee is warranted. Recent literature has begun to emphasize the impor-

tance of the first stage of the process, problem identification. Bergan and Tombari (1976) found that when problem solving was carried through the problem identification stage, the probability of a solution was almost always assured. Given the fact that their study involved the adoption of behaviorally oriented intervention plans, it seems logical that this first step would receive such a priority. Although other writers in the consultation field have also stressed the importance of this stage of consultation, it should be noted that what is often described in this chapter is an attempt to frame problems in ways that will lead to more productive problem solving rather than just defining the elements of the problem. Consultants are also problem finders, if you will, in that they "probe beneath the surface of a dilemma or a conflict in order to isolate the essential question, then attack it" (McPherson, Crowson, & Pitner, 1986, p. 271).

The prior discussion dealing with the problem solving of novices versus experts illustrated the dynamics of the problem-finding task. That orientation sets up a potential conflict with the consultee, as he or she may enter the relationship feeling this step has been completed or else why would the consultee have requested consultation. Once again, the role of the consultee has not been considered or is deemphasized. Of course, another scenario could find the consultee resisting any problem identification activities for ulterior motives. The potential conflict may be multiplied when the consultee is in a managerial position. Many of these professionals (managers) see themselves as rapid problem solvers, but in many cases the problems are not clearly defined. Often, quick solutions to prevent "institutional drowning" are identified as the priority (McPherson et al., 1986, p. 272). Problem identification time is wasted time for them. Some tips for problem identification are presented in the following list.

To emphasize again the relationship between consultant and consultee, both should agree:

1. To take stock of the situation together either as a review or refinement task.
2. That the consultant should evaluate the quality of the information provided by the consultee.
3. That the consultant needs to consider the expectations the consultee holds for the consultant.
4. That the consultant and consultee should collaboratively collect data in a systematic manner.
5. To conduct a process analysis of the problem. (Do contributing variables, identified problems, and problematic outcomes relate logically?)
6. To identify a (or several) competing hypothesis.
7. To consider the constraints affecting a problem solution.

Personality

There have been several attempts to take into account the emotional makeup of the consultee as a factor influencing the consultation process. Modeling his study after one dealing with a department's power within a university (Mann, 1972), Hirschman (1974) examined the relationship between an individual's perceived power within an organization and his or her willingness to utilize mental health consultation. Volunteers at a mental health center were

required to arrange a meeting with a consultant for client-related discussions following completion of their training. The volunteers rated the importance of their service at the facility, their influence over others, the importance of consultation in general, and the perceived help of the consultant. The consultant then noted the time that elapsed between the volunteers' first helping experience and their first request for consultation help. As in the Mann study, those who took the longest to contact the consultant held a high self-perception of their importance and influence. Some indirect evidence for the existence of this relationship can be found in earlier works that reported that individuals with limited experience and skill in an organization were more likely to be the ones to use mental health consultation (Iscoe et al., 1967).

It has been hypothesized that teachers' use of consultation *versus* referral services might also vary depending how much control they perceived they had in regard to a problem a student is presenting. For example, knowing little about how to help a client or even what their difficulty is would probably influence consultees to look to others to handle the problem. On the other hand, the more confident and in charge consultees feel with respect to a troublesome situation the more likely their orientation would be one of seeking out new ideas and strategies that increase their effectiveness. In this latter circumstance there is no felt need to have someone else take over and work with the client; the consultee feels in charge. The degree of control teachers feel they have in resolving a variety of student problems is closely related to their use of consultation, according to Gutkin and Ajchenbaum (1984).

Mischley (1973) reported a relationship between personality characteristics and the model of consultation preferred; consultees who reflected a general authoritarianism preferred a client-centered model while more introspective consultees preferred a consultee-centered model. In a related study, high dogmatic subjects (teachers) rated behavioral consultants more "facilitative" than they rated mental health consultants, and they rated mental health consultants less facilitative than did less dogmatic subjects (Slesser et al., 1990).

It is interesting to note that where a simple estimate of a consultee's internality-externality orientation (locus of control) is made, there seems to be no difference in how consultees (characterized along that personality dimension) prefer the consultant to work with them. There is an indication that all consultees, regardless of LOC score, prefer the collaborative approach (Pryzwansky & White, 1983). On the other hand, it may be that simply considering a person's generalized control expectancies, or even the influence of feelings of competency on those expectancies in particular cases, may be too limiting. However, in a recent study a consistent pattern of interaction between the method of consultation and locus of consultation and locus of control was reported (Slesser, Fine, & Tracy, 1990). In viewing a videotape of mental health consultation, teachers with an *external* locus of control (versus the internal subjects) gave those consultants higher ratings when asked how pleased they would be with the practitioner as well as the degree to which they were now able to deal with similar problems in the future. These differences were not found for behavioral consultation. Again, in another analogue-type study, it was found that teachers with a higher self-efficacy rate the consultants' effectiveness (regardless of the directness of consultant) and quality of intervention higher than those teachers with a low self-efficacy (DeForest & Hughes, 1992). Finally, teacher self-efficacy, perceptions of control, and attributions did not predict teachers' decisions to seek consultation or to refer a child under conditions in which the teacher is presented with vignettes describing classroom problems (Hughes, Barker, Kemenoff, & Hart, 1993).

An equally important factor involves the amount of control afforded by the consultee's role in the organization. For example, the constrained, powerless, lonely role of teachers (Lortie, 1975; Sarason, 1971) has been discussed at length in the literature. However, it has been argued that personality types compatible with the role gravitate toward the profession. Using teacher locus of control scores and their responses to a consultation problem-solving interview, Friedman (1977) identified four qualitatively different modal patterns of teacher consultation behavior termed *locus of control consultation styles*. These four styles, with a name attached to reflect the teachers' consultation behavior, are presented in Table 8.2. As evident from the table, the teachers' locus of control was considered from the perspective of their professional role as well as general self-concept, which yields four different consultee styles. From her consultation interviews, Friedman also specified both the content of consultation behaviors and the effect of each consultee style on impeding or facilitating the development of a consultation relationship.

In terms of Friedman's teacher consultation behavior patterns, internal consultation styles are referred to as *controllers* and *problem solvers* while external consultation styles are called *strivers* and *reactors*. The different orientations toward consultation of each style are evident in the reasons given to seek out consultation, and the effect they have on the process is quite different. For example, controllers seem interested in abdicating professional responsibility for a problem; they are particularly easy to work with if the consultant supports their perceptions. Strivers seek consultation to bolster their own threatened professional self-esteem and mitigate the discomfort of ambivalent emotional conflict about assuming professional responsibility for another (Friedman, 1977). By contrast, problem solvers and reactors hold congruent views of their personal and professional control. The behavior of problem-solver consultees suggests that consultants are seen as resources who can supplement their own professional competency. They are cooperative, and continuance in the relationship reflects judgment of the merit and efficiency of the consultant's recommendations. Reactors' interest in consultation tends to be one of compliance wherein they are pacifying or reacting to the pressures of external agents such as a principal or a parent. The most acquiescent of consultees, their cooperation is less likely to advance the problem-solving process from the standpoint of active contributions they might make. The progress of the interview is less effective and almost entirely the consultant's burden.

The framework that Friedman provides, albeit theoretical, argues for individualizing consultation behavior to fit the different professional needs, phenomenological perspective,

TABLE 8.2   Consultation Styles Based on Generalized and Situational Control Expectancies

	Generalized Locus of Control Belief	
Professional Power Expectancy	Internal	External
Role Power	Problem Solver	Strivers
Role Powerlessness	Controllers	Reactors

Adapted from L. P. Friedman (1977), p. 117.

and dynamics of the consultee. More accurate prediction of the consultant-consultee inter-action can help in facilitating effective consultation.

Consultants need to recognize the obvious—different consultees will need to be han-dled differently because of their personality. In particular, the way in which their own inclination toward handling problems meshes with their role at work needs to be taken into account. The reader is referred to Chapter 11 where the Friedman interview scale and cate-gorical system is presented as a helpful aid in evaluation.

Affect: Emotional State of the Consultee

An often overlooked condition considered critical to the outcome of consultee-centered consultation by Caplan (1970) is the emotional set of the consultee. For example, individu-als in crises are viewed as ready to take advantage of consultative input; in fact, one might argue that consultees who have voluntarily sought out consultation because of the intensity of their need for assistance will be more likely to follow through on ideas generated during the consultation. If nothing else, consultants, like therapists, need to be careful to reduce the anxiety of the consultee over working with a client to a level that they are no longer immo-bilized to take action.

Obviously, consultation is not always offered under crisis conditions. Also, the effect on the consultation process of the availability of other alternatives (for example, "Transfer the child to another class," or "Hang on, the year is almost over.") has not been empirically addressed. But it is safe to say that the psychological investment in the consultation enter-prise is affected by the intensity with which the consultee approaches the consultation problem.

The feeling state of the individual has been studied in terms of social interaction and decision making. In fact, positive affect has led people to be more helpful to others (Berkowitz, 1972) and influenced their decision-making strategies (Isen, Means, Patrick, & Nowicki, 1982). While the impact of these findings on problem-solving research is in its infancy there are tentative conclusions that need to be taken into account during the con-sultation experience. There is evidence that a person who is in a positive mood, while inclined to increase their helping of others generally, is protective of that good mood; if their future anticipated actions are likely to affect their feeling state in a negative way they will be less willing to cooperate. And although they may be more optimistic when faced with complex tasks, they are likely to be more conservative and reduce their risk-taking behav-iors. Paradoxically, they tend to see and use intuitive hypotheses so they usually work with more speed and are more efficient. That response, however, can lead to solutions that are sometimes biased and incomplete or incorrect. Yet if self-correcting feedback is inherent in the task, they are very responsive to that information and function as efficient problem solvers. A consultee who feels good about herself or himself in a role is likely to focus more on the problem at hand and contribute to the solving of the problem.

As is the case in most of the consultation research, there is rarely a simple relationship between two variables that can guide the consultant's behavior. The affective state of con-sultees in problem-solving situations is no exception. The nature and importance of the task(s) will have bearing on the consultee's approach as well as the feedback they receive in the task and their prior experience with affect of various kinds under situations requiring

different strategies. Thus, a positive mood can facilitate or impair performance depending on the circumstances involved.

One final point to be made with regard to affective states is consideration of the effects of different mood states. Isen et al. (1982) point out that the *valence* of the mood (positive or negative) is only one of four dimensions to consider. The *quality* of the emotion may have quite different consequences for behavior. That is, whether the consultee is anxious about dealing with a client versus angry with the client or significant others in the client's life can play a role. Similarly, the *intensity* and *arousal* dimensions may influence behavior. Low-level, everyday feeling states, such as have been used in the research of Isen et al., have been shown to interrupt and influence decision making so that relatively intense states may have differing influence. Finally, the degree of arousal, stimulating versus depressing, that consultees experience may have implications for their cognitive states.

In summary then, the consultee's mood, as well as other characteristics, cannot be overlooked as a potential factor affecting the process and outcome of consultation. The context of the problem situation and the interactional influence with other characteristics are also important. It is suggested that the consultant use a mental check-off system in which consultee characteristics and their potential impact are noted and considered when a consultation approach and specific interventions are planned. For example, the particular characteristics of consultative interventions affect what is or is not accepted by the consultee, and from an examination of this chapter's findings there is reason to expect that different consultees will respond differently to various intervention plans (Witt, Martens, & Elliot, 1984).

Consultee Training

Preservice training to use consultation services has received little attention in literature. Yet if employees are expected to take advantage of an organization's consultative resources, *how* to make effective use of consultants should receive some attention, For example, teachers should have specific information regarding the role and competencies of school support services staff such as the counselor, occupational therapist, resource teachers in the various areas of special education, social workers, speech and language specialists, and school psychologists. The ways in which resources could be utilized along with strategies consultees could employ to maximize their use would be important to include. Consultees should know *when* to request consultation, *methods* of presenting the problem to facilitate problem solving, *what* to expect from consultants, and *how* to make their style of working known to the consultant.

All too often, direct service providers are expected to have exhausted their repertoire of problem-solving skills before seeking any consultation or making a referral. The psychological consequence of such an orientation is to reduce the consultee to a position of incompetence, which not only makes the request for consultation difficult to make, but creates a situation in which those "weaknesses" will not only be reviewed but confirmed. Although it is not unreasonable to expect that the consultee has addressed the problem in some meaningful way, consultation is often more effective in terms of outcome and consultee growth if introduced early on in the consultee's engagement with a problem. The home base of the

consultant, whether internal or external to the system, as well as the resources a system has committed to consultation services are significant considerations that affect when entry by the consultant is made. The point to be made here is that the consultees' *orientation* toward consultation can be influenced during training and can significantly affect their involvement in the consultation process.

Consultees should also be trained in *methods* of framing the problem when it is presented to the consultant as well as preparing a data base that will enhance the consultation experience. For example, describing a problem through the use of specific examples not only reduces communication problems caused by professional jargon, but provides opportunities to examine intervention attempts and the reasons for their success or failure. The consultees' attempt to share all of their observations, whether of seeming relevance or not, in addition to any hunches or guesses as to the dimensions of the problem can prove valuable to consultants. Likewise, any data, whether of a formal or informal nature, that the consultee has should also be included.

The consultant's set is also important for the consultee to understand. An appreciation of the consultant's values (for example, problem finding is as important as problem solving) will help the consultee better understand the process itself. Similarly, knowing that a consultant emphasizes the problem identification stage of the consultation process and uses a systems orientation approach should help consultees appreciate and accept the service.

Consultees should also be trained to *discriminate* among the various consultation models they might expect or request. Negotiation may be the realistic outcome, but they should expect at the least that the range of their service needs be overtly stated. The scenario is all too common wherein a consultee is critical of the consultation received from a psychologist at the local mental health clinic. The reason for the criticism (for example, "The psychologist doesn't know what schools are about") sounds plausible enough but may, in fact, not reflect the primary source of frustration. Later observation may indicate that the consultant was perceived to have asked a lot of questions including the opinion of the consultee and to have left the problem in his or her lap. What the consultees expected, and even desired, was an expert who would tell them what to do. At the minimum, they had hoped for an "active" change agent. One consultee might legitimately opt for more of an expert approach, but they should then know what the trade-offs are. When consultees are given the information and power to discriminate, evaluation of the consultation is more likely to reflect those choices and the ensuing outcome than to result in a retrospective critique based on unclear parameters.

Finally, it is at the preservice level of training that any professionals who will eventually be expected to work together can most easily be trained together. Such preservice models have been described for promoting school based multidisciplinary teams (Buktenica, 1970). It would appear that similar experiences can be arranged regarding consultation training. In fact, collaborative efforts involving resource professionals, managers, and staff would seem to have the greatest probability of success. Such training could be both didactic as well as process orientated, serving to facilitate the training objectives of the individual professionals as well.

The objectives for consultee training, then, are: (1) the potential consultee needs to understand consultation as a process, (2) consultees need to know when consultation should be initiated and how the timing of the request can affect the process and outcome, and (3)

consultees must be able to make informed choices as to when consultation can be utilized in contrast to other available services.

Training during Consultation

More than likely, the consultee will not have experienced any of the preservice training described in the previous section. The consultant is then faced with a decision as to whether or not to incorporate this educative function into the problem-solving process and intentionally address those needs. If indeed all consultation should address consultee preferences/expectations as well as develop some skills, scales measuring consultation model preferences and objectives could be given to the consultee prior to the first consultation session (See Chapter 11). These scales could serve to sensitize the consultee to the critical parameters of consultation for them, function as a more natural way to begin discussion of these questions, and serve as the basis for finalizing a contract. While it is hardly reasonable to predicate consultation services on the consultees' willingness to undergo a workshop-type component of consultation, some of this emphasis seems justified. However, it may be that if the consultant takes on an educative role during the consultation process then a hierarchical relationship ensues, which is antithetical to the consultation model of choice. Indeed, beginning in a didactic fashion might contribute to either consultees' resistance to what they see as irrelevant for the task at hand or reinforcement of a passive role throughout consultation.

Zins (1993) reviewed a number of studies in which direct training of consultation-related skills was demonstrated; among the specific objectives included were the promotion of behavior consultation through knowledge of related principles, efficacy of modeling procedures for improving problem-solving skills, enhancement of communication skills, and the improvement of parent-teacher conferences. Based on the review, he proposes that consultees be trained directly in skills in order to improve the effectiveness of consultation interactions and enhance consultation outcomes. He reasons that the benefit of the training would be to increase congruence between consultants' and consultees' expectations. Although he is concerned with a specific consultation model, there are generic skills that the consultee could use regardless of the model being employed by the consultant.

The training question will continue to confront the consultant who wants to incorporate the educative function into the consultation process. For internally based consultants a particular skill or phase of consultee development may be solely emphasized during consultation on any one case. Future requests for consultation would then present opportunities for emphasizing another consultee skill or stage of consultation. In each instance, the needs of the consultee and problem situation should dictate the choice that is made. For the external consultant modeling or overt emphasis on the target area is recommended as the strategy of choice.

Professional Development Training

The training issue can be addressed as a staff development exercise for consultees in the field or as part of an eventual group consultation format. When there is an educational component prior to group consultation experiences, the motivation to learn may be high. If con-

sultees will eventually serve as co-consultants with the consultant or engage in peer consultation, the degree of involvement should increase even more. However, a staff development exercise that is geared to some potential future need of short duration may be of dubious value except for the inexperienced consultee.

Lambert, Sandoval, & Yandell (1975) describe the first stage in training of school-based mental health consultants as "learning how to be a consultee." Their premise was that the consultant must be aware of the different kinds of learning facing a consultee. The categories of understanding are presented here as one example of an outline for consultee training (Sandoval et al., 1977). They include: (1) recognizing how the consultation session is different from other professional contacts, (2) presenting information so the consultant understands and responds, (3) learning about the consultant, (4) learning what kind of help to expect and how to use the consultation experience, and (5) sensitizing oneself to the consultant's style of behaving in the work setting as it affects professional functioning.

Understanding of the contract provides the consultee with the behavioral limits on what can be said or done in consultation. Most importantly, as Sandoval et al. (1977) have pointed out, differentiating the role of consultant from that of the consultant's training (for example, mental health professional) is very important. The degree to which personal matters and peer professional relationships can or should be discussed also can be explored at this time.

The need to develop the skill of presenting information to the consultant along with any hypotheses developed by the consultees is important to the consultation process. The willingness to cooperate and jointly engage in the investigatory phase of problem finding will be invaluable to both participants, but requires acceptance on the consultee's part that risk taking will be involved. Finally, there must be recognition that some problems can lead to data base supported interventions, but other problems are at best conceptualized as hypotheses.

The remaining elements of training involve an understanding of the consultant's role and professional background. Closely related to issues involving the contract are issues of confidentiality that need to be explored. Consultees should hold realistic expectations and learn how they might maximize the strengths of their consultant. Consultees should know consultation can be pursued just as effectively when problems are seen to be developing rather than when they reach a crisis level. If consultation is to enhance the competence of the consultee, the range of opportunities throughout the consultation process must be apparent.

Summary

This chapter has attempted to sensitize the reader to an often overlooked or little emphasized aspect of consultation—the consultee. We need to consider what the consultee brings to the sessions, in terms of training for their role as well as cognitive and emotional characteristics, if consultation is to truly have an impact as a service delivery model. This premise is especially reinforced where the more active models of consultation are involved, although some would say that the degree of consultee involvement determines success in all models. The literature is clear that little training of consultees is being done, and even less

attention is being directed toward the expectations and preferences of consultees and their characteristics in terms of consultation model selection. When the consultee does receive attention, it usually involves the issue of resistance, and then the discussion revolves more around resolution than cause(s). Caplan has been one of the obvious exceptions to some of these general conclusions, having somewhat tied types of consultation strategies to types of consultee problems. In short, the literature reviewed in this chapter suggests that unless the consultee is more intentionally considered in the planning of consultation, we run the risk of reducing our understanding, if not effectiveness, of the process.

The consultee is treated as a variable in consultation in this chapter, but the consultee can be examined from any number of perspectives. And, in fact, the interaction of those many facets (variables) is what needs to be considered, whether in research or practice, if consultation is to be successful. Certainly the focus on any one characteristic may have its justification, but pursuing how age, personality, problem-solving ability, and so forth combine may lead to more effective consultee approaches. Finally, the consultee must be treated as a variable within the total consultation process involving the consultant, client, and setting.

Some final observations need to be made about the literature written about the consultee influence on consultation. For all practical purposes research on this important variable is in the beginning stages, so that in only a few instances do we have the semblance of data based working hypotheses. Furthermore, as in other areas of consultation research, the consultants in the studies are in training or rather inexperienced. Also the consultees tend to have a professional background themselves. The bulk of studies are done in schools. Consequently, those features must be kept in mind as we attempt to generalize the findings to specific situations.

Tips for the Practitioner

1. In the preliminary phase of consultation, determine the preconceived notions that consultees have about their roles, the process (e.g., amount of time required). Take steps to make sure that your expectations and theirs are approximately the same.

2. Similarly, try to determine the model of consultation preferred by your consultees. If possible, practice their preferred model. If you cannot, you must persuade them that the model of consultation you are practicing will be effective.

3. Be sensitive to the differences in perception that arise because of ethnic, socio-economic, and racial differences. Alter your style to accommodate consultees' preferences.

4. As you consult, try to determine the skills that the consultee brings to consultation. When deficiencies are discovered, arrange for indirect training experiences such as observation of other direct training, such as in-service training, to remedy deficiencies that will impede progress. It is inevitable that some training will have to occur during consultation.

Review Questions

1. What are the types of consultee preferences for consultation that are likely to be expressed? Identify cautions that must be kept in mind as such information is considered.

2. What advice would you give to a beginning consultant who uses the age of the consultee in determining the initial style of interaction?

3. What is likely to be one of the biggest differences in the problem-solving styles of consultees versus consultants?

4. Describe the personality attributes of the consultee that could influence outcome.

5. List some important skills that individuals should possess to enhance their role as consultees, thereby contributing to the positive outcome of the consultation process.

6. Why is it important that the consultant recognize the consultee as a crucial factor in the consultation activity?

References

Altrocchi, J. (1972). Mental health consultation. In S. E. Golann & C. Elsdorfer (Eds.), *Handbook of Community Psychology* (pp. 477–508). New York: Appleton-Century-Crofts.

Babcock, N., & Pryzwansky, W. B. (1983). Models of consultation: Preferences of educational professionals at five stages of service. *Journal of School Psychology, 21*, (4), 359–366.

Baker, H. L. (1965). Psychological services: From the school staff's point of view. *Journal of School Psychology, 3*, 36–42.

Bardon, J. I. (1977, August). *The consultee in consultation: Preparation and training.* Paper presented at the American Psychological Association Convention, San Francisco, CA.

Bergan, J. R., & Tombari, M. L. (1976). Consultant skill and efficiency and the implementation and outcomes of consultation. *Journal of School Psychology, 14*, 3–14.

Berkowitz, L. (1972). Social norms, feelings, and other factors affecting helping and altruism. In L. Berkowitz (Ed.), *Advances in experimental social psychology* (Vol. 6). New York: Academic Press.

Brady, M., & Schneider, O. (1973). The psychiatrist as classroom teacher: School consultation in the inner city. *Hospital and Community Psychiatry, 24*, 248–251.

Brickman, P., Rabinowitz, V. C., Karuza, J., Coates, D., Cohn, E., & Kidder, L. (1982). Models of helping and coping. *American Psychologist, 37*(4), 368–384.

Bronkowski, R. (1968). Mental health consultation and operation Head Start. *American Psychologist, 23*, 769–772.

Bucktenica, N. A. (1970). A multidisciplinary training team in the public schools. *Journal of School Psychology, 8*, 220–225.

Caplan, G. (1970). *The theory and practice of mental health consultation.* New York: Basic Books.

Clark, R. D. (1979). School consultants give teachers what they want—A straight answer? *Proceedings of the Eleventh Annual Convention, National Association of School Psychologists, 3.*

Coleman, S. (1976, August). *Developing collaborative-process consultation: Teacher and participant-observer perceptions and outcome.* Paper presented at the American Psychologist Association Convention, Washington, DC.

DeForest, P. A. & Hughes, J. N. (1992). Effect of teacher involvement and teacher self efficacy on ratings of consultant effectiveness and intervention acceptability. *Journal of Educational and Psychological Consultation, 3*, 301–316.

Duncan, C., & Pryzwansky, W. B. (1988). Consultation research: Trends in doctoral dissertations,

1978–1985. *Journal of School Psychology*, *26*, 107–119.

Duncan, C. & Pryzwansky, W. B. (1993). Effects of race, racial identity development and orientation style on perceived consultant effectiveness. *Journal of Multicultural Counseling and Development*, *21*, 88–96.

Friedman, L. P. (1976, August). *Teacher consultation styles: A theoretical model for increasing consultation process effectiveness*. Paper presented at the American Psychologist Convention, Washington, DC.

Friedman, L. P. (1977). Locus of control consultation styles: A theoretical model for increasing teacher-centered consultation effectiveness (Doctoral dissertation, University of Pennsylvania, 1976). *Dissertation Abstracts International*, *37*, 2074A.

Gibbs, J. T. (1980). The interpersonal orientation in mental health consultation: Toward a model of ethnic variations in consultation. *Journal of Community Psychology*, *8*, 195–207.

Gilmore, G., & Chandy, J. (1973). Teachers' perception of school psychological services, *Journal of School Psychology*, *11*(2), 139–147.

Gold, R. F. & Hollander, S. K. (1992). The status of consultant teacher services in special education on Long Island New York: 1989–1990. *Journal of Educational and Psychological Consultation*, *3*, 25–30.

Gutkin, T. B. (1980). Teacher perceptions of consultation services provided by school psychologists, *Professional Psychology*, *11*, 637–642.

————— (1983). *Variables affecting the outcomes of consultation as perceived by consultees*. Paper presented at the American Psychological Association Convention, Anaheim, CA.

————— & Ajchenbaum (1984). Teachers' perception of control and preferences for consultation services. *Professional Psychology: Research and Practice*, *15*(4), 565–570.

————— & Bossard, M. D. (1984). Impact of consultant, consultee, and organizational variables in teachers attitudes toward consultation services. *Journal of School Psychology*, *22*(3), 251–258.

Hilke, J. L. (1984). *An examination of the relationship between consultant variables and interpersonal problem solving skills for school psychology students, recent graduates and past graduates.*

(Unpublished doctoral dissertation, University of North Carolina at Chapel Hill).

Hirschman, R. (1974). Utilization of mental health consultation and self-perceptions of intraorganizational importance and influence. *Journal of Consulting and Clinical Psychology*, *42*(6), 916.

Hughes, J. N., Barker, D., Kemenoff, S., & Hart, M. (1993). Problem ownership, causal attributions, and self efficacy as predictors of teachers' referral decisions. *Journal of Educational and Psychological Consultation*, *4*, 369–384.

Iscoe, I., Pierce-Jones, J., Friedman, S. T., & McGehearty, L. (1967). Some strategies in mental health consultation: A brief description of a project and some preliminary results. In E. L. Cowen, E. A. Gardner, and M. Zax (Eds.), *Emergent approaches to mental health problems* (pp. 307–330). New York: Appleton-Century-Crofts.

Isen, A. M., Means, B., Patrick, R., & Nowicki, G. (1982). Some factors influencing decision-making strategy and risk-taking. In M. S. Clark & S. T. Fiske (Eds.), *Affect and cognition* (pp. 243–261). Hillsdale, NJ: Erlbaum.

Kolb, D. A. (1983). Problem management: Learning from experience. In S. Srvasta (Ed.), *The executive mind* (pp. 109–143). San Francisco: Jossey-Bass.

Lambert, N. M., Sandoval, J. H., & Yandell, G. W. (1975). Preparation of school psychologists for school-based consultation: A training activity and a service to community schools. *Journal of School Psychology*, *13*, 68–75.

Lortie, D. C. (1975). *School teacher*, Chicago: University of Chicago Press.

Macarov, D. (1968). *A study of the consultation process*. New York: State Committees and Association.

Mann, P. A. (1972). Accessibility and organizational power in the entry phase of mental health consultation. *Journal of Consulting and Clinical Psychology*, *38*, 215–218.

Mannino, F. U., & Shore, M. F. (1975). The effects of consultation. *American Journal of Community Psychology*, *3*(1), 1–21.

McPherson, R. B., Crowson, R. L., & Pitner, N. J. (1986). *Managing uncertainty: Administrative theory and practice in education*. Columbus, OH: Charles E. Merrill.

Medway, F. J., & Forman, S. G. (1980). Psychologists' and teachers' reactions to mental health and behav-

ioral school consultation. *Journal of School Psychology, 18,* 338–348.

Miller, J. N. (1974). Consumer response to theoretical role models in school psychology. *Journal of School Psychology, 12,* 310–317.

Mischley, M. (1973). Teacher preferences for consultation methods and its relation to selected background personality and organization variables (Doctoral dissertation, University of Texas at Austin, 1973). *Dissertation Abstracts International, 34,* 2312B.

Morrison, A. (1970). Consultation and group process with indigenous neighborhood workers. *Community Mental Health Journal, 6,* 3–12.

Noy, P., DeNour, A., & Moses, R. (1966). Discrepancies between expectations and service in psychiatric consultation. *Archives in General Psychology, 14,* 651–657.

Piersel, W. C. (1985). Behavioral consultation: an approach to problem solving in educational settings. In J. R. Bergan (Ed.), *School psychology in contemporary society* (pp. 252–280). Columbus, OH: Charles E. Merrill.

Pinto, R. F. (1981). Consultant orientations and client system perception: Styles of cross cultural consultation. In R. Lippitt & G. Lippitt (Eds.), *Systems thinking: A resource for organization diagnosis and intervention* (Chapter IV, pp. 57–74). Washington, DC: International Consultants Foundations.

Platt, J. J., & Spivak, G. (1975). *Manual for the means-end problem-solving procedure (MEPS): A measure of interpersonal cognitive problem-solving skill.* Philadelphia, PA: Hahnemann Medical College and Hospital.

Pryzwansky, W. B. & Vatz, B. C. (1989, April). *School Psychologists' solutions to a consultation problem: Do experts agree?* Paper presented at the National Association of School Psychologists Convention, Chicago, IL.

Pryzwansky, W. B., & White, G. (1983). The influence of consultee characteristics on preferences for consultation approaches. *Professional Psychology: Research and Practice, 14,* 457–461.

Roberts, R. (1970). Perceptions of actual and desired role functions of school psychologists by psychologists and teachers. *Psychology in the Schools, 7,* 1–25.

Sager, C., Brayboy, T., & Waxenberg, B. (1972). Black patient—white therapist. *American Journal of Orthopsychiatry, 42,* 415–423.

Sandoval, J., Lambert, N. M., & Davis, J. M. (1977). Consultation from the consultee's perspective. *Journal of School Psychology, 15*(4), 334–342.

Sarason, S. B. (1971). *The culture of the school and the problem of change.* Boston: Allyn & Bacon.

Schulte, A. C., Osborne, S. S., & Kauffman, J. M. (1993). Teacher responses to types of consultative special education services. *Journal of Educational and Psychological Consultation, 4,* 1–27.

Slesser, R. A., Fine, M. J., & Tracy, D. B. (1990). Teacher reactions to two approaches to school-based psychological consultation. *Journal of Educational Psychological Consultation, 1,* 243–258.

Solomon, M. H. (1984). *An approach to assessing the problem-solving skills of teachers.* Unpublished doctoral dissertation, University of North Carolina at Chapel Hill.

Sue, D., & Sue, E. (1977). Barriers to effective cross-cultural counseling. *Journal of Counseling Psychology, 24,* 420–429.

Vatz, B. C. & Pryzwansky, W. B. (1988, April). *The problem finding style of expert consultants in school psychology.* Paper presented at the National Association of School Psychologists Convention, Boston, MA.

Voss, J. F., Tyler, U., & Yengo, L. A. (1983). Individual differences in the solving of social science problems. In R. F. Dillon & R. R. Sneck (Eds.), *Individual differences in cognition,* Vol. I (pp. 205–323). New York: Academic Press.

Waters, L. (1973). School psychologists as perceived by school personnel: Support for a consultant model. *Journal of School Psychology, 11*(1), 40–45.

Weiler, M. B. (1984). *The influence of contact and setting on the ratings of parents for models of consultation.* Unpublished master's thesis, North Carolina State University, Raleigh, NC.

Wenger, R. (1979). School consultation process: Analysis, application and evaluation of a process variable—consultation. *Psychology in the Schools, 16*(1), 127–131.

White, G. W., & Pryzwansky, W. B. (1982). Consultation outcome as a result of in-service resource teacher training. *Psychology in the Schools, 19,* 495–502.

Witt, J. C., Martens, J., Elliott, S. N. (1984). Factors affecting teachers judgments of the acceptability of behavioral intervention: Time involvement,

behavior problem severity, and type of intervention. *Behavior Therapy*, *15*, 203–206.

Witt, J. C., Moe, G., Gutkin, T. B., & Andrews, L. (1984). The effect of saying the same thing in different ways: The problem of language and jargon in school-based consultation. *Journal of School Psychology*, *22*(4), 361–367.

Zins, J. E. (1993). Enhancing consultee problem-solving skills in consultative interactions. *Journal of Counseling and Development*, *72*, 185–190.

Chapter **9**

===================

Consultation with Parents

Goals of the Chapter

The goals of this chapter are to provide an overview of parental consultation including its empirical support and to provide a model for conducting parental consultation.

Chapter Preview

1. A brief history of parental consultation will be provided.
2. An eclectic model of parental consultation will be discussed and illustrated.
3. Consultation with parents and groups will be discussed.
4. Some of the unique problems involved in consulting with parents will be presented and some solutions offered.

The practice of consultation with parents has received relatively little attention in consultation literature until recently (Sheridan, 1993), probably because of the influence of Gerald Caplan (1970). The reader may recall that Caplan's definition of consultation posited that consultation is a process that occurs between professionals, and since Caplan's thinking has dominated much of the consultation literature until recently, parents have not been viewed as prospective consultees by many. However, Dinkmeyer & Carlson (1973) set forth an Adlerian-based model of parental consultation. In 1975, a model of parent consultation based largely upon operant psychology was presented (Brown & Brown, 1975), which was later expanded to include some Adlerian concepts (Brown, Wyne, Blackburn, & Powell, 1979). This chapter builds and expands upon some of this early thinking about consultation as well as the behavioral philosophy of training parents to intervene in the lives of their children by presenting an eclectic model of parental consultation. However, prior to the presentation of the model, an examination of the empirical support for family consul-

tation will be made and parental consultation will be differentiated from other types of interventions with parents.

Empirical Support

Because of the history of parental consultation, it is not surprising that the research in the area has focused on either Adlerian (see Frazier & Mathes, 1975; Palmo & Kuzniar, 1971) or behavioral approaches (see Weathers & Liberman, 1975, or the review by Cobb & Medway, 1978) with the latter approach being investigated far more frequently. The literature that has been produced to date does generally support the efficacy of parental consultation (Cobb & Medway, 1978) and when consultation with parents has been compared with other types of direct intervention such as individual or group counseling, it has proven to be as effective (Perkins & Wicas, 1971) or more effective (McGowan, 1969; Palmo & Kuzniar, 1971). However, it should be pointed out that many of the early studies on consultation did not have clear definitions of consultation and the interventions seemed more like parent education than parental consultation, a distinction that needs consideration and will be made in the next section.

Even though conclusions about the efficacy of consultation must be drawn cautiously, literature from a related area, parent education, supports the potential benefits of working with parents (Dembo, Sweitzer, & Lauritzen, 1985; Dumas, 1980). However, until specific research is conducted on the process and outcome of consulting with parents, generalizations must be made tentatively.

Parent Consultation and Other Parental Interventions

While definitions of consultation have been offered throughout the book, it is important to delineate the boundaries of parental consultation by differentiating it from two other parent-oriented processes: family therapy and parent education. Family therapy is a direct service to the entire family in which parents and children participate simultaneously with a therapist to correct a problem in the family (Goldenberg & Goldenberg, 1985). Parent education is an indirect approach aimed at teaching parents specific parenting skills. It is typically conducted in a group setting, follows a set curriculum determined by the instructor, and follows a specific timetable (Brown, Wyne, Blackburn, & Powell, 1979). Consultation, like parent education, is an indirect intervention, since only the parents are seen by the consultant.

Parent consultation has as one of its objectives the enhancement of parenting skills of the consultees, but it follows no set agenda. The process of parental consultation is determined collaboratively with the consultant and the consultee; it is aimed at determining problems that exist in the family system that are related to one or more children's maladaptive functioning; and it is designed to assist parents to increase their understanding of the problems they are experiencing with the children and to help them design and implement solutions to those problems. Parent consultation, like family therapy, assumes that an interpersonal relationship is essential to a successful outcome, an assumption that varies to some degree with parent education that is typically a more impersonal process. It should also be noted that parental consultation is typically a shorter term intervention than is family therapy.

Family consultation is viewed as an appropriate intervention for parents who lack basic knowledge of parenting principles, lack the skill to implement a solution to the problem, or have unrealistic or dysfunctional expectations of one or more of their children growing out of stereotypical perceptions or experiences with the child. It is not deemed appropriate for families in which the pathological behavior of the parents is the source of the family's problem. Nor is parent consultation appropriate for families in which there are severe marital difficulties that are influencing the parenting process.

As in all forms of consultation, the primary goal of the process is to help the consultee help the client. The gain for the client (child) should be improvement in educational or psychological functioning. The gain for the parent's consultation should be increased ability to facilitate the development of their children. The family unit as a whole should also benefit from parent consultation in that the unit should become more adaptable because of enhanced communication and problem-solving abilities. The family unit should also become more cohesive, although they should not become so intertwined in each other's lives that autonomy is not offered by the family structure (Olson, Sprenkle, & Russell, 1979).

Models of Family Consultation

Behavioral

As has already been noted, Behavioral models of parent education and consultation have been the dominant approaches to working with families. A Behavioral Model of consultation (Bergan, 1977; Bergan & Kratochwill, 1990) was set forth in Chapter Three. In 1981, Bergan and Duley attempted to expand on Bergan's earlier work by looking at the family as a system. More recently, Sheridan and Kratochwill (1992) have elaborated what they term a *Conjoint Behavioral Consultation Model*, which is defined as an indirect approach to consultation in which parents and teachers join with the consultant to address the needs of the child (Sheridan, 1993). The unique feature of this model is that it emphasizes collaboration between teachers and parents, an emphasis that most would agree is badly needed. Except for this different emphasis, the Conjoint Behavioral Consultation Model follows closely Bergan's (1977; Bergan & Duley, 1981) original propositions.

Eclectic Models: General Considerations

There are probably two theoretically pure models of parent consultation, Humanistic, Behavioral and Adlerian, only one of which will be addressed here. However, most family consultants are eclectic and have tried to some degree to incorporate systems principles into their approaches (e.g., Bergan & Duley, 1981; Sheridan & Kratochwill, 1992). The fact is that some theoretical approaches are incompatible with systems thinking. This is particularly true of traditional behavioral explanations of human behavior (classical and operant conditioning) and systems theory. Behaviorists subscribe to the basic scientific principle of cause and effect; systems thinkers reject this idea. Behaviorists endorse reductionistic thinking that suggests that all behavioral and environmental variables can be quantified;

systems thinkers believe that as soon as you start to analyze and quantify you destroy the essence of what is being examined. Behaviorists believe in an objective reality; systems thinkers are phenomenological. The point here is that these two theoretical approaches are antithetical and thus cannot be merged in any meaningful sense. However, less reductionistic theories can be melded with systems thinking to form meaningful approaches to family consultation.

An Eclectic Approach

The major goal of this chapter is to present an eclectic model of consultation with parents that relies upon concepts from the social learning theory (Bandura, 1977, 1978), mental health consultation (Caplan, 1970), and systems theory (Bateson, 1972; Capra 1982). Of these three influences, the model is most heavily tied to social learning theory and, in many ways, is quite analogous to the social learning model of consultation described earlier in this volume. However, Caplan's (1970) consultee-centered model of consultation has contributed to some of the ideas about assessment, although his ideas about theme interference as the major source of consultee problems have been rejected. The principles of systems theory were delineated in Chapter Four in a discussion aimed at increasing the reader's understanding of organizations. However, certain of these principles such as interdependence are quite useful in fostering the understanding of parent-child interactions and will be drawn upon in this discussion.

Another goal of this chapter is to illustrate how the approach to family consultation can be applied by providing concrete suggestions for conducting family consultation sessions. These suggestions grow out of the experiences of the authors and their students rather than from empiricism. It is therefore recommended that consultants-in-training accept these suggestions in the spirit in which they are offered, that is, as tentative guides to be tested in the crucible of consulting with parents and be retained or discarded based on the result.

The Assumptions of the Approach

From Social Learning Theory (Bandura, 1977, 1978)

1. Most behavior is acquired as a result of imitation of esteemed models. Since in most families parents are esteemed models, the origin of much childhood behavior is imitation of the parent or, in the case of the younger children, older siblings. When parents are either absent or not held in high esteem as models, other individuals will be imitated.
2. Cognition mediates the process of behavior acquisition. Cognitions regarding one's confidence that one can perform a task (self-efficacy), the importance attached to a task (appraisal), the outcomes associated with performing a task (expectations), and the standards one has developed with regard to performing a task are of major importance. Effective parents are confident, see child rearing as important, believe that they can make a difference, and want to do an outstanding job.

3. Self-efficacy can best be heightened by performance accomplishments. Vicarious modeling and verbal persuasion are also effective means of improving self-efficacy. Whenever anxiety is a barrier to performance, reducing that anxiety can improve self-efficacy by engaging parents in proximal goal setting and involvement in activities that are deemed important (appraisal) and achievable (expectation), self-efficacy regarding parenting can be improved.
4. Standards of functioning as a parent are probably acquired as a result of direct observation of one's own parents and observation of others. In consultation, vicarious modeling, verbal persuasion, and parental standards of functioning (e.g., how well they want to parent) are the mechanisms available for changing the standards of parents.

From Mental Health Consultation (Caplan, 1970)

1. Consultee problems can be classified as lack of knowledge, lack of skill, lack of confidence, and lack of objectivity. In this context, lack of objectivity refers to biases that are acquired either as a result of learning prior to the birth of a child (e.g., retarded children are to be shunned) or as a result of anxiety-laden experiences after the child is born (e.g., serious illness where child nearly dies).
2. The problems of knowledge, skill, self-confidence, and objectivity are often interrelated.

From Systems Theory (Bateson, 1972; Capra, 1982)

1. The nuclear family is a part of a broader suprasystem called the extended family. Many of the values of the nuclear family are based upon those of the suprasystem. These values, whether they be positive or negative, guide the parenting process.
2. The family interacts as a system. Healthy families are interdependent, but differentiated to the degree that individuals can have distinct identities; develop subsystems (e.g., parents and children); develop distinct mechanisms for regulating the behavior of their members based upon principles of supportive, open communication; and have their own values and goals.
3. Cause-and-effect is virtually impossible to ascertain in the family system. Therefore, blaming should be avoided.

The Process

The process of family consultation should be guided by the nine assumptions previously listed. However, the actual process of consultation with families is little different than that of other types of consultation. As described earlier in this volume, consultation is a problem-solving process that moves through certain stages: structuring and relationship development or assessment, problem identification, goal setting, intervention, and evaluation and follow-up.

One additional stage of consultation has been added to these five for parental consultation: explanation of psychological principles. This stage has been added because it is assumed that parents need to understand the *why* as well as the *what* of the intervention to be employed. It is also worth reiterating that these stages, while described as though they occur in a linear fashion, rarely do. However, for the sake of this discussion, the stages of family consultation will be described sequentially, while making every attempt to illustrate the dynamic nature of the process.

Relationship Development and Structuring

Initiating the Contact

Either one or both parents or the consultant may initiate the consulting relationship. In any situation, it is important to establish a collaborative contract from the outset. Some of the following statements *illustrate* how this may occur, although canned statements should be avoided.

Consultant: I've asked you to come in because we are quite concerned about Susan's progress in school. As you know, we've tested her for learning disabilities and other problems, and the results suggest that she is capable of doing good schoolwork. Her teacher believes the problem may be a motivational one. What I am proposing is that we work together to help Susan. There are certain things that we can do at school and other activities that might be carried on at home. If we work together, I am confident that we can get Susan on the track to learning at a pace that is more consistent with her potential.

OR

Consultant: John is responding well to the treatment, but substance abuse often returns unless there are some fundamental changes in the adolescent's environment. I believe it would be extremely helpful if we worked together at the clinic and in the home to help John eliminate substance abuse.

Once an overture for collaboration in the consultation process has been made, it is essential that power equalization occur. Parsons and Meyers (1984) suggest a number of strategies that may be useful in accomplishing power equalization that will be presented here. However, power equalization should begin with a forthright statement indicating that the consultation is to be a mutual process, that both parties are to contribute equally, and that the consultee ultimately has the power to accept or reject whatever solutions are generated by the consulting dyad. A statement such as the following illustrates this point.

Consultant: It is important for you to recognize how important you are in this process. Sometimes people involved in consulting relationships look to the consultant for "answers" and when they do that, they disregard their own ability and knowledge. My view of consultation is that we are equals. As parents, you know your child far better than I ever can and that knowledge is far more important in the success of this process than all the things I've learned about children. But if we combine the things I've learned about working with children with what you know about your own child, then I am confident that our work together can be successful.

Once a statement focusing upon the collaborative nature of consultation has been made, it is also important to set forth the goals of the process (e.g., assisting parents to deal with a child's problem more effectively).

In addition to the foregoing structuring statement, the following strategies may be useful in the establishment and maintenance of an egalitarian relationship.

1. Allow the consultee the freedom to accept or reject.
2. Encourage the consultee to contribute suggestions.
3. Emphasize the consultee's contributions.
4. Encourage consultee responsibility.
5. Require effort from the consultee.   (Parsons & Meyers, 1984, pp. 38–39)

Parsons and Meyers go on to suggest that the consultant act in a non-authoritarian manner, that questions be phrased so that the consultee feels as though he or she is actually contributing to the consultation rather than just providing data to the consultant, and that suggestions be made quite tentatively. The following excerpt from a consultation session with a parent illustrates some of these ideas.

Consultant: I'm delighted that we are going to be working together. It would be very helpful to me if you could share with me the ways in which you tried to stop the aggressive behavior and how these efforts have worked.

Consultee: (Mother is consultee.) Well, the main thing I've done is punish him. I've spanked him, but that just seems to make him angry. I've tried grounding him, but he ignores me. The only other thing that has worked is that I've taken away his allowance from time to time, but I really don't like doing that.

Consultant: So you have tried a number of things with varying success. Tell me a little more about what happened when you took away his allowance and why that is not an approach that you like.

Consultant: He responds pretty well when I threaten to take away his allowance, but I remember what it was like at 13 and having no money. I just feel bad about taking his allowance. So even when I threaten to take it, I often don't follow through even when he hits other people.

Consultant: So sometimes you follow through with your threats and sometimes you don't. It sounds a little like your own childhood memories get in the way.

Consultee: Yeah! I suppose they do.

Consultant: You've obviously thought about the problem. What types of suggestions would you make to yourself?

Consultee: (Laughs.) Be consistent. Everybody says be consistent. But it's harder than it sounds. I love Jeremy and I don't want to be too hard on him.

Consultant: It's obvious that you care deeply for Jeremy. I'm wondering if your present course of action is getting you where you want to go with Jeremy.

Consultee: No. I guess not. I know it isn't.

To some degree, the first few minutes of the consulting relationship set the tone for the remainder of the process. It is the consultant's responsibility to structure the relationship so that the power is equalized and then to maintain this stance throughout the consultation.

Relationship development: Relationship building and the structure of the power relationship go hand in hand. The relationship development techniques described in Chapter Five should be applied in parental consultation. However, because the process is so immediate, it is often the case that the consultant is (1) structuring the power relationship, (2) developing an interpersonal relationship with the consultee, and (3) beginning the assessment of the problem at the same time. While there never seems to be enough time to meet with parents and the problems that the consultee's child has are often severe, the use of appropriate relationship building techniques is still an essential ingredient of the consulting relationship. Consultation research literature confirms that the perceptions held of consultants by consultees are greatly influenced by their ability to employ relationship building techniques appropriately (Horton & Brown, 1990). It may also be a useful reminder to indicate that if a solid consulting relationship is not formed, parents may not disclose certain types of sensitive information that is necessary for accurate assessment of the problem or they may not develop sufficient trust in the consultant so that they will follow through with the interventions that are designed.

In addition to using the relationship building techniques described in Chapter Five, the following few tips may be useful in building relationships with parents.

1. If the parent is coming to a clinic or a school, be ready to greet them upon arrival since they may perceive these environments as hostile.
2. Immediately reassure parents that the purpose of their visit is to work collaboratively with you for the benefit of their child. Avoid any hint that the parents are being treated; focus on the client.
3. If others (e.g., teachers, psychologists) are to be involved, bring them into the process after parents have been made comfortable. Parents may be quite threatened initially by a group of strangers.
4. Discuss confidentiality as soon as possible. Parents may be quite defensive about what they think their child has told you or others about the home environment.
5. Establish an informal atmosphere. Offer coffee or soft drinks if possible. Have parents sit in comfortable chairs.
6. If the consultation is occurring in the consultee's home, be prompt, accept offerings of refreshment, and suggest that you have your discussion where the parents are most comfortable.

Assessment

As mentioned earlier, assessment, relationship development, and structuring the power relationship may often occur simultaneously. If both parents come to the consultation, the consultant should carefully observe their interaction as they enter the consulting room and the nature of their interaction throughout the consultation session. These observations may pro-

vide indicators of the nature of their relationship, the extent to which open communication occurs, and values differences with regard to child rearing. Statements such as the following can be quite revealing.

Consultee: This is the way I see it. Betty doesn't always agree, but—

Consultee: Sometimes, I just have to put my foot down.

Consultee: Then I told Darrell, just wait 'til your dad gets home.

Consultee: That's not the way it happens. He's finished his homework before you get home anyway.

It is also important to focus on the non-verbalizing parent when the other is talking to determine how he or she is reacting to what is being said. Non-verbal reactions can provide clues about whether parents are in agreement or disagreement about the nature of the child's problem and what is being done about it in the home. If there are differing perceptions of the child at home and/or in the way the child is being responded to by the parents, these differences need to be reconciled.

It seems to be more typical that consultation occurs with one parent because of the number of single family homes and work schedules. Effective consultation can occur in these situations even if the parent not living in the home is not involved *or* if the absent parent is *not* in agreement with the identified problem. These situations will be discussed in greater detail later in this chapter.

Some information comes to the consultant as a result of observations with the consultee. However, the majority of the data used in the assessment proves results from the verbalization of the consultee(s). In order to make an accurate assessment of the nature of the consultees' perceptions of their child's difficulty and the factors that may be contributing to the problem, the consultant needs to be able to get answers to the following questions.

Modeling Influences

1. What types of behaviors are modeled and reinforced in the home that may contribute to the child's problem?
2. Are there *outside* influences such as grandparents that influence the child's behavior? What is the nature of these influences?

Family Functioning

1. Is the child given the opportunity to perform significant tasks in the home and is his or her accomplishments recognized in the form of positive feedback?
2. Are siblings treated differently? Is one favored over another? Why? (Objectivity?)
3. Are the subsystems in the family well-differentiated? Do children assume parental roles, or conversely, do parents assume children's roles?

Communication

1. What type of expectations do the parents hold for the child? Are these communicated clearly and consistently?
2. Generally speaking, is communication clear in the family? Is it affirming?
3. Are children given the opportunity to express their individuality?

Importance of Problem

1. Do the parents see the child's problem as significant?
2. Do they "own" the problem or blame it on others or circumstances beyond their control?
3. Is "good parenting" important to the parents or do they have low standards of functioning as parents?
4. Do the parents believe that they can make an impact on the child?

As noted earlier, assessment begins as soon as the parents and the consultant meet. However, it is incumbent upon the consultant to identify information that will result in an accurate assessment of the influences that may be related to the child's behavior. Sonstegard (1964, pp. 74–75) suggested that the following outline be used when interviewing parents:

    I. Under what conditions did the complaint or problem arise?
        A. At what age?
        B. What has been its duration?

   II. What is the child's relationship to siblings?
        A. Position in sibling sequence
            1. Distribution of males and females?
            2. How are siblings different?
            3. How are siblings similar?
        B. With whom is the child compared?
            1. Whom is the child most like?
            2. Whom is the child least like?
        C. Nature and extent of
            1. Conflict?
            2. Rivalry?
            3. Competition? (Explain)
            4. Submission?
            5. Rebellion?
                a. Active?
                b. Passive?

  III. Environmental influences
        A. Relatives
            1. Grandparents
            2. Other relatives

        B. Other people living in the house
        C. Neighbors

  IV. What are you doing about the problem?
        A. Relate in detail the interactions
        B. Clarify if necessary: "What do you mean by that?"

  V. In what other ways does the child stand out?
        A. Conditions under which he functions adequately?
        B. In what way is he successful?

  VI. What is the nature of the daily routine?
        A. How does the child get up in the morning?
           1. Who awakens him?
           2. Is he called more than once?
           3. What about dressing?
           4. What about breakfast?
        B. Describe the lunch hour, dinner (each mealtime).
        C. How does the child get off to bed? At what time?

  VII. What happens when the family goes out together?
        A. Preparation for going out and special efforts
        B. What happens when away?

  VIII. How are the child's social relationships?
        A. Ability to make friends with others
           1. Neighborhood children
           2. Adults
           3. Children at school
        B. Does he have pets and does he take care of them?
        C. Attitude toward school
           1. Schoolwork
           2. Relationships with teachers
           3. How does he deal with people in authority?
        D. What impressions has he gained from the family situation?
           1. Has there been any tragedy in the family?
           2. Who is boss?
           3. What methods of discipline have been used?
           4. What kind of punishment?
           5. What kind of supervision?

  IX. What does the child think about his future?
        A. What does he want to be when he grows up?
        B. What is the occupation of other members of the family?

  X. Does the child have nightmares, bad dreams?

This is, of course, a lengthy and detailed interview schedule and Sonstegard cautions against rigid adherence to it. It should be noted that this interview schedule is based to some degree upon the needs of an Adlerian consultant. However, the format is useful to all consultants in that the means by which the family regulates the functioning of the children can be determined if it is followed.

The consultant should also focus upon the interactions of the children, the children and parents, and the children and other significant peers and adults. Sonstegard's interview schedule could be adapted quite nicely to ascertain which behaviors are being reinforced, the means by which they are reinforced, the nature of the behavior being modeled by the parents and significant others, and the maladaptive behavior that has developed as a result.

Let us assume, for example, that the consultation was initiated because the child consistently failed to complete seatwork in school. During the course of the interview, the consultee relates that the child seems unable to complete household chores, demands a great deal of help when doing homework, and generally is unable to care for himself. One possibility is that the child's helplessness in school is simply an extension of behavior that has been learned in the home.

During the assessment process, the consultant develops hypotheses about factors that may be contributing to the child's functioning. The following may illustrate this point.

Case 1: J is an emotionally disturbed fourth grader and has engaged in a long series of violent acts, including stabbing the emotionally handicapped teacher with a pencil. His parents have seen a number of family therapists, but they have proven to be ineffective. The reason for this failure seems to revolve around two points made by the mother in the first consultation session. At one point she said, "He (the therapist) treated us as though we were the ones with the problem." In another disclosure, she revealed that she hated all the counting and charting that one therapist had asked her to complete. She indicated that she always forgot to follow through on these assignments.

In the initial interview, the parents disclosed the following information:

1. J has a younger brother whom he has attacked with the result being that he and his brother are never left alone.
2. Spanking and yelling are the primary modes of punishment.
3. The father is uninvolved in the family, primarily because he works from 3 P.M until 12:00 A.M. The result is that the mother is responsible for child rearing.
4. Both parents are very much aware of the serious short- and long-term consequences of J's behavior and are committed to helping him.
5. Since the family is relatively poor, jobs are very important so that bills can be paid.
6. There is very little interaction (e.g., outings, games, etc.) as a family although the mother and the boys do some things together.
7. The parents estimate that 100 percent of their interaction with J is negative.
8. The younger brother has manifested none of J's aggressive behavior and in most ways is really fun.
9. J is compared openly and negatively to his younger brother.
10. The parents' goals for J are for him to grow up and be normal, get a job, and be happy.
11. School is seen as mildly important.
12. There are few, if any, outside influences on the family.

When the parents were asked to draw conclusions about J and what they might do to help him, they generated the following ideas.

1. Stop spanking him. It's not doing any good. ("One doctor told us this.")
2. Pay more attention to him. Stop leaving him with babysitters so much. ("We feel bad because we don't spend more time with him, but we're so busy.")

The consultant's analysis of the problem, which was not shared directly with the parents, was as follows.

Contributing Factors

1. Violence (spanking) modeled.
2. No expectations for positive behavior communicated directly.
3. No feedback when positive behavior does occur.
4. Negative comparison to sibling contributes to hostility.
5. Not enough time spent with child to influence behavior change.
6. No opportunity for child to observe normal positive human interaction since he goes to emotionally handicapped classroom.
7. Insensitive to their role in child's problem.

Goal Setting

The tentative hypotheses about factors in the family that may be contributing to the child's problem must ultimately be formulated into specific consultation goals. Just as is the case in other types of consultation, there are essentially two sets of goals to establish: client and consultee goals. Client goals are typically easily established since they are the antithesis of the behavior that led to the consultation. Goals such as getting and staying off drugs, being in less trouble at school, getting into less trouble with the law, are typical. Once the parents have verbalized how they would like for the child to function, then the obvious question is, "How can you as parents help your child?" Some parents will be able to answer this question directly, while others will have few ideas regarding the changes they need to make. The consultant can and should suggest goals to parents albeit tentatively. To return to the case of J for a moment, the consultant posed the following questions: "What would you think of establishing a more positive atmosphere for J as a beginning point?" The question was followed up with an explanation suggesting that at least a part of J's hostile behavior may be partially attributable to the fact that he receives no positive feedback. This suggestion builds on the parents' perceptions that they need to find an alternative to spanking and that they need to spend more time with him, thus validating the suggestion they have made.

The culmination of goal setting should be one or two goals that then become the focus of the consultation process.

Explaining Psychological Principles

Once goals have been agreed upon by the consultant and the parents, an explanation of the psychological principles to be utilized in designing the intervention seems necessary so that effective communication can take place (Brown & Brown, 1975).

Parents need to know some of the basic premises underlying any techniques that might be utilized in the intervention process. In addition to facilitating the communication process, an explanation of theoretical concepts seems necessary so that parents can understand the nature of their own problems with their children and begin to function independently of the consultant.

Explanations of theoretical propositions should always be made as simply as possible without losing the essence of the concepts involved. Brown and Brown (1975) point out that positive reinforcement can be explained as an event that increases the probability of a behavior occurring in the future. However, they go on to recommend that common-sense examples of positive reinforcement may be more readily understood by parents than this technical definition. Similarly, communication can be explained in terms of senders, receivers, channels of communication, nonverbal communication, and verbal communication. It can also be explained by illustrating the relationships among ways of talking, learning, and understanding. Finally, books on parenting illustrate the principles under discussion and can be given to parents.

The explanation of psychological principles should not be a one-way process. It should be conducted in a manner that allows parents to question the principles and/or to discuss ways in which the principles apply in their own family. Once it becomes apparent that parents have arrived at a high degree of understanding of the concepts to be utilized, it is time to proceed.

Once the psychological principles to be employed in the design of an intervention are fully understood by the parents, the consultant and the parents should review the existing family patterns. The consultant should encourage the parents to do this by asking them simply to analyze what is occurring in their particular situation. The process can be facilitated by pointing to specific examples. The consultant might use some of the following leads.

"You were telling me about the difficulties you were having with the siblings fighting and your role in these fights. How would you explain those now?"

"What types of behaviors are you reinforcing when you are attempting to get your children to complete their homework?"

"You were telling me that you have had a lot of trouble getting your teenagers to understand the financial situation in your family. Can you analyze what is going on in that area?"

This step is, in a sense, a check on parental understanding of the principles to be utilized. However, the focus at this time should be upon those areas that seem to be of a major concern to the family and, in that sense, is a prelude to the selection of strategies.

Selecting Intervention Strategies

Goal setting and the explanation of psychological principles are followed by the selection of strategies for goal attainment. Several guidelines should be followed in this process. First, interventions should be as simple as possible. Whether the consultees are single parents,

parents from blended families, or parents from intact families, they are typically involved with a variety of activities in addition to child rearing. It is necessary, therefore, to develop a strategy that will minimize parents' workload.

Second, the parent should choose the intervention. Consultants typically present options, but even this should be delayed until parents have generated their own list of possible interventions based either upon their own experience or those of other parents. Once parents' ideas about how to best resolve the problem are ascertained, the consultant may wish to make additional suggestions.

Third, parents must be trained to use the intervention. This training may be done through behavior rehearsal, use of assigned readings, direct modeling by the consultant, and even by involving parents who have successfully used the strategy to explain the problems they encountered in the process and how they overcame them.

Fourth, the potential consequences of the intervention, including those for the parents and siblings other than the client, must be anticipated. One consultant always warns parents that if one child begins to improve, expect another to get worse. While this may not always be the case, it is important for parents to think through the changes that may occur because the family system has been altered as a result of an intervention. Parents must also be prepared to alter their strategies if the children make valid observations about the need for change.

Fifth, plan to include the children, although the client in most parent consultation situations is a single child, all of the children in the family should be apprised of the goals that have been set and the strategies that are to be employed. Moreover, their input should be solicited regarding the efficacy of the strategies chosen and their suggestions solicited for improving both the goal(s) and its attainment.

When the changes that are to occur are discussed with the children, the potential impact of those changes for all children, and particularly the client, should be reviewed.

Once the consultant and parents are confident that the parents are ready to implement the strategy they have selected to deal with their child's problem, they should be advised to begin the intervention. They should also be cautioned that if problems arise in the course of the intervention, they should either call the consultant or discontinue the intervention until they have had an opportunity to discuss the problems they are experiencing with the consultant.

Follow-up and Evaluation

It is probable that the process outlined to this point will take one or two 90-minute sessions with parents. If two sessions are required to develop a relationship, set goals, design an intervention, and get the children involved, these should be scheduled relatively close together. However, it is suggested that sessions following intervention selection should be scheduled for two weeks later, so that parents will have an opportunity to fully implement the strategy that has been selected. It is also suggested that the consultant telephone the consultee between the strategy selection session and the first follow-up session in order to provide support and, if needed, technical assistance.

Follow-up consultation sessions should be opened with a review of the progress that has been made toward the goals that have been established. If goals have been attained, new

goals can be established, if needed, and then the session focuses upon the selection of an intervention to attain the new goal. However, if progress has either been slower than would be expected or is nonexistent, some troubleshooting must be conducted by the consultant with the purpose of determining the cause underlying the situation.

One of the first areas that should be examined in the trouble-shooting process is the parents' level of understanding of the psychological principles and strategies chosen. This can be accomplished by asking parents to relate what they did on a step-by-step basis as they implemented the intervention. At times, it is helpful to roleplay the interactions that occurred in order to attain additional insight into the difficulty that the parents have experienced. It is not uncommon to find that parents have been inconsistent in their efforts or that they did not fully understand the psychological principles involved. If the counselor ascertains that parents do not have a complete grasp of the psychological principles or the specific techniques, these should be carefully reviewed before any further action is initiated.

If the parents fully understood what actions were to be taken, the consultant should reexamine the home situation. It is possible that some vital factors were overlooked in the first interview. For example, the influence of peers, relatives, and siblings upon the client should receive special attention. So should factors such as parental disagreement about approaches to be utilized and the possibility of a family schedule that prohibits the systematic utilization of certain strategies. Typically, whenever progress has not been made, the consultant has either failed to explain the approaches to be used sufficiently or has overlooked key factors in the family. However, there is at least one other factor that may have contributed to this situation: resistance. This matter will be discussed in more detail later in this chapter.

Avoiding Therapy

When consulting with parents, there are often opportunities to lapse into therapeutic behavior since parents will often disclose material about their personal problems. For example, a single parent may burst into tears as she discloses, "My husband is no good. He's late with the child support again and I'm so depressed because I cannot pay the rent." A counselor or therapist might respond as follows.

Therapist: You're really angry because your husband's late with the child support again, but as angry as you are with him, you're still depressed because of your inability to pay the rent. Tell me more about your situation with your husband.

On the other hand, a consultant should respond in a manner that will refocus the consulting endeavor on the child (Randolph, 1985).

Consultant: I can understand your anger and the fact that you are quite unhappy about not being able to pay the rent. Is it likely that this emotion is going to influence your working with Jeremy?

Obviously if the parent persists in this manner, termination of consultation is in order.

Termination

Termination of the parental consultation process should occur whenever the parents are able to understand their own problems and act on those insights. Termination may occur earlier if either or both parents are in need of some type of therapeutic assistance, with the result that the problem interferes with the consulting process. In these situations, the consultant may renegotiate the consulting contract to a focus on personal counseling or make a referral.

It is suggested that approximately one month after termination, a follow-up note be sent to parents in order to determine whether or not progress has continued. This survey should also extend an opportunity for parents to reenter the consultation process if progress is not satisfactory. This serves to provide some evaluation of the process and to enable parents who either terminated or were terminated earlier to again consider the possibility of availing themselves of the consultant's services.

Group Parental Consultation

Dinkmeyer (1973) presented the idea of the "C" group, so labeled because it involves collaboration, consultation, and confrontation, and because it clarifies belief systems. His group consists of concerned and committed members, and is confidential. He goes on to enumerate the helping forces in the "C" group as acceptance, feedback, universalization or becoming aware that one's problems with children are not unique, altruism or stimulation through assisting others, and spectator therapy or the process of receiving help by observing others being helped.

Consultation groups, unlike parent education groups, do not have a set agenda. Typically, these groups are initiated by the consultant, usually through a mailed survey to parents. Dinkmeyer (1973) suggests that the groups be restricted to parents having children at a single grade level, that the groups meet for six-to-eight weeks, and that the meetings be approximately 90 minutes long.

The initial letter that is sent to parents should begin the structuring of the consultation group. Essentially, the group should be described as a place where parents share their concerns about their children and receive help with these concerns. This letter should also specify the time, place, and dates of the meetings. One additional component should be included in the first letter: the procedure for selecting participants. This is included because often more parents will volunteer for the group than can be accommodated initially. Therefore, the letter may need to contain dates for later sessions and a request that the parents list the dates in terms of priority.

The process of the consulting group is much the same as that described for individual consultation. The first session should be devoted to getting comfortable, establishing relationships, and establishing the roles of the members and the leaders. Subsequent sessions should focus on the general concerns of parents with a gradual shift to the particular concerns of individuals. Since a termination date has been established at the outset, this is generally not an issue. However, there are times when pressure will be brought to bear to continue the group. If this occurs, the consultant may encourage the group to continue independently or may meet with them, depending upon individual circumstances.

Parent groups allow consultants to use their time more effectively, and because other parents are involved, the resources available to the individuals in need of help are increased. Finally, parental consulting groups do not lend themselves well to confidentiality (Dinkmeyer, 1973). Since this is an important aspect of the consulting group, it is desirable to try to establish confidentiality as a rule in the group. As a matter of practical significance, it is not likely that confidentiality will exist and it may be wiser to acknowledge this from the outset.

Some Special Considerations

Resistance

As was noted in Chapter Six, resistance occurs in all forms of consultation. As Sheridan (1993) suggests, family consultants have drawn primarily upon the family therapy literature to explain resistance in consultation, probably because there are few explanations of this problem in the consultation literature. However, it seems likely that consultants will benefit by conceptualizing resistance in consultation as stemming from intrapsychic deficiencies (mental health problems, family systems variables, problematic marriages), broader systems concerns such as cultural norms, or normal concerns such as role overload. Approaches advocated by mental health specialists often run contrary to cultural ideas about the role of the child in the family and/or child rearing. Ideas such as children should be seen and not heard and that children should obey their authoritarian parents run deep in our culture and are constantly reinforced by the authoritarian nature of much of our societal structure. Democratic family structure and open communication are contradictory concepts of these traditional ideas and are thus either distorted or ignored by parents, in spite of the fact that they are experiencing difficulty in their relationships with their children.

Resistance can also develop because of a problematic marriage, particularly if the child (client) is a pawn in the marital dispute. For example, one parent may seek a child's favoritism by showering him or her with presents to compensate for the lack of love from the spouse. In other situations, the child may be neglected because the spouses are so engrossed in their dispute, parenting becomes of secondary importance. Whenever marital problems preclude follow-through, consultation should be terminated. Overwork may also be a source of resistance. It is not an overstatement to say that some parents are grossly overburdened by their roles as parent, worker, and child involvement with their own parents. Consultants may unwittingly exacerbate this problem by involving the parents in complicated interventions and/or pursuing too many goals at once. Resistance stemming from overwork should be avoided by anticipating the problem during strategy selection. However, if it is the problem, reducing the amount of work required may put the consultee back on track.

Fear of the unknown is also a source of resistance in parental consultation. This source of resistance can be summed up in the statement, "While things are bad now, they could get worse." In fact, consultation with parents seems to proceed best whenever parents are saying, "Things could not get worse." Fear of risk-taking appears to be at the

heart of resistance when parents are afraid that things could get worse. As noted earlier, some consultants warn parents that the family situation could get worse before it gets better. This type of statement seems to be a useful approach to avoid resistance from the consultee who, at the moment he or she senses things are getting worse, stops implementing the intervention. However, warning some parents that things may get worse may heighten resistance.

When resistance is present, two approaches to dealing with the problem are suggested. First, parents need to remind themselves that they came to consultation because one or more of their children is/are not functioning well. To accomplish this "self-reminding," parents can be asked, "What do you hope to accomplish with your children?" And then, "What are you accomplishing now?" Often the discrepancy between the two answers will be sufficient to motivate parents to return to the intervention. If this does not work, confrontation regarding the discrepancy between their stated goals for their children and what they are doing to establish these goals may be necessary.

Overcoming resistance resulting from mental health problems may be difficult. However, one technique that has proven to be of some use in overcoming parental resistance growing out of stereotypical views of children and/or parenting behavior is to ask parents what children are learning as a result of child rearing techniques. The first step in this process is to ask parents what behaviors or values they are trying to teach their children. The typical answers are honesty, loyalty, cooperation, good citizenship, independence, and so on. Then parents are asked to relate what their children are learning as a result of current parental treatment. The father who does not listen soon recognizes that one cannot teach cooperation without communication, just as the overly-protective parent recognizes that sheltering children and making decisions for them results in dependence rather than independence. Parents who expect their children to assume no responsibility in the home or who make excuses for them when they do not can hardly expect those children to become highly responsible citizens.

Working with One Parent

Several situations give rise to consultation involving one parent including divorce, one parent unable to attend the sessions because of scheduling problems, one parent being opposed to consultation, or a situation involving a parent that does not care enough about the client to become involved. These situations or others that result in the consultee being only one parent should not prevent consultation from occurring.

If a second parent is involved with the child by virtue of a visitation agreement or still living in the home, consultation should proceed by focusing on the child in much the same manner as described previously. The only addition to the process that may be necessary is that the consultee may need to develop skills in explaining the intervention that is to be made to the other parent and, if the possibility exists that the second parent will cooperate, skills in involving their spouse or ex-spouse as a collaborator in implementing the intervention.

Some Brief Case Studies

The Case of Jamie

Jamie was a kindergartner (five years old) who threw temper tantrums that were quite long (five to six minutes) and intense (kicking on the floor, breaking things, etc.). Her parents were middle-class and there was an older brother (eight years old). The parents were asked to come in to school to explore "ways that the school and the family could collaborate to help Jamie with her transition to school."

During the first session, several key facts were revealed. These included: Jamie's temper tantrums at home were very severe (she had kicked through a door); the punishment used had been spanking, but now the parents were trying to ignore the temper tantrums; the older sibling was a model child; and Jamie was the result of an unwanted pregnancy and the father resented her from the start. He also revealed that he "never showed his resentment." The father admitted that he had a terrible temper and that he had been known to throw some "fits" of his own.

An analysis of the events surrounding the temper tantrums strongly suggested that, in the home at least, whenever the father threatened Jamie, a temper tantrum resulted. As a consequence of this, he had withdrawn from involvement with her. It also appeared that this reaction had generalized, to some degree, because the mother reported a recent incident where she had corrected Jamie in the grocery store and Jamie had fallen on the floor, kicked her feet, and in doing so, had knocked over a large display of canned goods. (Follow-up with Jamie's teacher suggested that the worst temper tantrums occurred after reprimands.)

The initial goals established by the parents were (1) eliminate temper tantrums in the home, and (2) reestablish the father-child relationship. The strategies selected were to stop spanking Jamie, ignore the temper tantrums *completely* by leaving the room where the tantrum was occurring, stop modeling all violent behavior (father agreed to throw "fits" elsewhere), and provide Jamie with much more contingent and non-contingent positive feedback.

Establishing the father-daughter relationship proved to be problematic in that the parents reported in follow-up sessions that Jamie had engaged in temper tantrums whenever the father had tried to engage in several routine activities with her. After much discussion, it was learned that Jamie enjoyed swinging and often asked her mother to swing her. A strategy was adopted that required the father to be present whenever Jamie was being swung and to gradually approach her and engage in swinging her while carrying on routine conversation.

As expected, the older sibling who had received little, but always positive feedback from his parents began to manifest some negative behavior whenever the interventions were fully implemented. An analysis of the situation revealed that he had been neglected to some degree as the parents concentrated on Jamie. This situation was corrected and the problem behavior occurred significantly less often according to parental reports.

Because Jamie was experiencing problems both at school and at home, consultation with the teacher was also initiated.

Student Learning Activity 9.1

Analyze the case of Jamie by answering the following questions.

1. What parenting factors contributed (or may have contributed) to Jamie's problem?

	Yes	No
A. Parent's self efficacy	___	___
B. Parenting standards	___	___
C. Parent's approval of the situation	___	___

	Yes	No
D. Parent's standards	___	___
E. Parenting skills	___	___
F. Systems variables	___	___

2. What interventions can you suggest other than those adopted in this case?

3. Can you provide alternative explanations to why Jamie's sibling began to misbehave?

4. What would you do about the possibility of child abuse in this case?

Within two months (five sessions), the temper tantrums had all but disappeared. Unexpectedly, both children accompanied their parents to the final consultation session and all four sat on a couch with Jamie sitting by her father. The parents and the children agreed that the situation in their household had improved dramatically. One month later, a telephone follow-up revealed that while Jamie would still occasionally engage in a temper tantrum, they tended to be short in duration and of mild intensity.

The Case of Gerrard

Gerrard was placed in an inpatient substance abuse treatment center after repeated attempts at outpatient treatment had failed. He was 15 years old at the time he entered the center. One portion of the treatment plan called for ongoing family therapy that was to be initiated during Gerrard's eight-week stay in the facility and to be continued on an indefinite basis upon his release. Family therapy was rejected by the parents because "they were not the ones with the problem." A doctoral intern approached the parents and suggested consultation as an alternative to family therapy, indicating that the entire focus of the process would be to enhance their ability to parent Gerrard. The parents agreed to participate, although the level of their commitment seemed relatively low.

Gerrard's father was a professor at a major university and his mother was a housewife. They had three children of which Gerrard was the youngest. According to parental reports, the other children were "quite normal" in that they had done well in high school, gone on to college, and were either advancing in their careers or in graduate school. Gerrard, who is five years younger than his youngest sibling, was quite ill as a child and on one occasion, both parents expected him to die. At the time of consultation, Gerrard was experiencing no major health problems.

Both parents admitted that Gerrard had been treated differently than his older siblings in that expectations regarding academic achievement, out-of-school activities, and even in-the-home participation had been reduced. Both agreed that these lower expectations were partially because of Gerrard's health problems, but the father volunteered that Gerrard's

mother enjoyed her continuing role as mother and suggested pleasantly that Gerrard had been pampered by his mother.

When it became apparent in the middle of the elementary school years that Gerrard's health problems were virtually over, his father attempted to pressure him to do better in school and to generally raise his standard of performance. His mother, while not fully in agreement with the father's tactics, agreed with the general idea that Gerrard should be expected to function at a higher level.

Gerrard rebelled at the demands of his parents, but was usually somewhat passive in his rebellion. He declared that he was different from his siblings; and he started dressing dramatically differently in clothes that he purchased with his allowance at the PTA Thrift Shop. Most importantly to the parents, his grades continued to be in the C–D range with an occasional F even though test results indicated that he was capable of superior performance.

Once in junior high, Gerrard's academic performance fell even lower and while he "flirted" continuously with failure, he never actually failed a subject. He also fell in with the wrong crowd and was caught with a marijuana cigarette by one of his teachers. His behavior became more erratic and, once when his parents went to pick him up from a friend's house, he fell into the car, obviously inebriated. It became clear that he was using alcohol extensively near the end of junior high school and his relationship with his parents, and particularly his father, had deteriorated to the point where they interacted only on a superficial level. He failed two subjects during his sophomore year, was picked up by the police for possession of marijuana (less than an ounce), and what conversation went on at home was strained at best.

The parents agreed that they needed to:

1. Help Gerrard set some of his own goals instead of trying to impose their own goals on him.
2. Generally rebuild their relationship with him by communicating their concerned love instead of their expectations.
3. Accept his lifestyle (hair, clothes).
4. Help Gerrard develop self-confidence in areas of interest (e.g., music) by providing support in the form of lessons and purchasing instruments.
5. Model only the most responsible use of alcohol.

When Gerrard was told of his parents' plans to be more supportive of his interests and to stop the bickering over his clothes, hair, and so on, his response was one of extreme skepticism. In a subsequent visit to the hospital, his father, who was typically quite conservative, arrived wearing one earring, a vest with a Grateful Dead sticker on it, and with his hair spiked with mousse. While Gerrard was still skeptical, the ice was broken to some degree.

Throughout the remainder of Gerrard's stay in the hospital, the parents worked on helping Gerrard set some goals for himself and laying out plans for helping him achieve those goals. Gerrard was systematically reinforced for goal-setting behavior and any verbalization that related to increasing his standards of performance. Throughout these visits, the parents continuously expressed confidence in Gerrard's ability to take control of his life and in his ability to function in a wide variety of situations, including school (no great emphasis on this area).

Student Learning Activity 9.2

Analyze the case of Gerrard by answering the following questions.

1. What is the most likely explanation for Gerrard's behavior?
2. If you had known that the father was going to mousse his hair and wear an earring to the hospital, would you have advised it?

3. How do you explain the relationship of the health problem to the presenting problem?
4. What are alternatives to the interventions that appear to have been used in this case?
5. Would you make recommendations regarding assessment of the possibility of substance abuse?

After release from the treatment center, Gerrard returned to his high school where he continued to struggle academically, although he passed all subjects.

The open hostility that was present in the home prior to Gerrard's admission into the treatment center was greatly reduced, except when Gerrard's parents expressed reservations about his friends who were alcohol abusers, too. According to Gerrard's own statements, tension and conflict developed. Gerrard experienced two relapses during the three months of follow-up. Each time, his parents expressed disappointment and offered their continuing help in Gerrard's efforts to stop abusing drugs.

At the final session, the parents reported their relationship with Gerrard had improved dramatically, that his grades had improved to a small degree, and that he "was dressing better." They attributed this to the fact that his father occasionally appeared at the dinner table in an earring and a Grateful Dead vest.

Consultant's note: The unusual behavior engaged in by the father was not the result of a direct recommendation by the consultant. However, the father was encouraged to find ways to break the communication barriers between himself and his child. Had his behavior been viewed as a "put down" by the child, this approach would have exacerbated the situation.

Summary

Consulting with parents is a relatively new idea, primarily because of the influence of Caplan (1970) who viewed consultation as a process that occurs between professionals. However, consultants are embracing the idea with increasing vigor because they realize that consultation provides them with a tool that will allow them to intervene in the all-important family system.

The approach to consultation outlined here drew on social learning theory, systems theory, and Caplanian ideas. Eclecticism is decried by many purists, but, as was suggested earlier, current psychological theories are not comprehensive enough to provide the framework for something as complicated as family intervention. Perhaps this will change in the future, but for now the family consultant needs to draw upon a number of conceptual and practical frameworks to be effective.

Tips to the Practitioner

1. Interview several parents about the concerns they have about their children's educational development. Do they have complicated or simple explanations of the problems they perceive? Do they blame themselves or others?
2. Try to identify times in your own family or in the families of people you know when positive change in one child brought about negative change in one or more other children.
3. The systems principle of equafinality holds that there are many potential solutions to each problem in a system. Identify a student of any age who is experiencing a learning problem. Identify as many possible solutions as you can to the problem. How many of them involve parents? How many solutions did you generate?
4. Either observe a family therapy session or view a videotape of a session. How do these processes differ? How are they the same? What did you learn that you can use as a consultant to families?
5. If you can, attend a parent education session. How is this process similar to consultation? Different? What did you learn that you can use as a consultant?
6. Outline the process you expect to use as a family consultant.

Review Questions

1. Why are systems thinking and behaviorism incompatible?

2. What are the underlying assumptions of parent consultation?

3. Consider the impact that not caring how well you raise your children might have on the parenting process? How could that view be changed?

4. Consider the factors that need to be assessed in the consultation process. How many can you list? How will you assess the factors you have identified?

5. Discuss the pros and cons of parents' understanding the basis for the interventions which they are asked to implement. Where do you stand on the issue that parents need not understand the why of intervention, only the how?

6. What are the sources of resistance to consultation? Can you identify strategies that can be used to overcome these?

References

Bandura, A. (1977). *Social learning theory*. Englewood Cliffs, NJ: Prentice-Hall.

Bandura, A. (1978). The self system in reciprocal determinism. *American Psychologist, 33*, 344–358.

Bateson, G. (1972). *Steps to an ecology of mind*. New York: Ballantine.

Bergan, J. R. *Behavioral consultation*. Columbus, OH: Merrill.

Bergan, J. R., & Duley, S. (1981). Behavioral consultation in families. In R. W. Henderson (Ed.), *Parent-child Interactions: Theory Research and Prospects* (pp. 265–291). San Diego, CA: Plenum Press.

Bergan, J. R., & Kratochwill, T. R. (1990). *Behavioral Consultation and Therapy*. New York: Plenum Press.

Brown, D., & Brown, S. T. (1975). Parental consultation: A behavioral approach. *Elementary School Guidance and Counseling, 10*, 95–102.

Brown, D., Wyne, M. D., Blackburn, J. E., & Powell, W. C. (1979). *Consultation: Strategy for improving education*. Boston: Allyn and Bacon.

Caplan, G. (1970). *Mental health consultation*. New York: Basic Books.

Capra, F. (1982). *The turning point: Science, society, and the rising culture*. New York: Simon & Schuster.

Cobb, D. E., & Medway, F. J. (1978). Determinants of effectiveness of parental consultation. *Journal of Community Psychology, 6*, 229–240.

Dembo, M. H., Sweitzer, M., & Lauritzen, P. (1985). An evaluation of group parent education: Behavioral, PET, and Adlerian. *Review of Educational Research, 55*, 155–200.

Dinkmeyer, D. C. (1973). The parent "C" group. *Personnel and Guidance Journal, 52*, 252–256.

Dinkmeyer, D., & Carlson, J. (1973). *Consulting: Facilitating human potential and change processes*. Columbus, OH: Charles E. Merrill.

Dumas, J. E. (1989). Treating antisocial behavior in children: Child and family approaches. *Clinical Psychology Review, 9*, 197–222.

Frazier, F., & Matthes, W. A. (1975). Parent education: A comparison of Adlerian and behavioral approaches. *Elementary School Guidance and Counseling, 19*, 31–38.

Goldenberg, I., & Goldenberg, H. (1985). *Family therapy: An overview* (2nd ed.). Belmont, CA: Wadsworth.

Horton, E., & Brown, D. (1990). The importance of interpersonal skills in consultee-centered consultation: A review. *Journal of Counseling and Development*.

McGowan, R. J. (1969). Group counseling with underachievers and their parents. *School Counselor, 16*, 30–35.

Olson, D. H., Sprenkle, D. H., & Russell, C. S. (1979). Circumplex model of marital and family systems: Cohesion and adaptability dimensions, family types, and clinical applications. *Family Process, 18*, 3–28.

Palmo, A. J., & Kuzniar, J. (1971). Modification of behavior through group counseling and consultation. *Elementary School Guidance and Counseling, 6*, 258–262.

Parsons, R. D., & Meyers, J. (1984). *Developing consultation skills*. San Francisco: Jossey-Bass.

Perkins, J. A., & Wicas, E. (1971). Group counseling with bright underachievers and their mothers. *Journal of Counseling Psychology, 18*, 273–279.

Randolph, D. L. (1985). *Microconsulting: Basic psychological consultation skills for helping professionals*. Johnson City, TN: Institute of Social Services and Arts.

Sheridan, S. M. (1993). Models for working with parents. In J. E. Zins, T. R. Kratochwill, & S. N. Elliot (Eds.). *Handbook of Consultation Services for Children* (pp. 110–133). San Francisco: Jossey-Bass.

Sheridan, S. M., & Kratochwill, T. R. (1992). Behavioral parent-teacher consultation: A practical approach. *Journal of School Psychology, 30*, 117–139.

Sonstegard, M. (1964). A rationale for interviewing parents. *School Counselor, 12*, 72–76.

Weathers, L. R., & Liberman, R. P. (1975). The contingency contracting exercise. *Journal of Behavior Therapy and Experimental Psychiatry, 6*, 208–214.

Chapter *10*

Consultation with Teachers

Goal of the Chapter

The unique characteristics of the teacher role in the school setting and the implications for establishing a consultation service are discussed in this chapter.

Chapter Preview

1. The role expectations for the teacher are examined from the training and setting perspectives, with particular emphasis on factors affecting consultation contacts.
2. Several examples of approaches to consultation with the teachers are examined.
3. Two adaptations of individual consulting models tailored to the role and demands of the setting facing teachers are presented, for example, the 15 minute consultation and group consultation.

Of all the types of professionals that have been targeted as potential beneficiaries of consultation, teachers have to rank among the most frequently mentioned group. In fact, the term *teacher consultation* seems to be gaining popularity in special education literature to such a degree that we run the risk of it being incorrectly conceptualized as yet another unique model of consultation rather than simply a term used to identify the consultee.

It is rather obvious from a purely "impact" perspective why such a level of attention would be directed to this group of professionals. As primary caregivers who serve large numbers of students each year, as well as much larger numbers during their career, the potential impact that may ensue as a result of teachers generalizing what they learned in consultation to future students they teach becomes immediately apparent. In fact, if there is one rationale that appears to heighten the appeal of consultation to school administrators, it is the long-term benefit of consultation to both teachers and students. While the number

of school-based consultants available to teachers will always be limited, any factor that increases a teacher's independence will be valued.

Two additional reasons would seem to support the consideration of a consultation service for teachers. First, the preparation of the teachers is to a large degree focused on minimum entry-level competency. That is, until the recent renewal of interest in teacher credentials, teachers could be *permanently* certified upon college graduation with an undergraduate Bachelors degree. If a probationary period existed before permanent certification was granted, it was often less structured and rarely included formal supervisory reviews that focused on specific teaching skills improvement. There was no formal credentialing mechanism for becoming recognized as a *competent* teacher at any level of experience, let alone criteria for recognizing master teacher status. In spite of the acknowledged complexity of the teaching position, professional growth and development is experientially determined except in cases of continuing education activities associated with certification renewal requirements. Thus, consultation from experts would seem to be a valued resource for a practitioner group with an evolving professional identity. The teacher's task of managing instruction for such diverse populations as today's schools enroll would seem to require continued access to a variety of professional perspectives.

Second, the isolation of the teaching assignment (Lortie, 1975; Sarason, 1971) is yet another rationale for offering consultation services. Throughout the day, many teachers have minimum interaction with other professionals that allow for the professional exchange needed for brainstorming solutions to problems.

These two observations would seem to represent a persuasive argument for providing consultation services. However, in the absence of a database, the authors do not sense that the amount of teacher consultation taking place is overwhelming, and therefore, it does not seem to be a common service. While the advocacy for such services comes mainly from the professional groups doing the consultation, teachers, when asked, do not reject this model of service (Graden, 1989).

However, since the argument for teacher consultation originates with internal school professionals who are also expected to provide direct services (e.g., counselor, school psychologists, special educators), they must convince administrators that there be a reallocation of a proportion of their time commitment to direct services.

Administrators may be leery of providing support for that reallocation when caseloads are tied to program funding (e.g., assessment eligibility determination required for special education class placement), or the value of consultation is yet to be demonstrated through evaluation. Finally, the schooling enterprise, in contrast to other service areas in our society, has not been organized in such a manner that accommodates a service delivery strategy wherein several adults come together to discuss programs for individual and groups of students. There simply is little time during the school day for consultation, and the immediate period of time following the official school day is often scheduled with other responsibilities. Teachers are expected to be in charge of their class, or classes, throughout the day. For a teacher to miss a class, even with a substitute provided, is not encouraged, and with the current emphasis on the time-on-task effectiveness schooling notion, any activity that reduces instructional time is probably considered skeptically by many educators. Therefore, the time available to teachers may be the greatest impediment to consultation becoming utilized in a fashion that allows for its promise to be realized.

A rose is a rose, and consultation is consultation regardless of the professional identity of the consultee. However, as can be appreciated from previous observations, each professional group and their setting will reflect strengths and constraints that need to be considered. In this chapter, we will concentrate on those factors unique to the teaching profession, and in turn, for the consultant to keep in mind. In doing so, most of the information sprinkled throughout the book that arose out of consultation experiences with teachers (e.g., Gibbs' work dealing with the influence of the ethnic background of consultees on the consultation process—see Chapter Eight) will often be noted, but not repeated in any detail to avoid redundancy. Chapter Eight in general should be considered when this chapter is being read, since many of the "consultee" studies were done with teachers as subjects.

Constraints Limiting Teacher Consultation

In this section, we have the unpleasant task of reviewing what some have called the barriers that impede teacher consultations. It is unpleasant in that some of what we will present is not easily overcome by either the consultant or the teacher. Rather than appreciating the reality of the circumstances, some consultants have come to interpret teacher behavior associated with these constraints as resistance. Consulting with teachers does not imply that any exceptions should be made in terms of the sound principles of practice followed with other consultees. As with other consultees, an awareness of teacher role demands and their work environment is required, as well as the intentional incorporation of such information when interventions are planned. The absence of this perspective, or perhaps more accurately, the minimizing of such information may be a significant factor that has slowed the progress of introducing this service model in schools. Indeed, it would seem that the importance of such information needs greater prominence in the selection of the consultation approach used in the public schools than heretofore it has received (Pryzwansky, 1974). Thus, the role in setting characteristics that are to be presented should help in shaping that perspective of the teacher role and choice of model.

Training Orientation

In spite of all that has been written promoting the professionalism of teachers, much of the preparation seems to still reflect the technician rather than independent decision-maker orientation. The concentration of most preservice teacher training is methods oriented and emphasizes the curriculum guidelines adopted by particular states. Clearly, any consideration of the conceptualizations of the role gives way to the pragmatics of functioning in the role, and if the teacher-in-training is fortunate, some skill training that is directly applicable to the demands of the classroom. The expectation that all too often is reinforced is one in which the teacher delivers a predetermined curriculum using a prescribed set of materials to a classroom of students. Perhaps this description is a bit too extreme or harsh for some readers, but it should make the point that the independent, instructional decision making often expected of this consultee may simply not be reinforced in the teacher preparation program let alone realized in practice. This sophistication may develop over time with experience and further training.

More importantly, a second factor to be considered is the possibility that the match between the orientation of the teacher and the consultant may be incongruent. Teachers may

expect direct suggestions to handle problems since their initial training had dealt with questions in a prescriptive manner. Furthermore, they may reason that for the consultant to expect them to function in this way is unfair, because it neither matches their range of competencies, nor is it realistic in light of the prescribed set of responsibilities they have been assigned.

The technician orientation to teaching then, also may explain why consultative services are generally advocated by specialized personnel in the schools (e.g., special educators, counselors, school psychologists) rather than receiving the grass roots support one would expect from the teachers. While teachers are receptive to the offer of such assistance, they seem inclined to promote a service delivery model that involves direct treatment of students by specialists. Often, this preference reflects an honest judgment that the student requires more specialized assistance. This hierarchical model of interaction would certainly fit within the organization that has the teacher as the front line instructor of a group and/or subgroups of students; students who do not learn under this organizational scheme would then be shifted to other, more specialized personnel who teach in an alternative instructional environment such as a small class or individualized instruction.

Another important factor that may influence a teacher's acceptance of consultation is that there is an absence of a real understanding of the various educational specialties and school services, let alone the ways in which those services could be used *as part of the teacher's classroom program*. The availability of support services is not standardized, and the ways teachers can use those services is not part of the skills they receive. Not only do these circumstances need to be changed for a consultation service to be effective, but some minimal preparation as to how to make maximum use of the services available would seem advisable (see the consultee training section in Chapter Eight). Training in consultation could enhance the teachers' feelings of competency as consumers of such services in that their needs have a greater chance of being addressed. It might be important to add here as an example of this point that it is rare to find a text used in educational leadership training programs that deals with a description of specialized school professionals, let alone the different ways of deploying such staff.

Time to Consult

As noted in the introduction, use of school-based professional time is a critical variable affecting any teacher and student support service program. Indeed, a number of writers in the consultation field have acknowledged availability of time as a major factor affecting the initiation and quality of consultation (Johnson, Pugach, & Hammitte, 1988; Idol & West, 1987; Gutkin & Curtis, 1982). Obviously, an organization that assigns one adult per 20+ students and requires constant teacher-student contact will experience cognitive dissonance with proposals that interrupt that relationship. Even where "planning periods" exist, teachers set priorities on that time for planning so that it becomes as sacrosanct as instructional time. Such a scenario then, leaves the time before and after school as a period for consultation along with some stolen, but brief, period of time during the day. Thus, teachers who need and/or value consultation are going to be frustrated by organizational structures that impede implementation, and teachers whose orientation and priorities run counter to those associated with consultation will be equally frustrated. In part, the time constraint may account for the amount of time educational consultants report they actually spend in con-

sultation. Idol-Maestas, & Ritter (1985) reported only about 5 percent of resource/consulting teachers' time was spent consulting, with similar documentation characterizing the school psychologist's role (Gutkin & Curtis, 1982).

It seems imperative, then, that the consultant recognize this school system characteristic and deal with all of its ramifications in a realistic fashion. For example, one may have to give up the "50 minute" timeframe for the "15 minute consultation" (see a following section of this chapter) and adapt the model of choice. Use of supplementary contacts such as telephone consultation, electronic and facsimile mail are potential strategies, when combined with "quickie" or "15 minute consultations" can provide the follow-up and continuity that may be lost otherwise. Such abbreviated consultations must stay problem-focused within a circumscribed area. These targeted consults can also be bolstered by classroom observations where appropriate. Quade (1985) recommended that learning disability resource teachers "block" a period of time in their schedules for regular classroom teacher consultation and found that it promoted an expanded use of the service. Thus, the idea of the consultant posting a before/after school "office hour" may make sense in some districts. Additional strategies for dealing with time constraints have been provided in the literature (Idol, 1988; West & Idol, 1990). Whitaker (1992) highlights four areas in which time for consultation can be arranged, including the range of administrative support options that might be negotiated. She stresses the need to form a consultation committee as a means to demonstrate effectiveness across the variety of pilot projects that can be implemented. She also recommends that practitioners make use of existing groups in the organization as vehicles for consultation. Finally, the need for the consultant to have in place a workable communication network involving such strategies as a standard form for memo and/or progress reports and electronic mail is emphasized.

Administrative Support

The example of a superintendent of one school system who would not allow teachers to hold any type of conference during school hours underscores the rationale often heard that teachers are employed to directly serve the children. This "rule" was enforced by the superintendent's unannounced visits to the schools along with brief visits to the classrooms. Needless to say, professional contact time became a premium commodity in that system, particularly when one considers the other demands on teacher time outside the school day (including parent conferences, teacher meetings, activity supervision). Generally, administrators are receptive to the consultation model, particularly when the objective of increasing teacher competence to deal with similar problems to the one being discussed in consultation is explained. Additionally, the fact that specialized professionals can impact more students using the consultation service delivery model versus other models is also attractive.

However, the spoken or unspoken attitude of an administrator, e.g., the principal, toward teacher autonomy or, even more specifically, a service such as consultation, is emerging as a significant factor influencing teacher behavior *vis à vis* the consultant. Teachers are not only less likely to view consultation in a positive manner, but their use of such services is less likely to occur when they work under a controlling and threatening principal (Bossard & Gutkin, 1984; Gutkin & Bossard, 1984). Similarly, the degree of acceptability of interventions arising out of consultations on the part of teachers relates to the degree of administrative support that is perceived (Broughton & Hester, 1993). Such preliminary

findings lend credence to the notion that the consultants take into account the teacher's perception of how safe the consultation plan is as interventions are being planned.

The three common reservations expressed by administrators include the time demands on the teacher, the effect on the direct service commitments of the consultant, and accountability. Regarding the first two reservations, involvement of the administrator along with some teachers in designing a service mindful of time constraints and other perceived needs of the system will insure an initial commitment. Opportunities for such a group to serve an advisory role during the first year of the model could be further documentation of the consultant's interest in developing a relevant service, while insuring that all perspectives are taken into account as the program goes forward. There are ways of planning evaluations so that they can alleviate the administrative concerns over the effectiveness of the services and their acceptability by the teachers. Through the use of databased evaluations, Zins (1981) was able to expand school consultation services from one hour per week to a program in which consultation was the primary service offered. During the first year, the consultation time of the school psychologist was quite limited, but recognized. Evaluations of all consultations were conducted and reported at the end of the year. These evaluations included quantitative questionnaire data regarding the nature of consultation service itself (e.g., number and frequency of consultation contacts) and its quality (e.g., benefits of working with the consultant and consultant effectiveness).

Status

In Chapter Thirteen, we discuss the challenges inherent in asking for help. In a school system in which you are "the professional" responsible for a classroom of children, the erroneous expectation can arise (and often does) that you should know what to do, and any indication that you need "help" can only reflect negatively on the perceptions of your competencies. In an attempt to identify the factors that distinguish between teachers who seek consultation from school psychologists and those who do not seek such help, Stenger, Tollefson, and Fine (1992) found a number of such variables. First, the simple presence of a school psychologist in the building was an obvious important factor. However, the consultation help needs to be offered, and there is a greater chance of its being used than when the consultant waits for it to be requested by the teacher. Interestingly, only 30 percent of the teachers in this study reported its being offered! It would seem that one reason is the continued emphasis in the consultation literature on the relationship's being a voluntary one. Also, consistent with other research studies, teachers who described themselves as good problem solvers were more likely to seek consultation. However, another study found that teachers with a high self-efficacy score, i.e., rating their ability to solve a child's problem (when presented with a written description of a problem) were also likely to rate consultation as helpful in solving the problem; however, there was no relationship with a subsequent use of consultation or its outcome evaluation (Hughes, Grossman & Barker, 1990). Finally, Stenger et al. (1992) reported that the teachers' perceptions of school psychologists' having training in problem solving and their training as different from that of the teachers were likely to influence their seeking consultation.

As noted above, a voluntary teacher contact is often seen as critical to the offering of consultation service. Harris and Cancelli (1991) have conceptualized a continuum on which teacher consultees' level of volunteerism would be manifested at different stages of con-

sultation and different consultation models. In order to motivate the consultee to volunteer for consultation, they suggest that the consultant should concentrate on the needs that the consultee has produced, that the teacher should be encouraged to be an active participant in the process (i.e., avoid advice giving), that the strengths and weaknesses of the consultation discussion be evaluated by the teacher, and, finally, teacher ownership of the intervention be stressed. Consultation as a term has that common sense ring about it that an expert is telling you what to do. One of our colleagues recently shared an interesting insight into the power of the term. The teacher workshops offered by this colleague were once labeled "consultation," but now they are referred to as "collaborative problem solving" and are now not only well attended, but enthusiastically received. Hierarchical relationships with internally-based professional peers have the potential to elicit feelings of resentment and resistance on the part of teachers (Johnson et al., 1988). However, there may be exceptions of large systems in which the consultant is centrally located and dispersed to the school upon request, or the small school system with a limited staff of resource professionals may not be threatened by the consultant. Nevertheless, an internally-based consultant, with fairly regular contact with the staff, should pay particular attention to the manner in which indirect services are articulated and more importantly, actually delivered. The overwhelming consultee preference for collaboration noted in an earlier chapter suggests, at the very least, an expectation of being treated like a professional. The irony of that finding is that teachers expect collaborators to have expertise in another area than theirs and for that knowledge to be applied to their problem.

There have been several descriptions of consultation approaches targeted on the regular teacher as consultee and that carry a title to denote that emphasis. Obviously, any of the models presented in this text could be used effectively with teachers so that it could be argued that the "teacher consultation model" should be treated within the context of those models. Similarly, much of what is written in consultation for school psychologists has instructional staff as one of its target consultee group. However, given the growing use of the term *teacher consultation*, and its derivatives, it seems reasonable to briefly present the basic features of those descriptions. This terminology primarily grows out of the special education field wherein the objective is the facilitation of professional work between the special education teacher/resource consultant and the regular classroom teacher.

The Consulting Teacher Models

The idea of a teacher expert in content and/or instructional approaches available to assist other teachers in meeting the instructional challenges they face in the classroom is not new; in fact, this notion is embodied in the nature of educational supervision. However, as Blessing (1968) pointed out, the kind of assistance that was required changed as the training and professionalism of the teacher evolved; a dynamic, democratic supervisor was needed who facilitated growth and the fostering of meaningful change. For special education teachers, Blessing and his colleagues elected to use the term *resource consultant* to designate a new role and function for this education specialty, and envisaged this individual working not only with special education teachers, but with the regular classroom teachers, administrators, and other supportive school personnel as well. By the early 70s, this consultative

thrust was being embraced by special educators as one strategy that the special education teacher could use in delivering services to handicapped children, for example, working through the regular classroom teacher versus the resource teacher role or instructing in the special class. This alternative has certainly caught on recently, if the activity dealing with this theme from the middle of the 80s until now is any indication

In 1972, McKenzie described a consulting teacher approach, often referred to as the Vermont Consulting Teacher Model, in which "the consulting teacher assists regular classroom teachers to carry out diagnoses and to develop an intervention approach to facilitate a given child's educational development" (p. 103). He presented two considerations as a rationale for the model: (1) high cost estimates and the disruption that would result from local school system plans to bus students requiring special education to regional classes, and (2) the unfortunate byproduct of separate classes, for example, developing a reliance on special services versus services that can be provided in regular classes. Providing the special assistance as part of the regular classroom would obviate the necessity of labeling children, and thus, would decrease the need for evaluation services. The help that was envisioned to be provided by the consulting teacher would be "in the form of instruction regarding principles of the behavioral model of education and application of these principles" (McKenzie, 1972, p. 109). The consulting teacher in this model, then, is seen as an expert in applied behavior analysis, and it is this behavioral content that is delivered by the consulting teacher. The stages in this consulting service reflect the paradigm and priorities associated with that theoretical orientation (see Chapter Three). The consultant is viewed as an expert engaged in a trainer-of-teachers role.

By 1982, Heron and Harris were proposing a mutual problem-solving process for the *educational consultant* wherein the consultant and consultee share responsibility for an intervention outcome. They stress that education for handicapped students should take place within the least restrictive environment, and while eclectic in their coverage of strategies to accomplish this objective, still rely heavily on behavioral theory. Their work emphasized the new concepts and ideas pervading special education at that time, such as the content of the consultation rather than the process. The major exception is when behavioral approaches are discussed so that behavior management strategies and group classroom contingencies are dealt with in detail.

Although several different consultation models are available, special education models, for which program descriptions and outcome data are available for the most part, have employed a behavioral approach within a problem solving paradigm (Cantrell & Cantrell, 1976; Knight, Meyers, Paolucci-Whitcomb, Hasazi & Nevin, 1981; Nelson & Stevens, 1981 [see Chapter Three also]). In each of these studies, a problem-solving strategy was used in which general education teachers requested assistance from special education teachers in dealing with a child or group of children. The special education teacher then worked with the teacher to define the problem in measurable terms, collect data, develop and implement an intervention, and evaluate its effect. Given-Ogle, Christ and Idol (1991) describe a project in which school resource specialists formed a collaborative working group among themselves in addition to offering collaborative consultation to classroom teachers and building administrators. Preliminary evaluation data suggest that the project was effective in bringing selected students' reading skills to grade level, and their behavior to acceptable levels.

In contrast to this trend in special education consultation emphasizing the content of the consultation, Idol & West (1987; Idol, 1989) present the distinguishing conceptualization of the new role. They conceptualized consultation as an "artful science." The artful base refers to both the communicative/interactive skills, that allow rapport to be established in which information and problem solving competencies are shared, leading not only to good problem finding but to planning and evaluating solution strategies. The scientific base includes those technological and knowledge backgrounds that enhance the assessment demands of the role, but also contribute to substance of the solution, particularly when what is required is information based on theory and research. Idol & West reiterate the principle that one aspect without the other leads to at best, a friendly relationship with nothing of relevance to the problem shared between the professionals. Indeed, it seems as though the emphasis in instructional/teacher consultation writings has been on the technological side and little attention paid to consultation per se. In affirming a consultation service, Idol & West seem to be proposing a collaborative problem-solving model that is reflected in a preceding work (Idol, Paolucci-Whitcomb, & Nevin, 1986). Idol et al. (1986) defined collaborative consultation as a reciprocal arrangement "that enables people with diverse expertise to generate creative solutions to mutually defined problems" (p. 1). In terms of these special education-general education models, this approach seems to represent the only proposal that deals specifically with the question of how to provide an indirect service; the others primarily advocate that position while promoting a particular theoretical and/or methodical position.

Instructional Consultation

This approach obviously is geared toward the teacher as consultee. Bergan and Schnaps (1983) used the term in referring to an elaboration of *behavioral consultation* wherein the goal was "to modify teacher behavior to enhance the learning of all students in a class." In a similar vein, Rosenfield (1987) defined the term as integrating the growing knowledge base regarding instructional practices with classroom management, and utilizing consultation techniques that emphasize the collaborative relationship. She presents a rather comprehensive description of the process and content aspects of this approach which has as its overall goal, the improvement of school psychologists and other educational consultants work with teachers. What follows is a brief description of her ideas. The evolving work of special education consultation, which also targets the classroom teacher as consultee, is presented in the next section.

The role of the instruction consultant is conceptualized "not only as an indirect service method for working with children with academic problems, but also as a potentially powerful in-service training process . . ." (p. 7). Working in this role, Rosenfield puts forth some definitive assumptions about children with learning problems encompassing the idea that instructional mismatches underline the referred problem. The consultation interaction concerns itself with the vulnerable learner, inadequate instruction, and a "muddied conception of the task." The interaction of those three factors becomes the focus of Rosenfield's approach versus the "defective learner" assumption that she perceives to be the emphasis of current indirect services. She views the focus as indirect service to the referred child through the teacher, following the usual stages of consultation and elaborating on some of the basic skills required for collaborative (behavioral) consultation.

Rosenfield's approach essentially uses a behavioral problem identification and analysis strategy during the initial teacher interview. This information is then coupled with a classroom observation and Curriculum-Based Assessment (CBA). The instructional interventions that are developed take place in the classroom, either under the monitorship or through direct provision of the classroom teacher. In her book, Rosenfield (1989) summarizes several types of behavioral-observational and structured observation systems. The assessment of academic learning is defined as including CBA procedures as well as a task and process analysis. Finally, planning and conducting instructional interventions are defined as involving management of the learner (e.g. time management, physical changes in the classroom, contracting, and utilization of cooperative learning techniques) and management of learning (e.g. curriculum content and format changes, learning strategies, and the sequencing of instructional procedures).

An *abbreviated* example of a segment of the diagnostic interview might be as follows.

Consultant: Tell me about his trouble learning to read.

Teacher: He hasn't learned to read any words.

Consultant: What reading approaches has he had some success with?

Teacher: None, he still can't read a word. The next day, he can't remember words that have been learned.

Consultant: What have you tried?

Teacher: Phonics, whole word approach; nothing seems to work. (Teacher gives examples.)

Consultant: What words does he want to learn to read?

Teacher: I never asked him.

Consultant: Let's find out. He may be motivated to learn "his" words. He can choose any word he wants. It's important we don't put any value judgment on his choice. Then, we teach him that word, plus two others he chooses using configuration cues. (Consultant explains rationale and demonstrates.)

Specific task analysis is done upon initially finding the instructional level of the student. Then, the student's approach to the academic content is reviewed, for example, a process analysis. This latter step includes an analysis of errors made by the student. Thus, the consultant might recommend that the student is reversing letters and suggest that a small card with the letters commonly reversed, be arranged vertically (since this is an easier discrimination than when presented horizontally) and taped to the desk with a visual mnemonic in order to facilitate discrimination. Specific assessment and intervention steps are then taken.

This approach would fail to meet the criterion of a consultation model per se. Rather, it can be fairly stated that instructional consultation deals primarily with the instructional content expertise of the consultant, rather than the process of consultation itself. When the consultation process is described by Rosenfield, she mentions basic interpersonal skills, while drawing on the behavioral and collaborative models of consultation. However, the consultant's involvement in the intervention phase of consultation is not considered and as such

collaborative only to a point. Certainly, a special educator, who is engaged in offering some instructional intervention to the student either in the classroom or under a "pull-out" arrangement, would represent one prototype wherein a true collaboration between consultant and consultee would be realized. Another observation that needs to be made regarding the adoption of this approach involves the rather definitive set of instructional assumptions on which it is based. The degree to which the consultant explains those educational perspectives to the teacher, and in what detail, would seem to be critical questions affecting this helping relationship. Rosenfield provides little guidance on this point, let alone the question of whether or not the teacher can chose to disagree or reject those assumptions.

Education is characterized by a variety of instructional theories methodologies, aside from conceptualizations of the learner, that are not only diverse in the premises on which they are based, but may, in fact, be in conflict. Instructional consultation, as presented, would seem to have merit, but under the condition that the teacher's views are consistent with the consultant's. How to accomplish a knowledgeable choice on the part of the teacher when she or he enters this type of consultation needs to be developed by these consultants. What are the implications for the approach when teachers adopt a different set of assumptions? Similarly, at one point Rosenfield mentions that consultants help the teacher "shift" to a collaboration approach, but how that change should be dealt with represents another challenge for consultants using this approach. Both of these questions are dealt with in the issues chapter (13) of this text.

Group Consultation

Given the time constraints faced by teachers, the alternative of offering consultation in a group format would seem to have intuitive appeal. There are often groups of teachers who meet on a regular basis, such as grade level or department meetings. Scheduling some of that time on a regular basis for consultation might have some support, even if only part of the meeting or every third or fourth meeting were so designated. An even more fruitful advantage of this service strategy is that it serves as a forum for observing the problem-solving process on relevant problems and could lead to effective modeling of this skill. For example, in a study offering specific cognitive modeling exercises to undergraduates, it was found that the subsequent problem-solving behavior of observers was positively influenced (Cleven & Gutkin, 1987). Similarly, Curtis and Watson (1980) reported that teachers were more factual when they worked with colleagues who mastered a skill advancement training workshop on collaboration. Such collegial discussion, as might characterize group consultation sessions, may also serve to reduce any anxiety and self reproving attitudes contributing to a teacher's inhibition to explore challenges being presented by a student. Finally, there is the potential for "picking up ideas" and benefitting from listening to a colleague's strategies by generalizing to similar situations. Dinkmeyer & Carlson (1973) referred to this passive type of participation as *spectator therapy*, wherein an understanding of self is facilitated by listening to others problem solve.

In a review of mental health consultation to groups of school personnel, Cohen & Osterweil (1986) report that studies have reported substantive advantages such as reduction in referrals for direct service, increased knowledge of child development, and improved

communication among colleagues. Cohen & Osterweil point out that one major challenge facing the consultant using this approach is prevention of the sessions evolving into meetings with a psychotherapeutic objective; a number of authors usually limit discussion to work-related problems and deal with personal material in a generic manner (e.g., as universal phenomena) to prevent this from happening. Nevertheless, in spite of these benefits, Cohen & Osterweil offer their reflections on the type of group consultation that is case study oriented and find that there exists a number of disadvantages. The group can generate some anxiety among certain consultees, discussions can focus on limitations of consultees and in doing so reinforce an expert role for the consultant, and the experience may result in defensiveness or inhibition on the part of still other consultees.

While the impression exists that group consultation has been increasing and may accelerate, particularly in educational settings, there continues to be a paucity of empirical research (Gutkin, 1993) let alone case descriptions. As Gutkin argues, there is a need to develop significant research efforts in this area.

Task Groups

One type of group consultation that has been proposed for teachers is the *task* group, in which the objective is to learn to deal effectively with students (Brown, Wyne, Blackburn & Powell, 1979). These groups have been found to evolve through the same stages as other groups, so that the consultant must possess the necessary leadership background for the group to be successful; consultants must have knowledge of group dynamics and be able to facilitate group development. Thus, the consultant should be able to help the group clarify its purposes and working procedures. In addition, he or she is a group facilitator, sensitive to and promoting constructive verbal and nonverbal communication and problem resolution, while remaining a participant as well.

The "C" Group

Dinkmeyer and Carlson (1973) proposed the use of didactic-experiential groups for teachers that they called the "C" group. They reasoned that "unless there is personal involvement and opportunity to test out ideas, match them to ones style of life, internalize new concepts, and then exchange results with other professionals, little change will occur" (p. 223). Acknowledging that individual consultation can be hampered by a number of factors, working within teacher groups that were structured differently than the typical in-service education experience would be necessary if school-based consultants in the area of human behavior were to be effective. Thus, the "C" group concept was developed to assist teachers in examining their interactions with students with the objective of developing specific strategies for establishing different relationships. The specific components then, of the "C" group include collaborating, consulting, clarifying, communicating, being cohesive, confronting, being concerned, caring, being confidential, being committed and being willing to change.

Beginning with the collaboration factor Dinkmeyer and Carlson see the group working together on mutual concerns in a mutual help situation. Thus, consultation occurs among the teachers in the group with the consultant as a member of the group. The group then helps each teacher clarify his or her belief system and feelings in order to resolve discrepancies.

Confrontation is one technique that is encouraged, whether it's in the examination of one's own psychological make-up or in providing realistic and honest feedback to other group members. The objective of these factors is to show that the group is concerned and shows that it cares. Communication is reinforced to the point that teachers became involved with each other as individuals. Group cohesiveness enables their effectiveness to be realized. All discussions in the group are confidential to encourage open and frank discussions. Finally, members of the "C" group help each other to develop a commitment to change, and in particular, the notion that they must change their approach to problems. Part of the change also includes beliefs and attitudes; the group helps each other grow professionally and personally.

These writers form their "C" groups with teachers who either have similar concerns or who work with the same children. They also make the point that in forming the group, it is important to have a heterogeneous collection of teachers wherein age, experience, and theoretical/instruction approaches are represented. Involvement in their groups is always voluntary, and group involvement is preceded by an individual interview with the consultant to clarify the goals of the group as well as to establish concrete individual objectives for each teacher as each participate in the group. They report that leaders utilize the techniques that are used in group work in general. Before the group has its first meeting, leaders supply the members with written materials of a didactic nature describing the purpose, rationale, description, and benefits of the "C" group. Additionally, since Dinkmeyer & Carlson view most problems as "interpersonal and social" in nature, an explanation is provided of the Adlerian or socioteleological approach. This approach includes the basic assumptions underlying the development of personality according to Alfred Adler i.e., a) man is primarily a social being, b) man is self determined, c) man's behavior is purposive, d) man must be viewed subjectively, e) man is holistic. Finally, a chart for "making hypotheses about a child's mistaken goals" is given to the participants. The group then begins its first session by identifying a child and considering the following four questions.

1. What did the child do?
2. How did the teacher respond to his action?
3. How did the teacher feel when the child was misbehaving and the teacher was responding?
4. How did the child respond to the corrective efforts of the teacher?

In addition to this preliminary work, the consultant structures the group so that the purpose and focus are clear and the group is sensitive to feelings expressed in the sessions. The consultant links the ideas of group members, insures less verbal individuals can participate beyond the spectator therapy mode, keeps the group focused on its goals, promotes feelings of adequacy, insures consideration of alternative ways of solving challenges, and encourages changes in the behavioral pattern of teacher interaction with students.

Issue Groups

Cohen & Osterweil (1986) argue that an "issues-focused" versus "case seminar" method would meet the professional needs of the teacher focused group. Such teacher consultation groups provide a "safe" problem-solving environment. Rather than one teacher presenting

a case in the group mental health consultation model, Cohen and Osterweil advocate the consultant as "responsible for the choice, pacing, and timing of different consultation issues . . ." (p. 248) and various problems encountered by teachers related to the issue we addressed. Examples of issues addressed are "social relationships in the preschool," and "classroom rules and routines." These authors stress the importance of preparing for the sessions, including individual conferences with the teacher, choosing key questions in order to meet certain objectives, and evaluation.

Group consultation, whether case study or issue focused, seems to hold considerable promise as a school-based approach. As an alternative to the individual consultation approach, it may be appropriate to use in the school environment with many of the same advantages. Clearly, the objective(s) need to be clearly stated, and a volunteer, short-term (two-to-four meetings) commitment at a relatively stress-free time such as after school or piggy backed on another meeting are important to consider. In fact, group consultation approaches in schools may even serve as initial steps in shifting from a direct service approach.

The 15-Minute Consultation

To describe any teacher's day as "full" is truly to make an understatement. The expectations and demands competing for his or her time should seem to preclude only minimal meeting time opportunities being available after classroom responsibilities are discharged. It should come as no surprise then that most school resource professionals observe that teachers approach them for help when "on the run," that is, in-between classes, at breaks, or in the lunchroom. When they do arrange to meet with another professional regarding a "problem" it is typically for 30 minutes rather than the traditional one hour consultation time—and interruptions are not uncommon. Follow-up conferences become increasingly harder to arrange as the case progresses; this phenomenon may in part be due to the teachers limitation on how much time can be devoted to a single child in the class. Or again, the redistribution of limited time is affected by subsequent challenges that need attention, while a certain degree of intervention has already been generated through consultation on the student in question. Without a doubt, some problems are so complex that the time required for reflection and planning will be appreciated by the consultant and consultee. However, in the case of school-based teacher consultation, particularly from internal consultants, consideration of alternative and/or modified consultation may need to be considered. In this section one such alternative—the 15-minute consultation—is discussed.

It may be inevitable that we succumb to the temptation to add a mini adaption of the service approach addressed by this book. Our entire society increasingly is moving to what appears to be a reactive rather than reflective orientation, wherein speed coupled with efficiency is reinforced. It could easily be argued that problem-solving is one activity that doesn't adapt itself to this trend. Yet, whenever teacher consultation is discussed, the frequency with which time is mentioned as a factor is indicative of the importance of the problem. Given the number of times internally-based consultants are approached when the teacher is on-the-run, or in time-limited contexts such as the lunchroom or teacher workroom, it would seem advantageous to begin to deal with these interactions systematically.

Such requests will continue to arise and it would seem that they may simply be a way of life in the schools. These time limited contacts have the potential for developing into and/or generating the more classic type of consultation.

Constraints and Strengths

Several cautions must be noted when considering becoming involved in a brief consultation encounter. First, the teacher may distort or misrepresent the problem such as lack of cooperation from a senior high school student when the problem is the teacher's insecurity resulting from the student's probing, in-class questions. Because of the brevity of the session, the consultant is unable to discern contradictions that may inevitably surface during a longer session. Secondly, "quickie" diagnosis, which turn out to be incorrect, may discourage the teacher from continuing and/or negatively affect the credibility of the consultant with other teachers. Third, the complexity of the intervention(s) is limited because of the time factor. For that matter, even the time to fully explain the rationale for a particular intervention is constrained. Fourth, a brief approach may reinforce the notion that an expert model is the modus operandi of the consultant regardless of the time frame available for problem solving.

On the other hand, the advantages of this approach would suggest continued exploration of its potential and appropriate use. As argued above, the 15-minute consultation fits the teacher's time demands, and as such, reduces or even eliminates one source of resistance. Similarly, it relieves the concern of some administrators and school boards that instructional time will be sacrificed, and in the process the good of many will be jeopardized for the sake of one student. Certainly, the use of such an approach, even if on a restricted basis, allows the consultant to provide services to a greater number of teachers, particularly when individual consultation models are the alternative. Finally, a series of short, targeted problem-solving experiences spread out over an extended time period may be a more productive and efficient strategy to use for students than a concentrated, intense helping period. It meets the immediate needs of teacher and student, reinforces a developmental orientation to seeking and providing assistance, and gives the consultant a long-term perspective useful in providing a context for the presented problem. In summary then, both the constraints and strengths of this type of service option need to be kept in mind during such professional contacts.

Steps to Follow

The primary questions that consultants need to address in terms of maximizing their input involve both the type of assistance that the consultee is asking for, and, the nature of interaction that will facilitate the interaction. In terms of the former demand, the Caplanian topology of problems represents a rather straightforward system to use. You may recall from the discussion in Chapter Two that consultee's difficulties can be due to a lack of knowledge, skill, confidence, or objectivity. Definitive action can be taken by the consultant in terms of the recommendations made regardless of which of these difficulties are involved, but the purpose of those recommendations can be quite different. Similarly, Friedman's (1976) interview categories are helpful to keep in mind in assessing the consultee's style and determining the consultee's follow-through interest (see Chapter Eleven).

As far as style is concerned, Gibbs (1980; see Chapter Eight) noted that an interpersonal/instrumental (i.e., task orientation) preference for the interaction consultant style is manifested by some consultees. Furthermore, she reasoned that failure on the part of the consultant to function in that way during the initial phase of consultation (which is how the 15-minute consultation can be viewed) could negatively affect the outcomes of consultation.

A primary objective of 15 minute meetings for the consultant is to help the consultee prioritize the problems that seem to be of concern to him or her. Once problems are presented and prioritized, selecting from that list one problem that is important and lends itself to the time constraints of the session should contribute to the success of this effort. In terms of these choice points, it would seem wiser to let the teacher make these choices, and if the quality of the choices are an issue, that issue should be introduced during a later contact. Such a strategy will tend to increase the probability of greater involvement on the part of the consultee in the future.

Interestingly, Salmon & Lehrer (1989) reported that consultants' interpretations of problems are influenced by "their perceptions of the child's behavior, the teacher's sense of involvement with the child, and the teacher's beliefs about the causes of the child's behavior" (p. 173). In their analysis of two school psychologists' responses to a variety of presented problem scenarios, one consultant highlighted the technical aspect of consultation while the other consultant seemed to be attracted to the interpersonal concerns. Thus, in making quick analysis of the consultee's approach and style in consultation, the consultant must be sensitive to the effects of their own implicit theories of action influencing their interpretations of the problem. Finally, the advantages and disadvantages of this expert-oriented model versus other models for the 15-minute consultation deserves comment during this point in the contact.

During this problem finding/identification phase, it is extremely important to determine if the consultee has a hypothesis regarding the problem. Similarly, an iteration of the interventions that have been tried is invaluable in preventing the classic gaffe of recommending an approach that is perceived to be ineffective, determining the problem solving attitude and capability of the consultee, and gaining more insight into the problem.

Next, recommendations made by the consultant need to be made in the context of a brief explanation of the limitation of such conferences. The fact that only a tentative hypothesis can be made about the problem reinforces the advisability of focusing the attention of the consultant and consultee on a specific problem. It is advisable for this reason that the consultant share competing hypotheses, and stress the point that they could lead to different interventions.

Finally, the follow-up responsibilities of the consultant and consultee need to be agreed upon along with the next meeting date. The follow-up options involving further contact between the consultant and consultee (e.g., another brief meeting or telephone conference) should have some semblance of an agreed upon agenda and take place in the immediate future.

Telephone Follow-up

Perhaps one of the most underused follow-up approaches involves the use of the telephone. Telephone consultations would seem to have considerable potential, providing consultees know of the availability of the consultant on designated days and times. Consultation

by telephone, when used as a supplementary interaction to face-to-face approaches, helps to provide the support and review that may be the difference between a satisfied user of the service and a frustrated professional. Particularly when an agreed upon agenda is established prior to the call it is a way of touching base quickly and efficiently for the itinerant consultant internal to the system. Determination of the need for further scheduled face-to-face consultations can take place during these contacts along with further assessment of the initial problem identified hypothesis which was formulated.

In order to maximize the use of telephone consultation, the consultant should have regular hours during the day when he or she may be contacted. Nothing is more frustrating, discouraging, and perhaps disappointing in consultation than playing "telephone tag" with someone. Of course, it may be appropriate for the consultant to call the consultee, but for teachers, the only available time they may be free is in the evenings. However, giving the consultee responsibility for the contact sets an important expectation for them, and the timing and nature of the call gives the consultant valuable data about the effectiveness of the prior contact. It is also critical for the consultant to maintain a file so that they can be conversant about prior contacts to maximize the benefits of the call. Such notes should help the consultant improve the quality of future contacts of this sort.

The authors are not recommending either consultation by telephone for the first contact unless it is for preliminary discussions, or the sole means of subsequent contacts after an initial brief consultation. Phone consultations should be used with caution since obvious disadvantages are at the forefront of the consultant's consideration. However, even with those stipulations, it appears as an overlooked, potentially effective means of enhancing teacher consultations. Another option, of course, is to identify other school system resources that are more readily available or relevant to the expressed needs of the consultee or characteristics of the client such as a counselor, tutor, or family school coordinator. And, of course, there is the option of the observation that can be used as an adjunct to the brief consultation service.

Observations

When the idea of a 15-minute consultation is discussed with groups, one of the more common follow-up activities that is proposed involves classroom observation. On one hand, it allows first-hand observation of the student, especially when a consultee is perplexed and/or has trouble describing the behavioral/cognitive patterns—it is invaluable (especially if the consultee requests it). Sometimes the observation option is entertained for other reasons, occasionally unstated. Examples of such intents include the consultant who could provide objective validation as the teacher prepares his or her "case" against the student, or give support because once the consultant "sees how bad things are" he or she can be sympathetic and verify that the best instruction is being provided under the conditions. Observations can serve to supplement follow-up conferences, so that even if the teacher is unavailable for further timely conferences important information relevant to the discussions can be gained. However, the consultant should be cautious when suggesting observations since the message sent to the consultee may be a negative one and defensiveness may result.

At times, observations become the classical cop-out in the sense that when the professional feels unsure and overwhelmed, the observation provides some important delay time. Observations without an obvious purpose are questionable. They can convey a lack of trust

in the consultee, in the sense that the consultant does not consider the consultee's perceptions to be accurate. Observations suggest an expert model will be employed, which may be appropriate given the 15 minute scenario being discussed. However, if the consultant fails to offer insight into the problem, along with suggested interventions, and/or shift to another consultation model, it may create some confusion on the part of the teacher. Further, it can represent a problem-solving failure whenever the consultant errs in terms of identifying the reason the teacher has approached the consultant. The observation has the potential to shift the problem to a client or contextual focus. The observation should have a clear rationale suggesting this action.

Finally, there is one final question that needs to be asked in each problem-solving session, but especially in this consultation adaptation: "Is there anything else going on or any background information that would be important in understanding the situation that we haven't discussed?" It is surprising how this type of inquiry helps to "mine the memory banks." It seems that when consultees become intently focused on a problem, they overlook its salient features when they describe the problem to others. Perhaps, it is because those features have become so common to the consultee, that the obvious is not mentioned. In a conference with a teacher of a third-grade boy, the teacher presented a list of behaviors clearly indicating a lack of concentration and inattentiveness. The descriptions of restlessness and inability to organize thoughts on paper were leading the consultant to speculate on one type of disorder, commonly employed by school staff, although something, or some other information, seemed to be missing. Indeed, upon asking the previously emphasized question offhandedly upon preparing to leave the conference, a viable hypothesis presented itself in the teachers response. "Well, the parents do not want anyone to know, because they're afraid he'll find out, that he's adopted!"

What follows is an example of a series of six brief consultation contacts that illustrate some of the above points; moreover, they demonstrate how short contacts can be strung together to form a consultation.

Session One

The teacher presented himself in the school psychologist's office and made the following statements. "I just did something with John; I want you to tell me if I did it right." He then disclosed that because he was unhappy with John's attitude toward school, he had placed him in the in-school suspension program. When asked to be more specific, the teacher disclosed that John had failed to complete his homework for "weeks," and was only getting by because he was extremely bright. The teacher was told that it was impossible to assess the wisdom of the action without additional information and was asked if he wished to discuss it further. He responded affirmatively. Elapsed time: 5–7 minutes.

Session Two (later the same day)

The teacher began this session by telling the psychologist that he only had 15 minutes until he had to meet with a parent. The psychologist suggested that they use the time available to describe John's problematic behavior. The teacher consulted his grade book and responded that John had handed in one homework assignment in the first four weeks of

school and had completed only half of the assignment. He also reported that John seemed to be off task in class and at times closed his eyes and laid his head on his desk. However, John had passed all quizzes and a major examination. He had also attended class. The teacher, partially out of frustration, had placed John in the in-school suspension program for sleeping in class. A follow-up session was scheduled three days later. The psychologist asked the teacher to identify the goals for John and to contrast them with his own goals. Elapsed time: 15–17 minutes.

Session Three

The teacher reported at the outset that he wanted John to achieve at his potential, while John apparently was satisfied with passing his subjects. Discussion focused on factors that might increase John's aspirations and performance. The teacher also vented his feelings of frustration about underachieving students. At the end of the session, it was agreed that the consultant would design a potential intervention that would be approved by the teacher. Elapsed time: 20 minutes.

Session Four

The psychologist began the session by presenting the following intervention.

1. Teacher needed to readjust his short-term goals for student to perhaps raise his performance to average from the barely passing level, and lower his own expectations and appraisals.
2. The student needed to develop some reasonable expectations about the consequence of high and low school performance. The entire class was assigned an essay "Evaluating My Academic Success."
3. Teacher would engage the student in some goal setting that involved raising his grades.
4. Teacher would reinforce any rise in achievement and would ask parents to do the same thing to change performance standards.

Teacher agreed that plan was doable. Elapsed time: 20 minutes.

Sessions Five and Six

These sessions were brief (5–10 minutes) and were held for the purpose of monitoring progress. Teacher reported that he felt better and that John had made some modest, but discernible academic progress, although he was not achieving at the class average.

Some Final Thoughts about Teacher Consultation

It is natural to associate teacher consultation with challenges teachers face in dealing with learning and behavioral needs of students and overlook the consultant's needs. However, a problem such as loss of classroom control can really mirror the effect of burnout on the

teachers part, or personal problems that are intruding into dealing with his or her primary job effectively rather than management issues. In another example, what initially appeared to be concern about the behavior of some middle school boys was grounded in the fact that the teacher was propositioned in writing by them and in part felt flattered. The confusion caused by a search for appropriate strategy to deal with the situation, while at the same time dealing with such ambivalent feelings led to the teacher seeking out a school-based resource professional who did not know her. And herein lies the problem with the term "teacher consultation." Therefore, the school-based professional offering the consultation must be adept at identifying what is most appropriate in terms of the teacher request along with the limits of their competencies; a referral to and/or involvement of another professional may be indicated. As noted earlier, the consultant's perspective can influence problem identification so that the special educator may be tempted to see a mismatch between teacher instruction and the learner's learning approach, the counselor as a management problem, and the school psychologist theme interference; to complicate matters further, all may be partly correct in some cases. But, it is important to recognize that beginning the consultation too quickly, without considering all the possibilities, can result in wasted time and energies not to mention the frustration it causes.

Most of the time, the teacher request involves a student learning or behavior problem, and as such requests can be described as "straightforward," i.e., lack of information or skill. In turn, requests deserve rather straightforward resource help, rather than the typical verbal exploration that the consultant doesn't give answers, but brainstorms i.e., collaborates, which seems to be so prevalent. It is indeed true, that there is always greater commitment to an action by someone if they are involved in developing the action plan. But, that commitment can come about also through a discussion of the rationale for a recommendation and accountability in terms of a guarantee by the consultant to keep working on finding the workable intervention if the initial plan fails.

Finally, even with the "straightforward" situation, values, attitudes, and hypotheses/theories of how students learn and what constitutes good teaching will quickly arise. Teachers may be reluctant to spend too much time with an individual student because the rest of the class will suffer, yet the school-based professional is strongly committed to individualized instruction. Allowing the student to do something positive may be seen as "giving in" to the student. Similarly, student recommendations to have altered assignments raises concerns about equity and implication for grading. It seems imperative that the consultant be sensitive to such issues and deal with them directly. Meeting the needs of a student within the teachers framework (provided it is reasonable) should be considered rather than automatically planning to convert the teacher to one's own perspective. This orientation is perhaps most challenging in education where a range of interpretations and strategies may exist for a situation.

Summary

Teacher consultation has been widely discussed in the consultation literature. The teacher consultation process has also been widely researched. One result of the discussion and research is that we are aware that we can make an impact on students by consulting with

The Case of Frankie: An Example of Teacher Consultation

Frankie had been referred because of his antics in the classroom, which consisted of verbal outbursts, pulling chairs out from under students who were in the process of sitting down, mimicking the teacher when she turned her back, and making funny faces at classmates. When reprimanded, Frankie would immediately cease whatever he was doing, but return to those actions almost as soon as the teacher focused her attention elsewhere.

Frankie was 10 years old, had no learning disabilities, and tests of intellectual functioning placed him in the high average range. His grades were consistently in the high C to B range and he typically completed both his seatwork and homework, although the level of functioning in the seatwork area was consistently below his potential level of performance.

After three sessions with his counselor, which Frankie controlled by discussing off-task events and wisecracking about his teacher and fellow students, Frankie admitted that he really did want to change his behavior. At this time, counseling was terminated and the teacher was contacted to see if she wished to pursue a consulting relationship. She agreed reluctantly, admitting that complete frustration was her source of motivation.

In the first consultation session, the counselor and the teacher agreed to collaboratively address Frankie's problem by assessing the problem and designing an intervention that could be implemented by both parties. It was also agreed that, if both parties deemed it appropriate, the counselor would involve the parents in the consultation process. The consultant also solicited the teacher's perceptions of Frankie, which she indicated centered on his need for social recognition by his peers. The teacher observed that Frankie was not an unpopular child, but seemed to maintain his place in his peer group by telling jokes, engaging in witty reparté, and at times, taking physical risks, such as walking the top girder on a bridge between the school and the play area. Frankie did not have highly developed psychomotor skills and seemed to be involved in group activities more for his wit than his ability to contribute to the team effort. These perceptions were

supported by observations by the counselor in the cafeteria and on the playground, although the information growing out of the observation suggested that Frankie seemed "nearly desperate" for peer approval in that he seemed willing to go to great lengths to get attention. Specifically, Frankie would taunt other boys to "drop dead" during games, and as reported, walk a very narrow beam on top of the bridge between the school and the play area.

Because of the consultant's and teacher's concern for Frankie's safety, he was told immediately by his teacher that if he was observed on the girder again, he would be precluded from going to the play area and would be assigned to work with the assistant principal during play periods. The focus of the consultation was to develop ways of helping Frankie attain social approval without engaging in outrageous behavior such as that observed on the playground and in the classroom. A response cost system was initially put into place along with a program of supplemental verbal praise by the teacher. The response cost system was set up so that the teacher would receive one of five chips from his desk if he (1) punched or hit anyone, (2) blurted out-of-task utterances such as jokes or put downs, or (3) made faces or gestures to other students. If Frankie had at least one chip left at the end of the day, he was permitted to dismiss the class one row at a time.

Even though Frankie consented to the response cost system, it failed, probably because Frankie lost some social approval from his peer group. Alter four days he would blurt out, "There goes another one when he lost a token," and soon returned to his previous behavior.

After a bit of brainstorming, it was decided to change the reward associated with the response cost system. The teacher, Frankie, and the counselor agreed to replace one of the daily oral reading sessions with a talent show that Frankie would organize with the counselor and for which he would act as master of ceremonies. In order to earn the privilege, Frankie agreed to have at least one of three chips remaining three out of four days in one week. In the event that he did not earn the right to organize and

Continued

The Case of Frankie   *Continued*

narrate the talent show, Frankie was told that another child would be recruited to replace him. He was also told that in the future (unspecified), he would have to share the responsibility of the talent show with other children.

The responsibility of the teacher and teacher's aide was to provide social reinforcement. The counselor's responsibility was to develop an announcement regarding the talent show, to meet with Frankie to assist him in developing the skills needed to emcee the show, and to train the aide to run the project when the developmental work was done.

In five of the first six weeks of the talent show, Frankie was the emcee. At that point, the criterion was raised to having at least one chip each of four days (the talent and eventually the criterion was raised to every school day). During the eighth week, other emcees were recruited for the talent show. However, Frankie was retained by the planning group for the show and assisted in the training of emcees.

teachers and that, as a secondary benefit, teachers will be better able to deal with similar problems in the future. However, the process is not without its problems, and successful consultants consider the constraints placed on consultation by the school environment as well as the background of the teacher, and they work to overcome the limitations they present.

Tips for the Practitioner

1. The likely success of teacher consultation will be constrained by several factors such as time, administrative support, teachers' training orientation, and so forth. Prior to beginning consultation with a teacher, consider each of these variables, and answer the following questions on a preliminary basis:

   A. Has this teacher been oriented to using consultants?
   B. How much time will I have with this teacher?
   C. Does this teacher believe that the principal supports his/her involvement in consultation?

2. There are many advantages as well as disadvantages to group consultation. Prior to beginning a group effort, assess your own ability to facilitate groups.

3. Using a tape recorder, ask as many questions as you can in 15 minutes allowing the imaginary consultee two minutes to answer each question. You will find that only a limited number of questions (perhaps seven) can be posed. The implication is that you need to prepare for each consultation session by collecting as much information as possible through observation and by examination prior to the session and then focus your questions on the client at hand.

Review Questions

1. Identify and describe both the role and system factors influencing the teacher's use of consultation services.

2. Compare the "consultation with teachers" approach reviewed in this chapter with the models of consultation introduced earlier in the text.

3. Outline alternative methods of consultation that can be utilized when individual-oriented, relatively time-free consultation is not practical.

4. Compare and contrast two teacher group consultation services with different focuses.

5. How should classroom observations be used in conjunction with teacher consultation services.

References

Bergan, J. R., & Schnaps, A. (1983). A model for instructional consultation. In J. Alpert & J. Meyers (Eds.), *Training in Consultation* (pp. 104–119). Springfield, IL: Charles C. Thomas.

Blessing, K. (Ed.) (1968). *The role of the resource consultant in special education*. Washington, DC: The Council for Exceptional Children.

Bossard, M. D., & Gutkin, T. B. (1983). The relationship of consultant skill and school organizational characteristics with teacher use of school-based consultation services. *School Psychology Review, 12,* 50–56.

Broughton, S. F. & Hester, J. R. (1993). Effects of administrative and community support on teacher acceptance of classroom interventions. *Journal of Educational and Psychological Consultation, 4,* 169–177.

Brown, D., Wyne, M. D., Blackburn, J. E., & Powell, W. C. (1979). *Consultation*. Boston: Allyn & Bacon.

Cantrell, R. P. & Cantrell, M. L. (1976). Preventive mainstreaming: Impact of a supportive services program on pupils. *Exceptional Children, 42,* 381–386.

Cleven, C. A. & Gutkin, T. B. (1988). Cognitive modeling of consultation processes: A means of improving consultees problem identification skills, *Journal of School Psychology, 26,* 397–389.

Cohen, E. & Osterweil, Z. (1986). An "issue-focused" model for mental health consultation with groups of teachers. *Journal of School Psychology, 24,* 243–256.

Curtis, M. J. & Watson, K. L. (1980). Changes in consultee problem clarification skills following consultation. *Journal of School Psychology, 18,* 210–221.

Dinkmeyer, D. & Carlson, J. (1973). *Consulting*. Columbus, OH: Charles E. Merrill.

Friedman, L. P. (1976). Teacher consultation styles. Unpublished doctoral dissertation, University of Pennsylvania.

Gibbs, J. T. (1980). The interpersonal orientation in mental health consultation: Toward a model of ethnic variations in consultation. *Journal of Community Psychology, 8,* 195–207.

Given-Ogle, L., Christ, B. A. & Idol, L. (1991). Collaborative consultation: The San Juan Unified School District Project. *Journal of Educational and Psychological Consultation, 2,* 267–284.

Graden, J. L. (1989). Reactions to school consultation: Some considerations from a problem-solving perspective. *Professional School Psychology, 4,* 29–35.

Gutkin, T. B. (1993). Conducting consultation research. In J. Zins, T. R. Kratochwill & S. N. Elliott (Eds.). *Handbook of Consultation Services for Children* (pp. 227–248). San Francisco: Jossey-Bass.

Gutkin, T. B. & Bossard, M. D. (1984). The impact of consultant, consultee, and organizational/variables on teacher attitudes toward consultation services. *Journal of School Psychology, 22,* 251–258.

Gutkin, T. B., & Curtis, M. J. (1982). School-based consultation. In C. R. Reynolds & T. B. Gutkin (Eds.). *The handbook of school psychology,* pp. 796–826. New York: Wiley.

Harris, A. M. & Cancelli, A. A. (1991). Teachers as volunteer consultees: Enthusiastic, willing or resistant

participants? *Journal of Educational and Psychological Consultation, 2,* 217–238.

Heron, T. E., & Harris, K. C. (1982). *The educational consultant.* Boston: Allyn & Bacon.

Hughes, J. N., Grossman, P. & Barker, D. (1990). Teachers' expectancies participation in consultation, and perceptions of consultant helpfulness. *School Psychology Quarterly, 5,* 167–179.

Idol, L., & West, J. F. (1987). Consultation in special education (Part II): Training and practice. *Journal of Learning Disabilities, 20,* 474–494.

Idol, L. (1989). Reaction to Walter Pryzwansky's presidential address to the American Psychological Association on school consultation. *Professional School Psychology, 4,* 15–19.

Idol, L. (1988). A rationale and guidelines for establishing special education consultation programs. *Remedial and Special Education, 9*(6), 48–58.

Idol, L., Paolucci-Whitcomb, P., & Nevin, A. (1986). *Collaborative consultation.* Rockville, MD: Aspen Systems.

Idol-Maestas, L., & Ritter, S. (1985). A follow-up study of resource/consulting teachers: Factors that facilitate and inhibit teacher consultation. *Teacher Education and Special, 8,* 121–131.

Johnson, L. J., Pugach, M. C., & Hammitte, D. J. (1988). Barriers to effective special education consultation. *Remedial and Special Education, 9,* 41–47.

Knight, M. F., Meyers, H. W., Paslucci-Whitcomb, P., Hasazi, S. E., & Nevin, A. (1981). A four-year evaluation of consulting teachers service. *Behavioral Disorders, 6,* 92–100.

Lortie, D. C (1975). *School teacher.* Chicago: University Chicago Press.

McKenzie, H. S. (1972). Special education and consulting teachers. In F. Clark, D. Evans, & L. Hammerlynk (Eds.), *Implementing behavioral programs for schools and clinics,* pp. 103–124. Champaign, IL: Research press.

Merriam, S. B. (1988). *Case study research in education.* San Francisco: Jossey-Bass.

Nelson, C. M. & Stevens, K. B. (1981). An accountable consultation model of mainstreaming behaviorally disorder children. *Behavior Disorders, 6,* 82–91.

Pryzwansky, W. B. (1974). A reconsideration of the consultation model for delivery of school-based psychological services. *American Journal of Orthopsychiatry, 44,* 579–583.

Pryzwansky, W. B. (1989). School consultation: Some considerations from a cognitive psychology perspective. *Professional School Psychology, 4,* 1–14.

Quade, B. S. (1985). The effects of consultation time scheduling by elementary LD resource teachers on regular teachers' attitude and use of model. Unpublished doctoral dissertation. Southern Illinois University, Edwardsville.

Rosenfield, S. A. (1987). *Instructional consultation.* Hillsdale, NJ: Lawrence Erlbaum Associates.

Salmon, D., & Lehrer, R. (1989). School consultants' implicit theories of action. *Professional School Psychology, 4,* 173–187.

Sarason, S. B. (1971). *The culture of the school and the problem of change.* Boston: Allyn & Bacon.

Slesser, R. A., Fine, M. J. & Tracy, D. B. (1990). Teacher reactions to two approaches to school-based psychological consultation. *Journal of Educational and Psychological Consultation, 1,* 243–258.

Stenger, M. K., Tollefson, N., & Fine, M. J. (1992). Variables that distinguish elementary teachers who participate in school-based consultation from those who do not. *School Psychology Quarterly, 7,* 271–284.

West, J. F. & Idol, L. (1990). Collaborative consultation in the education of mildly handicapped and at-risk students. *Remedial and Special Education, 11*(1), 22–31.

Whitaker, C. R. (1992). Traditional consultation strategies: Finding the time to collaborate. *Journal of Educational and Psychological Consultation, 3,* 85–88.

Zins, J. R. (1981). Using data-based evaluation in developing school consultation services. In M. J. Curtis & J. R. Zins (Eds.). *The theory and practice of school consultation,* pp. 261–268. Springfield, IL: Charles C. Thomas.

Chapter *11*

Evaluation

Goal of the Chapter

This chapter is designed to introduce the major considerations that need to be taken into account in making evaluation an integral component of consultation.

Chapter Preview

1. The role of evaluation and research in consultation is explored along with the consultant's responsibility to consider both functions in his or her practice.
2. Evaluation purposes are presented as an important initial decision in planning the evaluation of the consultation.
3. The steps in planning and implementing the evaluation component are discussed.
4. Samples of instrumentation that can be used or adapted during the entry, process, and termination stages are provided along with commentary about strategies and concerns that need to be taken into account.

As we have seen throughout this book, consultation is an intervention technique that means many things to many people. It subsumes several theoretical orientations, techniques, and target populations. Perhaps partially because of the amorphous state of our understanding of consulting, the use of the term consultation seems to be growing and the literature becoming more complex. These conditions are ripe for creating myths and disillusionments among the participants in any consultation effort. Add to this state of affairs the fact that individuals are likely to question any alternative service to the traditional services they receive, and the prudent course for any consultant to follow would include a *proactive evaluation* plan. By this we mean, consultants should utilize an evaluation strategy during each consultation case as well as include this component of their service if they operate as an internal consultant.

Data based interventions are critical to professional functioning as we conceptualize it. Given the fact that consultation is usually time limited and goal directed, an accountability orientation on the part of the consultant is also prudent. The importance of documenting the nature and extent of consultation services and its impact from an accountability standpoint should be self-evident. Collected data can not only contribute to the evaluation of the model being used but, perhaps more importantly, be extremely helpful in the continuing development of consultation.

Evaluation refers to the data-gathering activity that allows the consultant to know what progress the consultee and/or client of the consultee is making or the overall success of the intervention. Evaluation questions relate to the needs of those two constituents, and a systematic procedure is followed in gathering data to answer these types of questions. Decisions can then be made regarding continuation or change in the interaction. This data also influences which consultation strategies will be utilized in future consultations, with similar consultees or similar problems. Finally, evaluation allows the consultant to document the effectiveness of his or her consultation service as well as provides information on the utility of such a service delivery approach.

What is being stressed in this chapter is that the consultant has responsibility for evaluation of the intervention versus assuming a program evaluator role or a research role. Often the level of skills and expertise needed by a program evaluator are different than those mastered by professionals functioning in a consultation role. Yet, most consultants are experienced and oriented toward evaluation. Although the content of this chapter is similar to what would appear in the program evaluation literature, the perspective or set emphasized here is on the evaluation responsibility of the consultant in the individual or group situation.

The distinction drawn between evaluation and research on the other hand often comes down to one of intent (Meade, Hamilton, & Yuen, 1982). Evaluation is usually done for some purpose related to the decision-making process; research (at least of the basic type) is done for its own sake. The problem to be solved usually defines the questions in the evaluation model and in that sense an atheoretical or descriptive result is expected. The opposite type of objective would be true for research efforts. The question of the practitioner's obligation to address both an evaluation and research objective, particularly with respect to his or her consultation cases, is addressed in Chapter 13.

Evaluation of consultation can take many different forms depending on the purpose(s), methodology, and resources available to conduct it. As we shall see, there are many purposes for an evaluation and they are not mutually exclusive. Although the purposes of any evaluation may vary, hopefully a multidimensional model will be adopted by the consultant. The consultant should pursue as many of the purposes as resources, time, and circumstances will allow. It is recognized, however, that even in the most supportive environment, routine collection of data on all consultation activities, and maintenance of a data base can be formidable.

Evaluation Models

In this first section a number of evaluation models are presented, in part from the program evaluation literature. Evaluation efforts have been categorized in different ways, so the intention of this brief review of several different frameworks is to help in conceptualizing

evaluation tasks as well as to help the individual consultant set priorities. Types of evaluations are discussed first and followed by a brief discussion of purposes of evaluation.

Formative-Summative

Scriven's (1967) model of formative-summative types of evaluation has been drawn upon heavily in the consultation literature. Essentially, two different kinds of evaluations are identified. *Formative* evaluation is concerned with the planning and implementation processes of consultation. It deals with questions of "how" and, as such, examines and/or monitors the process stages of consultation. It can be used to develop an intervention or to fine tune the consultation process. The planning and decision-making needs are addressed. Often referred to as *process* evaluation, it goes beyond consideration of the consultant-consultee relationship to deal with issues at all stages that are related to consultation improvement. Questions that might be addressed are as follows: Were objectives clearly identified for the consultation? How did the consultee feel about his or her participation during the problem identification stage? Was the consultant easy to relate to? How effectively was the relevance and success of the intervention monitored? Were meetings held regularly? What was the nature of the meetings that were held?

By contrast, *summative* evaluation deals with goal achievement concerns; questions of whether a program has been implemented and its degree of success are postulated. The impact of the consultation, then, is being addressed in this evaluation procedure. Another term used in describing this approach is *product* evaluation. This focus is concerned with the outcome of the intervention. For example, Was student achievement level positively influenced? Did the number of referrals decrease? Are the services being requested by more consultees within the organization? Was the consultation cost-effective? Did the outreach program reduce alcoholism? Was the agency able to communicate better with the community? Did fundraising activities increase? These types of evaluation data can address questions related to efficacy of the indirect service model as well as desirability of maintaining and/or expanding the service versus consideration of an alternative approach.

Evaluation Criteria

A slightly different emphasis in program evaluation is represented by Suchman's (1967) presentation of evaluation criteria. His levels of criteria represent considerations that the consultant may want to keep in mind both for individual case review as well as during an annual review of services. The evaluation criteria focus on effort, performance, adequacy, efficiency, and process. *Effort* refers to the quantity and quality of programmatic inputs such as the type and magnitude of effort of staff, money expended, and the number and type of clients served. *Performance* refers to measurement of the consequences of effort, that is, outputs. This aspect of the evaluations requires a statement(s) of short- and long-term goals specific to consultees, clients, and programs. *Adequacy* considers the relationship between effort and performance in relationship relative to the needs that exist. *Efficiency* considers the ratio between effort and performance (output divided by input if you will) in terms of cost factor such as money, time, personnel, and convenience. Finally, *process* criteria focus on the mechanisms by which effort is translated into outcome. The study of the means employed to produce results is involved in Suchman's view. Specifi-

cally, Suchman indicated that measurement of process should include the four areas: (1) identification of key program components that determine its effectiveness; (2) analysis of the effectiveness of an intervention with different consultees or clients; (3) specification of organizational conditions associated with smooth functioning of the intervention; and (4) delineation of the range of effects attributable to the intervention along with the strength of those results.

Purposes of Evaluation

Another evaluation framework that can assist further in planning evaluations has been proposed by Perkins (1977) in his listing of six major purposes of evaluation. They include strategic, compliance, design logic, management, intervention effect, and program impact. *Strategic evaluation* is akin to a needs assessment and consequently takes place before the intervention. One of the goals of this data collection activity is the identification of objectives. No comprehensive format has been proposed that can be used to assess the need for consultation (Schulberg & Jerrell, 1983), and consequently, attention should be paid to this issue when consultation services are instituted on a trial basis or if the services are scheduled for review. *Compliance* evaluation considers the "fit" or correlation between the objectives of a program and the system(s) of which it is an integral part. *Design logic* evaluations assess the degree to which assumptions are clear that link resources that are available for the intervention to outcome considerations. *Management* evaluations focus on the use of resources applied to reach the goals that have been identified. *Intervention* evaluations naturally attempt to assess the relationship of the intervention activity and the outcome, but may also consider the intervention process itself. *Program impact* evaluates the degree to which the intervention program achieved its goal(s). This last purpose is typically referred to as summative evaluation, while the other five purposes would be examples of evaluations that are formative in nature.

It should be remembered that consultants are responsible to at least two independent systems—their own and the consultee system. The individual consultant may be interested in improving his or her own skills and the eventual service, so feedback is considered to be a valuable asset in reaching that goal. Similarly, either as a means of justifying the service or extending it, data will be required. The consultee, by contrast, may have little need for information beyond the pragmatic one of "did it help." Their job performance may hinge on other demonstrated performance indices so that evaluation is seen as taking away from other important tasks and/or burdening an already overfilled schedule. Likewise, their training may have extolled the virtues of intervention while giving lip service to the idea of evaluation, let alone the notion that evaluation is an integral part of any intervention. A collaborative approach to evaluation based on principles of informed consent seems the most prudent course to follow. As Gallessich (1982) points out, when the consultant has some research purposes in mind or that becomes his or her prime role, these considerations need review from a collaborative perspective.

One final distinction needs to be made about evaluation approaches. The terms *cost-benefit* and *cost-effectiveness* are often thrown around when evaluations are conducted. A cost-benefit emphasis examines the relationship between input costs and outcome measures, usually in a ratio of dollars to dollars. Cost-effectiveness compares the dollar input

with the results of the program. The latter, then, concentrates on means of obtaining the results while the former is outcome oriented (Robinson, 1979).

Given the above array of evaluation options it is advisable that the consultant first clearly identify why the evaluation is being proposed. Then a model of evaluation can be chosen that corresponds to those purposes. Priorities can be more easily established and a rationale developed for sharing data with the consultee and/or organizational management. To the extent possible within organizational, resource, and personal constraints, the consultant should plan as comprehensive an evaluation plan as can be realistically implemented.

Steps in Consultation Evaluation

As with any stage or step model, arbitrary demarcations are made. The model that is used here is based upon the work of Paul (1979) and serves as one example of the type of formulation consultants should consider as the process of consultation unfolds. The steps include considerations of purpose, measurement, data collection techniques, data collection, and dissemination. Again, it is advisable to introduce the notion and rationale for evaluation during contract negotiation, to resolve questions of when it will be done and who has access to the findings. The issues of anonymity and confidentiality need to be explored with the consultee.

Determine the purpose(s) of the evaluation: Determining the purpose(s) of evaluation along the lines just discussed is important. To a large extent this step relates to the need for process and outcome data. As was seen in the foregoing section, these purposes may be subdivided in numerous ways. In large measure this decision guides the subsequent steps of evaluation. Likewise, there may be information needs of the consultee or management that need to be taken into account. Their involvement during this time will be affected by such considerations.

Practical matters associated with evaluations must also be dealt with at this time. The extent to which consultees provide or gather the data affects their involvement at this point. The opportunity to make choices that will affect the time that needs to be devoted to evaluation as well as the types of information that are collected will contribute to ownership of the evaluation. Finally, the use of the data and access by others within the system should be an issue for the consultee as well as the consultant. Confidentiality should be addressed in a direct manner and the consultant should be in a position personally and professionally vis-à-vis the consultee's employer to honor any commitments that are made. In the long run the cooperation that is experienced may be traced to this step.

Agree on measurements to be made: To the extent possible, process and product aspects of consultation have been addressed in the formulation of purposes or objectives. Measures that apply to both of these areas will have to be selected. These measures might also serve an educative objective for the consultant. The information that is included or required may sensitize the consultees to issues or perspectives they need to address in thinking about the problem. The bottom line in selection of measures, however, is that they can be defended as relevant indices of the intervention objectives and other stated purposes.

Identify data collection techniques: Paul describes this step as involving the selection of data collection techniques appropriate to the purpose of the evaluation. "The major goal here is to place the measures in a context which allows for their interpretation" (Paul, 1979, p. 39). He presents a scheme that recommends the matching of purposes, criteria, and methodological tools of evaluation in a tabular form so that the relationship among the three considerations can be visually inspected.

Set a data collection schedule: The actual points at which the data will be collected need to be spelled out and agreed to by the participants. These decisions include who will be involved and whether their role will be collection of information from others, filling out forms themselves, or in some other way participating in data collection, and the summarizing/scoring of the information. Decisions about follow-up, particularly measurement of long-term effects, also need consideration.

Develop a dissemination plan: The disposition of the data that are collected needs to be decided upon. That decision is dictated by the purposes of the evaluation, as well as other considerations such as confidentiality and with whom the data will remain. Data supplied to the consultee's supervisor could serve to reinforce some preconceived negative notions he or she holds or support merit review decisions. Such unintended consequences of data disseminations not only affects the eagerness and openness of the consultee toward future consultation contacts, but can influence the attitudes of other potential consultees in the organization. Similarly, evaluation of the consultant sent directly to his or her supervisor can certainly protect the anonymity of the consultee, but leaves the consultant with no option to add information important to the interpretation of the data.

In addition to providing information on the process and outcome of consultation dissemination can serve a number of other purposes. For example, it may be utilized to justify continuation of the consultation service. An organization or consultee may be willing to give indirect services a try, but both personal experience with consultation *and* data supporting the goals laid out for the service will be needed to convince those who have handled problems in a different way for years that change is beneficial. Data can also serve a public relations function. For example, a school-based psychological consultant may use the results (anonymously) obtained in a consultation to demonstrate some of the potential benefits of consultation.

Instrumentation

In their introduction to the special issue of *Professional Psychology* on evaluation of psychological service delivery programs, Perloff and Perloff (1977) lament the nonexistence of a taxonomy and listing of questionnaires and instruments. They reason that such a classification would save time and money if evaluators could use already developed instruments and forms. If a number of consultants used the same instruments then possibly reliable and valid information could be generated. More importantly, normative data would become available, that is, consultants would know the typical response to items or the typical answer given by certain consultee types. Such standardization would make utilization of the results generalizable. Indeed, such a list of instruments would be helpful in the consultation area

because of the paucity of such information. Of course, further development of instrumentation is still to be encouraged.

An initial step has been taken here to identify existing scales that might be considered. Some of these instruments have been designed with specific purposes in mind. Nevertheless, with some changes and/or in combination with other scales or sections of scales, they may prove more useful to consultants. If their only use is to serve as an impetus for development of other scales, the effort has been well spent.

Essentially, paper and pencil tasks such as questionnaires and surveys are presented. The use of data from observations and tapes (video and audio) are not ruled out; in fact, they are encouraged. However, these data-generating sources (types) have been used primarily in research on consultation. Observations present a challenge because they require an observer who is trained; some obvious cost in actual payment or loss in manpower time is also involved. Taping can be as expensive or more so than the use of observers, particularly if consultants must provide their own equipment. Both strategies require permission of the consultee, and it may be argued that they serve to inhibit communication. Nevertheless, both observation and taping should be seriously considered and utilized, if not routinely in all evaluations, then at least on a periodic basis. The value to the consultant would be immeasurable as a self-evaluation device or peer review type approach.

Beyond the consideration of using an already existing instrument versus one that exists in the literature the consultant needs to consider matching the evaluation methodology to the objectives of the plan. The idea of fitting one's instrumentation/methodology to the purpose of the evaluation seems like a rather simple one. Yet, it is one rule that is likely to cause confusion and even interfere with the consultation process if not followed. It makes little sense to employ an elaborate design and complicated methodology if rather simple, straightforward questions are being proposed. Conversely, comprehensive and specific purposes will require an array of measurement strategies. Finally, the model of consultation and theoretical orientation of the consultant may also dictate the evaluation format that is used.

What follows then are examples of proposed scales arranged by stage of consultation, that is, entry, implementation, and termination. The scales could be categorized as process or outcome measures, but it seemed logical to emphasize the concept of an ongoing evaluation approach to consultation. The emphasis in this section is on dyadic consultation. For information on organizational consultation instrumentation the reader is referred to Cooper and O'Connor (1993).

Entry

Model Preferences

During the entry stage the concern is with needs assessment type tasks. If we define the consultee as the individual who works with the consultant (in contrast to the administrator who sanctions the consultation arrangement), several approaches could be used. For example, it seems logical to expect a consultant to take into account a consultee's preferences and expectations for the consultation services. If such information can ever be collected and available to the consultant before the first session, it provides a starting point in selecting the approach/model to use during an initial meeting. Such a strategy also sensitizes the con-

sultee to the range in consultation approaches that is possible; this educative potential needs some follow-up by the consultant to determine what selected elements of the approach are critical to the consultee.

The Babcock and Pryzwansky (1983) Consultation Preference Scale allows the consultee to state a preference for one of four models of consultation during each of five stages of the process. Table 11.1 summarizes that information; the actual scale is presented in Table 11.2, along with the code for each item.

The Babcock and Pryzwansky scale can be modified in several ways. For example, with minor editing the model x stages can be combined for each model into a narrative. Consultees can be presented with the four narratives, each describing a different model, and asked to make a choice. A further modification would involve the addition of a group versus individual format, providing the consultant was able to offer such a choice. As pointed out in Chapter Eight, Mischley (1973) found equal numbers of consultees stating that they felt more comfortable under one or the other format.

Intake Forms

Paul (1979) recommends a simple intake form be maintained on consultation services similar to that used with direct services. Data that would be recorded on this form would include the consultee's organization, the problem, recommendations concerning the type of consultation indicated, and suggested disposition. Additional data could include information about consultant and consultee characteristics, the consultees "ideal" intervention plan at the time of the interview, and prognosis of the probability of success as a result of consultation.

Parsons & Meyers (1984) have developed a Formative Evaluation Checklist (see Table 11.3), which assists the consultant in summarizing issues related to the entry stage. The form also allows for similar review to be made on those same issues throughout five subsequent stages. The authors' overall objective is to provide a list of sample questions that can be asked continually throughout consultation. A form or checklist like this, with any additional relevant questions, can facilitate the process of monitoring consultation.

A somewhat related concept of intake involves Friedman's (1976) semi-structured interview scale. Her list of questions, although ultimately meant to identify a consultee style that in turn indicates a consultation approach, can again be adapted easily by the consultant for a variety of purposes. Her questions were framed in the student-teacher context, but the terms client-consultee could easily be substituted. Diagnostic information collected about the student (client) was as follows: Who is (are) the client(s)? What is the actual nature and extent of the problem(s) presented? What previous information has been collected that may be of use in understanding the nature of the current problem situation? What are the client's current performance capabilities? What are the client's strengths? weaknesses? What antecedent or consequent conditions maintain the behavior? What information is available about the client's social behavior? emotional functioning? What resources available within the environment may be used as reinforcers?

Diagnostic information about the teacher (consultee) included the following: What is the teacher's perception of the problem situation? What efforts has the teacher made to cope with the problem situation? What were the outcomes of those efforts, if any? Has the teacher formulated any hypothetical explanations of the problem situation? Does the

TABLE 11.1 Differentiation of Consultant Role and Objectives in Five Stages of Four Models of Consultation

Stage	Collaboration (C)	Mental Health (MH)	Clinical (CL)	Expert (E)
1. Consultant Goal	Work with cee[1] to identify problem, plan and carry out recommendations (recs)	Increase cee ability to deal with similar problem in future	Identify problem and develop recs for cee to carry out	Plan and carry our recs for problem identified by cee
2. Problem Identification	Both cee and clt[2] identify problem	clt helps cee identify problem by clarifying his/her perceptions of it	clt identifies problem	cee identifies problem
3. Intervention Recommendations	cee and clt suggest intervention recs	cee plans intervention with clt acting as facilitator	clt offers recs for cee to implement	clt plans intervention which he/she will implement
4. Implementation of Recommendations	cee and clt may each implement some recs	cee implements recs he/she developed	cee implements recs developed by clt	clt implements his/her recs
5. Nature and Extent of Follow-up	cee and clt engage in continuous follow-up to modify intervention if necessary	further consultation may be initiated at request of cee	clt may offer further advice to cee	none

[1] consultee
[2] consultant

265

TABLE 11.2 Consultation Preference Scale

INSTRUCTIONS Assume you will be consulting with a _____ concerning a _____. Below are twenty statements relating to your consultation. Please rate each statement by circling the number below it which best indicates your agreement with its content.

Code	Item

C1
1. The goal of the consultant should be to work with me to identify the problem, to plan and to carry out recommendations.

1	2	3	4	5
strongly disagree	disagree	neutral	agree	strongly agree

C2
2. The consultant and I should both identify the problem based on information we have collected.

1	2	3	5	5
strongly disagree	disagree	neutral	agree	strongly agree

MH3
3. I should plan the recommendations with the consultant offering suggestions.

1	2	3	4	5
strongly disagree	disagree	neutral	agree	strongly agree

CL4
4. I should implement the recommendations that the consultant has developed.

1	2	3	4	5
strongly disagree	disagree	neutral	agree	strongly agree

MH5
5. Further consultation should be initiated only at my request.

1	2	3	4	5
strongly disagree	disagree	neutral	agree	strongly agree

E1
6. The goal of the consultant should be to plan and carry out recommendations after I have identified the problem.

1	2	3	4	5
strongly disagree	disagree	neutral	agree	strongly agree

CL2
7. The consultant should identify the problem based on information he or she collects.

1	2	3	4	5
strongly disagree	disagree	neutral	agree	strongly agree

E3
8. The consultant should plan the recommendations which he or she will then implement.

1	2	3	4	5
strongly disagree	disagree	neutral	agree	strongly agree

C4
9. The consultant and I may each implement some of the recommendations.

1	2	3	4	5
strongly disagree	disagree	neutral	agree	strongly agree

CL5
10. It should be the role of the consultant to offer me any further advice.

1	2	3	4	5
strongly disagree	disagree	neutral	agree	strongly agree

TABLE 11.2 *Continued*

Code	Item

CL1 11. The goal of the consultant should be to identify the problem and develop recommendations that I will then carry out.

1	2	3	4	5
strongly disagree	disagree	neutral	agree	strongly agree

E2 12. I should be the one to identify the problem based on the information I collect.

1	2	3	4	5
strongly disagree	disagree	neutral	agree	strongly agree

C3 13. The consultant and I should both suggest recommendations that we will both then implement.

1	2	3	4	5
strongly disagree	disagree	neutral	agree	strongly agree

MH4 14. I should be the one to implement the recommendations that I develop.

1	2	3	4	5
strongly disagree	disagree	neutral	agree	strongly agree

E5 15. There should probably be no follow-up consultation after the recommendations have been implemented.

1	2	3	4	5
strongly disagree	disagree	neutral	agree	strongly agree

MH1 16. The goal of the consultant should be to increase my ability to deal with similar problems in the future.

1	2	3	4	5
strongly disagree	disagree	neutral	agree	strongly agree

MH2 17. The consultant should help me identify the problem by clarifying my perceptions of it.

1	2	3	4	5
strongly disagree	disagree	neutral	agree	strongly agree

CL3 18. The consultant should suggest recommendations that I will then implement.

1	2	3	4	5
strongly disagree	disagree	neutral	agree	strongly agree

E4 19. The consultant should implement the recommendations that he or she develops.

1	2	3	4	5
strongly disagree	disagree	neutral	agree	strongly agree

C5 20. The consultant and I should engage in continuous follow-up to modify the intervention recommendations, if necessary.

1	2	3	4	5
strongly disagree	disagree	neutral	agree	strongly agree

From "Models of Consultation" by N. Babcock and W. Pryzwansky, from the *Journal of School Psychology*, (1983) 21, pp. 359–366.

TABLE 11.3 Formative Evaluation Checklist

Directions: For each stage of the consultation process, feedback and request for corrective feedback from institutional representatives and consultees are both appropriate and desirable. The checklist provides a broad framework from which to conceptualize the specific formative function to be used within your particular consultation relationship.

Name of Institution _____ Name of Consultee _____ Date of Initial Contact _____

		Consultation Stage			
Formative issue	Entry	Goal Identification	Goal Definition	Intervention	Assessment
1. Record of contacts (record dates, length of sessions)					
2. Special focus of contacts; concerns emerging for later consideration					
3. Provide feed-back to highest relevant adminis-trator (acceptable direction, time line, cost tone)					
4. Request feed-back from con-sultee: Expecta-tions met? Specific concerns?					

TABLE 11.3 *Continued*

Formative issue	Entry	Goal Identification	Goal Definition	Intervention	Assessment
New needs? Suggestions for modification of program? Consultant style? Or administrative details (meeting times, rooms, and so on)					
5. Stage-specific concerns	All relevant personnel contacted? Collaborative atmosphere? Relationship skills?	Agreement on level of entry? Optimal entry point? Possible recontact?	Consultee's skill, cooperation; facility in data gathering/reporting? Data complete?	Feedback to consultee on joint ownership? Consultee accept? Agree? Understand? Modifications? Joint agreement?	Outcomes? Inputs? Process? Design? Decision options? Assessment as collaborative effort?
6. Counselor's perception of process to date—new paths tried					

From *Developing Consultation Skills* by R. D. Parsons and J. Meyers. Copyright © 1984 by Jossey-Bass. Reprinted by permission of the publisher.

teacher analyze student-teacher dyadic interaction to determine the possibility of reciprocal responsibility for the existence of a problem situation? What are the teacher's professional strengths? weaknesses? What is the teacher's attitude toward the student? What is the teacher's motivation in seeking consultation? How involved and committed is the teacher in devising solutions to the problem situation? What is the teacher's attitude toward the consultant? toward the consultation process? How willing does the teacher seem to be to retain professional responsibility for the student?

Next the consultee's information-reporting behaviors were categorized according to the alternatives in the following list. The answers were judged so as to conceptually group them together to identify one of four consultee styles as indicated by Table 11.4. This interview scale serves a dual function: it lends itself nicely to use as a diagnostic instrument and it allows the consultant to assess the success of his or her reactions to the various styles or characteristics of consultees. Such a review of consultant-consultee patterns of interaction can lead to different or refined consultation techniques in future cases.

Consultation Behavior Categories and Criteria

I. Consultee Information-Reporting Behaviors

    1. *Quantity of information reported*: This category allows the consultant to focus on the extensiveness of the teacher's available fund of observations. The following behavioral criteria are used in detailing observations:

        1a. The teacher reports a limited amount of information, narrow in range, and restricted to a few aspects of the problem.

        1b. The teacher reports a wide range of information about many different aspects of the problem.

        1c. The teacher reports an extensive amount of information about a few aspects of the problem.

TABLE 11.4   Four Consultee Styles

Situational Professional Expectancy	Generalized Locus of Control	
	Internal Orientation	External Orientation
Expectancy of Professional Role Power	*Problem-Solving*[a] *1b; 1d; 2a; 2c; 2e; 2f; 2g; 2i;* *3b; 3c; 3d; 4a; 4e; 4g; 4i;* *5b; 5e; 5h; 5i*	*Strivers*[b] *1b; 1d; 2a; 2c; 2e; 2f; 2h;* *2k; 3b; 3c; 3e; 3g; 4c; 4d;* *4f; 4h; 4i; 5c; 5e; 5i; 5k*
Expectancy of Professional Role Powerlessness	*Controllers*[b] *1a; 1d; 2a; 2c; 2e; 2f; 2g;* *2i; 3e; 3f; 3h; 4c; 4d; 4h;* *5a; 5d; 5g, 5h*	*Reactors*[a] *1a; 2b; 2d; 2e; 2h; 2i; 3a;* *3d; 3i; 4b; 4e; 4j; 5b; 5f;* *5j*

[a]Congruent professional and personal expectancies.

[b]Conflicting professional and personal expectancies.

1d. The teacher has used several sources of information to collect data about the problem.

1e. The teacher has used a few sources of information to collect data about the problem.

2. *Quality of information reported*: This category refers to differences in the quality of information reported by teachers. The following criteria are used:

   2a. The teacher's information is specific.

   2b. The teacher's information is vague.

   2c. The teacher's information is detailed.

   2d. The teacher's information is general.

   2e. The teacher primarily reports information obtained from observation of the external environment.

   2f. The teacher primarily reports information obtained from observations of his or her own feelings, thoughts, and personal reactions to the problem situation.

   2g. The teacher's information is selective and organized according to some personal hierarchy of relative importance.

   2h. The teacher's information is unorganized and does not reflect the use of any personal hierarchy of relative importance.

   2i. In response to consultation questions or comments, the teacher voluntarily offers primarily negative information about the problem situation.

   2j. In response to consultant questions or comments, the teacher voluntarily offers primarily positive information about the problem.

   2k. In response to consultant questions or comments, the teacher voluntarily offers both negative and positive information about the problem.

   2l. In response to consultant questions or comments, the teacher does not volunteer additional positive or negative information.

II. Consultee Resistance-Cooperation Behaviors

3. *Extent of Participation in Problem-Solving*: This category refers to the extent to which the teacher displays a willingness to cooperate as an equal status problem-solving partner during the consultation interview and the degree to which the teacher exhibits commitment to problem-solving activities.

   3a. The teacher limits responses to answering the specific question asked.

   3b. The teacher answers questions and voluntarily elaborates broadening the range of problem solving.

   3c. The teacher asks questions or requests information about the problem.

   3d. The teacher does not actively seek clarifying information about the problem.

   3e. The teacher avoids certain problem-solving activities.

   3f. The teacher engages in all three problem-solving activities.

   3g. The teacher demonstrates receptivity toward recommendations offered.

3h. The teacher rejects or refuses recommendations offered.

3i. The teacher restricts feedback about recommendations offered.

4. *Maintenance of the Interview Focus*: This category refers to those teacher verbal behaviors that either facilitate, impede, or have neutral effects on the consultant's attempts to structure the interview in an orderly sequence and maintain a problem-centered focus.

 4a. Teacher responses to consultant questions or comments are relevant to the focus of the problem-solving discussion and enhance the orderly progression of the interview.

 4b. Teacher responses to consultant questions or comments are relevant to the focus of the problem-solving discussion, but do not enhance the progression of the interview.

 4c. Teacher responses to consultant questions or comments are irrelevant or tangential to the focus of the problem-solving discussion and impede the orderly progression of the interview.

 4d. The teacher answers consultant questions, but in so doing changes the focus of the interview.

 4e. The teacher answers consultant questions, but maintains the focus of the interview.

 4f. The teacher interrupts problem-solving activities to discuss his or her own personal and/or professional concerns, changing the problem-centered focus of the interview.

 4g. The teacher sustains problem-solving activities and introduces additional personal and/or professional concerns at appropriate intervals without changing the problem-centered focus of the interview.

 4h. Consultant questions or comments elicit the teacher's negative affective involvement (in varying degrees of intensity) with the problem, which disrupts the maintenance of a problem-centered focus.

 4i. Consultant questions or comments elicit the teacher's positive affective involvement (in varying degrees of intensity), which maintain the problem-centered focus.

 4j. Consultant questions or comments elicit the teacher's neutral affective involvement, which maintains the problem-centered focus.

5. *Consultee Influence Attempts*: This category refers to those verbal behaviors that reflect the teacher's attempts to actively influence the consultant's perceptions of the problem situation in a positive or negative direction. They thus reflect the way in which teachers use information available to exert influence over the consultant's perceptions or interview behavior. It should be noted that four of the criteria presented under this category (5g; 5h; 5i; 5j) were also used to delineate certain consultant information-reporting behaviors (2i; 2j; 2k; 2l). They are included here because they also allow the consultant to observe how a specific type of information may be used by the teacher to facilitate or impede problem-solving efforts.

5a. From the outset of the problem-solving interview, the teacher offers a diagnosis and solution that limit any further exploratory problem-solving activities.

5b. The teacher suspends judgment about the diagnosis and solution and engages in exploratory problem-solving efforts.

5c. The teacher seeks confirmation of the validity of his or her perceptions of the problem situation.

5d. The teacher adheres to his or her perception of the problem situation despite the introduction of alternative explanations.

5e. The teacher is receptive to additional information or alternative explanations and considers them within the framework of his or her professional experience.

5f. The teacher does not clearly articulate his or her perceptions of the problem and both seeks and willingly accepts the consultant's "expert" interpretation.

5g. In response to consultant questions or comments, the teacher voluntarily offers negative information about the problem situation.

5h. In response to consultant questions or comments, the teacher voluntarily offers primarily positive information about the problem.

5i. In response to consultant questions or comments, the teacher voluntarily offers both negative and positive information about the problem.

5j. In response to consultant questions or comments, the teacher does not volunteer additional positive or negative information.

5k. In response to consultant questions, the teacher introduces additional information not sought by the consultant and irrelevant to the discussion in progress.

5l. In response to consultant questions, the teacher introduces additional information not sought by the consultant and relevant to the discussion in progress.

Setting Variables

No specific scale is presented here; nevertheless the need for a preliminary consideration of such factors is strongly encouraged. Such information can serve diagnostic and evaluative purposes. Formal assessment (use of instruments) of setting variables, particularly when it does not appear directly relevant to the consultation objective, can be a tricky process. While it might be helpful to know how much a consultee's behavior may be dictated by the atmosphere of the work setting, questions about leadership style of a supervisor can create problems. Administrator "paranoia" then is just one factor that can result to complicate matters. Except where specific consultation goals directly warrant use of such content scales, this information is best gathered informally (the organizational development literature can be useful if particular scales are needed). Halpin & Croft's (1963) Organizational Climate Scale is helpful to review in terms of identifying some of the relevant dimensions distinguishing open from closed systems. The involvement of an administrator/supervisor in the consultation case and the consultee's perceived support of those individuals (aside from their stated commitment) will also need to be gauged. Gallessich (1973) has also outlined

a number of considerations to be taken into account with this perspective. For example, she recommends that the consultant gather information related to organizational phenomena in the domains of *external* and *internal* forces (pressures) on the organization, the organization's *trajectory* (that is, history and future trends), and the staff *perceptions* of the consultant's role and service. Again, an informal, nonobtrusive assessment of these factors is recommended. The data can be helpful in planning current and future consultations.

Process

A number of authors have encouraged an ongoing evaluation plan rather than one that comes at the end of consultation. This goal can be accomplished informally or by using some type of instrument for a mid-point or "taking stock" purpose. A process summary form could call for a problem definition, description of the intervention process, documents collected, a statement of the extent of fulfillment of the working contract, and a prognosis for the future maintenance of progress effect. The consultee could also be asked to rate aspects of the consultation process (Paul, 1979), or both the consultant and consultee could fill out the same form or make the same ratings independently and then share those perceptions.

Consultee Satisfaction
Although this type of data is usually associated with the termination stage, there is no reason why such feedback cannot be collected at different stages of the consultation process. Parsons & Meyers (1984) suggest a format that considers the areas of consultant efficacy, expertise, administrative ability, and interpersonal style, while soliciting more general comments from the consultee (see Table 11.5).

Goal Attainment Scaling
Goal attainment scaling (GAS) builds on the general tradition of goal-oriented evaluation. That is, one starts by setting a goal, then implementing a program, and finally collecting information about goal attainment. That information is then used to plan future interventions. Originally developed to evaluate the progress of individual psychotherapy programs in mental health programs in mental health centers (Kiresuk & Sherman, 1968), GAS has been applied to counseling in schools (Maher & Borbrack, 1984) and seems applicable to consultation encounters. Although GAS has traditionally been used as an *outcome* measure, it does have the potential to be used as a monitoring device and, as a result, is introduced in this section as a measure for the process phase of consultation.

The uniqueness of GAS is that the target goals are placed in the center of a continuum of possible outcomes rather than posited as either attained or non-attained. Thus, the interviewers arrange their goals, or goal indicators as some have labeled them, along a discrete 5-point scale continuum of "most unfavorable" and "less than expected" on the one end, the "expected outcome" in the middle, and the "more than expected" and "best anticipated" on the other end (Kiresuk & Lund, 1978). Secondly, GAS makes use of a quantitative score in which a weighted average of scores on each goal has been formulated (usually three to five goals are selected). Goals are then weighted in terms of importance from 1 to 99 (some authors suggest weights of 1–5). The goals are then scaled, as indicated above by placing them along the continuum of expected five levels of outcome, which also have been quantified by an outcome score of –2 to +2 (see Table 11.6). The computation formula for the goal attainment score is as follows:

TABLE 11.5   Consultee Satisfaction Form

For each statement listed, check the most appropriate response as it applies to the current consultative interaction. Your response is viewed as extremely important to the ongoing improvement and facilitation of the consultation program and to the consultant's professional growth. Thank you for your assistance.

	1	2	3	4
	Strongly Agree	Agree	Disagree	Strongly Disagree

I. Efficacy of Consultation
  1. The goal definition was accurate complete, and sufficiently concrete
  2. The data-gathering procedures provided the necessary data
  3. The intervention plan makes sense for my unique situation
  4. The intervention plan has been easy enough to implement
  5. The intervention plan has been effective to this point

II. Consultant Expertise
  1. The consultant knows his or her "stuff"
  2. The consultant is apparently versed not only in the subject matter but in the process of helping others
  3. The consultant presents information and directions clearly

III. Consultant's Administrative Abilities
  1. The consultant makes efficient use of time
  2. The consultant is prompt in providing feedback
  3. The consultant has efficiently distributed work assignments

IV. Interpersonal Style
  1. The consultant is comfortable to talk with
  2. The consultant is a good listener
  3. The consultant is generally pleasant
  4. The consultant is self-expressive without being overpowering
  5. The consultant has encouraged me to be an active participant in the consulting process

V. General Comments (regarding your likes, dislikes, recommendations for improving this and future consultations)

From *Developing Consultation Skills* by R. D. Parsons and J. Meyers. Copyright (1984) by Jossey-Bass. Reprinted by permission of the publisher.

TABLE 11.6   An Example of a Goal Attainment Scaling (Equal Weights)

GAS Category/Level	Sample Scales 1	2
Best anticipated success +2	Never tardy	Client attempting, consistent, reaching goals
More than anticipated success +1	Tardy once/month	Client attempting consistently with some success
Expected level of success 0	Tardy twice/month	Client attempting
Less than expected success −1	Tardy 3–4/month	Client makes some attempt but . . .
Most unfavorable outcome −2	Tardy more than 4/month	Client makes no attempt

$$\text{Goal Attainment Score} = 50 + \frac{10\Sigma(W_i W_i)}{[.7\Sigma W_i^2 + .3(\Sigma W_i)^2]^{1/2}}$$

Thus, W_i is the weight assigned to the $_i$th goal scale, X_i is the attainment score (−2 to +2) on the $_i$th goal scale, and the summations are across all of the goal scores. The result is a GAS score in which 50 indicates the goal was expected, less than 50 a more negative interpretation, and more than 50 a better than expected outcome. Although this method may seem cumbersome and/or formidable to some because of a formula, its application is not. Furthermore, where each of the goals (scales) is weighted equally, Table 11.7 is a handy conversion aid. Such a guide as Table 11.6 can include a notation for the level of attainment at the time of initial referral and the different times of follow-up.

Consultant Style

Some feedback regarding interaction style could be helpful in some instances of consultation. The boxed questionnaire following each session (see p. 278) represents a form that could be used with consultees in between sessions. In a sense the use of such a scale not only forces some reflection on the pace and progress of consultation, but sets the stage for future contacts. For consultees who are busy and/or do not engage systematically in such exercises, this mechanism may be especially helpful and beneficial to the consultation process.

Termination

It is during this stage of consultation that we generally think of the evaluation function. However, a dilemma of sorts faces the consultant when the target of change is to be identified. Given that consultation is indirect, it could be argued that the consultant can only be held accountable for changes in the consultee. In fact, in some consultation models such as Caplan's the consultee is given considerable freedom in terms of the intervention plan that is followed, if any, and is not accountable to the consultant. Others would argue that the consultee's client is the ultimate object of change and, therefore, the only logical focus of out-

TABLE 11.7   Goal Attainment Score Conversion Table for Equally Weighted Scales

Total raw score (Sum of scale scores)	Number of scales					
	1	2	3	4	5	6
−12						19
−11						22
−10					20	24
− 9					23	27
− 8				21	26	29
− 7				25	29	32
− 6			23	28	32	35
− 5			27	32	35	37
− 4		25	32	35	38	40
− 3		31	36	39	41	42
− 2	30	38	41	43	44	45
− 1	40	44	45	46	47	47
0	50	50	50	50	50	50
1	60	56	55	54	53	53
2	70	62	59	57	56	55
3		69	64	61	59	58
4		75	68	65	62	60
5			73	68	65	63
6			77	72	68	65
7				75	71	68
8				79	74	71
9					77	73
10					80	76
11						78
12						81

Reprinted from *Goal Attainment Scaling*, T. J. Kiresuk & S. H. Lund (1978) by permission.

come measures. The outcome/efficacy question is not a simple one and may more appropriately be tied to the model that is used or nature of the problem when an answer to outcome measures is sought. Caplan (1970) noted the complicated evaluation design needed to demonstrate the "chain of interlocking factors—that is, consultation intervention, change in consultee perception and attitudes, change in consultee-client behavior, resulting in change in client behavior and performance" (p. 295) may be a formidable task even for a sophisticated team of research scientists. Yet some attempts at thorough evaluation by the consultant are necessary, particularly if the service is to be respected and supported. What follows then is a discussion of a range of options that are available.

A particularly difficult challenge faces the consultant who has as one objective the improvement of the consultee's handling of future situations resembling the referral at hand. It is not unreasonable to expect several such repetitions, but in each instance with notable changes in the consultee's analysis and problem solving of the case. However, this objective is dependent on the consultee working with a relatively homogeneous population so as to insure similarity in client population needs and a long-term consultation arrangement. One alternative assessment under such a consultation goal would be an assessment of

Questionnaire Following Each Session

1. The consultant helped me to identify what the problems were today.
   strongly disagree   disagree   unsure   agree   strongly agree

2. The consultant helped me to understand the problems better.
   strongly disagree   disagree   unsure   agree   strongly agree

3. The consultant seemed to understand what I meant when I said something.
   strongly disagree   disagree   unsure   agree   strongly agree

4. The consultant helped me to better understand what I was feeling.
   strongly disagree   disagree   unsure   agree   strongly agree

5. If the consultant did help you to understand the problem(s), did he or she do this by (check as many as apply):

   _____ sharing a similar problem she or he had
   _____ telling you about problems other teachers have had
   _____ talking about problems children have had

6. The consultant restated the problem for me in words I could understand.
   strongly disagree   disagree   unsure   agree   strongly agree

7. How often during the meeting did you feel that the consultant let you decide what you wanted to do?
   never   rarely   occasionally   usually   always

8. How often did both you and the consultant work together to discuss the problems you brought up?
   never   rarely   occasionally   usually   always

9. I think the consultant was sensitive to the problems we talked about today.
   strongly disagree   disagree   unsure   agree   strongly agree

10. I like the consultant's style in relating to me.
    strongly disagree   disagree   unsure   agree   strongly agree

11. Did something the consultant say or do affect any of your opinions or behavior?
    not at all   not very much   somewhat   very much   drastically

    a. If it did, what was it the consultant said or did?
    b. How did you respond to what the consultant said or did?

12. Overall, I feel very satisfied with what happened in today's session with the consultant.
    strongly disagree   disagree   unsure   agree   strongly agree

13. Is there anything that you would like to discuss in your consultation meeting next week as a result of today's session?
    Yes   No   If yes, can you be more specific about what it is that you would like to talk about?

changes in future "problem finding" skills of the consultee, that is, identifying elements of the problem, developing alternative hypotheses for explaining the problem, and generating more relevant intervention plans.

Client Changes

A number of authors have advocated the use of single subject designs for measuring client outcome changes (Brown, Wyne, Blackburn, & Powell, 1979; Meyers, Parson, & Martin, 1979; Meade et al., 1982). Given the difficulty of generating control groups and the one-to-one nature of some consultation, these designs need to be seriously considered by consultants. The options include the ABC design and reversal designs, multiple baseline designs, case studies, and mixed designs.

An ABC design compares the effect of one intervention (B) to a second intervention (C) and the baseline data (A). Reversal designs establish that an intervention designed as a result of the consultation process has indeed caused the behavior change. As the letters A B A suggest, this design establishes an uncontrolled baseline, then introduces an intervention, and finally returns to an uncontrolled baseline condition. Multiple baseline designs permit the evaluation of the effectiveness of the intervention strategy. They can involve: (a) two or more *behaviors* by the same individual in the same situation, (b) two or more *individuals* in the same situation, or (c) an intervention applied to the same behavior, but in different *situations*. Mixed designs combine multiple baseline and reversal designs. The case study will be explained later in this chapter.

More recently the term *time-series methodology* has been introduced to refer to these approaches that share a number of essential characteristics (Barlow, Hayes, & Nelson, 1984). The designs are "organized by the nature of their estimates of stability and the logic of their data comparisons" (p. 180). Again, these designs include the necessity of specifying an intervention, repeated measurements over a period of time, and baseline data. Barlow et al. (1984) note that replication of effects is expected to bolster confidence in the results. Finally, they argue for an *attitude of investigative play* on the part of the practitioner to insure the success of these approaches; their use is seen as a "dynamic-interactive enterprise in which the design is always tentative, always ready to change as significant questions arise in the process" (p. 178).

Barlow et al. (1984) identify three fundamentally different kinds of single-case experimentation: (1) within-series elements, (2) between-series elements and, (3) combined-series elements. The *within-series elements* design changes are considered within a series of data points across time. A single outcome measure or set of measures could be used. The traditional AB or ABA design is an example of what is meant. There are more complex variations of this design such as A/B + C/A or interactional designs but the overall logic remains the same. The *between-series elements* organize data across time by different conditions and not by time alone. Two basic types of designs are identified here: the alternating-treatment design and the simultaneous-treatment design. Alternating-treatment designs involve simply the rapid and random alternation of two or more conditions. Simultaneous-treatment designs involve the concurrent or simultaneous applications of two or more interventions in the same case. Finally, the *combined-series elements* basically combine between-series elements and within-series elements into a logically distinct and coordinated whole. The most common example is the multiple baseline design. Barlow et al.

(1984) suggest that the multiple baseline probably represents the best design for practitioners: "It does not require withdrawal, it is fairly simple, and applied opportunities for its use abound once systematic measures are being taken" (p. 263). For more in-depth treatment of these designs including their strengths and weaknesses the reader is referred to the references in this section.

It is important to take notice at this point that the client-outcome designs being discussed here are typical of what is recommended by behavioral consultants. They fit the theoretical model underlying that consultation approach. As such they may be less palatable or relevant to other consultants and to consultees. Client-outcome measures such as the GAS or paper-and-pencil measures may be deemed more appropriate. For example, changes in consultee attitudes and knowledge of self-concept may be of more interest in other models of consultation.

Consultee Satisfaction
Perhaps the one variable that has received the most attention in the research literature is consultee satisfaction. Conoley and Conoley (1982) suggest an open-ended evaluation approach that can be used as a paper and pencil instrument or serve as the core of an interview process (see box on p. 281). Another approach to consultation evaluation places a good deal more emphasis on the consultant's style, as noted in the boxed consultation evaluation survey (p. 282).

Consultant Assessment
Many of the scales contain items that can be used by the consultant as feedback for self-improvement purposes or, in certain circumstances, as an accountability measure. One of the more well-developed scales, developed specifically for evaluation of the consultant, has been proposed by Curtis and Anderson (1975). Their scale (see box on p. 284) was intended to be used in an observation context, but many of the items could be adapted for a questionnaire instrument. Again this scale, as others, reflects the priorities of the consultant in the evaluation model.

Secondary Outcomes
As noted earlier, some authors have recognized the purposes of consultation as including changes in the client group and the consultee. However, positive changes in the latter may be seen as a secondary benefit. A sample of items that address the benefits that may accrue to the consultee is presented in the box on p. 288. Again, these items can be rewritten and supplemented with others to fit the consultant's situation. Although these questions are designed for consultees, it may be useful for the consultant to complete the same questionnaire and then, with the consultee, compare perceptions of the gains made by the consultee.

Another scale is suggested by Zins (1981) who asked consultees if they had benefited as a result of consultation interactions in the following areas: understanding complexities of the problem situation in greater depth and breadth; clarifying/specifying the problem situation; seeing alternatives not thought of before; finding themselves trying out some of their own ideas; making their own decisions as to management of problems; and helping them to work more effectively with client(s). Needless to say, if the original consultation request was framed solely in terms of client need by the consultee (or the supervisor) the use of

---

Open-ended Consultation Evaluation Form

1. Compared with other teachers at your school would you say your contacts with the consultant were:

   considerably fewer
   fewer
   average
   more
   considerably more

2. With what aspect of the consultation have you been happiest last semester? least happy?

3. What would you like to see changed this semester?

4. How might the consultant be more available to you this semester?

5. What comments or suggestions do you have specifically about the consultant's work this past semester?

6. Based on the things the consultant did this past semester, how would *you* define the role of consultant?

7. Based on your experience with mental health consultation this year, you feel that mental health consultation is:

Extremely helpful						Not at all helpful
7	6	5	4	3	2	1

Reprinted with permission from J. C. Conoley and C. W. Conoley, *School Consultation*, copyright 1982, Pergamon Press.

---

such consultee-oriented questions may contribute to defensiveness on the part of the consultee or rumors regarding the consultant's hidden agenda among the staff. The latter outcome could seriously damage the credibility of the consultant for future consultation requests.

Case Study

Traditionally, a case study analysis usually suggests a nonexperimental, purely anecdotal report will be made. As such, case studies have been seen by traditional research methodologists as in a separate (and lower) class than experimental works (Barlow et al., 1984). Furthermore, since their primary use is to suggest hypotheses that can be an outcome of any activity, this attitude has contributed to discouragement among practitioners when it comes to analyzing their consultation cases using the case study. Consequently, using this approach as an evaluation strategy or for advancing the knowledge base of the consultant has received little attention recently. Ironically, it is this potential as a hypothesis generating tool that should be highly valued for an increasingly popular intervention service whose application far outstrips the available database on which to base its applications (Pryzwansky & Noblit, 1990).

Barlow et al. (1984) note that an openness to case analysis and case studies is a "cornerstone of applied time-series methodology" (p. 281). That methodology simply means that a series of measures are collected on the same individual over a period of time. The single case experiment design is an example of time-series methodology, but differs from the

Consultation Evaluation Survey

Your organization _____ Date _____

Consultant's name _____

Number of years you have worked in this type of organization _____

Sex (circle one):   Male   Female

Have you had previous experience with consultants?
Yes   No

To what extent have you made use of the consultant this year?
_____ Not at all
_____ Very little, 1 or 2 times
_____ To a moderate extent, about 3 to 6 times
_____ To a considerable extent, about 6 to 10 times
_____ To a great extent, more than 10 times

In general, how helpful has the consultation been to you? (Circle the number that is most descriptive)
Not at all   1   2   3   4   5   6   7   Very helpful

Did you work with the consultant in a group situation?
Yes   No

Did you work with the consultant on an individual basis?
Yes   No

Please respond to the following items by circling the number that best describes your perception of your consultant. Response options range from 1 (not at all descriptive) to 7 (very descriptive). If an item does not seem applicable to your consultant, circle N.A.

The consultant:

1. Offers useful information.	1	2	3	4	5	6	7	N.A.
2. Understands my working environment.	1	2	3	4	5	6	7	N.A.
3. Presses his or her ideas and solutions.	1	2	3	4	5	6	7	N.A.
4. Is skilled in forming good working relationships.	1	2	3	4	5	6	7	N.A.
5. Is a good listener.	1	2	3	4	5	6	7	N.A.
6. Helps me find alternative solutions to problems.	1	2	3	4	5	6	7	N.A.
7. Increases my self-confidence.	1	2	3	4	5	6	7	N.A.
8. Helps me identify resources to use in problem solving.	1	2	3	4	5	6	7	N.A.
9. Is not concerned with my point of view.	1	2	3	4	5	6	7	N.A.
10. Encourages me to make my own decisions.	1	2	3	4	5	6	7	N.A.
11. Helps me find ways to apply content of our discussions to specific situations.	1	2	3	4	5	6	7	N.A.

Consultation Evaluation Survey *continued*

12. Respects values that are different from his or hers.	1	2	3	4	5	6	7	N.A.
13. Fits easily into our work setting.	1	2	3	4	5	6	7	N.A.
14. Stimulates me to see situations in more complex ways.	1	2	3	4	5	6	7	N.A.
15. Relies on one approach to solving problems.	1	2	3	4	5	6	7	N.A.
16. Explains his or her ideas clearly.	1	2	3	4	5	6	7	N.A.
17. Has difficulty understanding my concerns.	1	2	3	4	5	6	7	N.A.
18. Encourages me to try a variety of interventions.	1	2	3	4	5	6	7	N.A.
19. Helps me in ways consistent with my own needs.	1	2	3	4	5	6	7	N.A.
20. Encourages communication between me and others with whom I work.	1	2	3	4	5	6	7	N.A.
21. Increases my understanding of basic psychological principles.	1	2	3	4	5	6	7	N.A.
22. Makes helpful suggestions.	1	2	3	4	5	6	7	N.A.
23. Does not appreciate the pressures of my job.	1	2	3	4	5	6	7	N.A.
24. Makes me feel comfortable in discussing sensitive problems.	1	2	3	4	5	6	7	N.A.
25. Encourages our work group to cooperate.	1	2	3	4	5	6	7	N.A.
26. Supports my efforts to solve problems.	1	2	3	4	5	6	7	N.A.
27. Has knowledge relevant to my work.	1	2	3	4	5	6	7	N.A.
28. Helps me understand myself better.	1	2	3	4	5	6	7	N.A.
29. Helps me develop a wider range of problem-solving skills.	1	2	3	4	5	6	7	N.A.
30. Rushes into premature solutions.	1	2	3	4	5	6	7	N.A.
31. Is sensitive to my feelings.	1	2	3	4	5	6	7	N.A.
32. Helps me to see my situation more objectively.	1	2	3	4	5	6	7	N.A.
33. Knows how and when to ask good questions.	1	2	3	4	5	6	7	N.A.
34. Is reliable about appointments.	1	2	3	4	5	6	7	N.A.

This consultant will not be consulting in the future. What suggestions do you have to help him or her improve in consultation skills? Remember, this information will NOT be used for grading: it will be extremely helpful to your consultant as feedback.

What did you like most about his or her work?
What did you like least about his or her work?
If you did not use this consultant, why not?

Consultant Observational Assessment Form (COAF)

Observer's Name _____

Consultant (or Session Number) _____

Date _____

ON EACH OF THE FOLLOWING DIMENSIONS, PLEASE *CIRCLE* THE NUMBER THAT *BEST* REFLECTS YOUR ASSESSMENT OF THE CONSULTANT'S FUNCTIONING ON THAT SPECIFIC DIMENSION.

1. *Expert-Facilitator*
   How would you assess the consultant's role during the session?
   (Expert)   1   2   3   4   5   (Facilitator)

2. *Relationship*
   How would you assess the consultee's role during the session?
   (Subordinate)   1   2   3   4   5   (Colleague)

3. *Value*
   To what extent did the consultant seem to try to impose his or her values on the consultee?
   (Not at all)   1   2   3   4   5   (Great extent)

4. *Empathy*
   To what extent did the consultant seem to empathize with the consultee?
   (Not at all)   1   2   3   4   5   (Great extent)

5. *Support*
   How much moral support did the consultant seem to provide for the consultee? (Support does not connote agreement.)
   (None at all)   1   2   3   4   5   (Great deal)

6. *Interest (Nonverbal)*
   How much interest did the consultant seem to express in the concerns of the consultee (nonverbally)?
   (None at all)   1   2   3   4   5   (Great deal)

7. *Interest (Verbal)*
   How much interest did the consultant seem to express in the concerns of the consultee (verbally)?
   (None at all)   1   2   3   4   5   (Great deal)

8. *Trust*
   To what extent was the consultant able to create an atmosphere of trust and acceptance?
   (Not at all)   1   2   3   4   5   (Great extent)

9. *Ventilation*
   How would you assess the consultant's allowance of ventilation by the consultee?
   (Far too much   1   2   3   4   5   (Optimal
   or far too little)   amount)
   If rated 1, 2, or 3, was the ventilation allowed _____ too much or _____ too little?

Consultant Observational Assessment Form (COAF)   *continued*

10. *Data Generation*

    How much relevant information was the consultant able to draw out?
    (None at all)   1   2   3   4   5   (Great deal)

11. *Follow Through*

    To what extent did the consultant seem to pursue or follow up on key comments by the consultee?
    (Never)   1   2   3   4   5   (Always)

12. *Questioning*

    How would you assess the overall effectiveness of the consultant's questioning techniques?
    (Not at all)   1   2   3   4   5   (Very effective)

13. *Summarization*

    How effectively did the consultant summarize what had transpired?
    (Not at all)   1   2   3   4   5   (Very effectively)

14. *Thought Clarification*

    To what extent did the consultant clarify his or her understanding of consultee statements?
    (Not at all)   1   2   3   4   5   (Great extent)

15. *Problem Clarification*

    How effective was the consultant in clarifying the problem?
    (Not at all)   1   2   3   4   5   (Very effective)
    Did the consultant attempt to develop a solution before the problem had been
    thoroughly clarified?
    _____ Yes   _____ No

16. *Strategy Generation*

    To what extent were strategies developed for solving the problem in focus?
    (Not at all)   1   2   3   4   5   (Thoroughly developed)

17. *Responsibility*

    To what extent did the consultant leave the responsibility for selection and pursuit of problem-solving
    strategy with the consultee?
    (Not at all)   1   2   3   4   5   (Totally)
    _____ Not applicable

18. *Follow-up*

    To what extent did the consultant leave the responsibility for follow-up or evaluation with the consultee?
    (Not at all)   1   2   3   4   5   (Totally)
    _____ Not applicable

19. *Evaluator*

    How evaluative did the consultant seem to be of the consultee or his or her ideas?
    (Great deal)   1   2   3   4   5   (Not at all)

Continued

Consultant Observational Assessment Form (COAF) *continued*

20. *Consultee Feelings*

To what extent did the consultant delve into the feelings of the consultee?
(Too deeply   1   2   3   4   5   (Only so far as
(Not enough)   necessary for rapport)

If rated 1, 2, or 3, indicate

_____ too deeply

_____ not enough

21. *Threat*

How much threat did the consultant's behavior pose to the consultee?
(Very   1   2   3   4   5   (Not at all
 threatening)   threatening)

Please identify any specific behaviors which you would consider to be threatening to the consultee.

What types of questions asked by the consultant, if any, would you consider to be threatening to the consultee?

22. *General Effectiveness*

How would you rate the overall effectiveness of this consultant?
(Low)   1   2   3   4   5   (High)

23. *Consultee*

As a consultee, how willing would you be to use this individual as a mental health consultant?
(Not at all)   1   2   3   4   5   (Very)

TOTAL SCORE:

ADDITIONAL COMMENTS

From *Consultant Observational Assessment Form*, M. J. Curtis & T. Anderson (1975). University of Cincinnati, Department of Special Education and School Psychology. Reprinted by permission.

anecdotal report typical of the case study. In the case study, data are collected repeatedly over a baseline period of time and then are also collected during an intervention period (the classic A/B design). If changes are noted under the B condition, in that the stability, trend, or level shown in A is changed, then an initial inference can be made about B. These authors note that the believability of intervention B effects are enhanced if they can be replicated, can be shown to have more applications, are consistent, are greater than could be expected, are immediate, and rule out alternative explanations. Since such "rules" of judging single-case data rely largely on logic, the findings could still be proved wrong.

The qualitative case study paradigm also has been proposed as one way for the consultant to improve his or her practice and potentially contribute to the knowledge base (Pryzwansky & Noblit, 1990). Through its regular use, insights can be provided into the

ongoing consultation process, intervention decisions regarding particular consultation cases can be facilitated, self or peer critiques promoted, and accountability proposes served. Thus, its value as an aid to improve the practice of consultants is an important enough reason to consider its use aside from any research utility. Qualitative case study approaches are particularly appropriate for answering the questions of "how" and "why" and can be much more than descriptive in terms of purpose. Merriam (1988) argues that this type of case study paradigm can serve interpretive and evaluative functions as well.

As participant-observer, the consultant can use session notes, retrospective notes from a journal, audiotapes, and follow-up interviews to develop his or her "notes on notes" from which a case record can emerge. This record begins to capture thoughts and tentative theories that can be read and coded multiple times to formulate a "text." Such texts serve as the basis for satisfying reliability and validity questions, thereby, increasing confidence in the case analyses made.

Finally, the use of a consultation diary/log is definitely recommended covering at least the first and last interview and including general information. A sample outline of a diary currently in use in some courses (Pryzwansky, 1989) is as follows.

Initial Interview

1. Nature of referral as seen by consultant and consultee.
2. Type of referral (e.g., academic, behavior) as seen by consultant and consultee.
3. Consultee's expectation for consultant style (see Chapter Eight).
4. What action does the consultee see as being most helpful for the client with all other factors being equal (i.e., discounting factors such as money, availability of community resources).
5. What is seen as the way(s) realistically that the consultant can be most helpful from the consultant and consultee perspective.
6. Prognosis for helping client as made by consultant and consultee.
7. Degree of cooperation consultant estimates to experience working this consultee.
8. Consultee analysis (e.g., see Friedman Scale in this chapter).
9. Model of consultation used by consultant.

Final Interview

1. Most helpful function(s) (e.g., information, support, active intervention) provided by consultant as seen by consultant and consultee.
2. From a retrospective perspective, consultant and consultee opinion if referral could have been resolved without consultation.
3. Changes consultant and consultee would make if they had it to do all over again.
4. Consultee opinion of consultation as a service.
5. Degree of success as rated by consultant and consultee.
6. Major concerns expressed by consultee during the consultation as a way to identify major issues to resolve in future consultations, e.g., student's problem is really a home problem, no time to follow through on recommendations, issue of favoring one student more than others.

7. Positive statements made by the consultee during consultation, e.g., "I like this client," "the parents are cooperative," "it's wonderful to have services like this available to me."
8. Actual services offered to the client by the consultant.

General Information

1. Consultee characteristics: age; sex; race; if teacher, what grade teaching and years of experience.
2. Person initiating the referral.
3. Consultees prior attempts to get assistance with the client and the result.
4. Number of consultation conferences.
5. Type(s) of recommendations made, and recommendations implemented.
6. In schools, type of classroom and organization if other than self-contained.
7. Organizational climate.

Consultee Benefits

Secondary outcome: Objectivity

1. I am better able to understand my students.
   Yes _____ No _____ Unclear _____
2. I have gained a new perspective regarding student behavior.
   Yes _____ No _____ Unclear _____
3. My biases no longer are the determining factor in the way I deal with students.
   Yes _____ No _____ Unclear _____

Secondary outcome: Problem Solving

1. I am better able to establish priorities.
   Yes _____ No _____ Unclear _____
2. I now use a more systematic approach to problem solving.
   Yes _____ No _____ Unclear _____
3. I can say with some certainty that I am a better decision maker.
   Yes _____ No _____ Unclear _____

Secondary outcome: Role Competency

1. I am a better teacher (parent, administrator, etc.).
   Yes _____ No _____ Unclear _____
2. I feel more confident about my ability as a teacher (parent, administrator, etc.).
   Yes _____ No _____ Unclear _____

3. I can deal more effectively with my classroom (home, school) situation.
   Yes _____ No _____ Unclear _____

Secondary outcome:
Understanding Human Behavior

1. I have gained greater understanding of the principles of human functioning.
   Yes _____ No _____ Unclear _____
2. I feel confident that independently of the consultant I can utilize the principles that I have learned.
   Yes _____ No _____ Unclear _____

Secondary outcome:
Facilitating Human Development

1. I am better able to design approaches that will be helpful to my students.
   Yes _____ No _____ Unclear _____
2. I have developed new approaches to students that will facilitate their overall development.
   Yes _____ No _____ Unclear _____
3. I feel confident that I can develop interventions (may specify) for students in the future.
   Yes _____ No _____ Unclear _____

From *Consultation*, D. Brown et al. (1979). Boston: Allyn & Bacon. Reprinted by permission.

The descriptive case study typically involves the collection of relevant data about the consultee and/or client (and system) along with careful description of the various stages of the consultation process. Buttressed by some initial conceptualization regarding the consultation approach that is used, the potential for a defensible qualitative analysis to take place is enhanced. One challenge, however, is deciding when enough information has been collected. The recommendation that all possible data that could be included should be recognized that the post hoc emphasis to the case study means one never knows until termination what all of the relevant data might be. However, the result, in part, is either to reduce the appeal of the case study approach or contribute to its loss of credibility even as an evaluation tool. The best advice may be that consultants using a case study approach should collect information to the degree it is practical for them to do so and that allows them to address the questions initially posed. Some compromises will obviously need to be made in this regard until single case experimental designs are feasible. Anserello and Sweet (1990) recommend that a final consultation report be completed for every consultation case. At minimum they believe the report should include the specific referral questions determined jointly by the consultant and consultee, a detailed list of services provided by the consultant, and detailed information regarding the intervention(s). For these authors, the report serves as an accountability device along with other service-related data compiled on an organization schedule so as to satisfy monitoring and evaluation purposes. Nevertheless, the use of case studies in providing accountability data as well as contributing to follow-up research investigations because of the hypotheses they suggest should not be overlooked by the consultant.

Uses of Evaluation Data

We have been stressing the use of an evaluation scheme as a means of improving the service. The advantages to the consultant are immediate, and, providing the consultee expects such services to be available and utilized in the future, it should have some meaning to the consultee. A visible, tangible indication of the consultant's use of the data should contribute to the consultee's willingness to participate in and even support this aspect of the consultant's role. The most logical rationale introduced at the beginning of consultation will not overcome the need for such evidence being supplied.

Beyond this immediate need, there is the very real need for the consultant to document the quantity and quality of consultative efforts. In addition to utilizing data from the type of instruments presented in this chapter, a follow-up schedule could be arranged for each consultation. For example, consultees are sent rating scales at two four-month intervals following the last consultation contact. Or all consultees (ongoing and terminated cases) receive an evaluation instrument at mid year and end of the year. This latter schedule permits the feedback to be collected in a way to insure the consultee's anonymity. In one of the few reported examples of the use of data to demonstrate the utility of consultative techniques and support its gradual expansion, Zins (1981) collected information over a three-year period on time spent usage, benefits to consultees, and ratings of consultative effectiveness. It seems reasonable to assume that until and unless consultants utilize a systematic evaluation plan the chances for using consultation as a viable means of delivering services remain precarious.

Finally, consultants are in a position to influence the consultation knowledge base, either through a case study methodology or action research paradigm. This area will be discussed in greater detail in the next chapter, but it should be made clear that practitioners have an important role to play with regard to the use of such research approaches. It is only when they are involved in sharing their experiences with their colleagues in a systematic manner that progress will be made in this research area. In a sense some of the very needs that support evaluation plans (for example, impact of consultee characteristics on outcome; relationship of intervention strategies) constitute basic questions for the researcher.

Summary

Consultants who are concerned about improving their service will develop an ongoing evaluation that looks not only at outcomes but at the process as well. Many criteria may be used to look at the outcomes of consultation ranging from behavioral indicators of client and consultee change to consultee satisfaction. Formative evaluation may focus on variables such as the quality of the individual consulting relationship, the expertise of the consultant, the match between the consultant's and consultee's expectations, and so forth. Perhaps the most important point made in this chapter is that evaluation requires careful planning or it will not yield useful information. Consultants must first determine the purpose(s) of the evaluation then devise a set of strategies for attaining those purposes.

Tips for the Practitioner

1. Familiarize yourself with the various approaches and instruments in this chapter. Select a strategy to evaluate the processes and outcomes of your next consultation.
2. Audiotape consultation session(s) for playback and general review and/or to improve skills or functioning during certain stages of consultation.
3. Arrange for peer consultation on audiotapes with a colleague.
4. Ask consultees for preferred manner of providing feedback on your "consultative" services.

Review Questions

1. Describe a comprehensive model of evaluation. Include the types of questions that could be addressed by a consultant.

2. What are some similarities and differences between evaluation and research?

3. Identify three guidelines that consultants should consider in planning an evaluation of their consultation.

4. Describe two different types of consultation outcome measures.

5. How does the traditional case study approach compare to time-series methodology?

References

Anserello, C. & Sweet, T. (1990). Integrating consultation into school psychological services. In E. Cole & J. A. Siegel (Eds.). *Effective Consultation in School Psychology* (pp. 173–199). Toronto: Hogrefe & Huber.

Attkisson, C. C., & Broskowski, A. (1978). Evaluation and the emerging human service concept. In C. C. Attkisson, W. A. Hargreaves, M. J. Horowitz, & J. E. Sorensen (Eds.), *Evaluation of Human Service Programs* (pp. 3–26). New York: Academic Press.

Babcock, N. L., & Pryswansky, W. B. (1983). Models of consultation: Preferences of educational professionals at five stages of service. *Journal of School Psychology, 21,* 359–366.

Barlow, D. H., Hayes, S. C., & Nelson, R. O. (1984). *The Scientist Practitioner.* New York: Pergamon Press.

Brown, D., Wyne, M. D., Blackburn, J. E., & Powell, W. C. (1979). *Consultation.* Boston: Allyn & Bacon.

Conoley, J. C., & Conoley, C. W. (1982). *School Consultation.* New York: Pergamon Press.

Cooper, S. E. & O'Connor, Jr., R. M. (1993). Standards for organizational consultation assessment and evaluation instruments. *Journal of Counseling and Development, 71,* 651–660.

Curtis, M. J., & Anderson, T. (1975). *Consultant observational assessment form.* Cincinnati, OH: University of Cincinnati, Department of Special Education and School Psychology.

Friedman, L. P. (1977). Teacher consultation styles, Unpublished doctoral dissertation, University of Pennsylvania.

Gallessich, J. (1973). Organizational factors influencing consultation. *Journal of School Psychology, 11,* 57–65.

Gallessich, J. (1982). *The Profession and Practice of Consultation.* San Francisco: Jossey-Bass.

Halpin, A., & Croft, D. (1963). *The Organizational Climate of Schools.* Chicago: Midwest Administration Center, University of Chicago.

Kiresuk, T. J., & Lund, S. H. (1978). Goal Attainment Scaling. In C. C. Attkisson, W. A. Hargreaves, M. J. Horowitz, & J. E. Sorensen (Eds.), *Evaluation of Human Service Programs* (pp. 341–370). New York: Academic Press.

Kiresuk, T. J., & Sherman, R. E. (1968). Goal attainment scaling: A general method for evaluating community mental health programs. *Community Mental Health Journal, 4,* 443–453.

Maher, C. A., & Borbrack, C. R. (1984). Evaluating the individual counseling of conduct problem adolescents: The goal attainment scaling method. *Journal of School Psychology, 22,* 285–297.

Meade, C. J., Hamilton, M. K., & Yuen, R. K. W. (1982). Consultation research: The time has come the walrus said. *The Counseling Psychologist, 10*(4), 39–51.

Merriam, S. B. (1988). *Case study research in education.* San Francisco: Jossey-Bass.

Meyers, J., Parsons, R. D., & Martin, R. (1979). *Mental Health Consultation in the Schools.* San Francisco: Jossey-Bass.

Mischley, M. (1973). *Teacher preferences for consultation methods and its relationship to selected background, personality and organizational variables.* Unpublished doctoral dissertation, University of Texas at Austin.

Parsons, R. D., & Meyers, J. (1984). *Developing Consultation Skills.* San Francisco: Jossey-Bass.

Paul, S. C. (1979). Consultation evaluation: Turning a circus into a performance. In M. K. Hamilton, & C. J. Meade (Eds.). *Consulting on Campus: New directions for student services* (pp. 33–46). San Francisco: Jossey-Bass.

Perkins, N. T. (1977). Evaluating social interventions: A conceptual schema. *Evaluation Quarterly, 1,* 639–656.

Perloff, R., & Perloff, E. (1977). Evaluation of psychological service delivery programs: The state of the art. *Professional Psychology, 8*(4), 379–388.

Pryzwansky, W. B. (1989). *Consulting Diary*. Author.

Pryzwansky, W. B., & Noblit, G. W. (1990). Understanding and improving consultation practice: The qualitative case study. Manuscript accepted for publication. *Journal of Educational and Psychological Consultation*.

Robinson, S. E. (1979). Evaluation research: An approach for researching applied programs. *Improving Human Performance Quarterly*, *8*(4), 259–267.

Schulberg, H. C., & Jerrell, J. M. (1983). Consultation. In M. Herson, A. E. Kazdin, & A. S. Bellack (Eds.), *The Clinical Psychology Handbook* (pp. 783–798). New York: Pergamon Press.

Scriven, M. (1967). The methodology of evaluation. In R. Tyler, R. Gagne, & M. Scriven (Eds.), *Perspectives of Curriculum Evaluations*, (AERA Monograph Series on Curriculum Evaluation) (pp. 39–83). Chicago: Rand McNally.

Suchman, E. A. (1967). *Evaluative research: Principles and practices in public service and social action programs*. New York: Russell Sage Foundation.

Zins, J. E. (1981). Using data-based evaluation in developing school consultation services. In M. J. Curtis, & J. E. Zins (Eds.), *The theory and practice of school consultation* (pp. 261–268). Springfield, IL: Charles C. Thomas.

Ethical and Legal Considerations

Goal of the Chapter

The goal of this chapter is to discuss the ethical and legal issues that relate to the consultation process.

Chapter Preview

1. The purposes of codes of ethics are discussed.
2. Six major ethical principles are presented and discussed. These concern the competence of the consultant, protecting the welfare of the client, confidentiality, public statements, ethical and moral issues, and relationships to other consultants.
3. The process to be followed in enforcing ethical standards is presented.
4. Legal issues relating to consultation are addressed.

Consultation is receiving increasing emphasis in training programs for counselors and psychologists (Zins, Kratochwill & Elliot, 1993). Not unexpectedly, interest in ethical practice has also increased. Although it is still true to some extent that consultants do not have a well-defined set of ethical principles to guide their behavior, the picture is changing rapidly. Both of the most recent revisions of the American Counseling Association (ACA) (1988) and the American Psychological Association (APA) (1992) codes of ethics reflect these changes. For example, in 1981 when APA published its newly adopted *Ethical Principles for Psychologists*, it contained four references to consulting or consultation (Robinson & Gross, 1985). The 1992 APA statement, *Ethical Principles of Psychologists and Code of Conduct*, contains at least 20 references to these words, half of which relate to the psy-

chologist as a consultant and half of which suggest that the psychologist needs to be a con-sultee in many instances. In its 1988 statement, *Ethical Standards of the American Coun-seling Association*, ACA added an entire section devoted to consultation. In the proposed revision to this document that will be adopted in 1995 or 1996, there are numerous refer-ences to the consulting process, competence in consultation, confidentiality in consultation, and so forth (ACA, 1993). Recent publications by Pryzwansky (1993) and Newman (1993) also address ethical issues in consultation. Clearly, counselors and psychologists are addressing the need to improve ethical guidelines for consultants.

Ethical standards are important to the consultation decision-making process. So are legal statutes. Most mental health professionals are aware of the potential legal actions against them if they engage in unethical or illegal behavior in the practice of assessment or counseling. However, legal issues associated with consultation have been largely unex-plored. The purposes of this chapter are to explore the ethical principles set forth in the ACA and APA codes of ethics, to detail some of the shortcomings of these codes, and to explore some of the legal issues facing consultants as well.

Purposes of Codes of Ethics

Codes of ethics are grounded in the highest moral standards of society (Pryzwansky, 1993). The introduction to the APA (1992) code contains the following statements:

> *The preamble and General Principles (of the code) are* aspirational *goals to guide psychologists toward the highest ideals of psychology. (p. 1598)*

and

> *If the Ethics Code establishes a higher standard of conduct than is required by law, psychologists meet the higher ethical standard. (p. 1598)*

These statements are meant to alert psychologists that special standards of conduct are expected, standards that go beyond those expected of the average citizen.

Codes of ethics are an attempt to guarantee members of the public that their welfare will be the first consideration of the group. This is done by adopting a set of values as well as by establishing standards of practice. Again the APA (1992) code is instructive. It states, "The Ethical Standards set forth *enforceable* rules for conduct as psychologists" (p. 1598).

Codes of ethics also serve the professional groups that promulgate them in several important ways. Every occupational group aspires to professional status, and one prereq-uisite to acceptance as a profession by society is a well-articulated, carefully crafted code of ethics. Once the code of ethics is in place and is enforced by quasi-legal bodies within the profession itself, the occupational group is ready to petition for formal recognition. Typi-cally this occurs through lobbying efforts that, if successful, culminate in licensure laws and licensure boards that are empowered to make rules governing the functioning of the group. Central to the rules adopted by these boards is a requirement that the code of ethics be

adhered to by licensed professionals. At this point the standards in the code of ethics are quite analogous to legal statutes.

Codes of ethics also serve occupational groups in other ways. Approximately 30 years ago, Greenwood (1966) set forth some of the roles codes of ethics play in regulating a profession. Ethical standards delineate the responsibilities of the professional to society, to her/his profession, specify certain types of acceptable and unacceptable practices, and set forth the values that are to guide the professionals' work in the absence of specific guidelines. Codes of ethics usually do identify some specific practices to be followed. They also identify the values that are adhered to by the profession. Since the practices identified in codes of ethics are rarely comprehensive enough to cover all of the situations in which professionals find themselves, the values contained in the documents are to be used by professionals as the basis for decision making (Pryzwansky, 1993). The introduction of the APA code of ethics specifically states, "The Ethical Standards are not exhaustive" (p. 1598). It is therefore important for professionals to understand the principles as well as the underlying values of the code that must govern their behavior.

Codes of ethics are complicated documents that deserve much study by the consultant. Since space will not permit a detailed examination of the codes of ethics followed by consultants, the discussion to follow will be directed to the general principles that underlie the codes of ethics of the ACA (1988) and APA (1992).

Ethical Principles

Principle One: Competence

All major codes of ethics contain statements admonishing practitioners to gain competence prior to practicing in an area and to retain that competence by constantly upgrading their skills. Principle Two of the APA (1992) code states in part:

> *They (psychologists) recognize the boundaries of their competence and limitations of their expertise. They provide only those services and use only those techniques for which they are qualified by training and experience. (p. 1599)*

The ACA (1988) code also addresses the matter of competency in consultation directly in an almost identical statement. It states:

> *Members (of ACA) recognize their boundaries of competence and provide only those services and use only those techniques for which they are qualified by training or experience.*

Although the ACA and APA standards dealing with competence seem clear, their interpretation is not (Brown, 1985; Lowman, 1985; Robinson & Gross, 1985). Unlike practitioners of assessment and psychotherapy, consultants have not established clearcut standards of training—an oversight that is likely to be corrected in the near future. However, as was noted in an earlier chapter on the characteristics of the consultant, there is increas-

ing consensus regarding the skills consultants need to be effective. These can be a temporary guide to the practitioners who are interested in evaluating their competency. However, as Newman (1993) notes in summarizing this issue, "the most basic requirement for consultants in ensuring competent practice is a thorough understanding of their own limitations" (p. 153).

Codes of ethics do provide guidelines in what are termed *emerging areas*, that is, areas for which standards of training and practice have not been fully articulated. For example the APA (1992) codes states:

> *In those emerging areas where recognized standards for preparation and training do not yet exist psychologists nevertheless take reasonable steps to ensure the competence of their work to protect patients, clients, students, research participants, and others from harm. (p. 1600)*

The ACA Code, Section E.1, states in part, "[Counselors] have a high degree of awareness of [their] own values, knowledge, skills, limitations and needs" which of course suggests that the counselor/consultants carefully assess their own competencies prior to engaging in various types of consultation. In making this assessment, other ethical values and legal questions must come into play. Is there potential harm to the client or the consultee if consultation is initiated and I do not have the skills to carry the process to a successful conclusion? [Welfare of the Client] If I engage in consultation and fail, will I tarnish the image of my profession and thus the ability of other professionals like myself to help members of society? [Professional Responsibility] If I engage in consultation without the proper skills am I likely to be charged with malpractice? [Professional Liability]

Ultimately, no one is served well by consultants who practice outside their areas of competence. If a mental health professional is uncertain about his or her competency to function in a given area, she or he probably is incompetent. However, consultation with others is an appropriate and ethical way both to determine competence to function and to improve competence if skills are needed to proceed with a consultation (APA, 1992).

Student Learning Activity 12.1: Principle One

1. The consultant agrees to work with a family who has an emotionally disturbed child. The thrust of the consultation is to assist the parents in developing a behavior management system that will ameliorate the child's difficulty. The consultant, who has no training in the educational area, is also asked to help the parents work on a study skills plans. He decides that the principles being employed in the behavior management system will generalize to the study skills areas and proceeds. Is this ethical?

2. A consultant is contacted by a hospital that is experiencing staff relationship problems. The consultant has no past training or experience in working with this type of problem, but accepts the job because he intends to gain the competence needed, although the job begins in four weeks. Are there any circumstances under which this consultant could be functioning ethically?

Principle Two: Protecting the Welfare of Clients

Protecting the welfare of clients served is the *sine qua non* of all codes of ethics, and the APA (1992) and ACA (1988) codes are no exceptions. They make it apparent that consultants are to keep uppermost in their minds both the immediate client and others who might inadvertently be affected by the result of the consultation service. As Robinson and Gross (1985) and Gallessich (1982) point out, it is anticipating the impact of consultation upon the "hidden client" that is difficult. However, Section E, 2, of the AACD code summarizes the position taken in both codes: "There must be an understanding and agreement between member and client for the problem definition, change goals, and *predicted consequences* (italics added) of interventions selected." Consultants who work in community agencies, with families, in business and industry, in schools, and in other settings need to concern themselves with the welfare of the consultee. However, because of the triadic nature of consultation they need to anticipate the consequences of their actions upon the client group who may be either the beneficiary or victim of their services.

These guidelines place tremendous burdens upon consultants to pay particular attention not only to their own behavior and the impact that it might make upon the welfare of the consumer, but also to the actions of the institutions that employ them. Thus, a school consultant who encounters de facto segregation during a program-centered consultation (for example, ability grouping) would be obligated to state his or her objection to the policy and to work to change the regulation. A consultant employed in business and industry to help establish a business information management system would be obligated to help ensure that data potentially injurious to the employees not be included in the system. Constant vigilance regarding the legal, civil, and human rights of consultees and clients is required of consultants.

Both the ACA and APA codes of ethics make it apparent that the welfare of consultees and clients need to be protected in the selection of assessment devices. Principle 2 of the APA code and Section C of the ACA code contain numerous references to the potential misuse of assessment devices and appropriate warnings regarding their use. Since consultants frequently use various assessment devices in the course of their work, reliability, validity, and appropriateness of norms must receive the same attention that they would in clinical settings. Since these assessment tools must often be developed by the consultant, the problems of reliability, validity, and appropriateness are even more acute because they must be developed using limited resources. Individuals who are given assessment devices have a right to a full explanation of the intended purpose of the assessment, regardless of how they were developed.

In Principles E & F of the APA code of ethics, consultants are told to avoid illegal practices and to keep the welfare of their clients uppermost in their minds. Moreover, consultants are instructed that, whenever institutional and/or governmental regulations are contradictory to their ethical guidelines, they are to adhere to the ethical principles and work to change the contradictory regulations. The ACA (1988) code goes one step further. It indicates that, whenever employer regulations are at odds with ethical principles, termination of employment should be considered if the conflict cannot be resolved.

Another aspect of concerning oneself for the welfare of the client is sensitivity to cultural differences (Jackson & Hayes, 1993). Consultants must be culturally sensitive to the

stereotypes they hold and must avoid these in their work (ACA, 1988; APA, 1992). Gibbs (1985) points out that training programs often neglect multicultural issues, thus consultants may not be equipped to deal with the complex issues that arise in cross cultural consultation. She goes on to assert that problems such as linguistic styles, interactional styles, and power-authority perceptions may impair communication in the consulting relationship. Many of the assessment instruments in current use also contain cultural biases. In order to protect the welfare of people from all cultures, differences must be considered actively during consultation and biased assessment instruments avoided. One obvious solution to this dilemma is for consultants to become sensitive to and skilled in dealing with cross cultural differences (Gibbs, 1985).

Protecting the welfare of consultees also pertains to fee setting. Consultants are generally advised that fee setting should be done with the best interests of the consultee in mind and that some services should be performed for little or no money (ACA, 1988; APA, 1992). In an unusual aspect of a code of ethics, counselor-consultants are held responsible for finding appropriate services if a suitable fee arrangements cannot be reached (AACD, 1988).

Consultants are told that protection of the consultee's welfare depends in part on avoiding dependency relationships, and they are instructed to terminate the consulting relationship when it is no longer productive. In the event of termination, both the APA and ACA ethical codes suggest that there is an obligation to make alternative sources of assistance available. These guidelines provide two major sources of difficulty for the consultant. The first of these is that they must make continuous assessment of the progress of consultation and to be constantly alert to the possibility that a particular consultation will be unproductive. Unfortunately, there are few guidelines except those acquired through experience to aid in making the determination that a consultation is going to be productive.

Making referrals to other consultants is the other source of difficulty. Since no training standards for consultants have yet been established (Brown, 1985), the consultant must rely upon word-of-mouth information to determine the effectiveness of other consultants in many instances. One of this book's co-authors was recently reminded how risky referrals can be. After 18 months of continuous work with a school district in the Northeast aimed at revitalizing certain aspects of its educational program, it became apparent that a friendship with one of the top administrators precluded effectiveness. A referral was therefore made to another consultant who, based on his professional reputation and informal feedback from individuals in the district who had observed him, was purported to be very effective. Unfortunately, the information turned out to be erroneous, at least as it applied to this particular consultative situation.

Student Learning Activity 12.2: Principle Two

The consultant working with several therapists in a correctional institution introduces aversive conditioning strategies as an historical example of "what not to do." She discovers that one of the techniques is being employed by one of the therapists. After warning the therapist that the technique is inappropriate she learns that the technique is still being employed. The consultant reports the therapist to the supervisor of the therapy program. Is this ethical?

Even though no empirical guidelines exist that provide definite answers regarding termination of consultations, the consultant is not absolved from responsibility to act. The best data available should be used to make this decision, and, above all, the welfare of the consumer must be protected. Similarly, the absence of training guidelines does not mean that the consultant has any less responsibility to make appropriate referrals (ACA, 1988; APA, 1992). It only means that the consultant may have to work harder to collect information about other consultants.

Principle Three: Maintaining Confidentiality of Disclosures

The matter of confidentiality of communication in consultation is addressed directly in both the APA (1992) and ACA codes of ethics. Consultants need to discuss the limits of confidentiality with all consultees and it is suggested that, unless otherwise indicated, this discussion should occur at the outset of the consulting relationship. Consultants need to consult the laws in their particular states that establish the limits of confidentiality (APA, 1992).

The APA (1992) code is clearer on consultants' responsibilities in the area of confidentiality than is the ACA (1988) code. It suggests that, in addition to establishing the limits of confidentiality, consultants need to discuss the "foreseeable uses of the information generated through their services" (p. 1606). In human services consultation, there are some foreseeable uses of information that might not be disclosed routinely to consultees. For example, information gained from a parent about childrearing might ultimately have to be disclosed if the consultant is ordered to testify in a child custody hearing, but the likelihood of this happening is rare. Clearly if the consultant knew that this was a possibility, the disclosure would have to be made.

Much information gained in organizational decision making is collected to inform the decision-making process. People who complete questionnaires and engage in interviews should be told the use to which the information may be put. However, the APA (1992) code indicates that confidential information gained from organizational clients should be discussed "only for appropriate scientific or professional purposes and only with persons concerned with such matters" (p. 1606). This ambiguous statement opens a virtual Pandora's box for the organizational consultant unless it is taken in the context of other principles such as protecting the welfare of clients. The problem is that the person who hires the consultant may want to have him or her disclose the "source" of information, which is contrary to good consultation practice and to ethical practice as well.

Student Learning Activity 12.3: Principle Three

A consultant is asked by the director of a small mental health center to tell him "what the staff really thinks of him." The consultant provides a general overview of the employees' perceptions of the director, many of which are negative. The consultant does not name names. Is this ethical?

One obligation of the consultant is to identify these and other areas of potential disagreement in the pre-entry phase (Kurpius, Fuqua, & Rozecki, 1993). The consultee should then be encouraged to communicate to others involved in the consultation that disclosures will be held in confidence (Robinson & Gross, 1985).

Internal consultants, and perhaps external consultants, will necessarily have to keep records that pertain to consultation. These records are also to be kept confidential according to current standards. Consultants should communicate this expectation to employers.

Principle Four: Responsibilities When Making Public Statements

Both the ACA (1988) and APA (1981) codes emphasize the importance of accuracy in all public statements. Although accuracy is indeed the watchword in issuing public statements offering consultation services, several guidelines must be followed to avoid deceptive practices. First, statements announcing the availability of consultation services should be restricted to naming highest academic degree, credentials (licensure), professional memberships, and type of service provided. Second, when listing professional membership affiliations, consultants should be careful not to imply sponsorship by a particular association or that membership in the organization is indicative of skill or credentials. Third, advertisements should not include testimonials from current clients. Fourth, consultants should not engage in direct solicitation. Currently there are no restrictions regarding the type of media that may be used for advertisements. Casual observation would lead the authors to believe that direct mail solicitations and the use of the telephone book yellow pages are the most common methods of advertising, although magazine and newspaper ads are also prevalent.

It is not unusual for consultants who have well-designed, accurate advertisements to find that their credentials have been misrepresented by consultees in brochures and other media devices aimed at publicizing their employment. Consultants should make reasonable efforts to correct these public statements (APA, 1992, ACA, 1988), just as they should correct misperceptions about their credentials when they are negotiating for a consulting job (Pfeiffer & Jones, 1977).

Public statements by internal consultants are less likely to be problematic than those by external consultants. Nevertheless, it is still important that internal consultants accurately describe the levels of their competence, outline the goals, techniques, and expected outcomes of the consultation, and make known their intent to adhere to the ethical principles of their profession.

Student Learning Activity 12.4: Principle Four

A well-trained, school-based consultant states in his or her introductory remarks to the faculty of a school the desire to become involved in consulting relationships with the teachers because he or she is confident that many of the learning problems encountered by children can be eliminated as a result of consultation. Is this ethical?

Principle Five: Social and Moral Responsibility

All occupational codes of ethics incorporate sections that deal with general moral standards as well as professional morality. They also include certain guidelines for regulating one's own ethical behavior and reacting to the ethical breaches of others. Of major concern in both the ACA (1988) and APA (1992) codes is that consultants be aware of personal needs and/or problems that might impair their functioning. When consultants are aware of their needs for status or esteem that may influence their functioning, they are expected to exercise appropriate restraint in meeting those needs at the expense of the consultee or the clients in the consultation. When they have personal impairments that restrict their effectiveness, consultants are expected to take action that will eliminate the impairment or avoid situations, including consultation practice, where the impairment will be a factor.

Backer and Glaser (1979) identified 19 potential ethical pitfalls for consultants and, as Robinson and Gross (1985) note, most of these are related to potential conflicts between the consultant's needs and those of the consultee. Unethical behavior that might grow out of the consultant's personal needs include (1) becoming the decision maker rather than fostering these skills in the consultee, (2) seeking significant favors from the consultee, (3) prolonging consultation as a means of maintaining income, (4) failing to recognize one's own limitations, (5) not taking stands against unethical/illegal behavior on the part of the consultee, (6) not considering readiness for consultation prior to initiating the consultation process, (7) failing to maintain objectivity and becoming embroiled in the politics of the setting in which the consultation occurs, (8) imposing one's own values, (9) not reporting accurately the outcomes of consultation, (10) not respecting consultants from other disciplines, and (11) resisting evaluation. If Kelman's suggestion for avoiding manipulation were applied to the consultation process, these pitfalls could be avoided.

As noted in the earlier discussion, it is the consultants' responsibilities to make their code of ethics known and to practice those codes even when contrary institutional policies and/or governmental regulations exist. It is also incumbent upon consultants to act to ensure that fellow colleagues act ethically as well (ACA, 1988; APA 1992). Generally speaking, the first step in correcting unethical behavior is to remind the guilty consultant of his or her ethical responsibilities. However, if the offense is severe, or if the offense is repeated after appropriate warnings have been offered, the consultant should be reported to the appropriate ethics committee.

Sexual intimacy with and harassment of clients and others have been pinpointed by the ACA and APA for special attention and, not surprisingly, both are prohibited. Consultants

---

Student Learning Activity 12.5: Principle Five

A consultant working out of a mental health center has been assigned to work with the police department to enhance its effectiveness in working with juveniles in the community. It is obvious that the consultant enjoys this association and it continues for two years. The evaluation of the project indicates that no progress has been made toward bettering police-juvenile relationships. Was this consultant functioning ethically?

Student Learning Activity 12.6: Principle Six

One consultant openly states that he is the best trained and most effective consultant in the area. He also indicates that persons from other specialties are not as well trained or effective as he is. An exami- nation of his vita shows that he has, in fact, received excellent training and reports show that he has been an effective consultant. Is he acting ethically?

---

who become involved in sexual intimacies with consultees, participate in sexual harass- ment, or condone either practice in the context of their work are acting unethically. Con- sultants are also admonished that dual relationships that might result in a conflict of interest should be avoided. For example, it is probably unwise to enter into a consulting relationship with a close friend, relative, business associate, or other individual where the nature of the personal relationship might attenuate the consultant's objectivity.

General standards of ethical and moral behavior are usually left to the individual. How- ever, consultants are expected to adhere to the moral and ethical norms of their communi- ties and not to act in ways that would diminish their profession (APA, 1992).

Principle Six: Relationships with Other Consultants

As was noted in the introduction to this chapter, a code of ethics attempts to insure harmony within professional groups by delineating standards for intragroup and interprofessional relationships. Several aspects of the ACA and APA codes are aimed at this function.

Consultants are generally expected to be familiar with and respect the expertise of practitioners from other disciplines. They are also to respect the client groups of other professionals and accord them the same courtesy they would individuals from their own discipline.

Consultants who make referrals to others should generally not expect remuneration for the referral. Neither should they accept payment whenever they are performing services that grow out of arrangements between the agency that employs them and another organization or agency.

Ethical Decision Making

It is obvious that consultants must often make decisions about ethical practice in situations without clearcut guidance from their codes of ethics. Pryzwansky (1993) suggests that one way to enhance ethical practice in this type of situation is to adopt a decision-making strat- egy that is rooted in ethical principles, concern for the dignity and free will of the individ- uals involved, and a concern for the norms of societies. He goes on to present the ethical decision-making model developed by Haas and Malouf (1989). According to these authors, the professional is obligated to start the ethical decision-making process by first determin- ing whether there is an existing ethical principle that provides a course of action to deal with the situation at hand. If a principle exists and there is no reason to deviate from it, such as a legal mandate, the consultant's decision making is relatively simple. If there is no clearcut

principle governing decision making in the situation, then the consultant is obligated to look at the underlying issues, such as the welfare of the client, competence, professional responsibility, respecting the dignity of the consultee and client, and his or her social responsibility as guides to decision making. Using these broader principles, the consultant should construct a plan of action, determine whether that plan of action poses any new ethical dilemmas, and proceed if no new ethical problems are apparent.

Consider the following situations:

1. A teacher-consultee seems to have a serious mental health problem that is interfering with his ability to deal with students effectively.
   A. Is there a clearcut principle involved?
      1. No. Generally consultants are admonished to concern themselves with the welfare of others and when the welfare of the students with whom the teacher works is at risk. However, the consulting conversation is confidential. Reporting the teacher's problem breaches confidentiality.
   B. Is there a viable solution?
      1. None that is clearcut. However, the consultant can confront the consultee with the problem and offer to assist him in getting help with the problem while managing his classroom more effectively. If this fails, the consultant's broader responsibility to the welfare of the children will have to be acted upon and the teacher's problem will have to be reported.

2. The director of a mental health center with whom you are consulting reveals that he takes cash paid by clients of the center to pay for his lunches. This information has nothing to do with the consultation, which is aimed at enhancing the out-reach program.
   A. Is there a clearcut principle involved?
      1. Yes. It is the principle that information gained in the consulting relationship is confidential.
   B. Are there reasons to deviate from the principle?
      1. Possibly, but given the small amount of harm that can result from not disclosing the information, the need to protect the client's privacy and adhering to a basic ethical principle seems to supersede other concerns.

3. You have been providing counseling services to a fourth-grade student. It has become clear that you need to enter into a consulting relationship with the parents to speed the process.
   A. Is there a clearcut ethical principle involved?
      1. Yes. Consultant's code of ethics warn against dual relationships.
   B. Is there any reason to deviate from the principle?
      1. Yes. The child's welfare may be better served if counseling continues along with consultation.
   C. Are there potential problems that need to be anticipated?
      1. Yes. Requests by the parents for confidential information; discomfort on the part of the client because parents are involved.
   D. How can these problems be resolved?

1. Explain reason for decision to the client and the limits of confidentiality to both parents and client. Get permission to disclose information from client if necessary.

To summarize and reiterate to a degree, consultants must understand the values upon which their codes of ethics are based, the principles that are set forth, and must adopt decision-making strategies that will reflect those values and principles. To do less is to act unethically.

Enforcing Ethical Standards

All professional organizations have clear-cut guidelines for accepting and adjudicating ethical complaints. These same organizations stress that it is the individual's moral stance that is the most basic ingredient in maintaining ethical behavior. Gallessich (1982) refers to this as self-discipline.

As we stated earlier, consultants also have a responsibility for the behavior of other consultants who belong to their professional group. Whenever unethical behavior is observed, the consultant should, if the breach seems to be an oversight or poor judgment, approach the guilty party and express concern, ask for an explanation, and explore with him or her the appropriate course of action. If the ethical breach is more serious, or if the unethical consultant fails to respond to informal resolution, a complaint should be filed with the state association ethics committee. Generally speaking, the complaint should contain a specific description of the unethical behavior including documentation if possible and should identify the areas of the code of ethics that have been violated.

Once complaints are received, the ethics committee will inform the accused party of the charges and ask for his or her response to them. Non-compliance with this request is in and of itself unethical and can result in disciplinary action. The ethics committee may also engage in any other data collection procedures they deem appropriate. When all data have been collected the ethics committee renders a judgment. If the ethics committee determines that an accused consultant is guilty of unethical behavior they may take a variety of actions. The mildest of these is to reprimand the offender. This reprimand usually includes an educational component, for example, instruction regarding ethical behavior. Harsher actions involve (1) placing the offender on probation for a specified period of time, (2) probation plus supervision, and (3) expulsion from the association. The committee may (and usually does) inform state licensing boards and certification agencies of its action. These boards then take appropriate action including initiating delicensure or decertification.

One note of caution should be inserted for the overzealous consultant regarding the filing of complaints. The accused party in these actions has the right to know who has lodged the complaint and the exact nature of the complaint. Therefore, inaccurate complaints may result in defamation suits, which, even if they are unsuccessful, can be time consuming and expensive. Therefore, caution is advised whenever action against a colleague is contemplated.

Potential Legal Difficulties

Just as consultants have not been carefully scrutinized by other professionals for unethical practice (Lowman, 1985), they appear to have escaped legal entanglements as well. And just as it can be expected that the ethical behavior of consultants will receive greater attention, the likelihood of legal difficulties is also increasing. This discussion is aimed at identifying certain areas where consultants are legally vulnerable.

Legal Actions against the Consultant

Malpractice suits have been lodged against counselors, psychiatrists, social workers, and psychologists for numerous reasons, only a few of which pertain to the consultant. Among these are negligence in rendering a service, misrepresentation, slander and libel (defamation), sexual misconduct, invasion of privacy, and breach of contract. Negligence can be charged if a plaintiff can establish that a breach of duty has occurred in the course of delivering services, if a loss or injury occurred as a result of the failure, and if a causal relationship between the two can be established, that is, the breach resulted in the damage. Defamation can either be written (libel) or spoken (slander). Generally speaking, defamation is an untrue statement about a person that diminishes their status or reputation. Schwitzgabel and Schwitzgabel (1980) point out that professionals are held to a higher standard, and even true statements that injure an individual may be viewed as defamatory by the courts. Misrepresentation of either credentials or the efficacy of one's services could involve either explicit or implicit communications that are essentially false. Sexual misconduct involves sexual intimacies growing out of professional relationships.

In considering the prospect of consultant negligence the first item of concern would, of course, be to determine the nature of the consultant's duty (Hopkins & Anderson, 1990). Often, because the specific duties of a consultant are not carefully delineated, and thus are hard to establish, some written consultation contracts delineate in detail what the responsibilities of all parties are to be during the consultation process. In this situation, the consultants are particularly vulnerable to malpractice suits if they do not fulfill their responsibilities and damage results. In other cases where the consultant is hired to assist with a specific task (for example, improve a specific service or develop an employee assistance program), the absence of a written contract would not necessarily preclude the identification of duty. A breach of the consultant's duty might involve failure to terminate the consultation process once one's expertise is exhausted, misassessing the consultee's or client's concern, violating standards of confidentiality, or undue use of one's influence during the course of consultation.

The problem for malpractice lawyers is, of course, to establish a causal link between the breach of duty and loss (Hopkins & Anderson, 1990). It is important to note that loss may be either tangible, such as profits, or psychological, such as stress or loss of self-esteem. It is not difficult to imagine that a liability could be established between shoddy practice by a family consultant and the psychological well-being of a child. It is even easier to see that a human service agency or business might suffer loss in effectiveness or profits as a result of the work of a consultant who has not functioned ethically or who has not used reasonable judgment in the consultation process.

Slander and libel suits can conceivably grow out of several aspects of the consultant's work. The inappropriate selection, use, and interpretation of various assessment devices might lead to suits if the scores or profiles resulted in damage to a consultee or client. So could breaches in confidentiality that injured either the consultees or clients involved in the consulting process. Reports that are not carefully prepared or that do not properly protect the persons involved from identification could also be considered defamatory in some instances if loss or embarrassment results.

Sexual misconduct is apparently a problem for a small minority of psychotherapists (Bouhoutsos, Holroyd, Lerman, Foler, & Greenberg, 1983). While there is no data supporting the idea that a similar problem exists among consultants, the consequences of such improprieties are sufficiently severe that a warning against them seems necessary, even in the presence of ethical taboos. Sexual liaisons that result in injury to consultees or to the organizations that employ them might serve as the basis of successful malpractice suits.

The use of inappropriate assessment devices may also serve as the basis of litigation regarding wrongful invasion of privacy, which is here defined as an intentional act that invades either the psychological or personal domain of an individual (Schwitzgabel & Schwitzgabel, 1980). As was discussed in the section on ethics, consultants may be involved in situations where employees, inmates, children, and others are subtly pressured into becoming a part of the consultation process. Because of the ethical expectation that this situation will be avoided, the person who can demonstrate that their privacy has been invaded may have the basis of a successful suit.

Misrepresentation of one's credentials as a consultant is unethical and legally dangerous. A consultant who lacks the stated credentials and fails to provide the expected service is at risk, both from actions that may be taken by the ethics committee of his or her professional association and by injured parties who may levy charges or fraud. Similarly, misrepresentation of the efficacy of a consultant's skills and techniques can be legally unwise.

A final area of legal concern to consultants lies in the area of breach of contract (Hopkins, & Anderson, 1990). In the presence of a written or formal contract, consultants are expected to (1) deliver the services specified in the contract and (2) follow the standards of practice of their profession while doing so. Failure to do so can result in a law suit. A carefully drawn contract may be the most effective means of avoiding legal entanglements concerning contractual issues. McGonagle (1981) has provided a set of guidelines for drafting consulting contracts that, if followed, would not only mitigate against breach of contract issues but other legal and ethical problems as well.

McGonagle suggests that a standard consulting agreement would contain 12 basic paragraphs. The first of these would state the terms of the agreement and would consist of a statement or two that identify the beginning and end of the consulting period.

Paragraph two of the consulting agreement would be a bit more complicated in that it would spell out in detail the nature of the consultant's activities during the consulting period. For example, a psychologist employed to provide case consultation for a mental health center might receive the following job description:

The consultant will review case material with staff members with the explicit purpose of identifying case management strategies. Monthly reports regarding consulting activities and other observed reports will be filed with the director. Within

30 days of the termination of the contract period a summary of activities is also to be filed with the director along with the consultant's informal evaluation of the outcomes.

Remuneration for consulting and expenses would be included in paragraph three of the agreement. This paragraph would normally stipulate the rate, the payment schedules, contingencies, if any (for example, filing reports), or the nature of allowable expenses. In some instances reimbursement for expenses follows local, state, or federal guidelines and these may simply be alluded to instead of providing a detailed statement. McGonagle points out that it is good practice to include clauses in paragraph three of the consulting contract regarding the relationship between progress on the work and payment as well as procedures for filing requests for payment.

Paragraph four of the consulting contract should cover work facilities. Will an office be provided? A secretary? Copying equipment? Consultant and consultees alike need not only to anticipate what facilities will be required to successfully complete a project, but to contractually stipulate which party will provide them.

Reports and work products should be addressed in paragraph five and a clause establishing the consultant as an independent contractor should be included in paragraph six. Normally, clauses regarding reports and work products stipulate when they are due and who owns the rights to reports and products. McGonagle indicates that the consultee normally retains the rights to all work products, but in some instances the consultant may wish to retain rights to materials developed for the consultee, such as assessment devices. Stipulating that an individual is an independent contractor is merely an indicator that the consultant is not an employee and thus provides the consultant with more latitude regarding the manner in which the work is performed. McGonagle (1981) points out, however, that the establishment of the consultant as an independent contractor does not protect the consultee from legal liability incurred as a result of the consultant's action.

Paragraph seven should deal with termination of the contract. Normally this involves only a simple statement that either party may terminate the agreement after a suitable notice period, usually 30 days.

Paragraph eight should make the material gained during the consulting relationship confidential according to McGonagle (1981). He suggests the use of the following phrase: "You agree that for the term of your appointment hereunder and for two (2) years thereafter, that you will not disclose to any person, firm, or corporation any confidential information regarding the corporation" (p. 88). Obviously this phrase is intended to protect the consultee. It is suggested here that in addition to this type of phrase that another be added to assert the intent of the consultant to follow ethical guidelines regarding confidentiality. In this way the consultee, the consultant, and the clients are served.

The last four paragraphs of the consulting contract should deal with assignability of the contract, arbitration of disputes, integration, and closing the contract. Assignability has to do with the consultant's legal right to assign all or part of the work set forth in the contract to another party. In some instances the consultee may wish to stipulate the work as non-assignable. Arbitration deals with the matter of settling disputes that arise from the contract. The consultee and consultant may wish simply to stipulate that a mutually acceptable third party will be used to resolve disputes. Integration is a statement or statements that stipu-

late that the contract can only be changed by written agreement by both parties and that the contractual document constitutes the entire agreement. This precludes either the contractor or the consultee from raising issues that were raised orally. Finally, in the last paragraph the contract is closed and approved by both parties. Since the contract is typically written by the consultee, this paragraph simply states that if the consultant agrees to the terms of the contract, he or she should sign in the designated place and return a copy to the contractor.

Defenses

It is not accidental that many areas of legal concern are addressed quite directly in codes of ethics. As was noted in the introduction to the chapter, promulgators of ethical codes seek to protect the profession and its members by establishing rules of conduct that avoid legal entanglements. Just as the litigation resulting from the Watergate scandal at the close of the Nixon administration diminished the reputation of lawyers, so does each successful suit against a consultant reduce the status of his or her professional group. Therefore, following one's code of ethics is the first defense against legal action.

A second and equally important defense involves following the standards of practices set down by a professional group. Unfortunately, there are no standards of practice for consultants at this time (Lowman, 1985). Therefore, consultants should take every precaution to insure that their practices are currently acceptable within their particular group. Two examples of techniques that might have been either suggested or utilized by consultants in the past are aversive conditioning techniques and encounter groups. Neither are supported as standard practices for dealing with consultee or client problems at this time, although encounter groups are still in use to promote personal growth in some instances.

Other Legal Concerns

Although direct suits against consultants are of concern, consultants may find themselves embroiled in other types of litigation. For example, a school psychologist or counselor might be subpoenaed to testify in a child custody suit. So might a family consultant working out of a mental health center. Also, an organizational consultant might be requested to testify in a suit against management. This type of situation automatically raises a concern about privileged communications.

Confidentiality is an ethical term that admonishes the consultant to maintain communications in confidence. Privileged communication is a legal term and refers to legislative recognition that certain communications can be held in confidence. Consultees of consultants who are licensed psychologists, counselors, or social workers have been accorded privileged communication in most instances. In many states, the consultees of school counselors, school psychologists, and others have also been accorded this right. However, Sheely and Herlihy (1984) point out that privileged communication has certain distinct limitations. The most common of these is that consultants may be compelled by a judge to disclose communications if he or she deems it in the best interest of justice. In other instances, privileged communication does not extend to children (for example, the statute for school counselors in California). As Sheely and Herlihy (1984) suggest, each consultant should become aware of the legal aspects of privileged communication in his or her own state.

Consultants may also be called on to serve as expert witnesses in litigation related to their area of expertise. Expert witnesses may be used by lawyers for either the defendant or the plaintiff and are typically paid for their services. Once an "expert" is contacted by the lawyer, it is the lawyer's responsibility to qualify the expert to the presiding judge. Ultimately, the judge determines whether the person may act as an expert in the particular case before the court.

Summary

Major codes of ethics have not yet been revised to accommodate the complexities of the consultation process. However, consultants from various disciplines are bound to abide by the ethical standards of the professional organizations to which they belong. A number of ethical principles keyed to the codes of ethics of APA and ACA were set forth in this chapter that can serve as the basis for ethical behavior in consultation. The major principles identified dealt with competence, welfare of the consumers of consultation services, confidentiality, public statements, ethical and moral responsibilities, and relationships to other consultants.

Legal entanglements have been largely avoided by consultants. However, a number of potential legal pitfalls were identified and discussed, including negligence, defamation, sexual misconduct, misrepresentation, confidentiality, invasion of privacy, and breach of contract. Guidelines for avoiding lawsuits were also presented.

Tips for the Practitioner

1. Make certain that you study your code of ethics carefully. Place an asterisk (*) beside each portion that deals with or has potential relevance for consultation.
2. Determine the legal basis for confidentiality in your state by reading the licensing laws that regulate your profession. If you work in a public school or other agency, determine whether there are privileged communication laws that accord confidentiality to any of the consultees with whom you might work.
3. Identify laws that impinge upon the statutes that regulate confidentiality in your state. For example, all states require mental health professionals to report child abuse. In other states, mental health professionals can be required to divulge information in pre-trial investigations if a court order is obtained.
4. Write the statement you will use to tell consultees about the confidentiality and its limits when you consult.
5. Try to determine whether a consultant has ever been sued for malpractice in your state. If the answer is yes, determine the allegations in the suit, the outcome of the suit, and the basis for the decision.

Review Questions

1. Identify at least four purposes of a code of ethics.

2. What are the problems associated with identifying competent consultants?

3. Who are the "hidden clients" in consultation?

4. Explain why the selection of assessment devices in consultation may be as problematic as it is in psychotherapy?

5. Outline an ethical public statement announcing the availability of consultation services.

6. Manipulation of consultees appears to be a major ethical problem for consultants. How can this be eliminated?

7. Ethically, how should you act as a consultant to avoid difficulties with other consultants?

8. Identify areas where consultants are vulnerable to legal action. How should a consultant act to reduce this threat?

9. Identify the elements of a comprehensive consulting contract.

10. Distinguish between the terms confidentiality and privileged communication.

References

ACA (1988). *Ethical Standards*. Washington, DC: American Association for Counseling and Development.

ACA (1993). ACA proposed standards of practice and ethical standards. *Guidepost, 36*, 15–22.

APA (1981). Ethical principles of psychologists. *American Psychologist, 36*(b), 633–638.

APA (1992). Ethical principles of psychologists and code of conduct. *American Psychologist, 47*, 1597–1611.

Backer, T. E., & Glaser, E. M. (1979). *Portraits of 17 outstanding organizational consultants*. Los Angeles: Human Interaction Research Institute.

Bouhoutsos, J., Holyroyd, J., Lerman, H., Foler, B. R., & Greenberg, M. (1983). Sexual intimacy between psychotherapists and patients. *Professional Psychology: Research and Practice, 14*, 185–196.

Brown, D. (1985). The preservice training and supervision of consultants. *The counseling psychologist, 13*, 410–425.

Gallessich, J. (1982). *The profession and practice of consultation*. San Francisco: Jossey-Bass.

Gibbs, J. T. (1985). Consultant training and supervision: Can we continue to be color-blind and class-bound? *The counseling psychologist, 13*, 426–435.

Greenwood, E. (1966). The elements of professionalization. In H. M. Vollmer & D. L. Mills (Eds.), *Professionalization* (pp. 2–28). Englewood Cliffs, NJ: Prentice-Hall.

Haas, L. J., & Malouf, J. L. (1989). *Keeping up good work: A practitioner's guide to mental health ethics*. Sarasota, FL: Professional Resource Exchange.

Hopkins, B. R., & Anderson, B. S. (1990). *The counselor and the law* (3rd ed.). Alexandria, VA: American Counseling Association.

Jackson, D. N., & Hayes, D. H. (1993). Multicultural issues in consultation. *Journal of Counseling and Development, 72*, 144–147.

Kurpius, D. J., Fuqua, D. R., & Rozezecki, T. (1993). The consulting process: A multidimensional approach. *Journal of Counseling and Development, 71*, 601–606.

Lowman, R. L. (1985). The ethical practice of psychological consultation: Not an impossible dream. *The counseling psychologist, 13*, 466–472.

Luke, J. R., & Benne, K. P. (1975). Ethical issues and dilemmas in laboratory practice. In K. D. Benne et al. (Eds.), *The laboratory method of changing*

and learning: Theory and applications (pp. 360–401). Palo Alto, CA: Science and Behavior Books.

McGonagle, J. J. Jr. (1981). *Managing the consultant.* Radnor, PA: Chilton Book.

Newman, J. L. (1993). Ethical issues in consultation. *Journal of Counseling and Development, 72,* 148–156.

Pryzwansky, W. B. (1993). Ethical consultation practice. In J. E. Zins, T. R. Kratochwill, and S. N. Elliot (Eds.), *Handbook of Consultation Services for Children* (pp. 329–350). San Francisco: Jossey-Bass.

Robinson, S. E., & Gross, D. (1985). Ethics in consultation: The Canterville ghost revisited. *The counseling psychologist, 13,* 444–465.

Schwitzgabel, R. L., & Schwitzgabel, R. K. (1980). *Law and psychological practice.* New York: John Wiley and Sons.

Sheely, V., & Herlihy, B. (1984). *Privileged communication in 50 states.* Paper presented at Southern Association of Counselor Education and Supervision Convention, Nashville, TN.

Van Hoose, W. V., & Kottler, J. A. (1977). *Ethical and legal issues in counseling and psychotherapy.* San Francisco: Jossey-Bass.

Zins, J. E., Kratochwill, T. R., & Elliot, S. N. (1993). Current status of the field. In J. E. Zins, T. R. Kratochwill, & S. N. Elliot (Eds.), *Handbook of Consultation Services for Children* (pp. 1–14). San Francisco: Jossey-Bass.

Issues in Consultation

Goal of the Chapter

This chapter will address issues related to the theoretical and applied aspects of the consultation process.

Chapter Preview

A number of issues related to the use of consultation by human service professionals will be presented, and the available literature relevant to each issue will be discussed.

Throughout this book the critical challenges facing human service professionals have been addressed. There are few commonly held conclusions about consultation; most are debated if not controversial. However, given the relative newness of consultation as an intervention used by human service professionals, the fact that there are controversial issues is not surprising. In fact, it could be argued that the tension arising from these issues might actually be positive, resulting in a more sophisticated theoretical and empirical base. As long as professionals remain enthusiastic and maintain an open, flexible stance regarding consultation, we can expect continued progress.

With regard to the organization of this chapter, the issues that cut across chapter content, that is, have relevance for several chapters, are presented here so redundancy is kept to a minimum. Therefore, the reader should consider the implications of each issue for the various aspects of consultation presented throughout the book. However, there were some instances where the issue warranted special treatment, and it was also included in this chapter. Finally, there was no intent to prioritize issues by placement within the chapter or by their order of presentation.

Direct or Indirect Services

Consultation was originally defined as an indirect service to client groups. In human services agencies such as schools, mental health agencies, college counseling centers, and departments of social welfare, the tradition has been to provide direct services through counseling, therapy, assessment, educational programs, and other approaches where the professional interacts directly with the client. This tradition is only recently being examined and questioned (Monroe, 1979; Gutkin & Curtis, 1982; Reynolds, Gutkin, Elliot, & Witt, 1984). The focus of this questioning is how best to identify the intervention strategy given a particular set of circumstances.

Reynolds et al. (1984) suggest that there are three criteria that may be utilized in making this selection: effectiveness, cost, and acceptability. Some research has addressed the effectiveness issue by comparing consultation with one form of direct intervention, counseling (Alpert & Kranzler, 1970; Lauver, 1974; Palmo & Kuzniar, 1972; Randolph & Hardage, 1973), and has concluded that consultation is more effective. It should be pointed out that most of these studies were conducted in school situations, however, and for the most part cannot be generalized outside of that setting. Comprehensive reviews of the literature support the efficacy of consultation in other settings with a variety of consultees (Fullan, Miles, & Taylor, 1980; Mannino & Shore, 1975b; Medway, 1979), but the studies reviewed do not make a comparative analysis of consultation with direct service approaches. Future research will need to focus on the relative effectiveness of direct and indirect services as they relate to specific problem situations.

Acceptability of consultation has been studied to some degree within school psychology (Reynolds et al., 1984) with the result being that few definitive conclusions can be reached at this time. Witt, Elliot, and Martens (1985) studied the criteria utilized by teachers in accepting interventions and concluded that time needed to learn and implement an intervention, the potential risk to the client, and the potential negative impact on other children were the primary considerations in deciding whether to accept or reject the intervention. Kazdin (1980) has also suggested that an overall criterion of acceptance of an approach revolves around the perception of whether the expected outcome justifies the effort needed to implement the intervention. Again, no research has looked specifically at giving potential consultees alternative approaches to dealing with a problem in the form of direct services.

Which type of intervention is the most efficient: direct or indirect? In an era of shrinking resources human resource professionals must concern themselves with cost/benefit factors. Unfortunately, this issue is virtually unexplored in the professional literature. Consultation appears to have an edge on this dimension when compared to more labor-

Student Learning Exercise 13.1

Contrast consultation and counseling with regard to efficiency (amount of time spent by the professional) and acceptability to the recipient of the service. With these criteria, which intervention has the advantage?

intensive direct interventions such as counseling (Reynolds et al., 1984). However, no empirically based indicators or even guidelines have developed.

The tradition among professionals working in human services agencies has been one of direct service to clients. To be sure, school psychologists have adopted consultation as a primary service delivery vehicle (Bardon, 1982; Meyers, 1973; Meyers, Parsons, & Martin, 1979). However, the issue to be faced is not whether direct interventions such as counseling are to be preferred to consultation, but which intervention will best meet the clients' needs given the criteria for success or effectiveness, efficiency, and acceptability? Given the state of research in this area, this is likely to be a long-standing issue.

Classification Schemes

Although the practice of consultation has increased among the various human services professionals and the writings and research literature has reflected this increase, professionals are still struggling with the formulation of a working typology or classification scheme of consultation models. Several have been proposed (Blake & Mouton, 1976; Caplan, 1970; Gallessich, 1985; Schein, 1969), but as yet none has really taken hold. They range from relatively straightforward descriptions of different types (e.g., Schein, 1969) to complex matrices involving several dimensions on which the consultant must correctly identify the point of interaction among those dimensions to theoretically expect a successful consultation (e.g. Blake & Mouton, 1976).

Some curious mixtures have resulted in the conceptual discussions related to this topic. There is a tendency to mix individual approaches with organizational models, to concentrate on the theoretical underpinnings of the model (for example, behavioral) versus the professional identity of the consultant (for example, resource teacher consultation, psychiatric consultation), and to emphasize process (for example, process consultation, collaboration) versus product (for example, technical consultation). Semantics often confuse and confound efforts to develop a typology. What is still clearly needed is a taxonomy of consultation models based upon a well articulated rationale.

One starting point in building such a taxonomy would be to concentrate on the purpose of consultation (change, helping), the values of the consultant, and the parameters of the consultation act itself (content, goal, targets). For example, Chin and Benne (1976) reason that any planned change must be based on current knowledge of change; likewise, technologies should be utilized based on current knowledge of change as a process. They have categorized different strategies and procedures of change that have a few important elements in common. The first type of change strategy they label as *empirical-rational*. This group of strategies begins with the assumption that individuals are rational and will act to protect their self-interest in a rational manner. Such strategies, then, are information- and knowledge-based, and individuals are expected to change when confronted with data and a logical rationale. What has often been referred to as "expert consultation" is an example of this approach. Medical or clinical consultation and to a certain extent behavioral consultation also fall into this category.

The *normative–re-educative* strategy is the second type of change strategy. Although embracing to some degree the assumptions of the empirical-rational strategy, this second

type assumes that sociocultural norms are equally important in human motivation. Consequently, when change occurs it involves changes in attitudes, values, skills, and significant relationships. Social norms must be addressed by consultants, then, if they expect to be successful. The Caplanian consultation category of consultee-centered consultation would certainly apply here as would a number of organizational development approaches.

The third type of strategy, *power-coercive*, is based on the application of power in some form. Economic and political pressures are common illustrations of this approach, but the use of moral power, such as playing on the emotions of guilt and shame, would also be included. Such a strategy often relies on legitimate power, such as the principal who says "My teachers will use the materials if I tell them to!" In summary, then, all change models, including consultation models, are initially conceptualized in terms of the assumptions upon which they rest. The change strategies are not differentiated in terms of the size and target of the change. Chin and Benne (1976) argue that there are similarities in the processes of changing regardless of the target of consultation. Differentiation among consultation models can, theoretically, be developed from the point at which a change strategy is identified.

An alternative classification was proposed by Gallessich (1985) and had the objective of unifying "currently scattered and heterogeneous concepts" (p. 336). Theory and practice are seen as lagging far behind the increasing range of consultation applications. Her consultation "meta-theory" proposes to identify general characteristics of four different consultation conceptions or models. She proposes that the universal *characteristics* (dyadic, triadic, external) of consultation should be identified along with the consultation *parameters* (content, goals, role, and relationship rules) and *fundamental variants* (value systems or ideologies of consultants). Gallessich reasons that theory building and research efforts will be given an important boost as a result of this higher level conceptualization, which incorporates the three factors of characteristics, parameters, and variants in a way resembling the Blake and Mouton (1976) matrix. Bardon (1985) suggests that yet another step involving "identification of reasonably consistent patterns of interactive variability" will probably also need to be taken into account before cogent descriptions of consultation are to emerge (p. 359).

The challenge of formulating a consultation classification scheme may be with us for some time, but the conceptualization represented by the above-referenced authors and others should be considered by consultants as they plan to work with consultees. The model approach that is chosen should be clearly understood in terms of its assumptions and characteristics, the locus of the consultant's employment and target of change identified, characteristics of the consultee and his or her setting as well as the nature of the problem delineated. Consultants should get used to thinking about intervention in this complex way in approaching their day-to-day interactions, reading the literature, and conducting evaluation or research.

Consultation as a Profession

The definitions of consultation range from Webster's "to give advice" and the common sense help we can expect from a friend to the sophisticated models described in this text. For the most part, the assumption underlying any use of the term is that the consultant, either by virtue of his or her life experience or training and experience, is respected enough

to have his or her opinion solicited. The former image implies a common sense attribute while the latter notion clearly reflects expertise in a content area.

In his book on mental health consultation, Caplan (1970) specifically addresses this question of expertise or common sense versus a new profession. He argued that consultation was a method of communication, a special way in which professionals may operate, and not a new profession. Although consultation is often distinguished from other roles such as supervision, counseling, and testing, the distinction is not always clear in the consultee's and even the consultant's mind. The fact that there are so many different definitions and other activities that consultants can engage in seems to be the source of this confusion.

By contrast, Gallessich (1982) argued that consultation is an emerging profession. She defended her notion of a new field by pointing out that consultation is a complex process requiring specialized training, and that consultants share a common role and purpose and as a result need a common body of knowledge and code of ethics. Levin, Trickett and Kidder (1986) come to a similar position after reviewing the topics addressed in a handbook on mental health consultation. They concluded that "the increasing knowledge base, the assertion that ethical issues in consultation are not easily clarified by the ethical standards of other professional roles, and the clear evidence that consultation activities are proliferating across populations and settings argues that the preconditions for consultation as a primary professional identity are discernible" (p. 509).

Such diverse opinions can either contribute to the confusion that exists or serve as a unifying step. For now, a simple, straightforward definition will have to suffice. Consultants are sought out for some reason related to their expertise and not necessarily the manner in which they offer services. They have something in the way of knowledge or skills that is not possessed by the consultee. In some instances the consultant's objectivity, as a result of being external to the system, plays a role in selection, but his or her bailiwick is the prime criterion for involvement. For the present, it is most useful to think of consultation, conceptually and practically, as an intervention approach.

The Limits of Consultation

It is important to remember that just because a consultee requests consultation and a consultation is begun, there are no reasons to continue it in the face of later information that contradicts this intervention approach. Caplan (1970) has recommended that consultants keep the possibility in mind of aborting the process, thereby reminding us of the realistic limits of this method. As an example he notes that if the consultee's actions have the potential of endangering the client, the consultant should set aside his or her consultant role and give advice or take action from the consultant's professional frame of reference, which the consultee does not have the option to reject.

The employment base of the consultant, that is internal or external, and dual role responsibilities can be a factor in such a decision. External consultants certainly should not allow poor judgment on the part of a consultee to continue; an organization can expect such a level of responsibility from the consultant. By contrast, the internal consultant has more of a dilemma in that technically he or she is as responsible for the client's welfare as

his or her fellow employee, perhaps not to the degree as the consultee, but responsible nevertheless. The question of boundaries between the role of a consultant versus the professional identity of the consultant can further complicate the deliberation of when to step outside the consultant role. For example, as a counselor the consultant may do things very differently from what he or she observes as the practice of the consultee. The important question is not whether a theoretical or stylistic difference exists between consultant and consultee but whether in fact the consultee's behavior is harmful or is clearly indefensible from what is known in the literature about the matter at hand. (See Student Exercise 13.2.)

Asking for Help

For some consultation models it is important that the consultee ask or request the service. The motivation to seek assistance is considered an important element in the success of the consultation. In other models this question does not seem to be of much concern; it could be that the impetus for change is assumed, or the nature of the change process or its target relies less on the "felt need" of the consultee in order that some degree of consultation

---

Student Learning Activity 13.2

A principal and teacher request a consultation with the psychologist assigned to their school. Their concern involves a fourth-grade girl who they suspect of stealing money from the teacher's purse. The principal is worried that a lot more objects will turn up "missing" as reported to him by the teacher, and the teacher fears the child is becoming a kleptomaniac. As the session progresses, the consultant discovers that the consultees are interested in his or her capability as the psychologist to test the youngster and confirm that she is the culprit. Following more discussion, it turns out that over the past two years little of any significance has been reported stolen (two quarters and a pencil box). A weak documentation of circumstantial evidence is presented by the consultees and includes an incident wherein the student broke one of the teacher's earrings, left on her desk during the time this student and another were alone in the room to clean the blackboard. The teacher has already had the police in her class to investigate the incident and they talked with the student. The student's parents have approached the principal relaying their child's fear that the teacher suspected her. Both consultees have proposed that a situation be set up wherein the child would be given an opportunity

to steal. This entrapment approach is thoroughly explored with all its impending consequences. Following further discussion of the student's background and other information that builds a case against the student, the session appears to be winding down with the principal and teacher seemingly still disposed to arrange a scenario wherein the student might transgress which could lead to a confession of the precipitating incident and some rehabilitative intervention.

As a consultant, how would you proceed from this point in the consultation? What type of action might be taken that would not challenge the integrity of the consultees since the consultees are employed by the school district and will need to work in this school in the future? Should the principal have been involved in the consultation? What purpose did his presence serve? Write out your assessment of this consultation session as you understand the dynamics so far, and what you would do. If you have a chance, role play the session with another student in your class. Now read the consultant's response and consider how the consultant handled this situation. Do you agree with that approach?

success be realized. Yet we know little about the dynamics of asking for help, particularly consultation assistance. It could be a powerful variable determining who does and does not seek consultation, how involved they become, and the nature of the intervention planning and implementation (see Chapter Nine).

It has been proposed that one's views of who is to blame for a problem as well as who should be responsible for its solution can lead to different ways of behaving (Brickman, Rabinowitz, Karuza, Coates, Cohn, & Kidder, 1982). These orientations of whether or not individuals are responsible for causing their problems and solving them were further linked to models of helping and coping in the minds of helpers and recipients of the help. Brickman et al. (1982) proposed four such models: (1) people are responsible for problems and solutions; (2) people are not responsible for problems but are responsible for solutions; (3) people are not responsible for problems or solutions; (4) people are not responsible for solutions but are responsible for problems. In many instances, the help giver and help recipient are applying models that are out of sync with one another. Brickman et al. then go on to identify the *dilemma of helping*. It derives from the notion of help itself, because help would imply that recipients are not responsible for solving a problem.

Ironically, Brickman et al. present evidence showing that help givers benefit from helping even when recipients of the help do not. Assumptions of helping may benefit the helper more than the recipient of help. As a result of such findings they present a number of research questions that require follow-up such as: Are some models uniformly better than others or are different models best for different clients? Are models that tend to be discrepant from the client's initial assumptions more or less effective? Should models be applied consistently or change as consultees change their attributions? Do help givers burn out less using one model(s) versus another?

Based on the data in his study of consultation outcome, Macarov (1968) examined the psychological constraints associated with help. He noted the difficulty of asking for and taking help that some consultees experience. Consultees might present problems that were not real, or were not the one most important to them, or the one problem they faced. For example, in one situation a consultant was distracted from developing a classroom management plan with a teacher by the consultant's own frustrations with a similar situation many years earlier when she was a teacher. The present consultee (a young teacher) broke down and cried, explaining she was really afraid and felt totally overwhelmed, which was the real reason she asked for classroom management consultation. Consultants must recognize that it is not easy to ask for help in a society that idolizes a "take charge," "on top of it" facade. In fact, seeking out help may be seen as a sign of weakness or at least may suggest that one's work needs to be monitored for other signs of shortcomings.

Macarov (1968) even detected problems on the part of consultees in accepting the word consultation because of its association with the act of receiving help. For example, the consultees in his study could accept help if it was described as occurring on a sharing or informational level or in some other way that suggested an informal context. By contrast, the label consultation seemed to imply a formal activity involving high-level expert help. Consultees clearly were uncomfortable in describing the service they received as consultation. As further support for this impression that help seems to be sought out in an informal context, Cowen (1982) has suggested that the overwhelming bulk of society's interpersonal help-seeking and help-giving commerce involves non-mental health professionals.

The Consultant's Response to Student Learning Activity 13.2

The consultant became very direct with the principal and teacher in terms of describing the negative consequences of any attempt to "trap" this student in a stealing episode. In doing so, many of the consultees' observations of the disadvantages of such a solution to the problem which they mentioned in response to indirect probing by the consultant earlier in the session were reiterated. The consultant directly withdrew support for such a plan and advised against it. In order to positively redirect the teacher's apparent need to do something more and to ostensibly deal with her concern for the student (and save face) the consultant recommended the following: 1) the teacher keep a list of reported missing items, 2) follow up be made to determine if the items showed up, 3) the principal request similar information from other teachers who also had this student in class, 4) a follow-up conference be planned in two weeks, if none seemed to be necessary before then. At the second session no stealing or other incidents involving the student were reported nor were there reports of other thefts. The teacher did report a more positive relationship did develop between her and the student. In fact, no changes were reported for the rest of the school year.

Finally, Macarov (1968) found a clear preference among consultees in his study for information over advice. Information seemed to be easier to ask for and to have admitted receiving than other assistance.

Consultants, at minimum, should keep in mind these characteristics related to the process of helping, not only in terms of how terminology may affect the consultee but also what it means to the consultee. Consequently, it may be advantageous to emphasize the nature of the service rather than what it's called. As noted in the "Teacher as Consultee" chapter, a "collaborative problem solving resource" may be a mouthful, but tastier than "consultant."

Dealing with Consultee Feelings

In any problem situation there are likely to be feelings experienced by the consultee related to his or her self-concept, the client, or significant others in the organization. The issue of whether the consultant should deal directly with those personal feelings or choose an approach that deals with them only as they relate to the work problem was clearly more prominent in the early consultation writings (Caplan, 1970). At that time, the mental health consultation model was popular, and consultants were influenced by their therapeutic experiences and possibly psychodynamic training. Also, the nature of the presented problems in mental health consultation (that is, involving emotional needs of clients) were such that it could be argued the needs of clients were likely to influence the emotional state of the consultee. As consultation methods evolved out of behavioral theories and consultation was offered under less "crisis" conditions, the consultee affect received less emphasis. Consequently, the priority of consultee-affect may be related partly to the theoretical orientation of the consultant.

For Caplan (1970), recognition of personal feelings is important, but the explicit content of the consultation session is the work-related problem and ways of dealing with that

problem. Although the technique of theme interference reduction is one exception to this rule, even that strategy is one in which relevant aspects of the problem remain the focus. Finally, mental health workers may by virtue of their stereotypic role in society and even style of interpersonal interaction suggest a degree of sanction for personal problems to be expressed by the consultee (Caplan, 1970).

Within the mental health consultation model Altrocchi (1972) identifies two variables that can be related to the choice of dealing directly or indirectly with consultee feelings: the personality of the consultant and group versus individual consultation. Some consultants are more comfortable in discussing emotions while being relatively open and communicative individuals. There are some advantages in such a focus, but it can unnecessarily complicate the consultation effort and even shift the emphasis more in the direction of counseling or therapy.

Altrocchi finds support for a direct approach when mental health consultation takes place with groups. He argues that groups stimulate affect and support its expression, but at the same time naturally tend to control such expression by setting limits. Providing the affect is shared by the group and does not reflect pathological qualities and is directed to the work problem, he recommends discussing such reactions under general rules set up and sanctioned by the group.

The consultee's personality and the nature of the problem are two additional considerations that need to be assessed in making this decision. In general, however, it seems best to acknowledge affect and its immediate influence on the consultation; to do otherwise would be insensitive. Consultants should be supportive resources for identifying appropriate professionals that can help consultees with personal problems.

The Involvement of the Consultant

The degree to which consultants should take some active intervention on behalf of consultees should be one of the questions addressed by consultants as they engage in the consultation process. For example, should consultants participate in acquiring information for consultees, contact individuals on their behalf, advocate in their interests, and in general help turn the planning of consultation into action?

Decisions regarding the consultant's behavior of "doing for" the consultee are attributed to tactical and ethical viewpoints (Macarov, 1968). In the tactical view such behavior preempts the growth of the consultee. It clearly may result in a quicker and more efficient resolution of a problem. However, the long-term objectives of fostering better problem solving and increasing the degree to which consultees handle such matters in the future may be diminished. From the tactical perspective, the preferences, needs, and competencies of the consultee will play a role in determining involvement, but so will the model of choice, an issue addressed in earlier chapters. It seems reasonable, then, that the involvement decision be built into an evaluation mechanism to determine the extent to which consultees learn to function without involvement of the consultant, or the extent to which consultees see such activities on the part of the consultant as acceptable and helpful. Another tactical consideration for consultants when deciding on the degree of consultee learning to promote is the amount of turnover in the organi-

zation. If the board member receiving the consultation is in his or her last term or last year, or the consultee-teacher's husband is soon to graduate from the local university with a Ph.D., the advisability of active consultation versus a growth-centered variety of consultation takes on other dimensions. Growth-centered consultation goals might be more defensible economically when used with consultees who will remain with their organization.

The second consideration influencing involvement is of a more ethical nature. It involves the "right" of the consultant to encourage a consultee to intervene or take action of a certain type. Should the consultant influence those with whom he is working to consider and/or adopt goals or activities particularly when they do not coincide with those originally requested by the consultee? Under what constraints, if any, should the consultant operate? Such questions need to be explored by the consultant prior to any consultation and perhaps discussed with the consultees under each contract. Certainly, taking action on behalf of the consultee should be addressed. As this review is conducted, the consultant needs to take note that consultees may wish them to be directive and action oriented, particularly as the consultee's anxiety and/or lack of confidence increases and the client problem looms prominently in their mind. "Yet, the questions of self-determination, the right to participate in decisions affecting one, the knowledge that one is responsible for the success or failure of an effort, remain" (Macarov, 1968, p. 126).

The ethical consideration also has its more practical component. The reinforcement of a dependent relationship is one outcome that the consultant must be aware of and guard against. Stringer's (1961) observation from the early consultation era still seems to be true. "No one, apparently, will object to being called a consultant. The term has prestige value, the quietly unassailable dignity of a hallmark" (p. 85). Appreciative feedback from the consultee who relies on an assertive consultant can be very seductive.

The limits on the consultant stem from his or her personal philosophy, training, consultation model(s), and experience. As mentioned earlier, there are limits to the model that is practiced, the ethics of the consultant's profession, and the expectations of the organization. Other roles filled by the consultant in the organization may also come into play. Finally, the nature of the request as well as the preference and experience of the consultee will also need to be assessed when considering involvement. Consultation does not need to be confined to the communication between the consultant and consultee, but the consultant should carefully consider the implication of his or her actions on behalf of the consultee.

To Manipulate or Not to Manipulate

The term manipulation generally has such a negative connotation that consultants sometimes overreact when asked about its role in their professional practice. To some, it permeates all interpersonal interactions; to others, manipulation represents the intentional act of one person to influence another in a secretive manner. Still others may take a more positive view of manipulative acts when they are conceptualized as a professional technique. This issue has an obvious relationship to the one just presented—the involvement of the consultant—and should be read with the former discussion in mind.

It has been argued that consultation involves change and as such the professional change agent is a potential manipulator (Lippitt, 1973). Lippitt argues that consultants should be proactive in demonstrating their values and beliefs about how consultees learn and change. The question is not whether the consultant has a right to change others, but rather, "What right have I to withhold myself and skills from helping change to take place in a direction consistent with my convictions?" However, Lippitt also stresses that an *ethical methodology* based on those values and beliefs about the change process should guide the process of deciding what changes are needed and evaluating the changes that take place. Using such an ethical methodology, the consultant considers his or her task-oriented motivation, level of collaboration, experimental problem solving, approach toward coping, and accountability. Briefly, the consultant should be task oriented rather than prestige oriented, meaning that the resulting change is better than what existed before, and the matter of who gets credit for it is not important. In addition, all individuals affected by the change should be involved in the planning and development. The methods of problem solving are seen as experimental; from this position, all plans have the potential of being tried. Next, Lippitt argues that the method of change in addition to being democratic and scientific should leave those involved in a better position to solve future problems. Finally, consultants are accountable to themselves and others affected by their efforts.

Kelman (1965) has taken a slightly different tact in dealing with the question of manipulation. He acknowledges that the practitioner (consultant) is faced with a basic dilemma, that is, if that consultant believes in the fundamental value of a human being's freedom of choice, then manipulation of others' behavior constitutes a violation of that right. Kelman does recognize however, that behavioral change will inevitably involve some degree of manipulation, and since consultants constantly are involved in change activities, they are faced with an ethical problem. The two horns of the dilemma are: (1) manipulation of others violates a fundamental value; and (2) there is no system or formula for arranging conditions wherein manipulation is totally absent. Kelman argues that the practitioner must remain conscious of the potential for imposing values on the consultee. Otherwise the consultant may become totally insensitive to this phenomenon and/or get carried away with good intentions so that no controls will be considered.

Kelman recommends three steps to deal with this challenge. First, as was already hinted at, the consultant should increase awareness of the manipulative characteristics of the consultation intervention. The consultant must be able to recognize and label the values that permeate his or her approach to consultation and change and communicate those orientations to the consultee. In a sense, this notion of sharing introduces a sense of mutuality between the consultant and consultee that serves as a control on the manipulative aspects of the relationship; in Kelman's notion, the consultee is able to "talk back" to the consultant.

Student Learning Activity 13.3

Take the three steps recommended by Kelman (described in the "manipulation" section of this chapter) and identify specific ways they could be implemented during an initial consultation session. Roleplay specific strategies if possible.

Secondly, he encourages building "into the change process itself procedures that will provide protection and resistance against manipulation" (p. 42). Thus, he would minimize the consultant's values while maximizing the consultee's values as the dominant criterion for change. Kelman strongly advises the practitioner to minimize the direct and indirect constraints he places on the consultee. Finally, he recommends that the consultants use their professional skill as well as their relationship with consultees to increase the consultees' range of choices and ability to choose. This latter point involves the value of enhancing the freedom and creativity of consultees.

The above discussion presents some ideas regarding a characteristic of consultation that has had less attention than it deserves—the abuse of the consultation service. The issue perhaps is not that consultants are or have become unscrupulous in their practice, but rather need to recognize the role of their values in the process. Given such awareness they are less likely, in Kelman's terms, "to make full use—either unwittingly or by design—of the potential for manipulation that they possess" (p. 43).

Another variation on this manipulation theme has become more prominent since the first edition of this book. It involves the growing research on the acceptability of interventions by the teacher which was presented in an earlier chapter: that research has grown out of a concern that interventions may be under-utilized or improperly implemented (see Witt & Elliott, 1985). Skinner and Hales (1992) found that teachers in their study operated from a different theoretical perspective than the behavioral consultant. Therefore, they suggested that such consultants should foster an atmosphere in which teachers feel free to adapt ABP procedures to fit with their particular teaching style. They also encourage the behavioral consultant to be aware of the differences between themselves and the consultees, and modify their own language.

In another twist on this matter it was reported that in *behavioral* consultation the consultants with higher dominance scores (i.e., an interpersonal relationship in which one person frequently accepts the other's conversational direction) were judged to be more effective by consultees (Erchul, 1987). It has been argued that consultant dominance involves *cooperation*, in that "cooperation suggests there is a leader and a follower," and *teamwork*, in that "teamwork subsumes and implies further that who leads and who follows may change over the course of the consulting relationship" (Erchul, 1992, p. 365). Indeed, the use of interventions by the consultee is a concern worthy of serious attention by consultants. If perceived time to implement interventions is a critical factor influencing the consultee's receptivity to those ideas, then it is also a critical variable to understand. However, as it may be discerned that lukewarm acceptance or even failure to cooperate may be due to differences in the theoretical orientation of each of the participants some thorny questions arise. What are the implications of making the language describing an intervention more palatable so that the consultee does not recognize the theoretical orientation of the consultant? This approach of "making the medicine go down" raises questions about the consultant's attitudes toward the consultee and values in the consultation process. If nothing else, such motivation to practice in this manner suggests the consultant embraces an expert model of consultation, which is not negative in itself, except if the consultee is led to believe the consultation is collaborative. Thus, the motivation and use of this strand of research findings needs careful reflection by the consultant.

The Consultant as Researcher

The consultant's role as practitioner must have first priority in the resolution of the presented problem. The most appropriate intervention applied in the least time-restricted manner is expected by the consultee and the organizational leadership. Anything less than an all-out effort to achieve the goals of the consultation is very questionable. At the same time, we argued in Chapter Eleven for the importance of accountability and the need for a data-based approach to consultation. But what of the responsibility of the consultant to contribute to the knowledge base regarding consultation from the perspective of the practitioner? Should the consultant's research expertise be in the area of consuming empirical findings and/or applying those findings, or should they be expected to advance the state of the art via more research?

Lewin (1946) was the first to advocate for an "action research" approach for social scientists as a means to help solve practical problems in specific social situations. Thus, research was undertaken but often with the objective of addressing a specific problem. As Rapoport (1970) stated, this type of research "aims to contribute both to the practical concerns of people in an immediate problematic situation and to the goals of social science by point collaboration within a mutually acceptable ethical framework" (p. 499). This position clearly attempts to capitalize on both the evaluation and research potential in any data collection strategy. However, Meade, Hamilton, and Yuen (1982) note that those working from an action research model seem prone to subordinate research to action and those working from the evaluation paradigm tend to subordinate raising questions to providing answers.

But the blurring of the intent of the activity, that is, research versus evaluation, can lead to some serious ethical problems. Consultants should never do research in the name of evaluation. The consultant needs to face up squarely to the reasons for asking certain questions or using certain measures. Similarly, if the data collection techniques result in higher costs or delayed services, the practices may be questionable additions to the consultation service.

TABLE 13.1   The Distinction between Evaluation, Consultation Evaluation, Consultation Research, and Research

Objective	Pure Evaluation	Consultation Evaluation/ Research	Consultation Research/ Evaluation	Pure Research
Contribution to scientific knowledge	None	Secondary	Primary	Primary
Problem Solving for Consultee/ Client Benefit	Primary	Primary	Secondary	None

From *The Scientist Practitioner*, J. I. Barlow, S. C. Hayes, & R. O. Nelson, (1984). New York: Pergamon Press. Copyright 1984 by Pergamon Press, Inc. Adapted by permission.

Finally, there may be a "review of research with human subjects" committee that may need to be contacted in the organization to review the consultant's plans as well as the need to consider written consent from the consultees to collect certain data. Again, this committee can be helpful in making these determinations as can reference by the consultant to his or her professional ethical codes of conduct. For further discussion of these points, the reader may want to consult Barlow, Hayes, & Nelson (1984). In addition, Table 13.1 provides a summary of the distinctions between purely evaluative or research effort in consultation versus a data collection approach that emphasizes both to varying degrees.

Research Directions

The consultation area is not suffering from a dearth of research studies. From 1978 to 1985 approximately 173 data-based studies in consultation were referenced in *Psychological Abstracts* and 81 doctoral dissertations reported in *Doctoral Dissertations International* (Pryzwansky, 1985). Also, the research seems to be relatively evenly distributed among the training as well as process and outcome dimensions of consultation. Although reviews of that research period are not currently available, at least two reviews have found similar outcome effectiveness results in mental health consultation and school consultation. It has been reported that 76 to 78 percent of the reviewed studies reported a partial success rate (Mannino & Shore, 1975b; Medway, 1979). However, the interpretation of those findings remains highly qualified due to the nature of the research. Methodological difficulties and fragmented studies often characterize research in this area.

The problem most often associated with consultation research is the lack of control groups or inadequate comparison groups. It is understandably difficult to find an appropriate control as it is questionable for the practitioner to withhold a service that can be of immediate assistance to a consultee because of a research objective. It is for that reason that time series designs are recommended for research considerations (Medway, 1979; Meyers et al., 1979; Meade et al., 1982). Outcome type studies are badly needed, particularly outcome research that measures multiple outcomes and is based on actual consultation efforts. All too often consultants in training serve as the "consultant" in the study without much thought given to this factor as an influence on the results. The need seems to be for more illustrations of cases on which data have been collected in a systematic manner. In their review of directions in consultation research, Froehle and Rominger (1993) echo the call of earlier authors for an operationalizing of the scientist-practitioner orientation for the consultant.

The available research also seems to be plagued with the definitional problems discussed in this book. Meade et al. (1982) have recommended that process studies of consultation be operationally based on the actual model of consultation being investigated. The theoretical propositions of the model should be spelled out to avoid the atheoretical (and thus unreproducible) studies that often typify the research studies. Specifically, Meade et al. (1982) point out that little has been done in the way of investigating different consultant behaviors at the various stages of consultation. The authors go on to identify a second implication for doing research in this area: The advantage of defining explicitly what is taking place in the consultation process. It has been suggested that all researchers provide a mini-

mum set of information data for their studies. In addition to describing the consultation model and descriptions of the problem dimensions, consultation goals and evaluation should be delineated (Pryzwansky, 1986). Such standardization of information would help others in generalizing the findings and provide a structure for future applications. There has been an agreement in the literature that case study designs are badly needed and do not have to be subjective; designs can be of the quantitative type (Kratochwill, 1985) or the qualitative type (Pryzwansky & Noblit, 1990). The hypothesis-generating value of the latter type investigations can be extremely helpful to this still-new service delivery approach. Similarly, Gutkin (1993) has stressed the importance of analogue research to the literature.

Finally, it seems that consultation research will need to mirror the complexity of the process itself. Thus, multiple measures of process and outcome dimensions of consultation involving consultee and client variables should be employed in an attempt to establish interrelated interactional relationships among independent and dependent variables. At the same time, greater collaboration between consultants and trainers will need to occur, especially during this time of limited resources. It seems that only when we shift to this more complex plane of investigation and conceptualization will we be able to realize the full potential of consultation.

Choosing a Consultation Model

At times when one is reading consultation literature, it would seem that only the model under discussion is the one to use. Seldom is the question "Which model for which problem?" addressed. On the one hand it could be argued that consultants should use the model consistent with their more general theoretical and personal bases as it would prove difficult if not impossible for the consultant to do otherwise. However, shouldn't a consultation approach be chosen based on the nature of the presented problem, the characteristics of the consultee, the setting resources and constraints, or some combination of those variables? Granted, the research is not definitive as far as this question is concerned, but given what is known, the consultant should at least consider the implications of using an alternative approach in the self-evaluations that are conducted of his or her consultation. At least two writers have explicitly considered a multimodel approach, and their ideas will be briefly reviewed.

Caplan's (1970) types of consultation (client-centered, consultee-centered, program-centered, administrative, and consultee-centered administrative) are an administrative response to a need to take into account the nature of the problem (case versus administrative) and the goal of consultation (improving the problem-solving capacity of the consultee versus the giving of specialized opinion). Caplan cautioned that while most consultants may not exactly fit one of these categories, a predominance of elements will "load up" in one of the four categories. The consultant will then be in a better position to gauge the most effective strategies to use. Caplan goes on to further categorize four types of consultee-centered case consultation, which again has implications for the responses of the consultant. Finally, Caplan notes that external consultants may go through a series of successive stages before consultee-centered consultation is requested. For example, liaison expectations may constitute the initial response of host agency/institution and its consultees. A staff educator role may follow, with then some requests for a client-centered case consultation.

Pursuing this stage progression idea one step further, it may be prudent to approach some individual consultations with a stage concept system of consultation in mind. That is, the consultee may not be ready to enter into a collaborative problem-solving relationship or feel comfortable with a consultee-centered focus. Similarly, consultant misconceptions about a theoretical approach may preclude problem formulations of a certain type. Also, the possibility exists that some consultees prefer differential consultant styles dependent on the consultation stage that is at hand (Babcock & Pryzwansky, 1983). For example, a consultee may expect the consultant to offer expert opinions in terms of problem identification, but expect to be very much involved in deciding what to do about the problem, or vice versa. Whether consultants *should* shift from one consultation approach to another is yet to be determined as well as whether they *can* be trained to function in this way.

A prescriptive use of consultation models was advocated by Conoley and Conoley (1981), which led to their recommendation for the training of consultants to be as broad as possible. They recommend selecting (prescribing) a consultation model based on characteristics of the consultee and the problem. In studying the question of the consultant's discriminant use of models according to contextual variables, Conoley and Conoley analyzed the logs and audiotapes of 46 consultation trainees in 24 service sites (elementary and secondary schools as well as mental health oriented agencies). They found that consultee characteristics were very important in the choice of behavioral consultation; most prominent were the roles of the consultee and comparative gender. Behavioral consultation was used with teachers, parents, and residential unit staff, but seldom above the elementary level. Also, consultants tended to choose this model when the consultee was of the opposite sex.

By contrast, the consultant's preference for mental health consultee-centered consultation was the largest contributor to its use. It was also seldom used at the elementary level and seemed to be employed in work with school administrators. When client-centered consultation was used it was not clearly separated from behavioral or mental health consultee-centered consultation, although it tended to be more closely allied with the behavioral approach. The very limited use of program-centered models or advocacy approaches was attributed to the trainee status of the "consultants" in the Conoley and Conoley study. In fact, that finding plus the lack of information regarding the nature of the prescriptive training (that is, were only models emphasized or were selection criteria also emphasized?) underscores the preliminary status of their report.

Since proposing this issue in our first edition, it has received little attention in the literature. First, most of the research studies on consultation (75%) have involved primarily one approach, the behavioral paradigm (Martens, 1993). Also, unproductive criticism of the collaborative model (Witt, 1990) (sometimes based on erroneous assumptions of the model) such as its "minimum emphasis on intervention, let alone concern for measuring it or as an adult oriented" model (Fuchs & Fuchs, 1992) have been the level of the discussions which are now found in the literature. This finding leads us to the conclusion that professionals may still be searching for the *one* consultation model. One example of an exception to this conclusion was the Tindal, Parker, and Hasbrouck (1992) exploratory study that analyzed 10 individual consultation cases and found little orderliness to the stages and activities that were employed. Engaging two experienced teachers who were enrolled in a

program wherein they were receiving special education-consultation training, the researchers trained the teachers to be responsive to the critical variables in each case when selecting a consultation approach to employ. In addition to raising some provocative questions based on their findings, such as the continued wisdom of "demarcating the consultation process into artificial stages," the emphasis on training professionals to apply the same skills in all cases received an empirical test. The choice of using a single consultation model routinely versus a prescriptive model or tailoring the model to the situation remains a challenging decision for consultants and trainers alike. It is hoped that the future will bring additional, systematic consideration of this issue.

Summary

It is important to recall that consultation is an evolving strategy and, as a result, there are many unresolved issues. Should the consultant control the process? What is the best way to establish the limits of consultation? Which is better: direct or indirect services? Perhaps the major implication of these unresolved issues is that consultants who are trained today need to keep abreast of tomorrow's developments, both in the theoretical and the empirical domains.

Tips for the Practitioner

1. Make a list of the issues identified in this chapter. What is your opinion about the "rightness or wrongness" of the opposing points of view surrounding these issues? Write about how your opinions about these issues are likely to influence your practice.

Review Questions

1. Identify an additional issue that belongs in this chapter and present the current position that exists with respect to that issue.

2. Make a list of the positions you would take with respect to each of the issues presented in this chapter.

3. After reading this chapter, make a list of the issues that have been raised in Chapters 1–12 that were not covered in this chapter.

4. What will be the strategy you use in selecting a consultation approach?

5. Should consultants do research? Present a rationale for your answer.

References

Alpert, G., & Kranzler, G. D. (1970). A comparison of the effectiveness of behavioral and client centered approaches for behavioral problems of elementary school children. *Elementary School Guidance and Counseling, 5,* 35–43.

Altrocchi, J. (1972). Mental health consultation. In S. E. Golann & C. Eisdorfer (Eds.), *Handbook of community mental health.* New York: Appleton-Century-Crofts.

Babcock, N. L. & Pryzwansky, W. B. (1983). Models of consultation: Preferences of educational professionals at five stages of service. *Journal of School Psychology, 21,* 359–366.

Bardon, J. I. (1982). School psychology's dilemma: A proposal for its resolution. *Professional Psychology, 13,* 955–968.

Bardon, J. I. (1985). On the verge of a breakthrough. *The Counseling Psychologist, 13*(3), 353–362.

Barlow, D. H., Hayes, S. C., & Nelson, R. O. (1984). *The scientist practitioner.* New York: Pergamon Press.

Blake, R. R., & Mouton, J. S. (1976). *Consultation.* Reading, MA: Addison-Wesley.

Brickman, P., Rabinowitz, V. C., Karuza, J., Coates, D., Cohn, E., & Kidder, L. (1982). Models of helping and coping. *American Psychologist, 37*(4), 368–384.

Caplan, G. (1970). *The theory and practice of mental health consultation.* New York: Basic Books.

Chin, R., & Benne, R. D. (1976). General strategies for effecting changes in human systems. In W. G. Bennis, K. D. Benne, R. Chin, and K. E. Corey (Eds.). *The planning of change* (pp. 22–45). New York: Holt, Rinehart and Winston.

Conoley, J. C., & Conoley, C. W. (1981). Toward prescriptive consultation. In J. C. Conoley (Ed.), *Consultation in schools* (pp. 265–293). New York: Academic Press.

Cowen, E. L. (1982). Help is where you find it. *American Psychologist, 37,* 385–395.

Erchul, W. P. (1987). A relational communication analysis of control in school consultation. *Professional School Psychology, 2,* 113–124.

Erchul, W. P. (1992). On dominance, cooperation, teamwork, and collaboration in school based consultation. *Journal of Educational and Psychological Consultation, 3,* 363–366.

Froehle, T. C. & Rominger III, R. L. (1993). Directions in consultation research: Bridging the gap between science and practice. *Journal of Counseling and Development, 71,* 693–699.

Fuchs, D. & Fuchs, L. S. (1992). Limitations of a feel-good approach to consultation. *Journal of Education and Psychological Consultation, 3,* 93–97.

Fullan, M., Miles, M. D., & Taylor, G. (1980). Organizational development in the schools: The state of the art. *Review of Educational Research, 50,* 121–183.

Gallessich, J. (1982). *The profession and practice of consultation.* San Francisco: Jossey-Bass.

Gallessich, J. (1985). Towards a meta-theory of consultation. *The Counseling Psychologist, 13*(3), 336–354.

Gutkin, T. B., & Curtis, M. J. (1982). School-based consultation: Theory and techniques. In C. R. Reynolds & T. B. Gutkin (Eds.), *The handbook of school psychology* (pp. 519–561). New York: John Wiley & Sons.

Kazdin, A. E. (1980). Acceptability of alternative treatments for deviant child behavior. *Journal of Applied Behavior Analysis, 13,* 259–273.

Kelman, H. C. (1965). Manipulation of human behavior. *Journal of Social Issues, 21*(2), 31–46.

Kratochwill, T. R. (1985). Case study research in school psychology. *School Psychology Review, 14,* 204–215.

Lauver, P. J. (1974). Consulting with teachers: A systematic approach. *Personnel and Guidance Journal, 52,* 535–540.

Levine, G., Trickett, E. J., & Kidder, M. G. (1980). The Hemes promise, and challenge of mental health consultation. In F. V. Mannino, E. J. Trickett, M. F. Shore, M. G. Kidder & G. Levin (Eds.), *Handbook of Mental Health Consultation* (DHHS Publication No. ADM 86-1446, pp. 505–520). Washington, DC: US Government Printing Office.

Lewin, K. (1946). Action research and minority problems. *Journal of Social Issues, 2,* 34–46.

Lippitt, G. L. (1973). *Visualizing change.* Fairfax, VA: NTL Learning Responses Corp.

Macarov, D. (1968). *A study of the consultation process.* New York: State Communities Aid Association.

Mannino, F. V., & Shore, M. F. (1975a). Effecting change through consultation. In F. V. Mannino,

B. W. MacLennon, & M. W. Shore (Eds.). *The practice of mental health consultation* (pp. 478–499). New York: Gardner Press.

Mannino, F. V., & Shore, M. F. (1975b). The effects of consultation: A review of empirical studies. *American Journal of Community Psychology, 3*, 1–21.

Martens, B. K. (1993). A behavioral approach to consultation. In J. E. Zins, T. R. Kratochwill & S. N. Elliott (Eds.), *Handbook of Consultation Services for Children* (pp. 65–86). San Francisco: Jossey-Bass.

Meade, C. J., Hamilton, M. K., & Yuen, R. (1982). Consultation research: The time has come, the walrus said. *The Counseling Psychologist, 10*(4), 39–51.

Medway, F. J. (1979). How effective is school consultation?: A review of recent research. *Journal of School Psychology, 17*, 275–282.

Meyers, J. (1973). A consultation model for school psychological services. *School Psychology Review, 11*, 5–15.

Meyers, J., Parsons, R. D., & Martin, R. (1979). *Mental health consultation in the schools.* San Francisco: Jossey-Bass.

Monroe, R. (1979). Roles and status of school psychology. In G. D. Phye & D. J. Rechly (Eds.), *School psychology: Perspectives and issues* (pp. 39–65). New York: Academic Press.

Palmo, A. J., & Kuzniar, J. (1972). Modifications of behavior through group counseling and consultation. *Elementary School Guidance and Counseling, 6*, 258–262.

Pryzwansky, W. B. (1986). Indirect service delivery: Considerations for future research in consultation. *School Psychology Review, 15*, 479–488.

Pryzwansky, W. B. & Noblit, G. W. (1990). Understanding and improving consultation practice: The qualitative case study approach. *Journal of Educational and Psychological Consultation, 1*, 293–307.

Randolph, D. L., & Hardage, N. C. (1973). A comparison of behavioral consultation and consultation with model-reinforcement group counseling for children who are consistently off task. *Journal of Educational Research, 67*, 103–107.

Rapoport, R. N. (1970). Three dilemmas in action research. *Human Relations, 23*, 499–513.

Reynolds, C. R., Gutkin, T. B., Elliot, S. N., & Witt, J. C. (1984). *School psychology: Essentials of theory and practice.* New York: John Wiley & Sons.

Schein, E. H. (1969). *Process consultation.* Reading, MA: Addison-Wesley.

Skinner, M. E. & Hales, M. R. (1992). Classroom teachers' "explanations" of student behavior: One possible barrier to the acceptance and use of applied behavioral analysis procedures in the schools. *Journal of Educational and Psychological Consultation, 3*, 219–232.

Stringer, L. (1961). Consultation: Some expectations, principles, and skills. *Social Work, 6*(3), 85–90.

Tindal, G., Parker, R. & Hasbrouck, J. E. (1992). The construct validity of stages and activities in the consultation process. *Journal of Educational and Psychological Consultation, 3*, 99–118.

Witt, J. C. (1990). Collaboration in school-based consultation: Myth in need of data. *Journal of Educational and Psychological Consultation, 1*, 367–370.

Witt, J. C., & Elliott, S. N. (1985). Acceptability of classroom intervention strategies. In T. Kratochwill (Ed.). *Advances In School Psychology, Vol. 4* (pp. 251–288). Hillsdale, NJ: Lawrence Erlbaum Associates.

Witt, J. C., Elliott, S. N., & Martens, B. K. (1985). The influence of teacher time, severity of behavior problem, and type of intervention on teacher judgments of intervention acceptability. *Behavior Disorders, 17*, 31–39.

Name Index

Kahn, R. L., 6, 13, 80, 84, 122
Karuza, J., 191, 318
Kast, F. Z., 153, 155
Katz, D., 6, 13, 80, 84, 122
Kauffman, J. M., 45, 188
Kaufman, H., 153
Kazdin, A. E., 62, 73, 122, 313
Keller, H. R., 5, 53, 65
Kelley, M. L., 122
Kelly, J. G., 24, 27, 108
Kelman, H. C., 322–323
Kemenoff, S., 191, 196
Kendell, G. K., 41
Keyser, V., 68
Kidder, L., 191, 318
Kidder, M. G., 40, 316
Kiresuk, T. J., 274, 277
Klein, D., 154
Knight, M. F., 240
Koeppl, G., 122
Kolb, D. A., 175
Kranzler, G. D., 313
Kratochwill, T. R., 3–4, 52–57, 60, 62–64, 68–69, 71, 75, 106, 116, 137, 149–150, 170, 178, 210, 293, 326
Krumboltz, J. D., 72
Kubr, M., 157
Kuhn, A., 80, 83
Kundert, D., 19, 40, 43–44
Kurpius, DeWayne J., 4–5, 10–11, 81, 85, 92–94, 96–100, 106, 139, 156, 171–175, 178–179, 300
Kuzniar, J., 209, 313

Lambert, N. M., 175, 202
Lauritzen, P., 209
Lauver, P. J., 313
LeBow, H., 41
Lehrer, R., 248
Lerman, H., 306
Leske, G., 68
Levine, A., 2
Levine, G., 316
Levine, M., 2
Lewin, Kurt, 2, 13, 84, 90–91, 324
Liberman, R. P., 209
Lin, N., 98, 153, 155
Lindemann, Erich, 20
Lippitt, Gordon L., 3–7, 9–11, 14, 81, 84–86, 92–93, 97–98, 106, 112, 146–149, 154–155, 157, 159, 322
Lippitt, Ronald, 3–7, 9–11, 86, 97, 106, 112, 146–149, 157, 159

Loevinger, L., 171–172
Lortie, D. C., 197, 234
Lowman, R. L., 295, 305, 308
Lund, S. H., 274, 277

Macarov, D., 186, 191, 318–321
Maher, C. A., 172–173, 274
Maitland, R. E., 127, 131, 140, 174
Malouf, J. L., 302
Mann, P. A., 195
Mannino, F. V., 4, 11, 185, 313, 325
Margullies, N., 147
Martens, B. K., 3, 10, 122–123, 313, 327
Martens, J., 199
Martin, R., 2, 5, 19, 106, 131–133, 279, 314
Matthes, W. A., 209
McClelland, D. C., 178
McFarlane, I. R., 85
McGehearty, L., 190
McGonagle, J. J., Jr., 306–307
McGowan, R. J., 209
McKenzie, H. S., 240
McMahon, R. J., 122
McPherson, R. B., 195
Meade, C. J., 4, 106, 140, 258, 279, 324–325
Means, B., 198
Medway, F. J., 11, 40–41, 63, 189, 209, 313, 325
Meichenbaum, R., 68
Meier, S., 106
Mendoza, D. W., 150
Merriam, S. B., 287
Meyers, H. W., 240
Meyers, Joel, 2–5, 10, 19, 21, 23–24, 40, 43–45, 106, 108, 113, 127, 131, 175, 178, 213–214, 264, 268–269, 274–275, 279, 314, 325
Miles, M. D., 313
Miller, J. N., 189
Mischel, W., 68
Mischley, M., 189–190, 196, 264
Modafferi, C., 19, 131
Moe, G. L., 122–123, 194
Monahan, J., 2, 63
Monroe, R., 313
Moos, R. H., 69
Morasky, R. L., 80, 83, 87–90, 163-164
Morrison, A., 192
Morrill, W. H., 11-12
Morrison, A., 192
Moses, R., 187

Mouton, J. S., 92, 94–96, 146, 314–315

Nelson, C. M., 240
Nelson, R. O., 279, 324–325
Nevin, A., 45, 240–241
Newman, J. L., 294, 296
Noblit, G. W., 281, 286, 326
Nowicki, G., 198
Noy, P., 187

O'Connor, Jr., R. M., 263
Oetting, E. R., 11
Oldham, G. R., 93
Olson, D. H., 210
Osberg, J. W., 40
Osborne, S. S., 45, 188
Osterweil, Z., 243–246

Palmo, A. J., 209, 313
Paolucci-Whitcomb, P., 45, 240–241
Parker, R., 327
Parsons, R. D., 2, 5, 19, 43, 45, 106, 113, 175, 178, 213–214, 264, 268–269, 274–275, 279, 314
Paskewicz, C. W., 174
Patrick, R., 198
Paul, S. C., 261–262, 264, 274
Perkins, J. A., 209
Perkins, N. T., 260
Perloff, E., 262
Perloff, R., 262
Peters, T. J., 90
Peterson, R. L., 123
Phillips, J. R., 90
Piaget, Jean, 106
Pierce, R. M., 160
Pierce-Jones, J., 190
Piersel, W. C., 52–53, 185
Pinto, R. F., 160–161, 192
Pipes, R. B., 107–103, 112
Pitner, N. J., 195
Poggio, J. P., 127, 174
Ponterotto, J. G., 181
Powell, C., 5
Powell, W. C., 42, 127, 208–209, 244, 279
Price, R. H., 2
Pryzwansky, W. B., 5, 40, 44–46, 53, 176–177, 185, 188, 194, 196, 235, 264, 266–267, 281, 286–287, 294–295, 302, 325–327
Pugach, M. C., 236

Subject Index